T0209154

VA Handbook for Veterans and Advocates

How to file for VA Benefits and Appeal Your Claim

Tyson Manker

authorHOUSE®

AuthorHouse™
1663 Liberty Drive
Bloomington, IN 47403
www.authorhouse.com
Phone: 833-262-8899

Published by AuthorHouse 11/28/2020

ISBN: 978-1-6655-0421-8 (sc)
ISBN: 978-1-6655-0420-1 (hc)
ISBN: 978-1-6655-0422-5 (e)

Library of Congress Control Number: 2020920212

Print information available on the last page.

This book is printed on acid-free paper.

Contents

Va-Handbook.com xi

Foreword xv

Introduction.. xix

Chapter 1. A History of Veterans Benefits in the United States

1.1 — Organic Era 2

    1.1.1 — Organic Era — Colonies.. 2

    1.1.2 — Organic Era — Revolutionary War 3

    1.1.3 — Organic Era — Civil War... 8

1.2 — 20th Century Pre-Modern Era 13

1.3 — Post-1988 Modern Era.. 20

1.4 — An American Tradition 22

Sources... 24

Chapter 2. Veterans Law

2.1 — Legal Authorities... 49

2.2 — Structure of the Department of Veterans Affairs 58

2.3 — VA Claim / Appeals Hierarchy 60

2.4 — Strongly and Uniquely Pro-Veteran System 65

Chapter 3. Claims for Disability Compensation

3.1 — Service-Connected Disability 71

3.2 — Veteran Status 73

    3.2.1 — Character of Discharge... 77

    3.2.2 — Unlawful COS/CSD Denials by VA of Veterans
          with Less-than-Honorable Discharges..........................81

3.3 — Bars to Benefits..82
    3.3.1 — Statutory Bars to Benefits 82
    3.3.2 — Regulatory Bars to Benefits..83
    3.3.3 — Compelling Circumstances Exception.......................85
    3.3.4 — Willful Misconduct 87
    3.3.5 — Suicide 90
3.4 — *Requirements for Establishing Service-Connection of a
Current Disability* 91
    3.4.1 — Current Disability..93
    3.4.2 — In-Service Injury...95
    3.4.3 — Nexus / Link 95
3.5 — NEXUS | 5 THEORIES to Establish Service-Connection........104
3.6 — Burden of Proof..107
3.7 — Standards of Proof...108
3.8 — Post-Traumatic Stress Disorder.......................................111
    3.8.1 — Combat – Stressor 116
    3.8.2 — Fear of Hostile Activity – PTSD Stressor 121
    3.8.3 — Sexual Assault – PTSD Stressor 122
3.9 —Agent Orange Herbicide Exposure 127
    3.9.1 — Presumption of Causation...130
    3.9.2 — Presumption of Exposure 132
    3.9.3 —Actual Exposure (Agent Orange) 136
    3.9.4 — Blue Water Navy Veterans 136
        3.9.4.1 — Blue Water Navy Veterans Act of 2019.......137
        3.9.4.2 — VA "Ship List" 139
        3.9.4.3 — Retroactive Effective Date of Benefits
            for Blue Water Veterans 142
    3.9.5 — Lawsuits against Agent Orange Manufacturers..........142
3.10 — Claims for Diseases Associated with Exposure to
Contaminated Drinking Water at Camp Lejeune 144
    3.10.1 — Claims for Medical Care (Lejeune Water)................145
    3.10.2 — Claims for Disability Compensation (Lejeune
        Water) 147
3.11 — Most Common Service-Connected Injuries.....................149
3.12 — Disability "Ratings" 150
3.13 — Effective Dates 152
3.14 — Individual Unemployability (IU).....................................153

Chapter 4. VA's Duty to Assist

4.1 — Duty: Provide Free Forms and Information..............................162
4.2 — Duty: Give Notice of Incomplete Claims 166
4.3 — Duty: Give Notice about Information Needed to
      Substantiate a Claim 167
4.4 — Duty: Obtain Records to Substantiate a Claim...........................169
4.5 — Duty: Provide Medical Examination/Opinion...........................175
4.6 — Duty: Liberally Read Pro Se Filings, and Fully and
      Sympathetically Develop Claims................................178
4.7 — Duty: Infer all Claims and Maximize Benefits 181
4.8 — Duty: Consider the Entire Record of Evidence........................183
4.9 — Duty: Resolve Questions of Reasonable Doubt in Favor of
      the Veteran 183
4.10 — Duty: Notice Of Decision Regarding Benefits........................186

Chapter 5. How to File a Claim for VA Disability Benefits

5.1 — Gather Records..190
     5.1.1 — How to request a Veteran's military personnel
        and medical records....................................190
     5.1.2 — Gather private medical / other records 194
5.2 — Appoint Representative..195
5.3 — "Intent to File" Claim..195
5.4 — File Claim for Disability Compensation Benefits......................197
     5.4.1 — File Claim for Service-Connected PTSD...................198
     5.4.2 — File Claim for Service-Connected PTSD caused
        by Sexual Assault....................................201
5.5 — File Claim for Health Care Benefits..........................204
5.6 — Initial Claim Review 204
     5.6.1 — Character of Discharge Review..........................204
     5.6.2 — Compensation & Pension Examination 205
5.7 — VA Issues Rating Decision..205
5.8 — Finality of Decisions 206
     5.8.1 — Clear and unmistakable error ("CUE")....................206
     5.8.2 — Supplemental claims with new evidence 208

Chapter 6. Appeals

6.1 — Modern Review System 210
6.2 — How to appeal a claim...211
    6.2.1 — Supplemental claim 211
    6.2.2 — Higher-level review...212
    6.2.3 — Notice of Disagreement 212
        6.2.3.1 Direct Review 213
        6.2.3.2 Evidence Submission Review 213
        6.2.3.3 Hearing with a Veterans Law Judge 213
6.3 — Legacy Claims & Appeals...217
6.4 — Requesting your claims folder (C-file)............................219

Chapter 7. Help Filing a Claim

7.1 — Accreditation 240
7.2 — Veterans Service Organization Representation 241
7.3 — State Dept. of Veterans Affairs Representation 243
7.4 — Representation by Attorneys..245
7.5 — Representation by Claims Agents 247
7.6 — Fee Agreement (Contract) 249
7.7 — Fees... 250
    7.7.1 — When Fees May Be Charged 251
    7.7.2 — CAVC | Fees and Fee Agreements 253
    7.7.3 — Equal Access to Justice Act Fees...............................253

Chapter 8. Other Benefits for Veterans and Dependents

8.1 — VA Education Benefits.. 256
    8.1.1 — Vietnam Era VEAP 257
    8.1.2 — Montgomery GI Bill..258
    8.1.3 — Post-9/11 GI Bill 259
8.2 — Vocational Rehabilitation and Employment 260
8.3 — Dependent Education Assistance (DEA)................................ 263
8.4 — VA Home Loan 264
8.5 — Veterans and Survivors Pension 265

8.6 — Dependency and Indemnity Compensation.............................. 266
8.7 — Burial and Memorial Death benefits..271

Forms Appendix 277
Case Index..325
Index 331
Poem 341

VA-HANDBOOK.COM

Additional information, forms and resources can be found online:
https://VA-handbook.com

The password for protected areas is: honest1

Dedication

This handbook is dedicated to every person who ever wore the uniform of the United States of America, and those who advocate for us. I salute you.

To my angel mother, thank you for everything.

Foreword

V A Handbook was written by a combat veteran / attorney for fellow veterans who were injured during their active duty military service and now want to file a claim with the Department of Veterans Affairs ("VA") for disability compensation, health care and other benefits. Advocates and family members will also find it useful.

Especially if you experienced trauma during your service, whether in combat, from sexual assault, or from some other stressful incident and are now living with post-traumatic stress ("PTSD"), it is important that you are able to begin healing as soon as possible. That includes having peace of mind as you go through the process of filing a claim with VA. You have already been through enough. That is why I assembled the information in this Handbook.

While I am a licensed attorney, the information contained in this handbook also comes from my personal experiences in working with the State of Illinois Department of Veterans Affairs and county-level veterans service officers ("VSOs") to file my own claims (for free, at no charge), plus my time interacting with VA administrators, nurses and doctors who provided the highest levels of care and utmost courtesy along the way. Countless veterans have asked me, "Is it worth pursuing?" a VA claim for a service-connected injury, and my answer is always, YES!

For me personally, VA played a key role in stabilizing my health after I returned from war and left active duty, because VA's diagnosis of my PTSD finally gave me confirmation that I wasn't having issues for no reason, but that I was experiencing the serious side effects of combat trauma that for years had gone unchecked. Moreover, VA's diagnosis was an acknowledgement by the federal government that my combat service as an infantry Marine had taken its toll. Being able to trace my symptoms to a medical issue—PTSD—made all the difference in the world. The financial compensation for income lost to PTSD offered peace of mind and helped put me back on solid ground.

I share with you my experiences in the hopes that you too will be motivated to begin pursuing your benefits, or get back in the fight for treatment and recognition for your military injuries, even if you or your loved one have been previously denied. More than a decade after my own service, some of my closest veteran friends are still filing claims and appeals for their injuries, and I continue to advise and cheer them on. Justice and good health should always be a top priority.

In many ways, VA fixes what the military breaks. After all, the Department of Veterans Affairs exists solely to provide care for Americans who "borne the battle" — while the Department of Defense ("DoD") exists to fight wars and defend our nation from attack. Though criticizing VA remains popular sport online and in the media, critics and ideologues fail to understand the remarkable work that VA does in improving the lives of millions of veterans and their families every single day. The fact remains that the vast majority of veterans who receive VA care and benefits are extremely satisfied, not to mention grateful.

Whatever situation you currently find yourself in, I encourage you to start the process of applying for VA benefits as soon as possible. Make sure to do your homework and develop a sound strategy. This mission, like all missions, requires reconnaissance (*research*) and planning. When armed with the right information, the process of filing a VA claim becomes far less daunting and your chances for success improve greatly.

As you prepare, always keep in mind the 7 Ps:

Proper Prior Planning Prevents Piss Poor Performance

I assembled this handbook with straightforward information to help guide your strategy and success, and I hope you find it useful.

Semper Fidelis

Tyson Manker
U.S. Marine Corps (0341)
Iraq OIF/OEF vet.

"The VA disability compensation system is not meant to be a trap for the unwary, or a stratagem to deny compensation to a veteran who has a valid claim." *Coomer v. Peake*, 552 F.3d 1362, 1369 (Fed. Cir. 2009)

"The Department of Veterans Affairs is required to reject a disability claim if the claimant fails to put forth sufficient evidence showing that he suffered an injury or incurred a disease during service." *Holton v. Shinseki*, 557 F.3d 1362, 1370 (Fed. Cir. 2009)

"The government's interest in veterans cases is not that it shall win, but rather that justice shall be done, that all veterans so entitled receive the benefits due to them." *Barrett v. Nicholson*, 466 F.3d 1038, 1044 (Fed. Cir. 2006)

"In the context of veterans' benefits where the system of awarding compensation is so uniquely pro-claimant, the importance of systemic fairness and the appearance of fairness carries great weight." *Hodge v. West*, 155 F.3d 1356, 1363 (Fed. Cir. 1998)

"The contrast between ordinary civil litigation . . . and the system that Congress created for the adjudication of veterans' benefits claims could hardly be more dramatic ... [the latter having] laws that place a thumb on the scale in the veteran's favor." *Henderson v. Shinseki*, 131 S. Ct. 1197, 1205 (2011)

Introduction

VA disability claims are how military veterans communicate to the Department of Veterans Affairs that they were injured during active duty service and now as a result of that injury their ability to find and keep work is hindered, or disabled. It is a relatively straightforward system, and is the focus of this VA Handbook.

VA claims are settled on the basis of evidence and law. In other words, VA claims examiners are required to review the entire record of evidence and follow the law when adjudicating individual disability claims. Veterans law includes the U.S. Code, Code of Federal Regulations, case law, and various internal VA guidelines. VA is not allowed to deviate from these established legal rules.

VA must always follow the law.

If you currently have a disabling illness or injury that stems from your active duty service and you present credible evidence of your condition and its link to your service, then you should qualify for disability benefits and receive a VA "rating" for your disability. Of course, this does not always happen, and veterans regularly have to appeal inaccurate ratings and erroneous denials—both of which are covered by this handbook.

A vast majority of claims fall short, not because someone evil at the VA hates veterans, but because veterans, at no fault of their own, sometimes fail to include with their claim enough evidence of their illness or injury and its connection to military service to permit VA to render a favorable decision under the law. While VA does have a legal duty to assist veterans who file claims, VA will not assign a disability rating if the evidence does not support such a conclusion. When insufficient evidence of a service-connected disability exists, VA is required by law to deny the claim.

Two important (albeit non-mandatory) items that veterans commonly fail to include with their disability claims are (1) private medical evidence of their current illness or injury, and/or (2) a medical professional's written opinion ("nexus letter") stating that military service is a possible source of their injury.

When you provide private medical and treatment records of a disabling illness or injury, VA must acknowledge that evidence and give it the proper weight. (*see* 38 U.S.C. §§ 1154(a), 5107(b), 5125; 38 C.F.R. § 3.303 requiring due consideration of all pertinent lay and medical evidence). If you do not submit private medical evidence of a current disabling condition, the entire decision of whether a current disability exists is made by a single VA medical examiner. Likewise, a VA Regional Office ("VARO") claims adjuster will make the ultimate determination about whether an injury is service-connected from the available record. As such, private medical evidence can be invaluable for establishing the record so that VA employees can more accurately discern the nature and origin of a veteran's condition.

In addition, private physicians, medical counselors and other health care providers generally have the benefit of treating a veteran for their condition over a period of time, sometimes for many years, which gives them great insight about the nature and cause of the disabling injury. In contrast, when making its determinations about a veteran's disability, VA provides a brief medical inspection, called the Compensation & Pension examination, or "C&P" exam, which generally lasts one hour or less. (*see* 38 U.S.C. § 5103A(d); 38 C.F.R. § 3.159(c)(4) requiring VA to provide medical examinations when necessary to decide a claim). Because private medical providers have the benefit of documenting a veteran's condition more thoroughly over time, their diagnosis and treatment history of the veteran carries great weight and should always be included with every VA disability claim.

Private medical records not only corroborate the existence of a veteran's illness or injury, but can also show the extent of their disability. Of course, veterans do not always seek care for their ailments, and in many cases cannot afford to. These issues aside, proving that a veteran's illness or injury has caused problems since discharge is made significantly easier in cases where a history of treatment exists. Not to mention, **VA is allowed to draw a negative inference when there is an absence of complaints or treatment sought by the veteran for an extended period**. As a veteran's service-connected illness or injury becomes more severe and bothersome, it becomes more likely that they will seek medical care.

Lastly, the VA disability benefits system is designed to ensure that injured military veterans receive all of the benefits that they are lawfully entitled to. It is intended to operate as a non-adversarial process. VA has a "duty to assist" veterans (*see* Chapter 4, Duty to Assist) in developing their claims—from the moment they file their first application until the claim has been approved or denied. VA does not submit evidence or make arguments against the veteran. There is no statute of limitations for claims, which can be reopened at any time with new evidence. Relaxed rules of evidence allow veterans to file for and receive their benefits without the need for legal representation. And a "Benefit of the Doubt" rule (*see* Section 4.9, Duty: Resolve Questions of Reasonable Doubt in Favor of the Veteran) affords veterans a relaxed legal standard of proof that requires VA to award benefits for a service-connected injury unless there is affirmative evidence to the contrary—i.e. a preponderance of the evidence against the claim. In general, veterans who include private medical records with their disability claims are likely to succeed sooner than those who do not.

Because VA claims examiners are legally required to consider all credible and relevant evidence, veterans are strongly encouraged to include private medical records with their compensation claim. In addition, successful claims often include a "nexus letter" from a private physician, therapist or other health care provider stating a professional opinion that the veteran's injury was incurred or aggravated by active duty military service. ("As likely as it is not") Once service-connection has been established by VA, additional nexus letters from private medical providers are unnecessary. Keep in mind, however, that private medical records are not mandatory, and disabled veterans can still file claims without them and let the VA make its diagnosing decision based solely on a C&P examination plus a review of their service records.

VA Handbook contains information about how to file a claim for VA disability benefits, and if necessary, how to appeal a wrongful denial or inaccurate rating. It includes battle-tested tips to help you succeed with your claim sooner than later. VA ratings decisions can be somewhat predictable if you familiarize yourself with the process. Veterans who take the time to learn the rules and submit the necessary evidence will reduce the amount of time spent on appeals. Like my father used to tell me, the best way is to "measure twice, and cut once…"

Lastly...

An important note about the terminology and citations that are used throughout this handbook. In veterans law, applicants for VA benefits are generally referred to as "claimants." (*see* 38 U.S.C. § 5100) However, I have made the assumption that most readers are either veterans, military family members, or advocates. As such, I have chosen to replace "claimants" with **veterans**. Military veterans deserve the proper acknowledgment, and it keeps things simple. In addition, I refer to VA employees who review claims as *examiners, adjudicators, adjusters* or *reviewers*. These different references are meant to be synonymous.

Unless otherwise noted all sections of the U.S. Code and Code of Federal Regulations come from Title 38, both of which pertain to veterans disability and other benefits. To save space, in some places I have intentionally omitted the title number. (ex. 38 U.S.C. § 5100 appears simply as § 5100). Additionally, all U.S. Code and C.F.R. provisions are current to the year 2021.

This handbook does not cover:

- State, local and private benefits for veterans with service-connected illnesses and injuries;
- How to sue the Department of Veterans Affairs for injuries stemming from medical procedures performed at VA facilities;
- Discharge upgrades;
- Records corrections.

Legal Disclaimer

This handbook and the information it contains is not intended to serve as a medical diagnosis for PTSD or any other illness or injury, or provide legal advice about any particular claim. It does not establish an attorney-client relationship with the author and is not affiliated with the U.S. Department of Veterans Affairs. Veterans are strongly encouraged to consult with a medical professional prior to filing a claim for VA disability benefits. Veterans are also encouraged to consider enlisting the help of a free claims advocate to assist in filing their claim at no cost, whether it be a county-level veterans service officer ("VSO") who is employed by your State Department of Veterans Affairs, or a representative from a Veterans Service Organization, like Veterans of Foreign Wars ("VFW"), Disabled American Veterans ("DAV") or American Legion. Only an "accredited" individual may assist veterans and qualifying family members in the preparation and filing of VA claims. Whether you enlist help from an advocate or file your own claims, the information in this handbook will prove invaluable in helping guide you through the process.

Acronyms

AF (USAF)	U.S. Air Force
APA	Administrative Procedures Act
AMA	Appeals Improvement and Modernization Act (2000)
AMVETS	American Veterans (organization)
AO	Agent Orange
AOJ	Agency of Original Jurisdiction
AVF	All Volunteer Force
BCD	Bad Conduct Discharge
BVA	Board of Veterans Appeals
CAC	Clear and Convincing Evidence
CAVC	Court of Appeals for Veterans Claims
CDC	Center for Disease Control
C&P	Compensation and Pension Exam
C-file	Claims file/folder
CFR	Code of Federal Regulations
CMA	Change Management Agent
COD	Character of Discharge
COE	Certificate of Eligibility
CSD	Character of Service Determination
CUE	Clear and Unmistakable Error
DAV	Disabled American Veterans
DBQ	Disability Benefits Questionnaire

DCE	Dichloroethylene
DD	Dishonorable Discharge
DD214	Discharge Certificate
DEA	Dependents Education Assistance
DIC	Dependency and Indemnity Compensation
DoD	Department of Defense
DVA	Disabled Veterans of America
EAJA	Equal Access to Justice Act
FDC	Fully Developed Claim
GAR	Grand Army of the Republic
GUHC	General Discharge Under Honorable Conditions
HD	Honorable Discharge
IOM	Institute of Medicine (now NAM)
ITF	Intent to File
IU	Individual Unemployability (also TDIU)
MCM	Manual for Courts-Martial
MEB	Medical Evaluation Board
MGIB	Montgomery GI Bill
MOPH	Military Order of the Purple Heart
MRE	Military Rules of Evidence
MST	Military Sexual Trauma
MTF	Medical Treatment Facility
NAM	National Academy of Medicine
NARA	National Archives and Records Administration
NAS	National Academy of Sciences
NCA	National Cemetery Administration
NLS	National Legislative Service (VFW)

NOD	Notice of Disagreement (Board of Veterans Appeals)
NPRC	National Personnel Records Center
NRC	National Research Council
NVLSP	National Veterans Legal Services Program
NVS	National Veterans Service (VFW)
OGC	Office of General Counsel
OIF	Operation Iraqi Freedom
OIG	Office of Inspector General
OEF	Operation Enduring Freedom
OMPF	Official Military Personnel File
OTH	Other (Less) Than Honorable Discharge
PCE	Tetrachloroethylene
PDHA	Post Deployment Health Assessment
PDHRA	Post Deployment Health Reassessment
PIV	Personal Identification Verification
POW	Prisoner of War
PTSD	Post-Traumatic Stress Disorder
PVA	Paralyzed Veterans of America
RAMP	Rapid Appeals Modernization Program
RCM	Rules for Courts-Martial
SCOTUS	Supreme Court of the United States
SOC	Statement of Case
SSA	Social Security Administration
SSOC	Supplemental Statement of Case
SMR	Service Medical Record
SRTs	Service Treatment Records
TCE	Trichloroethylene
TBI	Traumatic Brain Injury

UCMJ	Uniform Code of Military Justice
USC	United States Code
USCG	U.S. Coast Guard
USMC	U.S. Marine Corps
USN	U.S. Navy
VA (DVA)	U.S. Department of Veterans Affairs
VACO	Veterans Affairs Central Office
VASRD	Veterans Affairs Schedule for Rating Disabilities
VARO	Veterans Affairs Regional Office (also RO)
VBA	Veterans Benefits Administration
VBMS	Veterans Benefits Management System
VCAA	Veterans Claims Assistance Act (2000)
VEAP	Veterans Education Assistance Program
VEVRAA	Vietnam Era Veterans' Readjustment Assistance Act
VFW	Veterans of Foreign Wars
VJRA	Veterans Judicial Review Act (1998)
VHA	Veterans Health Administration
VLJ	Veterans Law Judge
VR&E	Vocational Rehabilitation and Employment
VRC	Vocational Rehabilitation Counselor
VSO	Veterans Service Organization
VSO	Veterans Service Officer
VSR/O	Veterans Service Representative/Officer
VVA	Vietnam Veterans of America
WWP	Wounded Warrior Project

VA Handbook

Chapter 1

A History of Veterans Benefits in the United States

C aring for military veterans who serve to protect the American way of life is a tradition older than the United States itself. In fact, the history of veterans law in this country predates the U.S. Constitution by over 100 years, starting with the first Pilgrims to the New World. This precedent of supporting injured veterans and their families set by the separatist Puritans helped to establish one of America's oldest traditions—more than 450 years before the U.S. Department of Veterans Affairs was created by Congress.

Veterans law in the United States evolved over the course of three distinct periods. First, an *Organic Era* gave birth to veterans law in the original Thirteen Colonies, lasting through the Revolutionary 1770s all the way to the 1860s and the Civil War. During this period, benefits were "limited" to massive parcels of land and pensions for service or disability. Following the Civil War, the last decades of the nineteenth century saw Congress liberalize the benefits system to the extent that by the year 1900 military disability pensions were the largest expenditure of the federal government. Next, the twentieth century saw the emergence of a *Pre-Modern Era* as social attitudes began to evolve about reintegration and the kinds of resources (other than money) military veterans needed to successfully transition back into society after wartime service. During this period, Congress worked to expand vocational, educational and housing benefits for veterans of both World Wars, Korea, and Vietnam. The pre-modern era saw the birth of the VA home loan, the GI bill, and the Veterans Administration—the precursor to today's VA. And finally, the current

Modern Era of Veterans Benefits commenced in 1988 (thanks in large part to the lobbying efforts of Vietnam Veterans) when Congress elevated the Veterans Administration to a Cabinet-level Department, renaming it the U.S. Department of Veterans Affairs, and removed the 50-year ban on appealing VA claims decisions. For this, the 1988 Veterans' Judicial Review Act created the U.S. Court of Appeals for Veterans Claims and provided a pathway for veterans to appeal to the federal courts. In the more than thirty years since, veterans law has experienced an extraordinary renaissance that continues to this day. Entitlement to VA disability benefits is now a constitutionally protected property interest. Not to mention, thanks to the tireless efforts of past generations, a plethora of benefits now exist to help ease the often turbulent transition from military back to civilian life. For legal practitioners boundless opportunities exist to not only serve those who served, but with focused and strategic litigation, to create new binding case law.

The following is a brief history of veterans law in the United States.

★ ★ ★

§ 1.1.1 — Organic Era — Colonies

Before debarking their ship, *Mayflower*, in 1620, the Pilgrims of Plymouth, in what is now the State of Rhode Island, signed what became known as the "Mayflower Compact" to establish rules of self-governance for their new colony. By **1636**, the local government had enacted one of the earliest known veterans benefits laws of the New World. The law, titled "maimed soldiers to be maintained," promised lifetime care for injured veterans.

> It is enacted by the Court that if any man shalbee sent forth as a souldier and shall return maimed hee shalbee maintained competently by the Collonie during his life.[1]

Veterans benefits laws became common in the Colonies as officials sought to recruit able-bodied individuals for expeditions and to help guard settlements against attack. In Maryland, a **1661** "Act for Encouragement of Such Soldiers as shall Adventure in the Defense of the Country" guaranteed that injured veterans would receive "maintenance from the Country according to his disability for maintaining himself."[2]

A New York recruiting law promised healthcare and pensions for disabled veterans, "If any person upon any invasion or other publick military service be wounded or disabled he shall be cured and maintained out of the Publick revenue."[3] To apply, injured veterans petitioned their local Court, which served as the colonial governing body.[4]

In **1676**, when an injured veteran named John Braudon appealed for benefits, the Massachusetts Bay Colony Court created the first standing committee to review veterans claims. "There be many in like nature that stand in like neede," the Court found, and appointed four local citizens to form the committee.[5]

It was common for colonial governments to pay disabled veterans lump sums of money in addition to annual or monthly stipends as compensation for their service injuries.[6] Early U.S. colonies also saw fit to provide death benefits for the families of fallen veterans. In **1678**, Maryland started the custom of providing pensions to widows and minor children of "every person slaine in the service of this Province."[7] In the century leading up to the Revolution and formation of a national government, most colonies passed veterans benefits laws that guaranteed some form of compensation[8] for disabled veterans and their families.[9]

Ten years of fighting in the French-Indian War **(1754-64)** brought additional wounded in need of relief.[10] Needless to say, by the start of the revolution colonial citizens who relied upon military protection for safety were entirely accustomed to providing veterans benefits.

★ ★ ★

§ 1.1.2 — Organic Era — Revolutionary War

In the Spring of **1775**, battles with the British at Lexington and Concord marked the start of war, and a Second Continental Congress soon convened in preparation for American independence. Notably, veterans benefits were as much a topic of conversation for the founders as the creation of the new government itself.

In **1776**, as the Declaration of Independence was being drafted, future general Nathanael Greene wrote to future War Secretary and President John Adams and urged him to adopt a national veterans disability benefits system, like those of the colonies, for wounded soldiers and their families. Greene wrote:

> The peculiar situation of American affairs renders it necessary to adopt every measure that will engage people in the service. The danger and hardships that those are subject to who engage in the service, more than those who do not, is obvious to everybody which has the least acquaintance with service, tis that which makes it so difficult to recruit. The large force that is coming against America will make it necessary to Augment our forces. If I am to form a judgment of the success of recruiting from what is past, the time is too short to raise the troops and be in readiness to meet the enemy and as every argument has been made use off upon the present plan of recruiting to engage people in the service there must be some new motives added to quicken the motions of the recruiting parties.
>
> From the approaching danger recruiting will grow more and more difficult. If the Congress was to fix a certain support upon every Officer and Soldier that got maim'd in the service or upon the families of those that were kild it would have as happy an influence towards engageing people in the service and inspire those engagd with as much courage as any measure that can be fixt upon ... It puts those in and out of Army upon a more equal footing than at present. ... The desperate game you have got to play and the uncertainty of War may render every measure that will increase the force and strength of the American Army worthy consideration.[11]

Weeks later, Greene wrote Adams again, arguing forcefully that the new national government should incorporate a robust veterans benefits scheme. "I have the happiness to find you agree with me in sentiment for the establishing a support for those that gets disabled in the Army or militia; but I am sorry to find at the same time, that you are very doubtful of it taking affect: I could wish the Congress to think seriously of the matter, both with respect to the Justice and utility of the measure."[12] The military leader puzzled, "Is it not equitable that the State who receives the benefit should be at the expense?" The idea that injured veterans should be cared for by the public will ultimately "be reduced to a National principle," he predicted.

REDUCED TO A NATIONAL PRINCIPLE - Nathanael Greene

Calls from Greene and others[13] prevailed, when on Thursday, **June 20, 1776**, the Continental Congress established the first national committee for veterans benefits "to consider what provision ought to be made for such as are wounded or disabled in the land or sea service."[14] This committee, formed prior to the Declaration of Independence, established veterans law as a key feature of American jurisprudence, and caring for veterans as a quintessentially American value. The Congress continued to pass individual disability benefits legislation for individual veterans as the system took shape.[15]

After proper debate, on Monday, **August 26, 1776**, the Continental Congress created the first national pension system for injured and disabled veterans.[16] The "pension law"—as it was called—guaranteed half pay for life for all disabled veterans regardless of rank or level of disability. Though payment obligations were initially left to the States, this first veterans benefits law set into motion the "National Principle" envisioned by Greene.

The Framers also saw fit to give military veterans parcels of land (awarded through "Bounty-Land Warrants") as a recruiting tool and also as a reward for those who had already served.[17] The federal government continued to give veterans large tracts of real property as a "thank you" for their service for the next 80 years until **1855**, when the final bounty-land law granted 160 acres to every enlisted and volunteer soldier since 1790.[18]

The Revolutionary War came to a close in **1783**, but without a strong national government, States that were loosely organized under the *Articles of the Confederation and Perpetual Union* were often unable or unwilling to meet their financial obligations.[19] The **1786-87** uprising known as *Shays' Rebellion*, led by Revolutionary War veteran Daniel Shays, was in part a hostile reaction to the government's failure to pay veterans of the recent war their pensions as promised.

Well aware of the issue, in **1789** one of the first laws passed by the new

Congress under the U.S. Constitution was the authorization of a disability benefits system for injured veterans, then referred to as "Invalids" [in-vuh-lid]. On its final day in session, Tuesday, **September 29, 1789**, Congress passed "An Act Providing for the payment of the Invalid Pensioners of the United States" that shifted the financial burden of paying for veterans pensions back onto the federal government.[20] While the same benefit still exists, modern "invalid-pensions" are now regarded as "disability compensation" for service-connected injuries.[21]

Society of the Cincinnati

At the close of the war the regular army was disbanded, and veteran officers who wanted to stay connected formed the nation's first veterans organization, The Society of the Cincinnati. The group proved to be extremely controversial, however, as suspicious citizens, having just survived a war of independence from an autocratic king, were in no mood for another hereditary class system.[22] The controversy surrounding the Society "embarrassed George Washington, distressed John Adams, alarmed Thomas Jefferson, amused Benjamin Franklin, and in some way stirred the lives of nearly all leading Americans."[23] The Society of the Cincinnati still exists today as a hereditary-based group that promotes its history. (see societyofthecincinnati.org/)

The responsibility of administering America's first veterans benefits system was initially placed with the District Courts of the newly created judicial branch, and federal judges were tasked with adjudicating claims and reporting to the Secretary of War. However, immediate pushback from the judiciary (in a conflict that was ultimately before the Supreme Court[24]) caused Congress in **1793** to amend the law with a different system.[25] Under the new scheme, district court judges took testimony from veterans under oath, then forwarded the evidence to the Secretary of War, who in turn put each case before Congress to pass individual legislation for each veteran found deserving of benefits. By **1803**, Congress granted the War Department the authority to adjudicate invalid-pension claims on its own without Congressional approval—although individual pension legislation continued for decades.[26]

Notably, in November of **1800**, as the federal government was in the process of relocating from Philadelphia to the District of Columbia, a massive fire broke out in the temporary offices of the War Department, destroying nearly all Revolutionary War service and pension records.[27] Despite the setback, in **1802** Congress passed an act[28] guaranteeing disability compensation to qualifying veterans of the "peace establishment" that served as the fundamental authority for all invalid-pension claims for the next sixty years up to the Civil War. An **1805** law[29] acknowledged for the first time that disabilities from service injuries don't always appear right away—sometimes not until years later. In **1816**, when disability compensation rates were increased, Congress announced that the national goal was a public benefits system to enable injured veterans to support themselves *"plentifully and comfortably."*[30]

Two years later in **1818** at the urging of President Monroe,[31] Congress created an entirely new benefit for impoverished elderly Revolutionary War veterans of all ranks.[32] Unlike previous disability benefits that required a service-connected injury, "service pensions" were offered to any qualifying former servicemember in need, a benefit that is still offered today to wartime veterans with non-service connected injuries.[33] Additional service-pension laws were passed (in addition to bounty-land warrants) for veterans of the War of **1812**, the Mexican War (**1846-48**), and the various so-called Indian Wars.

In **1833**, Congress saw fit to create a "Pension Office" within the War Department (led by a Senate-confirmed Commissioner of Pensions) to assist the otherwise-preoccupied Secretary of War with reviewing disability claims and administering pension payments.[34] When the Interior ("Home") Department was created in **1849**,[35] it assumed control of the pension office, which was renamed the "Bureau of Pensions." Adjudication of all pre-WWI veterans benefits remained the responsibility of the Pension Bureau until 1930, when it was merged with other agencies into the Veterans Administration.[36] In **1848**, Congress made it illegal for attorneys, claims agents and other businessmen in the burgeoning pension claims industry to require of widows and dependents an assignment or other acquisition of rights to their pension benefits.[37]

★ ★ ★

§ 1.1.3 — Organic Era — Civil War

The U.S. Civil War began on **April 12, 1861** when a southern militia launched an attack on Fort Sumpter, South Carolina. Days later, on April 15, President Lincoln issued a national proclamation calling for seventy-five thousand loyal volunteers to protect and defend the Republic.[38] Lincoln put out a second call two weeks later for another forty-two thousand volunteers.[39] Congress then quickly passed legislation[40] to recruit 500,000 army regulars, but because benefits were only extended to the volunteers who had enlisted under the act—not those militiamen who answered Lincoln's calls—additional legislation was needed.

On **July 14, 1862,** President Lincoln, "with practically no opposition from either house,"[41] signed into law an act known as the "**General Law**" that created a disability pension system for U.S. Civil War veterans and their families.[42] The general law was rather remarkable in that it covered mental as well as physical injuries, and instituted a medical ratings system to rank the nature and severity of an injury and its impact on a veteran's ability to work—a precursor to today's disability ratings system. The law set the effective date of a claim for benefits as either the date of discharge, if filed within one year, otherwise from the date of the application. Under the law veterans could retain an attorney or claims agent to help file their claim, but in an attempt to prevent fraud and abuse, Congress capped the fee that veterans could be charged at $5.[43] As later described:

> In many ways the pension law of 1862 was epoch making. Mothers and orphan sisters had never before been provided for in our national legislation. The pensions allowed to other classes, particularly to widows and orphans and to disabled seamen, were largely increased. Greater uniformity in the rates of army and navy pensions was also secured. As a whole the act explicitly committed the federal government, early in the war, to a pledge of pensions to all disabled Union soldiers and also to a similar provision for the dependent relatives of those who should lose their lives in the service.[44]

The Grand Army of the Republic (GAR)

In **1866** at the close of the Civil War, a group of veterans formed the Grand Army of the Republic ("GAR"). Unlike the Society of the Cincinnati, membership in the GAR was open to all Union veterans, regardless of rank or billet.[45] As a result, with help from the National Tribune newspaper, the GAR grew into a national political powerhouse of more than 400,000 members at its height. The so-called "Grand Army vote" is credited with deciding multiple elections, including the 1888 Presidential election in favor of Civil War General Benjamin Harrison over incumbent Grover Cleveland, who was staunchly opposed to veteran pensions.[46] By organizing around political and legislative change, the influential GAR, awarded its congressional charter in 1924,[47] paved the way for modern Veterans Service Organizations ("VSOs") of the twenty-first century[48] and beyond. The final GAR encampment, held in Indianapolis in 1949, was attended by six surviving Civil War veterans. [49]

Over the next decade a number of amendments to the 1862 general law eventually caused "a confused mass of laws," which, as noted by the Commissioner of Pensions, required updating.[50] In **1873** the "Consolidation Act" restructured all existing veterans benefits laws as the federal government prepared for a surge of post-war claims.

As veterans aged and the post-Civil War disability system grew, an industry of attorneys and claims agents emerged, ready to help veterans and their dependents with filing pension claims. With each step to liberalize the pension scheme, however, came abuse. Notably, fraud committed by claims agents during this period greatly impacted later views of the pension system, and caused Congress to tightly restrict attorney involvement with veterans benefits for the greater part of the twentieth century.

Of note, in **1877** a Civil War veteran named George Lemon, who was also a savvy businessman and claims attorney, founded a monthly (then weekly) newspaper called the National Tribune[51] to promote the veteran cause—and his personal business.[52] The Tribune was quite successful[53] in this regard, and with a wide readership[54] became the primary tool of the GAR to promote its membership and organize around veterans legislation. In addition to owning and editing the newspaper, Lemon helped thousands of readers who saw his advertisements to file their disability claims. At one point, Lemon's firm was handling over 125,000 disability claims—more than all other veterans claims firms[55] combined—and he employed up to seventy clerks—as many as the Pension Bureau itself.[56] Through the Tribune and his claims business, Lemon became quite influential[57] and he used his power for the benefit of all veterans, including himself. In one instance, Lemon is notoriously credited (or perhaps blamed)[58] with singlehandedly influencing the passage of an 1884 provision[59] —opposed by the GAR— that allowed the Commissioner of Pensions to withhold the $25 representation fee directly from the veteran's stipend. For his efforts Lemon became a millionaire, amassing a fortune[60] from the disability claims that were directly impacted by his lobbying efforts. Lemon was respected by clients and fellow veterans, while others called him a "scoundrel."[61] Their motives aside, Lemon and other claims attorneys played a major part in expanding the country's first veterans disability benefits system.

CLAIMS ! CLAIMS !

This Claim House Established in 1865!

GEORGE E. LEMON,
Attorney-at-Law.

OFFICES, 615 Fifteenth St., (Citizens' National Bank,)
WASHINGTON, D. C.

P. O. DRAWER 325.

Pensions.

If wounded, injured, or have contracted any disease, however slight the disability, apply at once. Thousands entitled.

Heirs.

Widows, minor children, dependent mothers, fathers, and minor brothers and sisters, in the order named, are entitled.

War of 1812.

All surviving officers and soldiers of this war, whether in the Military or Naval service of the United States, who served fourteen (14) days; or, if in a battle or skirmish, for a less period, and the widows of such who have not remarried, are entitled to a pension of eight dollars a month. Proof of loyalty is no longer required in these claims.

Increase of Pensions.

Pension laws are more liberal now than formerly, and many are now entitled to a higher rate than they receive.

From and after January, 1881, I shall make no charge for my services in claims for increase of pension, where no new disability is alleged, unless successful in procuring the increase.

Restoration to Pension Roll.

Pensioners who have been unjustly dropped from the pension roll, or whose names have been stricken therefrom by reason of failure to draw their pension for a period of three years, or by reason of re-enlistment, may have their pensions renewed by corresponding with this house.

Desertion

from one regiment or vessel and enlistment in another, is not a bar to pension in cases where the wound, disease, or injury was incurred while in the service of the United States, and in the line of duty.

Land Warrants.

Survivors of all wars from 1790, to March 3, 1855, and certain heirs are entitled to one hundred and sixty acres of land, if not already received. Soldiers of the late war not entitled.

Land warrants purchased for cash at the highest market rates, and assignments perfected.

Correspondence invited.

Prisoners of War.

Ration money promptly collected.

George Lemon, 1882 veterans claims advertisement. Source: The National tribune. (Washington, D.C.), 28 Jan. 1882. Chronicling America: Historic American Newspapers. Lib. of Congress. <https://chroniclingamerica.loc.gov/lccn/sn82016187/1882-01-28/ed-1/seq-7/>

One of the coalition's first major victories came in **1879** with the "**Arrears Act**" that paid arrears, or back pay, from the date of discharge (or death) to thousands of disabled veterans and their dependents — rather than the date the claim was filed, as the 1862 general law called for. This controversial piece of legislation, promoted in large part by claims agents like George Lemon,[62] caused a flurry of new claims, many of which resulted in large lump-sum payments. "This was the claims agents' harvest time," said one historian.[63] A 1955 House report later described one effect of the Arrears Act:

> Although professional claims agents, or attorneys, had made their unsavory appearance long before this time, this act gave rise to their period of liveliest activity. No previously considered legislation had offered a greater potential gain for the thousands of claims agents throughout the country. Even though from time to time previous legislation had sought to limit their percentage take from the individual pensioners and their dependents, in actual practice they were skilled and successful at evading legal restrictions.[64]

In **1890**, President Benjamin Harrison, himself a former Civil War General elected with help from the "Grand Army vote," fulfilled his campaign promise to push veterans benefits even further by signing into law the "**Disability-Pension Act**," which, unlike previous benefits before it, granted disability pensions to all disabled veterans regardless of their financial situation or how they were injured. Unlike the 1862 General Pension Law and its amendments, including the 1879 Arrears Act, which were tied to *service-connected* disabilities, the 1890 law provided disability compensation for literally *any injury*, even if it was not service related. Death benefits, granted upon the death of a soldier or sailor, were approved for virtually all dependents who applied. By end of the century, the U.S. Government was spending more on pensions than the entire military defense, even as it ramped up multiple overseas campaigns.[65]

The 1890s also saw America's first major international conflicts and mass overseas deployments of American troops: to Cuba for the Spanish-American War (**1898**), to China during the "Boxer Rebellion" (**1899-1901**), and for the so-called "Philippine Insurrection" (**1899-1902**).[66] Unlike Civil

War veterans, however, these veterans of foreign wars returned home to serious hardships that were exacerbated by legislative gaps in benefits, including the absence of medical care and pensions upon discharge. To compound matters, these first veterans of foreign engagements were shunned by the GAR, as they were ineligible to be members, and an unconcerned public had grown indifferent to their needs. As predicted by then-Colonel "Teddy" Roosevelt, "The world will be kind to you for ten days."[67]

Veterans of Foreign Wars

Realizing a need for organization, on **September 29, 1899**, a group of Spanish-American war veterans met in Columbus, Ohio to plan their collective future.[68] They called themselves the "American Veterans of Foreign Service." The following year on **August 13, 1900**, a group of Philippine veterans gathered in Denver to form the "National Society of the Army of the Philippines." These and other associations[69] operated separately until **1913**, when they consolidated as the "Veterans of Foreign Wars." The VFW (36 U.S.C. Ch. 301) received its congressional charter in 1936,[70] and continues to provide direct assistance to veterans and their families, as well as active duty troops, through its National Veterans Service ("NVS"). VFW has accredited claims officers in every state.

As the nineteenth century came to a close, so too did the organic era of U.S. veterans benefits. From the Pilgrims to the Framers to the Civil War and our first overseas wars, each of the earliest generations of Americans made it a priority to provide benefits from the public revenues for not just wounded warriors, but for all who served. These earliest traditions established the principles of veterans law from which all progress since has been built.

★ ★ ★

§ 1.2 — 20th Century Pre-Modern Era

Benefits granted to Civil War veterans and their dependents under the General Laws reached their peak just after the turn of the century, when, after extensive lobbying efforts by the GAR, in **1904** President Theodore "Teddy" Roosevelt issued Executive Order No. 78, that for the first time granted disability benefits for *old age* under the act of June 27, 1890.[71] The order declared that "when a claimant has surpassed the age of sixty-two years old he is disabled one-half in the ability to perform manual labor."

Congress codified Roosevelt's order three years later in **1907**, by passing what became known as the "**Old Age Pension**"[72] law that granted disability benefits to all veterans upon reaching the age of 62. Lawmakers explicitly barred attorneys from receiving *any compensation* for helping veterans file Old Age Pension claims. The law required "That no pension attorney, claim agent, or other person shall entitled be entitled to receive any compensation for services rendered in presenting any claim to the Bureau of Pensions, or securing any pension, under this Act."

Although the Civil War-era general pension laws would have provided coverage for disabled WWI veterans, America's **1917** entry into the first World War called for a new era of veterans benefits. Congress anticipated a conflict like no other that would involve a lengthy readjustment period for returning service members. As attitudes about reintegration evolved, lawmakers sought new ways to provide services and care for veterans that would proactively avert some of the negative developments seen after wars of recent memory. (i.e. the forgotten disabled and infirm veterans of the Civil War, Spanish-American War in Cuba, "Boxer Rebellion" in China, and the "Philippine Insurrection")

The **1917** "War Risk Insurance Act"[73] amendment created an entirely new framework for World War I Veterans to receive benefits. Unlike prior pensions, which continued to be administered by the Bureau of Pensions in the Department of the Interior, a new "Bureau of War Risk Insurance" was created in the Treasury Department to administer benefits. In addition to offering optional death or disability insurance up to $10,000, and other benefits, the War Risk Act standardized disability compensation for the first time by eliminating the distinction between officer and enlisted troops and calling for the creation of a disability rating schedule which is still in use for compensation claims today.

The following year, in **1918** the law was amended to cap the fee that veterans could be charged to file a claim at $3.[74] In doing so, members of Congress made clear that their intent was to create a veteran-friendly system that provided maximum benefits with minimal intervention from attorneys:

It is not the intent of Congress that these mercenary claim-agent leeches should sap the blood of any financial benefit from the Government by putting up these false claims and establishing their right to this 10 percent commission for doing nothing, and doing what the Government itself intends to do in every individual case... Unless there is still some joker we have not discovered, enactment of this bill will absolutely prevent applications being made by claim agents in behalf of beneficiaries under the act who would prevent them from obtaining all that is justly their clue.[75]

1918 also saw the launch of the Vocational Rehabilitation program[76] to train disabled veterans for new employment—a major benefit that continues to be utilized by tens of thousands of disabled veterans.[77]

The American Legion

The American Legion (36 U.S.C. Ch. 217) was established by a group of politically connected World War I combat veterans that included the former President's son, Teddy Roosevelt, Jr., on **July 4, 1919** at a gathering in Paris, France, and received its congressional charter the following month.[78] Today the American Legion offers trained, accredited service officers at locations in all 50 states to help veterans file claims and appeal denials to the Board of Veterans Appeals.

Disabled American Veterans

Disabled American Veterans (36 U.S.C. Ch. 503) was also founded by WWI veterans at the end of 1919. The group held its first national caucus the following year, on **September 25, 1920**, but was not chartered by Congress until 1932.[79] Like other national VSOs, DAV offers free accredited claims officers to represent veterans and help file claims for benefits.

In **1921**, Congress consolidated all of the functions of the Bureau of War Risk Insurance, including WWI disability payments and rehabilitation programs, from the Treasury Department into a new independent "Veterans Bureau." In addition to creating the first federal agency specifically for Veterans, the 1921 Act also established presumptions of service-connection for pulmonary tuberculosis, caused by toxic exposure, and neuropsychiatric disease, a precursor to PTSD.[80]

After the war, in **1924** Congress passed the "World War Adjusted Compensation Act," also known as the "Bonus Act," as an economic stimulus for unemployed veterans. The Bonus Act sought to assist those struggling veterans who returned home to find that their jobs had been filled, by creating a service-pension system that awarded "service credits" based on the length of service. $1 of credit was granted for each day of domestic service, and overseas service was worth $1.25.[81]

Under the Bonus Act, starting in 1925 veterans were issued an interest-bearing "Adjusted Service Certificate" on their birthday worth an amount equal to their time amount of service. The unfortunate catch, however, was that the veteran had to wait 20 years (or die!) before their certificate could be reimbursed. Hard times from the Great Depression caused restless, impoverished veterans who were unable to wait until 1945 to march on the U.S. Capitol in 1932. Their massive demonstration and march on Washington, D.C., led at one point by revered Marine Corps General Smedley Butler,[82] became known as the "Bonus Army."[83]

A few months after the Bonus Act, Congress passed the **1924** World War Veterans' Act[84] to revise and consolidate the various laws pertaining to World War I Veterans (War Risk Insurance, Vocational Rehabilitation, medical and domiciliary, etc.) and expand the duties of the recently-created Veterans Bureau. The act also increased the fee for helping to file a claim from $3 back to $10 where it remained until 1988.[85]

In **1930**, at the urging of the VFW, American Legion and the public, Congress passed legislation authorizing President Hoover to consolidate the separate Veterans Bureau and Bureau of Pensions with veterans hospitals and other agencies into a new "Veterans Administration."[86] As further evidence of the close and unique relationship between VSOs and the federal government, in **1931** Congress passed a resolution to print the annual proceedings of each major VSO as an official House document to be delivered each year to Congressional armed services committees.[87]

In **1933**, at the low point of the Great Depression, President Franklin

Delano Roosevelt urged Congress to quickly pass "An Act to Maintain the Credit of the U.S. Government," known as the "National Economy Act"[88] which, in addition to granting new, sweeping powers to the Executive Branch, resulted in the first ever significant cuts to veterans benefits. So drastic were its reductions, the 1933 law was described as "one of the most unjust and unfair measures ever enacted in regard to compensation for veterans."[89] Despite virtually no debate on the matter, a far-reaching provision of the 1933 law, Section 5, prevented veterans from seeking judicial review of their claims. It read:

> All decisions rendered by the Administrator of Veterans' Affairs ... shall be final and conclusive on all questions of law and fact, and no other official or court of the United States shall have jurisdiction to review by mandamus or otherwise any such decision.

To the bane of veterans everywhere, this provision "to remove the possibility of judicial relief"[90] remained in place for more than half of a century until 1988, when the "Veterans Judicial Review Act" opened VA decisions to appellate review by the courts.[91]

With his new powers, FDR began building the agency and in **1933** created the Board of Veterans Appeals ("BVA") that is still in operation today.[92] Though far short of full judicial review, the BVA for the first time gave veterans and their dependents an opportunity for appeal. From 1933 until 1988, the BVA existed as the one-and-only way to appeal denied VA claims, although its decisions were final and could not be appealed. (The BVA still operates in Washington, D.C., but its decisions are now appealable to the U.S. Court of Appeals for Veterans Claims, which can be appealed to the U.S. Court of Appeals for the Federal Circuit).

Over FDR's veto, in January of **1936** Congress passed the "Adjusted Compensation Payment Act," which amended the similarly-named 1924 law by replacing adjusted service certificates that weren't redeemable until 1945 with Treasury bonds that were immediately payable.[93] Later that year, Congress revisited the attorney fee issue and opted to maintain the maximum charge for helping to file a claim at $10.[94]

Despite attempts to remain neutral, the U.S. was forced into the second World War when, on **December 7, 1941**, the Japanese attacked Pearl Harbor, Hawaii. With America's return to war came expansions of veterans benefits and the VA structure. Shortly after the allied invasion at Normandy on D-Day, FDR signed into law the groundbreaking "Servicemembers Readjustment Act" of **1944**, also known as the "GI Bill of Rights," that elevated the Veterans Administration to "an essential war agency" and prioritized VA funding as second only to the war departments.[95] In recognizing the difficulties of overseas service, a new focus was placed on helping all veterans make a successful transition from the military back to civilian life. The law authorized VA to create a home and business loan program, which still exists, and allocated funding for education and training programs, a benefit known today as "the GI Bill."[96]

Also in **1944**, Congress passed a "Mustering Out Payment Act"[97] as an economic stimulus for returning war veterans in an attempt to prevent another great depression. Under the act, Veterans with at least 60 days of overseas service were granted a single $300 payment, or just over $4,000 in today's currency.[98] Disability compensation rates were also raised.[99] For the first time, in **1946** Congress made clear the distinction between *service-pensions* and *disability compensation*. "Veterans Administration monetary benefits ... for service-connected disability ... shall be designated "compensation," and not "pension."[100]

American Veterans (AMVETS)

American Veterans, or AMVETS (36 U.S.C. Ch. 227), is credited as the first World War II veterans organization. AMVETS was founded as the American Veterans of WWII and received its charter on **July 23, 1947**.[101] Membership in the AMVETS is open to all honorably discharged veterans regardless of overseas service or disability. Like other VSOs, AMVETS has a national network of accredited claims officers who are trained to help veterans file disability claims free-of-charge.

In **1952**, the "Veteran's Readjustment Assistance Act" (known as the "Korean GI Bill of Rights")[102] extended benefits of the 1944 law to veterans of the Korean war. Several years later in **1957**, Congress overhauled all of the existing benefits laws into a more modern form, organized by title.[103] In **1958** veterans benefits laws were permanently placed as Title 38 of the U.S. Code.[104] Basic entitlement for disability compensation, as defined in

1958, remains virtually the same. Confederate widows were also granted service-pensions that year.[105] A **1959** amendment further expanded pension benefits to widows of both World Wars and the Korean War.[106]

The Vietnam War beginning in the early **1960s** created another generation of veterans with distinctive injuries in need of their own benefits legislation. Specifically, for the duration of the war, the United States deployed a toxic liquid herbicide named "Agent Orange" as a defoliant to kill and clear jungle vegetation. Troops on patrol were routinely doused by spray planes or otherwise exposed to the toxic liquid during its transport.[107]

The "Veterans Readjustment Benefits Act" of **1966**[108] extended GI Bill education, home loan and other benefits to Vietnam Veterans while the war was still raging. After the war had ended but before the dangers of Agent Orange were acknowledged, in **1974** the landmark "Vietnam Era Veterans' Readjustment Assistance Act" ("VEVRAA")[109] expanded vocational and education programs and sought to prevent discrimination against Vietnam Veterans, who often faced ungrateful aspects of society upon their return home. The law allows veterans who feel they have been discriminated against to file a complaint with the Labor Department, among other provisions.

On July 12, **1973**, a massive fire at the National Personnel Records Center ("NPRC") in St. Louis destroyed millions of military service records. As it was later described, "The fire was one of the worst losses of records in U.S. history, destroying 80 percent of the Army records and 75 percent of the Air Force records: an estimated 16 to 18 million individual files. The old building was not equipped with a sprinkler system…"[110] That same year, Congress abolished mandatory conscription by ending the draft and instituting in its place an all-volunteer force ("AVF").

Vietnam Veterans of America

Vietnam Veterans of America ("VVA") (38 U.S.C. Ch. 2305), like their predecessors, felt unrepresented upon their return from an unpopular overseas war that claimed the lives of more than fifty-thousand U.S. troops and exposed millions of service members to deadly Agent Orange. VVA traces its roots to a **January 1978** gathering in Washington, D.C, with Congress granting its charter[111] the following decade on May 23, 1986.[112] Unlike other modern veterans service organizations, VVA has a limited existence, with membership limited to veterans "who served on active duty during the dates established by federal law for the Vietnam War."[113] In addition to lobbying efforts, VVA has remained a notable litigant in the courts, pushing tirelessly for positive change. Like other national VSOs, VVA offers accredited claims officers to help veterans file and appeal claims for benefits at no cost.

In **1979**, Congress authorized and appropriated funding for local health facilities called "Vet Centers" to provide all returning veterans with mental health counseling services.[114] Today, Vet Centers, which are smaller than VA medical centers, continue to provide mental health counseling and other critical veterans services in communities across the country.

Also in **1979**, the "Veterans Health Programs Extension and Improvement Act" authorized the first comprehensive health study of "persons who, while serving in the Armed Forces of the United States during the period of the Vietnam conflict, were exposed to any of the class of chemicals known as "the dioxins" ... (including the herbicide known as "Agent Orange") to determine if there may be long-term adverse health effects in such persons from such exposure."[115]

With the "Agent Orange Act" of **1991** [116] the government finally acknowledged the lasting damage caused to Vietnam Veterans by the deadly poisonous herbicide. The 1991 law, like previous benefits laws, granted Vietnam Veterans a presumption that certain diseases were incurred as a result of their service in Vietnam and exposure to toxic Agent Orange, making it easier to obtain compensation and healthcare benefits for their conditions without having to prove their direct exposure or service-connection.[117]

★ ★ ★

§ 1.3 — Post-1988 Modern Era

In 1988, fifteen years after Congress ended the draft in favor of an all-volunteer military, the current modern era of veterans benefits began with the passage of two landmark pieces of legislation.

The Department of Veterans Affairs Act of **1988** [118] elevated the Veterans Administration from an independent agency to a cabinet-level executive branch department, renaming it the U.S. Department of Veterans Affairs. Three years later the new department provisions were restated and codified[119] in Title 38 of the U.S. Code where they remain.

Later that year, the Veterans Judicial Review Act—Veterans Benefits Improvement Act ("VJRA") of **1988** [120] removed the longstanding bar to judicial review of VA decisions[121] set in 1933 at the low point of the Great Depression, and for the first time gave veterans the ability to appeal their claims to the federal judiciary. The VJRA also created the Court of Veterans Appeals, an administrative Article I court later renamed the U.S. Court of Appeals for Veterans Claims,[122] to review decisions of the Board of Veterans Appeals. The VJRA opened the door for veterans to obtain expert legal representation, and allowed decisions of the CAVC to be appealed to the federal circuit. As a result, veterans case law since 1988 has developed as an important part of American jurisprudence.

In the nearly thirty years since the passage of these two landmark laws, other critical pieces of legislation have helped to shape and define the mission of the modern Department of Veterans Affairs.

The Veterans Claims Assistance Act of **2000** ("VCAA") established VA's "Duty to Assist" veterans with their applications for benefits. Congress passed the VCAA in response to a U.S. Court of Appeals for Veterans Claims ruling[123] that VA had no obligation to help a veteran develop their claim for benefits if it was missing certain information. The multi-faceted "Duty to Assist" veterans and their dependents legally requires VA to obtain substantiating service and medical records, provide a medical examination, and otherwise assist in developing a claim. (*see* Chapter 4, Duty to Assist) The non-adversarial pro-claimant nature of the VA claims system is most apparent when the VA fulfills its VCAA obligations (although improper denials do occur, which must then be appealed).

On September 11, 2001, terrorists attacked the United States. Within months, U.S. forces were on the ground in Afghanistan engaged in direct combat. Less than two years later, on March 19, 2003, the U.S. launched an invasion of Iraq, followed by an occupation that quickly spiraled out of control.[124] Over the next decade, millions of U.S. troops served in Afghanistan and Iraq, some deploying multiple times to both countries.

With a new generation of veteran claimants on the horizon, in **2006** Congress passed the "Veterans Benefits, Health Care, and Information Technology Act."[125] One major change was to begin allowing accredited attorneys to represent veterans with their denied disability claims. Under the 2006 law, veterans could retain legal counsel or non-attorney claims agents to represent them before VA after they filed a Notice of Disagreement ("NOD").

Most recently, in **2017** the "Veterans Appeals Improvement and Modernization Act" ("AMA") restructured the outdated and overwhelmed VA appeals system for improved accuracy and efficiency. Under the AMA, which went into effect on February 19, 2019, veterans can retain legal representation even earlier than was permitted by the 2006 law. For all modern appeals, veterans may now retain legal counsel once the agency of original jurisdiction ("AOJ"), generally the VA Regional Office, has issued a decision on an original claim. In an effort to streamline the appeals process, the AMA created three "lanes" of appeal: (1) supplemental claims with new evidence, (2) higher-level review of the same evidence by a senior claims adjuster at the regional office, (3) appeal to the Board of Appeals by filing a Notice of Disagreement. Veterans who appeal to the Board may also request an in-person hearing and present new substantiating evidence. Appeals are the focus of Chapter 6.

★ ★ ★

§ 1.4 — An American Tradition

It is important to appreciate the long and colorful history of veterans benefits law in the United States of America. To have a basic understanding of how previous generations fought to create our modern veterans benefits system might spur 21st-century veterans to be more aware about their own claims. Even better, perhaps they will become socially and politically engaged like our predecessors who labored so hard to advance the cause. No manmade system is ever perfect or maintenance-free, and veterans of the future will stand to benefit from the work of twenty-first century veterans and veteran advocates.

Because the VA claims process can seem daunting, military veterans often decide that it is not worth their time or energy to apply for benefits. Or they may attempt to file an application for benefits, but because they do not understand the process or how to respond to VA correspondences, they do not complete the claim. Sometimes one failed attempt is all it takes for a veteran to decide that their claim is not worth pursuing.

Despite all of the good that it does, VA, like all institutions, sometimes makes mistakes that have a negative impact on people's lives. Though a minority of cases, veterans I have heard from who are unhappy with VA are generally disappointed about one of three things: (1) a denied disability claim or inaccurate (low) disability rating, (2) the length of time it takes for VA to process disability claims and appeals, and (3) long waits for medical appointments.

The first issue, improper denials and inaccurate ratings, are not always due to VA errors, or as is widely believed, a secret desire of the VA to "screw over" veterans. When a veteran does not provide enough evidence to establish their claim, VA is required by law to deny the (unsubstantiated) claim based on the available record—even though the decision may not accurately reflect the veteran's true condition. While the veteran perceives the denial as an incompetent or uncaring VA, in countless cases I have seen the veteran simply failed to submit ample, or in some cases, *any* substantiating evidence to accompany their claim. Veterans can avoid this pitfall by making sure to include substantiating evidence with their disability claim.

The second issue, lengthy claims appeals, are in the process of being addressed by the new "modernized" appeals system that went into effect on February 19, 2019. VA is currently in the process of eliminating the backlog of so-called "legacy" claims appeals that were filed prior to the AMA, and, with the creation of the modern system, will completely phase out the legacy program over time. All original claims filed after the effective date of the AMA, February 19, 2019, are automatically classified as "modern" claims. Thus, for the foreseeable future, when filing an appeal veterans and advocates should determine whether the claim being appealed is a "legacy claim" or "modern claim" and proceed accordingly.

Lastly, it is important to understand that the current, primary cause of long delays for VA medical appointments is the more than 49,000 vacancies in VA hospitals and medical facilities nationwide.[126] The unnecessary and entirely preventable shortage has been caused primarily by officials who want to eliminate all forms of government healthcare, including VA care for injured military veterans, on *ideological* grounds. Despite the long and bipartisan history of providing healthcare as a benefit to sick and wounded veterans (dating back to the Pilgrims and George Washington), certain politicians are locked in an effort to push disabled veterans out of the VA healthcare system and into private care facilities and, in an act of sabotage, have intentionally avoided addressing VA's staffing shortages.[127] The desire of anti-VA ideologues to undo centuries-old American traditions and cripple the VA is all the more reason to understand and share the history of veterans benefits. Until VA is allowed to fully staff its facilities with the doctors and nurses and other professionals that are needed to provide for millions of veterans, VA healthcare will continue to see unnecessary delays and deaths.[128]

The current system of veterans benefits administered by the VA Department is a culmination of centuries of progress fought by and on behalf of America's frontline warriors. By participating in this system, today's veterans are continuing an American tradition older than the United States itself. Millions of veterans from every generation have collected trillions of dollars in compensation and health care for their selfless service and their injuries. Millions since 1944 have taken advantage of free college education and VA home loans guaranteed by the GI Bill. Needless to say, every veteran who fights for their claim to earn VA recognition is a part of this long and storied American tradition.

★ ★ ★

1. Sources

1   Massachusetts. *Records of the Colony of New Plymouth in New England. Laws. 1623-1682.* (p. 182) Boston: Press of W. White, 1861, *HathiTrust*, hdl.handle.net/2027/cool.ark:/13960/t0xp7km8p.

2   Maryland. *Proceedings and Acts of the General Assembly of Maryland, January 1637-38 to Sept. 1664, Vol. I.* (p. 408) Baltimore: 1883, msa.maryland.gov/megafile/msa/speccol/sc2900/sc2908/000001/000001/html/am1--408.html.

3   New York. *The Colonial Laws of New York From the Year 1664 to the Revolution.* Vol. I. (p. 234) Albany: J. B. Lyon, state printer, 1894, *HathiTrust*, hdl.handle.net/2027/umn.31951002158537d.

4   Massachusetts. *Records of the Governor & Company of the Massachusetts bay in New England. 1644-1657. Vol. III.* (p. 387) Boston: Press of W. White, 1854, *Google Books*, books.google.com/books?id=u0IOAQAAMAAJ.

5   Massachusetts. *Records of the Governor & Company of the Massachusetts bay in New England. 1674-1686. Vol. V.* (p. 80) Boston: Press of W. White, 1854, *Google Books*, books.google.com/books?id=wm9OAQAAMAAJ.

"In ansr to the petition of John Braudon, a wounded souldjer, for releife, there being many in like nature that stand in like neede, the Court judgeth it meet to appoint Mr. Edward Ting, Mr. Joseph Dudley, Capt. Hugh Mason, & Mr. Wm Parkes to a standing committee to consider petitions of this nature, and make their report of what hey judge meet donn to this Court, and to continue till the Court take further notice."

6   Virginia. House of Burgesses. *Journals of the House of Burgesses of Virginia, 1761-1765.* (p. 349) Richmond, VA: The Colonial Press, 1907, *HathiTrust,* hdl. handle.net/2027/mdp.39015039496164.

"Resolved, That the petition of *Thomas Brown,* a wounded soldier, is reasonable, and that he ought to be allowed by the Publick the Sum of £20 for his present relief, and the sum of £5 per Annum during Life."

7   Maryland. *Proceedings and Acts of the General Assembly of Maryland, October 1678 to November 1683, Vol. VII.* (p. 58) Baltimore: 1889, msa. maryland.gov/megafile/msa/speccol/sc2900/sc2908/000001/000007/html/ am7--58.html; *HathiTrust,* hdl.handle.net/2027/umn.31951d02897618v.

"That every person that shall adventure as a Soldier in any warr in defence of this Province and shall therein happen to be maimed or Receive hurt soe as he thereby be render Incapable of getting a Livelyhood as aforesaid shall according to his disability receive a yearely pension to be raysed out of the Publick Leavy of this Province for the time of such his disability & every person Slaine in the service of this Province & leaveing behind him a wife and Children such wife and Children shall alsoe be allowed a Competent pension the wife dureing her widdowhood and the Children till they be of yeares able to gett their Liveings or be putt out apprentices."

8   Virginia. House of Burgesses. *Journals of the House of Burgesses of Virginia, 1659/60-1693.* (p. 70) Richmond, VA: The Colonial Press, 1914, *HathiTrust,* hdl.handle.net/2027/mdp.39015006970571.

Disabled veterans were at times paid out of the public treasury with tobacco, which was a primary source of revenue for colonial governments.

"It is ordered, that Richard Jones who was wounded and disabled in his Majesty's service at James City be allowed Annually out of the Public Levy, 500 pounds of tobacco, upon his producing annual certificates, from the Magistrates or County Collector where he lives that he continue disabled by reason of his said wounds or hurt."

9   Franklin, Benjamin. *The Papers of Benjamin Franklin, Vol. 3, Jan. 1, 1745, through June 30, 1750.* "Proposal to the Associators, [21 March 1748]." New Haven: Yale University Press, 1961, pp. 279–281, *NARA Founders Online,* founders.archives.gov/documents/Franklin/01-03-02-0115. Franklin publicly supported "Pensions to poor Widows whose Husbands should happen to fall in Defence of their Country."

10 Virginia. House of Burgesses. *Journals of the House of Burgesses of Virginia, 1761-1765.* (p. 214) Richmond, VA: The Colonial Press, 1907, *HathiTrust*, hdl.handle.net/2027/uva.x001603217.

(1764) "A Petition of *James Wilson*, praying some Compensation for the Loss of the Use of his right Arm, occasioned by a Musket Shot in an Engagement with a large Body of Indians in September last."

"Also a Petition of *Robert Clandening*, setting forth that he being drafted out of the Militia of Augusta County was sent out under the Command of Captain Moffat, to repel the hostile Invasions of the Indians on the Frontiers of this Colony; that in an Action between a Large Body of Indians ... he was dangerously wounded in his right Arm by a Musket Ball, which has deprived him of the use thereof, and rendered him entirely incapable of getting his Livelihood; and praying to the Consideration of the House therein, was presented to the House and read."

(p. 220)

(1764) "Resolved, That the petitions of *James Wilson* and *Robert Clandening* be allowed the Sum of £40 each, to enable them to discharge the Demands of the Doctor, and other Expenses, incurred by the Wounds they received in the Service of their Country."

"Resolved, That the said *James Wilson* and *Robert Clandening* by allowed the Sum of £10 each per Annum, for their Support during their Lives, they having both lost the Use of their right Arms in the said Service."

Virginia. House of Burgesses. *Journals of the House of Burgesses of Virginia, 1766-1769.* (p. 24) Richmond, VA: The Colonial Press, 1907, *HathiTrust*, hdl. handle.net/2027/uva.x001603216.

(1766) "A Petition of *John Harwood*, setting forth that he had served as a Soldier under Colonel George Washington and was wounded in the first Engagement at the Meadows, and was also wounded in General Braddock's Defeat, and the draughted to go to the Northward where the Hardships he met with, and his other Infirmities, rendered him incapable of supplying himself with the common Necessaries of Life; and praying for Relief, was presented to the House and read."

(p. 32)

(1766) "Resolved, That the Petition of *John Harwood*, a wounded Soldier, for Relief from the Publick, is reasonable; and that he ought to be allowed the sum of £5 for his present Relief, and the further Sum of £5 per Annum during Life, as a Recompense for the Wounds he received in the Service of the Colony."

Virginia. House of Burgesses. *Journals of the House of Burgesses of Virginia, 1770-1772.* (p. 8) Richmond, VA: The Colonial Press, 1906, *HathiTrust*, hdl. handle.net/2027/uva.x001603227.

(1770) "A Petition of *Henry Townsend*, late a Soldier in the Virginia Regiment, was presented to the House, and read; setting forth that the Petitioner had

served upwards of four Years in the said Regiment, and on the twelfth Day of November in the year 1758, was so wounded in his left Breast and Arm, that he is unable to labour; and therefore praying that this House will take his Case into Consideration, and grant him such Relief as to them shall seem reasonable."
(p. 18)

"A Petition of *John Welch*, late a Soldier in the Virginia Regiment, was presented to the House, and read; setting forth that the Petitioner had served in the said Regiment seven Years, and was not discharged until he was disbanded at Fort Lewis in March 1762; and that during that Time he suffered much from Inclemency of Weather, which has brought on him a Rheumatism and Weakness, and disabled him from getting his livelihood; and therefore praying that this House will grant him such Relief as they shall think meet."
(p. 31)

(1770) "Resolved, That it is the Opinion of the Committee, that the Petition of *Henry Townsend*, late a Soldier in the Virginia Regiment, is reasonable; and that he ought to be allowed the Sum of Ten Pounds for his present Relief, and the further Sum of Ten Pounds per Annum, during his Life, in Consideration of the Wound he received in the Service, and of his being thereby rendered incapable of getting a Livelihood."

"Resolved, That it is the Opinion of the Committee, that the Petition of *John Welch*, late a Soldier in the Virginia Regiment, is reasonable; and that he ought to be allowed the Sum of Five Pounds for his present Relief, and the further Sum of Five Pounds per Annum, during his Life, in Consideration of the Hardships he suffered in the Service, and of his being thereby rendered incapable of getting a Livelihood."
(p. 266)

(1772) "A Petition of *John Burton*, late a Soldier in the Virginia Regiment, was presented to the House, and read; setting forth that the Petitioner, whilst he was in that Service, was so wounded in an Engagement by two Musket Balls, one of which, lodged in the small of his back, could never be extracted, that he is unable to by his own Labour, and hath no other Means to maintain himself, and that he suffers continual Pail, and is in great Distress; and therefore humbly praying Relief."
(p. 270)

(1772) "Resolved, That it is the Opinion of this Committee, that the petition of *John Burton*, late a Soldier in the Virginia Regiment, is reasonable; and that he ought to be allowed the Sum of ten Pounds for his Present Relief, and the further Sum of five Pounds per Annum during his life, in Consideration of the Wounds he received and the Hardships he suffered in the Service, and of his being thereby rendered incapable of getting a necessary Subsistence."

11 Greene, Nathanael. *The Adams Papers, Papers of John Adams, vol. 4, Feb–Aug 1776*, ed. Robert J. Taylor. (pp. 213–214) Cambridge, MA: Harvard University Press, 1979. "To John Adams from Nathanael Greene, 26 May 1776." *NARA Founders Online*, founders.archives.gov/documents/Adams/06-04-02-0092.

12 *Supra* note 11. "To John Adams from Nathanael Greene, 2 June 1776." founders.archives.gov/documents/Adams/06-04-02-0100.

13 *Supra* note 11. "From John Adams to Nathanael Greene, 22 June 1776." founders.archives.gov/documents/Adams/06-04-02-0129.

Adams told Greene that his idea to establish a national veterans disability compensation system was "extremely just" and that whether it should be adopted, along with veterans hospitals and other care, was "a Matter of Importance" and that "the Plan should be well digested."

Your Reasoning, to prove the Equity, and the Policy of making Provision for the Unfortunate Officer, or soldier, is extremely just, and cannot be answered, and I hope that when We get a little over the Confusions arising from the Revolutions which are now taking Place in the Colonies, and get an American Constitution formed, Something will be done. I should be much obliged to you for your Thoughts upon the subject. What Pensions should be allowed or what other Provision made? Whether it would be expedient to establish an Hospital &c. It is a Matter of Importance, and the Plan should be well digested.

14 Library of Congress. *Journals of the Continental Congress, 1774-1789, Vol. V.* (p. 469) Washington: Govt. Printing Office, 1906, bit.ly/cc-v-469.

(20 June 1776) "Resolved, That a committee of five appointed to consider what provision ought to be made for such as are wounded or disabled in the land or sea service, and report a plan for that purpose."

15 *Supra* note 14. *Vol IV.* (p. 273) bit.ly/cc-iv-273.

(April 1776) "Resolved, That the sum of thirty dollars be advanced to John Harkness, a wounded soldier, who was discharged at Cambridge without pay."

16 *Supra* note 14. *Vol. V.* (pp. 702-705) bit.ly/cc-v-702.

"Resolved, That every commissioned officer, non-commissioned officer, and private soldier, who shall lose a limb in any engagement, or be so disabled in the service of the United States of America as to render him incapable afterwards of getting a livelihood, shall receive, during his life, of the continuance of such disability, the one half monthly pay from and after the time that his pay as an officer or soldier ceases..."

"[T]he Continental Congress promised to provide to those disabled in the cause of American Independence." *D'Amico v. West Jr.*, 209 F.3d 1322, 1327 (Fed. Cir. 2000) (citing *Lauran v. West*, 11 Vet.App. 80, 85 (1998).

17 *Supra* note 14. *Vol. V.* (p. 763) bit.ly/cc-v-763.

(1776) "That Congress make provision for granting lands, in the following proportions: to the officers and soldiers who shall so engage in the service, and continue therein to the close of the war, of until discharged by Congress, and to the representatives of such officers and soldiers as shall be slain by the enemy: To a colonel, 500 acres; to a lieutenant colonel, 450; to a major, 400; to a captain, 300; to a lieutenant, 200; and to an ensign, 150; each non-commissioned officer and soldier, 100."

18 An Act in Addition to certain Acts granting Bounty Land to certain Officers and Soldiers who have been engaged in the Military Service of the United States. (March 3, 1855, ch. 207, 10 Stat. 701) loc.gov/law/help/statutes-at-large/33rd-congress/session-2/C33s2ch207.pdf.

19 Library of Congress. *Journals of the Continental Congress, 1774-1789. Vol. VIII.* (p. 290) Washington: Govt. Printing Office, 1907, bit.ly/cc-viii-390.

20 An Act providing for the payment of the Invalid Pensioners of the United States. (September 29, 1789, ch. 24, 1 Stat. 95) loc.gov/law/help/statutes-at-large/1st-congress/session-1/c1s1ch24.pdf.

"Be it enacted by the Senate and House of Representatives of the United States of America in Congress assembled, That the military pensions which have been granted and paid by the states respectively, in pursuance of the acts of the United States in Congress assembled, to the invalids who were wounded and disabled during the late war, shall be continued and paid by the United States, from the fourth day of March last, for the space of one year, under such regulations as the President of the United States may direct."

21 38 U.S.C. § 101(13); 38 C.F.R. § 3.4

22 Burke, Aedanus. *Considerations on the Society or Order of the Cincinnati.* By "Cassius." Charleston, S.C.: A. Timothy, 1783. *Google Books*, books.google.com/books?id=XrF4nQEACAAJ. The Society first came under public attack from Aedanus Burke, a South Carolina Judge. Burke penned a 15-page pamphlet under the pseudonym "Cassius" that warned "the order of Cincinnatus does in truth establish a nobility in the heart of America." (p. 46) A society composed of the generals and officers of the army and navy of the United States of America, has been established in all the provinces which form the American confederation. This society takes the name of the *Cincinnati*, and has already arrived at a very great degree of maturity. Its strength increases every day. It is hereditary, perpetual, richly endowed, and boasts to have the most distinguished personages of America, including General Washington, amongst its members. (p. ix)

The Cincinnati have also instituted a badge of honor, by which their members are to be known and distinguished. It is a medal of gold in the figure of an eagle, with an inscription on the face and reverse, alluding to the time establishing that order, and to their having saved the republic ... The ribbon and medal are to be word by each member of the society, in the same manner as crosses, and other insignia of knighthood, are worn in Europe. (pp. xi-xii)

Having been asked to serve as the Society's first President, Washington found himself caught in an embarrassing public spectacle. From his home at Mount Vernon, he wrote Thomas Jefferson to ask his friend to "give me your opinion of the Institution of the Society of Cincinnati." Washington mentioned Aedanus Burke's pamphlet, saying "I am told had its effect. People are alarmed..." *The Papers of Thomas Jefferson, vol. 7, 2 March 1774–25 February 1785,* ed. Julian P. Boyd. (pp. 88–89) Princeton: Princeton University Press, 1953. "To Thomas Jefferson from George Washington, 8 April 1784." *NARA Founders Online,* founders.archives.gov/documents/Jefferson/01-07-02-0076.

See also: *George Washington's Correspondences Concerning The Society of the Cincinnati.* Baltimore: The Johns Hopkins Press, 1941, *HathiTrust,* hdl.handle.net/2027/wu.89058491358.

Jefferson replied to Washington that he understood the well-intended desire of recently discharged veterans to stay in touch, and to band together to promote mutual interests, but that he didn't believe, once peace was restored, that men who served together would remain friends. In fact, he predicted that partisan politics would sour friendships forged in battle. Jefferson advised:

When the army was about to be disbanded, and the officers to take final leave, perhaps never again to meet, it was natural for men who had accompanied each other through so many scenes of hardship, of difficulty and danger, who in a variety of instances must have been rendered mutually dear by those aids and good offices to which their situations had given occasion, it was natural I say for these to seize with fondness any propositions which promised to bring them together again at certain and regular periods. And this I take for granted was the origin and object of this institution: and I have no suspicion that they foresaw, much less intended those mischiefs which exist perhaps in the forebodings of politicians only. I doubt however whether in its execution it would be found to answer the wishes of those who framed it, and to foster those friendships it was intended to preserve. The members would be brought together at their annual assemblies no longer to encounter a common enemy, but to encounter one another in debate and sentiment. Something I suppose is to be done at those meetings, and however unimportant, it will suffice to produce difference of opinion, contradiction and irritation. The way to make friends quarrel is to pit them in disputation under the public eye. An experience of near twenty years has taught me that few friendships stand this test; and that public assemblies where every one is free to speak and to act, are the most powerful looseners of the bands of private friendship. I think therefore that this institution would fail of its principal object, the perpetuation of the personal friendships contracted thro' the war.

Jefferson further warned that "experience has shown that the hereditary branches of modern governments are the patrons of privilege and prerogative, and not of the natural rights of the people, whose oppressors they generally are." See: *The Papers of Thomas Jefferson, vol. 7, 2 March 1774–25 February 1785,* ed. Julian P. Boyd. (pp. 105–110) Princeton: Princeton University Press, 1953. "From Thomas Jefferson to George Washington, 16 April 1784." *NARA Founders Online,* founders.archives.gov/documents/Jefferson/01-07-02-0102.

23 Hoey, Edwin. "A New and Strange Order of Men." *American Heritage.* Vol. 19, issue 5 (August 1968) https://web.archive.org/web/20200926145401/https://www.americanheritage.com/new-and-strange-order-men.

24 *U.S. v. Yale Todd* (U.S. 1794)

Ritz, Wilfred J. "United States V. Yale Todd (U.S. 1794)." 15 Wash. & Lee L. Rev. 220 (1958), scholarlycommons.law.wlu.edu/wlulr/vol15/iss2/5.

The federal judges looked upon the procedures set forth in the Act ... with disfavor. They thought that the provisions of the statute were contrary to the Constitution in that: (1) the business directed by the act was not of a judicial nature, and (2) their judgments were subject to suspension by the Secretary of War and to revision by Congress.

25 An Act to regulate the Claims to Invalid Pensions. (February 28, 1793. ch. 17, 1 Stat. 324) loc.gov/law/help/statutes-at-large/2nd-congress/session-2/c2s2ch17.pdf.

Sec. 2: "And be it further enacted, That the judge of the district shall District judge transmit a list of such claims, accompanied by the evidence herein directed, to the Secretary for the department of War, in order that the same may be compared with the muster-rolls, and other documents in his office; and the said Secretary shall make a statement of the cases of the said claimants to Congress, with such circumstances and remarks, as are to be stated may be necessary, in order to enable them to take such order thereon, as to Congress. they may judge proper."

26 An Act to make provision for persons that have been disabled by known wounds received in the actual service of the United States, during the Revolutionary war. (March 3, 1803. ch. 37, 2 Stat. 242). loc.gov/law/help/statutes-at-large/7th-congress/session-2/c7s2ch37.pdf.

27 *Hodgson v. Dexter,* 1 Cranch 345, 2 L.Ed. 130, 5 U.S. 345 (1803) Joseph Hodgson, a property owner who leased his buildings to the War Department, filed a civil suit against the Secretary of War, Samuel Dexter, for his losses from the fire. The case, ultimately decided by the Supreme Court, helped to establish the legal doctrine that public officials are not personally liable for public contracts. loc.gov/item/usrep005345/.

Annals of Congress of the United States. Sixth Congress. *Books and Papers Destroyed by fire in the War Department, in 1800.* (p. 1357) Washington, D.C. (1851) "Not a book or paper of the office was saved." bit.ly/aoc-1357.

Everly, Elaine C. and Howard H. Wehmann. "The War Office Fire of 1800." *Prologue,* Vol. 31, pp. 22–35 (Spring 1999) *HathiTrust,* hdl.handle.net/2027/

osu.32435062692728. "A fire broke out in the building in which the War Office was temporarily located, and within a few hours the flames had ruined two new brick houses and consigned to ashes all of the books and papers of the secretary of war."

"Papers of the War Department" is a project funded through grants from the National Endowment for the Humanities to restore the records destroyed by the 1800 fire. See: wardepartmentpapers.org/. NEH grant numbers: RZ-20557-00 and RZ-20982-02. See also: neh.gov/explore/the-papers-the-war-department-1784-1800.

28 An Act fixing the military peace establishment of the United States. (March 16, 1802, ch. 10, 2 Stat. 132) loc.gov/law/help/statutes-at-large/7th-congress/session-1/c7s1ch9.pdf.

Sec. 14: "And be it further enacted, That if any officer, non-commissioned officer, musician or private, in the corps composing the peace establishment shall be disabled by wounds or otherwise, while in the line of his duty in public service, he shall be placed on the list of invalids of the United States, at such rate of pay, and under such regulations, as may be directed by the President of the United States..."

29 An Act in addition to "An Act to make provision for persons that have been disabled by known wounds received in the actual service of the United States, during the revolutionary war. (March 3, 1805, ch. 44, 2 Stat. 345) loc.gov/law/help/statutes-at-large/8th-congress/session-2/c8s2ch44.pdf

"...the provisions contained in the first section of "An Act in addition to "An Act to make provision for persons that have been disabled by known wounds received in the actual service of the United States, during the revolutionary war" ... are hereby extended to all those persons in service of the United States ... who, in consequence of known wounds received in the actual service of the United States, have at any period since, become and continued disabled, in such manner as to render them unable to procure a subsistence by manual labour."

30 American State Papers. Documents, Legislative and Executive of the Congress of the United States, Claims. Vol. I. (pp. 473-474) 14th Congress, 1st Session. "Increase of the Rate of Pensions" No. 307. bit.ly/asp-473.

31 President James Monroe, State of the Union Address. December 12, 1817. presidency.ucsb.edu/node/205560.

"In contemplating the happy situation of the United States, our attention is drawn with peculiar interest to the surviving officers and soldiers of our Revolutionary army, who so eminently contributed by their services to lay its foundation. Most of those very meritorious citizens have paid the debt of nature and gone to repose. It is believed that among the survivors there are some not provided for by existing laws, who are reduced to indigence and even to real distress. These men have a claim on the gratitude of their country, and it will do honor to their country to provide for them."

32 An Act to provide for certain persons engaged in the land and naval service of the United States, in the Revolutionary War. (March 18, 1818, ch. 19, 3 Stat. 410) loc.gov/law/help/statutes-at-large/15th-congress/session-1/c15s1ch19.pdf. "That every commissioned officer, non-commissioned officer, musician, and private soldier ... who served in the war of the revolution until the end thereof, or for the term of nine months, or longer, at any period of the war ... who is yet a resident citizen of the United States, and who is, or hereafter, by reason of his reduced circumstances in life, shall be, in need of assistance from his country for support ... shall receive a pension from the United States..."

33 38 U.S.C. § 101(15); 38 C.F.R. § 3.3

34 A Resolution in relation to the execution of the act supplementary to the "Act for the relief of certain surviving officers and soldiers of the revolution. (March 2, 1833, 4 Stat. 668) loc.gov/law/help/statutes-at-large/22nd-congress/session-2/c22s2ch97.pdf.
    U.S. Bureau of Pensions. Service Monographs of the U.S. Government, No. 24. *The Bureau of Pensions. Its History, Activities and Organization.* books.google.com/books?id=A5olAAAAMAAJ.

35 An Act to establish the Home Department. (March 3, 1849, ch. 108, 9 Stat. 395) loc.gov/law/help/statutes-at-large/30th-congress/session-2/c30s2ch108.pdf.

36 U.S. Executive Office of the President [Herbert Hoover]. Executive Order No. 5398: *Consolidation and Coordination of Governmental Activities Affecting Veterans.* July 21, 1930. (p.623) *Google Books,* books.google.com/books?id=2cmSQH4Ype4C.

37 An Act for the Relief of certain surviving Widows of Officers and Soldiers of the Revolutionary Army. [Sec. 2] (July 29, 1848, ch. 120, 9 Stat. 265) loc.gov/law/help/statutes-at-large/30th-congress/session-1/c30s1ch120.pdf
    U.S. v. Hall, 98 U.S. 343, 356 (1878)

38 "Proclamation by the President. Seventy-Five Thousand Volunteers and an Extra Session of Congress." *New York Times,* 15 Apr. 1861, nyti.ms/38jB2Uz.

39 "The Great Rebellion. By the President of the United States. A Proclamation to Dispatch to the Associated Press." *New York Times.* 3 May 1861, p.10, nyti.ms/2PnirhR.

40 An Act to authorize the Employment of Volunteers to aid in enforcing the Laws and protecting Public Property. (July 22, 1861, ch. 9, 12 Stat. 268) loc.gov/law/help/statutes-at-large/37th-congress/session-1/c37s1ch9.pdf.

41 Glasson, Henry. "Federal military pensions in the United States." New York: Oxford University Press, 1918, p. 125, *HathiTrust,* hdl.handle.net/2027/hvd.32044010562718.

42 An act to grant pensions. (July 14, 1862, ch. 166, 12 Stat. 566) loc.gov/law/help/statutes-at-large/37th-congress/session-2/c37s2ch166.pdf

SEC. 6. And be it further enacted, That the fees of agents and attorneys making out and causing to be executed the papers necessary to establish a claim for a pension, bounty, and other allowance, before the Pension Office under this act, shall not exceed the following rates: For making out and causing to be duly executed a declaration by the applicant, with the necessary affidavits, and forwarding the same to the Pension Office, with the requisite correspondence, five dollars.

See debate: Cong. Globe, House, 37th Cong., 2nd Sess. 3 May 1862, p. 2101, *Lib. of Congress*, bit.ly/cg-37-2-2101.

43 As noted by the dissenting justices in in *Walters v. Natl. Assoc. of Radiation Survivors*, 473 U.S. 305, 359-360 (1985), Congress set a $5 fee for veterans claims in 1862 (*supra* note 42), which was raised to $10 two years later in 1864.

An Act supplementary to an Act entitled "An Act to grant Pensions," approved July fourteenth, eighteen hundred and sixty-two. [Sec. 12] (July 4, 1864, ch. 247, 13 Stat. 387, 389) loc.gov/law/help/statutes-at-large/38th-congress/session-1/c38s1ch247.pdf.

Frisbie v. U.S., 157 U.S. 160, 15 S.Ct. 586, 39 L.Ed. 657 (1895); Supreme Court ruling that $10 fee restriction was a Constitutional exercise of legislative power.

In 1870, due to the aggressive lobbying efforts of influential claims agents, Congress raised the fee that an attorney could charge for filing a claim to $25. Attorneys who were able to convince naïve veterans and their dependents to sign a fee agreement could now collect $25 instead of $10. The *Walters* Court may have overlooked this provision.

An Act to define the Duties of Pension Agents, to prescribe the Manner of paying Pensions, and for other Purposes. [Sec. 7] (July 8, 1870, ch. 225, 16 Stat. 193) loc.gov/law/help/statutes-at-large/41st-congress/session-2/c41s2ch225.pdf.

44 Glasson, *supra* note 41, p. 128.

45 Wilson, Oliver. M. "The Grand Army of the Republic Under Its First Constitution and Ritual. Its Birth and Organization." Kansas City: Franklin Hudson Pub. Co., 1905. (pp. 214-15) citing GAR Constitution, Art. II Qualification of Members. GAR only required that its members be honorably discharged, "No soldier or sailor, who has been convicted by court-martial or desertion, or any other infamous crime, shall be eligible for membership."

46 McConnell, Stuart. "The William Newby Case and the Legacy of the Civil War." *Prologue*, Vol. 30, No. 4 (pp. 246-255) Winter 1998. *Google Books*, books.google.com/books?id=jtdLAQAAMAAJ.

Blanck, Peter. "The Right to Live in the World": Disability Yesterday, Today, and Tomorrow – the 2008 Jacobus tenBroek Disability Law Symposium. *Texas Journal on Civil Liberties and Civil Rights*, 13 (2008), 367-401.

Glasson, *supra* note 41. Noting that the "pension issues ... may even have been the deciding factor in the November elections." The "Grand Army Vote" was "believed to have carried some states in the 1888 election." (p. 225)

47 An Act For the incorporation of the Grand Army of the Republic. (June 3, 1924, ch. 242, Pub. L. 68-184, 43 Stat. 358) loc.gov/law/help/statutes-at-large/68th-congress/session-1/c68s1ch242.pdf.

48 Ortiz, Stephen R. "Beyond the Bonus March and GI Bill. How Veteran Politics Shaped the New Deal Era." New York: New York University Press, 2010. "The Grand Army's success in building the Civil War pension system offered a sterling example for the organizations that would lobby the government on behalf of World War veterans." (p.13)

49 Six Civil War veterans attended the final GAR encampment in 1949.
   Miller, Francis. "Civil War veterans (L-R) Theodore A. Penland, Charles L. Chappel, Albert Woolson, Joseph Clovese, Robert Barrett and James A. Hard at the last GAR convention." *Getty Images, LIFE Picture Collection*, 1 Jan. 1949. gettyimages.com/detail/news-photo/civil-war-veterans-theodore-a-penland-charles-l-chappel-news-photo/50775170.
   "Robert Barrett, 104, Union Army Veteran; Opposed Disbanding of G.A.R." *New York Times*, 14 Jan. 1951, p. 84. nyti.ms/34b3ANF.
   "Last G.A.R. Negro Dies at Age of 107; Joseph Clovese, Drummer Boy and Infantryman in Civil War, Left Plantation to Serve Worked on River Boats." *New York Times*, 14 July 1951, p. 13. nyti.ms/2OawBDq.
   Harris, Kent. "Vicenza civilian to honor Union soldiers." *Stars and Stripes*, 25 May 2009. stripes.com/news/vicenza-civilian-to-honor-union-soldiers-1.91936 "Theodore Penland was commander-in-chief of the [GAR] when he died at the age of 101 in 1950."

50 United States, Secretary of the Interior. *Annual Report*. (1873) p. 325, *Google Books*, books.google.com/books?id=HDxgAAAAcAAJ&hl.

51 In a project called *Chronicling America*, the Library of Congress has digitized hundreds of American newspapers from the 1780s through the 1960s for free public access. At <chroniclingamerica.loc.gov/lccn/sn82016187/>, the LOC describes the Tribune:
   During its first few years of publication, the National Tribune covered Congressional news related to pension laws and the Pension Office, as well as providing narratives, tables, and statistics about past wars. Relying on his background as a lawyer, Lemon frequently printed simple, yet valuable advice to veterans on claiming their pensions. The paper also covered lighter topics and included anecdotes, poems, and jokes. Large illustrations many drawn by Thomas Nast, a well-known political cartoonist for Harper's Weekly, appeared on its front page. Later the Tribune became known for its regular feature, "Fighting them Over: What Our Veterans Have to Say About Their Old Campaigns," which solicited memoirs from veterans of all ranks

and backgrounds. This column established the National Tribune as a forum for discussion, debate, and reminiscence for veterans around the country, eventually becoming the official paper of the Grand Army of the Republic.

52 The National tribune. Vol. 1, No. 1 Washington, D.C. (October 1877) Chronicling America: Historic American Newspapers. *Lib. of Congress*, chroniclingamerica.loc.gov/lccn/sn82016187/1877-10-01/ed-1/seq-6/.

George Lemon announced in the first publication of the National Tribune five objectives for the newspaper to help the veterans movement accomplish. Unheralded, without previous announcement of any sort, a new candidate for public favor introduces itself into the journalistic world. There is a necessity for its existence. It is intended to fill a vacancy in journalism that should not have been left unfilled so long. Its life will depend upon its sustenance. When the motives which impel its publication no longer exist, and the objects toward which its devotion is to be directed are accomplished, it will remain then to be seen whether there is need for it longer. Seldom is a periodical established with a well-defined object; with an actual, expressed motive. The purposes of newspapers are often intentionally concealed; and a pretense may often cover a variety of objects far from the one expressed. But, in the publication of this paper, the intention is, to advocate, particularly, five great measures:

I.   The passage of a law by Congress equalizing the bounties paid to soldiers of the late war.

II.   The passage of an act by Congress, 'under which the pension of a wounded, injured, diseased soldier, or the family of a dead soldier, may begin from the time of death, or the date of discharge on account of disability.

III. The extension of the pension laws, so as to include soldiers of the Mexican war.

IV.   Putting on pension rolls all survivors of the war of 1812, and all widows of such, married prior to 1850, regardless of the period of service of the soldier.

V.   Action by Congress to remedy innumerable defects (in the pension laws, which will be pointed out from time to time, particularly the repeal of section 4717 of the Revised Statutes.

These objects are of direct and personal interest, not only to us, but to every pensioner in the United States, to every soldier who fought under the Union flag, to every widow and every child of a soldier, and generally, to every soldier's friend. The amount of influence to be exerted by these pages will depend entirely upon the circulation this paper receives. The subscription price has been placed low, so that it is within the reach of all. Let those who receive this copy circulate it among their friends, particularly among the soldiers of their locality. Our interests and the interests of soldiers are mutual. By helping us, you help yourselves. Do not allow yourselves to be drawn into the support of irresponsible advertising sheets, but concentrate your energies here, where they will be directly applied to the purpose' you and we wish to accomplish. A strong effort will be made during the approaching session of Congress to bring about such legislation as we ask above. In order to aid this effort, it was thought best, among some of the friends of the soldiers in Washington, to issue monthly such a paper as this, that in its columns might be recorded what is necessary to be done, the progress that is made, and the reasons why its accomplishment is wise and just. Let every comrade lend us a hand. The near approach of Congress makes it essential that, whatever is to be done, be done immediately. Let us hear from you quickly.

Library of Congress. All issues of the National Tribune 1877-1911: chroniclingamerica.loc.gov/lccn/sn82016187/issues/.

53 Part of the Tribune's success can be attributed to its ability to stir emotions. One front page depicted graphic images of malnourished former prisoners of war, and described their horrific conditions at Andersonville. See: The National Tribune. Vol. 1, No. 5 (February 1878) chroniclingamerica.loc.gov/lccn/sn82016187/1878-02-01/ed-1/seq-1/.

The Tribune also alerted veterans when the executive or legislative branches were taking actions harmful to veterans. Notorious pension opposer, President Grover Cleveland, began to purge veterans from the pension rolls immediately upon taking office in 1893. The Tribune was quick to warn veterans. See "Suspended." *The National Tribune.* Washington, DC. October 5, 1893, p.2 chroniclingamerica.loc.gov/lccn/sn82016187/1893-10-05/ed-1/seq-2/.

54 Dearing, Mary. *Veterans in Politics. The Story of the G.A.R.* Baton Rouge: Louisiana State Press, 1952. In 1884, the National Tribune claimed a circulation of 80,000 paid subscribers. (p. 288)

Blanck, Peter, and Chen Song. "Civil War Pension Attorneys and Disability Politics." *University of Michigan Law Reform.* 35 (Fall 2001 – Winter 2002) 137-216. (p. 150) In January 1885, Lemon testified to a House committee than the Tribune had jumped to 112,000 subscribers. repository.law.umich.edu/cgi/viewcontent.cgi?article=1432&context=mjlr.

55 Rowell, George Presbury. *Geo. P. Rowell and Co.'s American Newspaper Directory.* New York: George P. Rowell & Co. Publishers, 1882. (p. 1081) *Google Books*, books.google.com/books?id=TJkQAAAAYAAJ. The National Tribune was not the only veteran-themed newspaper owned and operated by a claims agent. Nathan Ward Fitzgerald, a competitor to George Lemon, operated the newspaper *World and Citizen Soldier.* In 1882, it boasted 25,000 subscribers and 100,000 weekly readers.

At the time, it was perfectly legal for firms and claims agents to buy and sell interests in veterans disability benefits—this "market" for claims helped to fuel public distrust in the system. In 1884, a dispute arose between Fitzgerald and Lemon over who was entitled to payment for filing veterans claims. See: United States Congressional Serial Set, Volume 2330. (pp. 45, 70, 119, 142-43) *Google Books*, books.google.com/books?id=ZDlHAQAAIAAJ.

56 Oliver, J.W. *History of the Civil War Military Pensions, 1861-1865.* Bulletin of the University of Wisconsin, No. 844. Madison, Wisconsin (1917) p. 99, *Google Books*, books.google.com/books?id=zOdRAAAAMAAJ.

57 Dearing. *supra* note 53, p. 268. George Lemon "exerted the most potent single influence on the veteran movement."

58 Oliver, *supra*, note 56, p. 98-102. "That the act of July 4, 1884 was virtually the work of one claim agent cannot be doubted." (p. 101) "Mr. Lemon was largely, if not entirely, responsible." (p. 102)

59 An act making appropriations for the payment of invalid and other pensions of the United States for the fiscal year ending June thirtieth, eighteen hundred and eighty-five, and for other purposes. (July 4, 1884, ch. 181, 23 Stat. 98, 99) loc.gov/law/help/statutes-at-large/48th-congress/Session%201/c48s1ch181.pdf.
SEC. 4785. No agent or attorney or other person shall demand or receive any other compensation for his services in prosecuting a claim for pension or bounty land than such as the Commissioner of Pensions shall direct to be paid to him, not exceeding twenty-five dollars;

60 "The Will of Capt. Lemon." *New York Times.* 29 Dec. 1897. nyti.ms/2LxM3rU.

61 Glasson, *supra* note 41, p. 216.

62 Glasson, *supra* note 41, p. 172. Footnote 2, Treasury Secretary denounces the law, "this bill was not demanded by the pensioners, but by the claims agents."

63 Glasson, *supra* note 41, p. 174.

64 U.S. House Committee on Veterans' Affairs. *The Provision of Federal Benefits for Veterans. An Historical Analysis of Major Veterans Legislation, 1862-1954.* Washington, DC: Government Printing Office, December 1955. (p. 11) *HathiTrust*, hdl.handle.net/2027/mdp.39015019907974.

65 "The Democrats and The Pensions." *New York Times*, 9 Dec. 1898, nyti.ms/2RvmWK2.

66 38 U.S.C. § 101(6)

67 Bottoms, Bill. "The VFW. An Illustrated History of the Veterans of Foreign Wars." Rockville, MD: Woodbine House, 1991. (p. 1)

68 "Columbus Mileposts | Sept. 29, 1899: Roots of VFW took hold in local tailor shop." *The Columbus Dispatch.* 29 Sept. 2012. dispatch.com/article/20120929/news/309299776

69 United States Congress. *Proceedings and Debates of the Congress. Appendix.* (p. A333) 26 Jan. 1965. Washington, DC: Govt. Printing Office. *Google Books*, books.google.com/books?id=3Yah_o9r5V4C. A history of the consolidation of various veterans groups into the Veterans of Foreign Wars (VFW) from the Congressional record:

1. American Veterans of Foreign Service, organized as a national body in Columbus, OH, September 23, 1899. Chartered by the State of Ohio, October 11, 1899. Elected J. C. Putnam as commander in chief.
2. Colorado Society Army of the Philippines, organized at Denver, CO, November 1899. Gen. Irving Hale, organizer. Became a national society Army of the Philippines on August 13, 1900.
3. Philippine War Veterans, organized at Altoona, PA, July 7, 1901. H. O. Kelley, organizer. In July 1902, reorganized with C. O. Knoghton as President.
4. Philippine War Veterans, organized at Pittsburgh, PA, October 13, 1901. G. H. Smith being elected commander. On April 27, 1902, reorganized as Foreign Service Veterans with Jacques La Belle as commander. William A. Wein commander, May 26, 1903.
5. American Veterans of the Philippine and China Wars, organized at Philadelphia, PA, June 24, 1902, by Capt. Robert S. Hansbury.

Numbers 3, 4, and 5 above met together September 10-12, 1903, at Altoona, PA, and formed the American Veterans of Foreign Service. In September 1905 the original American Veterans of Foreign Service, formed September 23, 1899, and this later one, formed September 1903, united and formed a society of the same name which in August 1913 at Denver, united with the Army of the Philippines under the temporary name of Army of the Philippines, Cuba, and Puerto Rico, the name being changed within the year to Veterans of Foreign Wars.

70 An Act to Incorporate the Veterans of Foreign Wars of the United States. (May 28, 1936, ch. 471, Pub. L. 74-630, 49 Stat. 1390) loc.gov/law/help/statutes-at-large/74th-congress/session-2/c74s2ch471.pdf.
See also: 36 U.S.C. Ch. 2301 — Veterans of Foreign Wars of the United States.

71 Glasson, *supra* note 41, pp. 246-47.

72 "Old Age Pension" | An Act Granting pensions to certain enlisted men, soldiers, and officers who served in the civil war and the war with Mexico. (February 6, 1907, ch. 468, Pub. L. 59-63, 34 Stat. 879) loc.gov/law/help/statutes-at-large/59th-congress/session-2/c59s2ch468.pdf.
Blanck, Peter. Civil War Pensions & Disability. 62 Ohio St. L.J. 109, 127 (2001) kb.osu.edu/bitstream/handle/1811/70436/1/OSLJ_V62N1_0109.pdf. Between 1870 and 1910, the percentage of Civil War and other veterans receiving disability benefits rose from 5% to 93%. (p. 127)

73 "War Risk Insurance Act" | An Act To amend an Act entitled "An Act to authorize the establishment of a Bureau of War Risk Insurance in the Treasury Department," approved September second, nineteen hundred and fourteen, and for other purposes. (October 6, 1917, ch. 105, Pub. L. 65-90, 40 Stat. 398) loc.gov/law/help/statutes-at-large/65th-congress/session-1/c65s1ch105.pdf.

74 An Act To amend an Act entitled "An Act to authorize the establishment of a Bureau of War Risk Insurance in the Treasury Department," approved September second, nineteen hundred and fourteen, and an Act in amendment thereto, approved October sixth, nineteen hundred and seventeen. [see "limit on attorneys' fees" - "shall not exceed $3 in any one case."] (May 20, 1918, ch. 77, Pub. L. 65-151, 40 Stat. 555) loc.gov/law/help/statutes-at-large/65th-congress/session-2/c65s2ch77.pdf.

See also: *Margolin v. U.S.*, 269 U.S. 93 (1925)

75 56 Cong. Rec. Pt. 5, 5222 (April 17, 1918) govinfo.gov/app/details/GPO-CRECB-1918-pt5-v56.

Not all lawmakers were oblivious to the potential impact the $3 fee would have on restricting attorney representation.

If a claimant today in any. State in the Union goes out and tells an attorney that he is limited to $3, that he has waited three or six months to get action on his claim, he is going to get no legal service that can be of any value to him, and I think a provision which would keep a claimant from applying to people who can be of service to him would be a mistake. (p. 5225)

76 Vocational Rehabilitation Act | An Act to provide for vocational rehabilitation and return to civil employment of disabled persons discharge from the military or naval forces of the United States, and for other purposes. (June 27, 1918, ch. 107, Pub. L. 65-178, 40 Stat. 617) loc.gov/law/help/statutes-at-large/65th-congress/session-2/c65s2ch107.pdf.

77 38 U.S.C. Ch. 31; 38 C.F.R. Part 21

78 An Act to Incorporate the American Legion. (Sept. 16, 1919, ch. 59, Pub. L. 66-47, 41 Stat. 284) loc.gov/law/help/statutes-at-large/66th-congress/session-1/c66s1ch59.pdf.

See also: 36 U.S.C. Ch. 217 — The American Legion

The American Legion Weekly. Vol. 1. New York. July 4, 1919. hdl.handle.net/20.500.12203/2816.

79 An Act to incorporate the Disabled American Veterans of the World War. (June 17, 1923, ch. 268, Pub. L. 72-186, 47 Stat. 320) loc.gov/law/help/statutes-at-large/72nd-congress/session-1/c72s1ch268.pdf.

80 An Act To establish a Veterans' Bureau and to improve the facilities and service of such bureau, and further to amend and modify the War Risk Insurance Act. (August 9, 1921, ch. 57, Pub. L. 67-47, 42 Stat. 147). loc.gov/law/help/statutes-at-large/67th-congress/Session%201/c67s1ch57.pdf.

(Sec. 18, 42 Stat. 153) Provided further, That an ex-service man who is shown to have an active pulmonary tuberculosis or neuropsychiatric disease (of more than 10 per centum degree of disability ...) developing within two years after separation from the active military or naval service of the United States shall be considered to have acquired his disability in such service, or to have suffered an aggravation of a preexisting pulmonary tuberculosis or neuropsychiatric disease in such service ... but nothing in this proviso shall be construed to prevent a claimant from receiving the benefits of compensation and medical care and treatment for a disability due to these diseases ... at a date more than two years after separation from such service."

81 World War Adjusted Compensation Act ("Bonus Act") | An Act To provide adjusted compensation for veterans of the World War, and for other purposes. (May 19, 1924, ch. 157, Pub. L. 68-120, 43 Stat. 121); (*see also* 38 C.F.R. Part 11). loc.gov/law/help/statutes-at-large/68th-congress/session-1/c68s1ch157.pdf.

82 Manker, Tyson. "A Duty to Speak. America needs more vocal military leaders like Smedley Butler to drown out the silence of people like former defense secretary James Mattis." *The Nation*. October 2019. thenation.com/article/trump-mattis-military-dissent/.
Gen Butler Urges Bonus Army to Stick. (July 20, 1932) *New York Times*, p. 2. nyti.ms/2QGd1AI.

83 The Bonus Army: How a Protest Led to the GI Bill. *NPR. All Things Considered*. 11 Nov. 2011. npr.org/2011/11/11/142224795/the-bonus-army-how-a-protest-led-to-the-gi-bill.
"Weary Bonus Army Reaches Capitol by Truck." (May 30, 1932) *New York Times*, p. 1. nyti.ms/2s1cNtD.
"Bonus Army Asked to Leave Capitol." (June 9, 1932) *New York Times*, pp. 1, 19. nyti.ms/35mjbKw.
"Bonus Army Calls for 50,000 New Recruits." (June 11, 1932) *New York Times*, pp. 1-2. nyti.ms/2KEQQHd.
"5,000 in Bonus Army Jam Capitol Steps." (July 2, 1932) *New York Times*, p. 2. nyti.ms/2s5MPp4.
"Bonus Army Boos Hoover at Capitol." (July 6, 1932) *New York Times*, p. 2. nyti.ms/2r9cWed.
"Hoover Signs $100,000 Bill for Bonus Army." (July 9, 1932) *New York Times*, p. 2. nyti.ms/2QE69UD.
"Bonus Army Begins an All-Night Siege." (July 13, 1932) *New York Times*, p. 2. nyti.ms/33aXawC.
"Bonus Army Digs in to Stay Until 1945." (July 19, 1932) *New York Times*, pp.1-2. nyti.ms/2XBsDqw.
"Hoover Orders Eviction." (July 29, 1932) *New York Times*, pp. 1-2. nyti.ms/2KIm54q.
"Anacostia Camp No More." (July 29, 1932) *New York Times*, pp. 1, 3. nyti.ms/2O6ywJq.
"V.F.W. Assails Hoover on Bonus Evacuation." (September 1, 1932) *New York Times*, p. 19. nyti.ms/35oqRMo.
"Bonus Army Moves to Organize Nation." (October 7, 1932) *New York Times*, p. 3. nyti.ms/35kRfGQ.

84 World War Veterans Act. (June 7, 1924, ch. 320, Pub. L. 68-242, 43 Stat. 607) loc.gov/law/help/statutes-at-large/68ᵗʰ-congress/session-1/c68s1ch320.pdf.

In *Silberschein v. U.S.*, 266 U.S. 221, 225 (1924), the Supreme Court upheld the finality of decisions made by the Veterans Bureau, while leaving open the possibility of district court suits under an "arbitrary or capricious" standard similar to the later Administrative Procedures Act, which was enacted later, in 1946.

We must hold that his decision of such questions is final and conclusive, and not subject to judicial review, at least unless the decision is wholly unsupported by the evidence, or is wholly dependent upon a question of law, or is seen to be clearly arbitrary or capricious.

See also: *U.S. v. Williams*, 278 U.S. 255 (1929); *Meadows v. U.S.*, 281 U.S. 271 (1930).

85 Section 500 of the 1924 World War Veterans Act set the maximum fee for helping a veteran file a claim at ten dollars:

SEC. 500. That payment to any attorney or agent for such assistance as may be required in the preparation and execution of the necessary papers in any application to the bureau shall not exceed $10 in any one case.

See also: *Hines v. Lowrey*, 305 U.S. 85 (1938)

86 An Act To authorize the President to consolidate and coordinate governmental activities affecting war veterans. (July 3, 1930. ch. 863, Pub. L. 71-536, 46 Stat. 1016) loc.gov/law/help/statutes-at-large/71ˢᵗ-congress/session-2/c71s2ch863.pdf. (*see also* Executive Order No. 5398, supra, 31)

87 Publications of proceedings of veterans' annual encampments authorized | Joint Resolution To print annually as separate House documents the proceedings of the National Encampment of the Grand Army of the Republic, the United Spanish War Veterans, the Veterans of Foreign Wars of the United States, the American Legion, and the Disabled American Veterans of the World War. (March 2, 1931, ch. 378, Pub. Res. 71-136, 46 Stat. 1481) loc.gov/law/help/statutes-at-large/71ˢᵗ-congress/session-3/c71s3ch378.pdf.

88 National Economy Act | An Act To maintain the credit of the United States Government. (March 20, 1933, ch. 3, 48 Stat. 8) loc.gov/law/help/statutes-at-large/73ʳᵈ-congress/session-1/c73s1ch3.pdf.

House of Representatives. *Congressional Record 77, Pt. 1* (March 11, 1933) p. 198. govinfo.gov/app/details/GPO-CRECB-1933-pt1-v77/GPO-CRECB-1933-pt1-v77-5-2.

89 Carlson, Frank (KS). *Congressional Record* 83 (4 May 1938) p. 6252, *Google Books*, books.google.com/books?id=22EUQZYNkZsC.

90 *Lynch v. U.S.*, 292 U.S. 571, 587 (1934)

91 *Johnson v. Robinson*, 415 U.S. 361 (1974), the Supreme Court upheld the finality of BVA decisions, ruling that statutory bar against judicial review of individual disability claims decisions made by the VA does not prohibit

federal courts from reviewing Constitutional questions of the veterans benefits system enacted by Congress.

92 Executive Order No. 6230, Veterans Regulation No. 2(a), July 28, 1933. For a complete history of the Board of Veterans Appeals from 1933-1983, see: *HathiTrust*, hdl.handle.net/2027/mdp.39015081891452.

93 Adjusted Compensation Payment Act of 1936 | An Act To provide for the immediate payment of World War adjusted service certificates, for the cancelation of unpaid interest accrued on loans secured by such certificates, and for other purposes. (January 27, 1936, ch. 32, Pub. L. 74-425, 49 Stat. 1099) loc.gov/law/help/statutes-at-large/74th-congress/session-2/c74s2ch32.pdf.

94 An act to liberalize the provisions of Public Law Numbered 484, Seventy-third Congress, to effect uniform provisions in laws administered by the Veterans' Administration, to extend the Employees' Compensation Act with limitations to World War Veterans and other persons, and for other purposes. (June 29, 1936, ch. 867, Pub. L. 74-844, 49 Stat. 2031) loc.gov/law/help/statutes-at-large/74th-congress/session-2/c74s2ch867.pdf.

95 Servicemen's Readjustment Act | An Act To provide Federal Government aid for the readjustment in civilian life of returning World War II veterans. (June 22, 1944, ch. 268, Pub. L. 78-346, 58 Stat. 284) loc.gov/law/help/statutes-at-large/78th-congress/session-2/c78s2ch268.pdf.

96 The 1944 GI bill, most widely known for its educational benefit, was actually a wide-ranging Bill of Veterans Rights that encompassed a variety of service members entitlements. (i.e. home loans, unemployment insurance, education and training, medical care)
U.S. Congressional Research Service. GI Bills Enacted Prior to 2008 and Related Veterans' Educational Assistance Programs: A Primer (October 6, 2016; R42785) by Cassandria Dortch. fas.org/sgp/crs/misc/R42785.pdf.
U.S. Congressional Research Service. The Post-9/11 GI Bill. A Primer. (August 1, 2018; R42755) by Cassandria Dortch. fas.org/sgp/crs/misc/R42755.pdf.

97 Mustering out Payment Act | An Act to provide for mustering-out payments to members of the armed forces, and for other purposes. (February 3, 1944, ch. 9, Pub. L. 78-225, 58 Stat. 8) loc.gov/law/help/statutes-at-large/78th-congress/session-2/c78s2ch9.pdf.

98 Mustering-out payments are a tax-free benefit, like disability compensation, and their provisions still appear in the tax code. *See* 26 C.F.R. § 1.113-1.
For the purposes of the exclusion from gross income under section 113 of mustering-out payments with respect to service in the Armed Forces, mustering-out payments are payments made to any recipients pursuant to the provisions of 38 U.S.C. 2105 (formerly section 5 of the Mustering-out Payment Act of 1944 and section 505 of the Veterans' Readjustment Assistance Act of 1952).

99 An Act to increase the service-connected disability rates of compensation or pension payable to veterans of Worlds War I and World War II. (May 27, 1944, ch. 207, Pub. L. 78-312, 58 Stat. 229) loc.gov/law/help/statutes-at-large/78th-congress/session-2/c78s2ch207.pdf.

100 An Act to clarify the terms "compensation" and "pension" under laws administered by the Veterans' Administration. (July 9, 1946, ch. 545, Pub. L. 79-494, 60 Stat. 524) loc.gov/law/help/statutes-at-large/79th-congress/session-2/c79s2ch545.pdf.

101 An Act to incorporate the AMVETS, American Veterans of WWII. (July 23, 1947, ch. 298, Pub. L. 80-216, 61 Stat. 403) loc.gov/law/help/statutes-at-large/80th-congress/session-1/c80s1ch298.pdf.

102 Veterans Readjustment Assistance Act | An Act To provide vocational readjustment and to restore lost educational opportunities to certain persons who served in the Armed Forces on or after June 27, 1950. (July 16, 1952, ch. 875, Pub. L. 82-550, 66 Stat. 663) govinfo.gov/app/details/STATUTE-66/STATUTE-66-Pg663.

103 Veterans' Benefits Act of 1957 | An Act To consolidate into one Act, and to simplify and make more uniform, the laws administered by the Veterans' Administration relating to compensation, pension, hospitalization, and burial benefits. (June 17, 1957, Pub. L. 85-56, 71 Stat. 83) govinfo.gov/app/details/STATUTE-71/STATUTE-71-Pg83.

104 Veterans' Benefits Enactment as Title 38, U.S. Code | An Act To consolidate into one act all of the laws administered by the Veterans Administration, and for other purposes. (September 2, 1958, Pub. L. 85-857, 72 Stat. 1105) govinfo.gov/app/details/STATUTE-72/STATUTE-72-Pg1105.

105 An Act To increase the monthly rate of pension payable to widows and former widows of deceased veterans of the Spanish-American War, Civil War, Indian War, and Mexican War, and to provide pensions to widows of veterans who served in the military or naval forces of the Confederate States of America during the Civil War. (May 23, 1958, Pub. L. 85-425, 72 Stat. 133) govinfo.gov/app/details/STATUTE-72/STATUTE-72-Pg133-2.

106 Veterans Pension Act of 1959 | An Act to modify the pension programs for veterans of World War I, World War II, and the Korean conflict, and their widows and children. (August 29, 1959, Pub. L. 86-211, 73 Stat. 432) govinfo.gov/app/details/STATUTE-73/STATUTE-73-Pg432-2.

107 Associated Press. (April 1, 1989) "First of Agent Orange Grants Given to Veterans' Agencies." *New York Times*, p. 7. nyti.ms/35osJ7L.
Associated Press. (July 19, 1989) "Veterans Dept. Offers Agent Orange Change." *New York Times*, p. 14. nyti.ms/35kPvxi.
Associated Press. (July 3, 1991) "Vietnam Veterans to Get Benefits For Ailment Tied to Agent Orange." *New York Times*, p. 6. nyti.ms/37tfbtl.

Haberman, Clyde. (May 11, 2014) "Agent Orange's Long Legacy for Vietnam and Veterans." *New York Times*. nyti.ms/1ouNfIT.

108   Veterans Readjustment Benefits Act of 1966 | An Act To provide readjustment assistance to veterans who serve in the Armed Forces during the induction period. (March 3, 1966, Pub. L. 89-358, 80 Stat. 12) govinfo.gov/app/details/STATUTE-80/STATUTE-80-Pg12.

109   Vietnam Era Veterans' Readjustment Assistance Act of 1974 (December 3, 1974, Pub. L. 93-508, 88 Stat. 1578) govinfo.gov/app/details/STATUTE-88/STATUTE-88-Pg1578.

110   Seibert, William, et al. "Personnel Records Are Consolidated At New Location In St. Louis." *Prologue*, Vol. 43, p.8 (Fall 2011) archives.gov/publications/prologue/2011/fall/nprc.html.

111   "Veterans to Get Charter." *New York Times*, 22 May 1986, p. 42. nyti. ms/38cFHHP.

112   An act to grant a Federal charter to the Vietnam Veterans of America, Inc. (May 23, 1986, Pub. L. 99-318, 100 Stat. 474) govinfo.gov/app/details/STATUTE-100/STATUTE-100-Pg474.

113   Vietnam Veterans of America, Inc., *Constitution*, as amended, Art. I Sec. 3A. https://va-handbook.com/vva-constitution/.

114   Veterans Health Care Amendments of 1979 | An Act To amend title 38, United States Code, to revise and improve certain health-care programs of the Veterans' Administration, to authorize the construction, alteration, and acquisition of certain medical facilities, and to expand certain benefits for disabled veterans; and for other purposes. (June 13, 1979, Pub. L. 96-22, 93 Stat. 47) govinfo.gov/app/details/STATUTE-93/STATUTE-93-Pg47.

115   "U.S. Defoliant is Linked to Liver Cancer in Vietnam." *New York Times*, 6 May 1979, p. 25. nyti.ms/2QFVPLU.

Coalition to Study Effect of Agent Orange on G.I.'s." *New York Times*, 17 July 1979, sec. A p. 10. nyti.ms/35hCvZg.

New Bill Would Aid Vietnam Veterans. *New York Times*, 11 Oct. 1979, sec. A, p. 9. nyti.ms/2OBBYKY.

Pentagon Is Disputed on Exposure Of Troops to Herbicide in Vietnam. *New York Times*, 25 Nov. 1979, p. 1. nyti.ms/2s1bQl3.

U.S. Panel Asking a Broad Study of Toxic Agents of Vietnam War. *New York Times*, 18 May 1981, sec. A, p. 17. nyti.ms/2OvLsaE.

American Legion to Sue U.S. Over Agent Orange. *New York Times*, 2 Aug. 1990, sec.A, p. 16. nyti.ms/2KHnN5Q.

116   Agent Orange Act of 1991 | An Act To provide for the Secretary of Veterans Affairs to obtain independent scientific review of the available scientific evidence regarding associations between diseases and exposure to dioxin and other chemical compounds in herbicides, and for other purposes. (February

6, 1991, Pub. L. 102-4, 105 Stat. 11) govinfo.gov/app/details/STATUTE-105/STATUTE-105-Pg11.

Under the Act, veterans who served in Vietnam during the period when the U.S. used Agent Orange (January 9, 1962 to May 7, 1975), and who develop specified diseases associated with exposure to Agent Orange, are *presumptively* entitled to disability benefits. 38 U.S.C. § 1116(a)(1)(A)

117 *Procopio v. Wilkie*, 913 F.3d 1371 (Fed. Cir. 2019), the Court of Appeals for the Federal Circuit ruled in favor of so-called "Blue Water" veterans, who had previously been denied the same presumptions of service-connection for Agent Orange diseases as veterans who served on land. Congress later codified the provision (see Blue Water Navy Act of 2019 below)

Blue Water Navy Vietnam Veterans Act of 2019 | An Act to amend title 38, United States Code, to clarify presumptions relating to the exposure of certain veterans who served in the vicinity of the Republic of Vietnam, and for other purposes. (June 25, 2019, Pub. L. 116-23, 133 Stat. 966) govinfo.gov/app/details/PLAW-116publ23.

See: 38 U.S.C. § 1116A. Presumptions of service connection for veterans who served offshore of the Republic of Vietnam.

118 Department of Veterans Affairs Act | An Act To establish the Veterans' Administration as an executive department, and for other purposes. (October 25, 1988, Pub. L. 100-527, 102 Stat. 2635) govinfo.gov/app/details/STATUTE-102/STATUTE-102-Pg2635.

119 Department of Veterans Affairs Codification Act | An Act To amend title 38, United States Code, to codify the provisions of law relating to the establishment of the Department of Veterans Affairs, to restate and reorganize certain provisions of that title, and for other purposes. (August 6, 1991, Pub. L. 102-83, 105 Stat. 378) govinfo.gov/app/details/STATUTE-105/STATUTE-105-Pg378.

120 Veterans Benefits Improvement Act of 1988 | An Act ... to establish a Court of Veterans' Appeals and to provide for judicial review of certain final decisions of the Board of Veterans' Appeals. (November 18, 1988, Pub. L. 100-687, 102 Stat. 4105) govinfo.gov/app/details/STATUTE-102/STATUTE-102-Pg4105.

121 "Veterans Press Senators for Right To Appeal Claims to U.S. Courts." *New York Times*, 29 Apr. 1988, p. 18. nyti.ms/2PomQkN.

122 Veterans Programs Enhancement Act of 1998 | An Act To amend title 38, United States Code, to improve benefits and services provided to Persian Gulf War veterans, to provide cost-of-living adjustment in rates of compensation paid to veterans with service-connected disabilities to enhance programs providing health care, compensation, education, insurance, and other benefits for veterans, and for other purposes. (November 11, 1998, Pub. L. 105-368, 112 Stat. 3315) govinfo.gov/app/details/PLAW-105publ368.

See also: 38 U.S.C. § 7251

123 *Morton v. West*, 12 Vet.App. 477 (1999), opinion withdrawn and appeal dismissed sub nom. *Morton v. Gober*, 14 Vet.App. 174 (2000) (per curiam order)

124 Photo of the author on the third day of the 2003 Iraq invasion. "US Marine Corps (USMC) Corporal (CPL) Tyson Manker, assigned to Charlie Company, 1ST Battalion, 7th Marines, displays a PG-76 Anti Tank Grenade found in a weapons cache on the side of the highway near Az Zubayr, Iraq, during Operation IRAQI FREEDOM." 24 May 2003. *National Archives.* National Archives Identifier: 6651698. catalog.archives.gov/id/6651698.

125 Veterans Benefits, Health Care, and Information Technology Act of 2006 | An Act To amend title 38, United States Code, to repeal certain limitations on attorney representation of claimants for benefits under laws administered by the Secretary of Veterans Affairs, to expand eligibility for the Survivors' and Dependents' Educational Assistance Programs, to otherwise improve veterans' benefits, memorial affairs, and health-care programs, to enhance information security programs of the Department of Veterans Affairs, and for other purposes. (December 22, 2006, Pub. L. 109-461, 120 Stat. 3403) govinfo.gov/app/details/STATUTE-120/STATUTE-120-Pg3403.

126 Davidson, Joe. "VA Struggles to fill hospital jobs. It has 49,000 openings across the country." *The Washington Post*, 5 Nov. 2019. washingtonpost.com/politics/va-struggles-to-fill-hospital-jobs-it-has-49000-openings-across-the-country/2019/11/05/91fbd4fe-ff4f-11e9-9777-5cd51c6fec6f_story.html.

127 Shulkin, David. "It Shouldn't Be This Hard to Serve Your Country." New York: Public Affairs, 2019.

128 The Department of Veterans Affairs serves as our nation's backup healthcare system in case of war or national emergency—an important role in the national security apparatus. *See*: "The V.A. Prepares to Back Up a Health Care System Threatened by Coronavirus." *New York Times*. 15 Apr. 2020. nytimes.com/2020/03/15/us/politics/veterans-affairs-coronavirus.html.

★ ★ ★

Chapter 2

Veterans Law

Veterans law comes from a hierarchy of legal authorities.

§ 2.1 — Legal Authorities

1. THE CONSTITUTION

Not only do all military service members take an oath to protect and defend the U.S. Constitution, the founding document that created our national government also forms the basis of all laws in America, including those that govern veterans benefits. The Constitution sets the guiding principles of lawfulness in America, and serves as a "measuring stick" for determining the legality of Congressional and Executive acts. Actions that violate the Constitution are declared "unconstitutional" by the judiciary, making them null and void.

Article I of the U.S. Constitution created the legislative branch of our federal government, and Section 8 vests in the Congress specific "enumerated powers" to —among other things— declare war, raise and support armies, provide and maintain a navy, and make rules to regulate the land and naval forces. The Constitution further instructs Congress to create laws, called *statutes*, that are necessary to fulfill these obligations.

Article II entrusts enforcement of the laws passed by Congress in an executive branch. To assist the President in performing these duties Congress has over time enacted legislation to create various departments and agencies, including the Department of Veterans Affairs and its different sub-agencies. (*see* 38 U.S.C. § 301) The VA in turn makes rules, called *regulations*, that inform the public about how it will implement the laws.

Because the executive branch is the largest of the three branches in terms of manpower and the functions it serves, its various departments, agencies and employee workforce are often referred to as "the federal government."

Article III established the federal judiciary, including the Supreme Court, and entrusted the courts it created with judicial powers. Ever since the landmark 1803 Supreme Court decision *Marbury v. Madison*, the judicial branch has exercised review over the other two co-equal branches, deciding when and how legislative and executive actions are in violation of the Constitution. Federal courts also have the power to review decisions of lower courts. Published court decisions, called opinions, orders, holdings or rulings are known as ***case law*** or common law.

★ ★ ★

2. STATUTES

Think Article I. Legislative statutes are the laws passed by Congress. Congress' power to pass laws comes from Article I of the Constitution. All statutes start as ***bills*** in the House of Representatives and the Senate, where they need a majority of votes for passage before being sent to the President for veto or signature into law. Once signed, statute provisions are "codified" and consolidated into a comprehensive body of law called "The Code of Laws of the United States of America," the U.S. Code, or simply U.S.C. The U.S. Code contains 50 Titles covering all subjects of Congressional jurisdiction. Veterans Benefits appear as Title 38.

On its journey from bill to law, a statute takes several forms.

A Bill. When a **bill** is proposed, it is assigned a bill number to identify where it was introduced and the session of Congress.

Example. H.R. 5288 (100th) The Veterans Judicial Review Act

HR	5288	100th	The Veterans Judicial Review Act
House of Representatives	Bill Number	100th Congress	Name of bill

★ ★

Public Law. When a bill is passed and becomes law, it is assigned a chapter number to identify which Congress passed the law. For example, when H.R. 5288 became law it was assigned the chapter number 100-687. It was the 687th law passed by the 100th Congress.

Example. Pub. L. 100-687

Pub. L.	100	687
Public Law	100th Congress	Number law passed that year by Congress

★ ★

Statutes at Large. At the end of every 2-year Congressional session, all of the laws passed by Congress over the previous two years are compiled chronologically into a series of books called the U.S. Statutes at Large. Every statute is given a citation to identify the volume and page where it is published. For example, at the end of the 100th Congress, when Public Law 100-687 was published in the Statutes at Large, it was assigned the citation 102 Stat. 4105.

Example. 102 Stat. 4105

102	Stat.	4105
Volume number	Statutes at Large	Page number

★ ★

U.S. Code. Modern laws contain amendments to the U.S. Code, which is organized by subject. Ultimately, the Code is the primary binding source for citing statutes.

Example. 38 U.S.C. § 7252. Jurisdiction; finality of decisions (1988)

38	U.S.C.	§ 7252	Jurisdiction	1988
Title number	U.S. Code	Section symbol and section number	Name	Date of statute edition

To summarize, members of Congress offer Bills, which, if passed by both houses and signed by the President, become Public Laws that amend the U.S. Code. At the end of each 2-year Congressional session, all Public Laws from the previous two years are published together as a set and assigned an additional Statutory citation. As such, each piece of enacted legislation has multiple identifiers, including title, short title, public law number, and statute number, with changes to the U.S. Code.

For example, the Agent Orange Act of 1991:

BILL TITLE: H.R. 556. An Act: To provide for the Secretary of Veterans Affairs to obtain independent scientific review of the available scientific evidence regarding associations between diseases and exposure to dioxin and other chemical

SHORT TITLE: Agent Orange Act of 1991

PUBLIC LAW: Pub. L. 102-4—Feb. 6, 1991.

STATUTE: 105 Stat. 11

U.S. CODE: 38 U.S.C. § 1116. Presumptions of service connection for diseases associated with exposure to certain herbicide agents; presumption of exposure for veterans who served in the Republic of Vietnam (2021) (formerly § 316)

★ ★ ★

3. REGULATIONS

Think Article II. Regulations are official rules used by executive agencies and departments to enforce the law, and are found in the "Code of Federal Regulations," or C.F.R. ("the Code"). VA regulations appear at C.F.R. Title 38 as Pensions, Bonuses, and Veterans Relief.

Example. 38 C.F.R. § 3.155 – How to file a claim. (2014)

38	C.F.R.	§ 3.155	How to file a claim	2014
Title	Code of Federal Regulations	Section symbol and number	Name	Date of Code Edition

When legislation, court orders, petitions and other factors make new regulations necessary, VA gives notice of its intent to updates its rules by publishing the new, proposed regulation in the ***Federal Register***, the official daily journal of the United States.[1] A subsequent public commenting period gives the public a chance to submit remarks with input about the proposed regulations, after which time a final binding rule is published. Unless nullified by Congress or found unconstitutional by the Courts, the new regulations are incorporated into the C.F.R.

Timeline for New Regulations

1. Public Law / Order / Other	2. Federal Register Notice: Proposed Rule	3. Federal Register FINAL Rule	4. Code of Federal Regulations

Example. 83 Fed. Reg. 39818 (August 10, 2018) *proposed rule*
84 Fed. Reg. 138, 140 (January 18, 2019) *final rule*

84	Fed. Reg.	138	140	Jan. 18, 2019
Volume	Federal Register	Starting page number	Page that contains cited information	Date Published

In additional to formal regulations, VA also uses informal rules and guidelines to implement its mission.

---

[1] Federal Register Act | An Act To provide for the compiling and publishing of the Official Register of the United States. (August 28, 1935, ch. 795, Pub. L. 387-74, 49 Stat. 956) loc.gov/law/help/statutes-at-large/74th-congress/session-1/c74s1ch795.pdf.

- **VA Office of General Counsel[2] (OGC) opinions** provide additional guidance on specific issues and are binding on all VA claims adjudicators, Regional Office employees, and the Board of Veterans Appeals ("BVA").[3] OGC opinions are only binding on the VA and may be reviewed by the CAVC.[4] The OGC is led by a Senate-approved chief legal officer who assists the VA Secretary on all legal matters. A summary of precedent OGC opinions through 2019 appears in the Federal Register,[5] which can be found by Google searching "VA OGC opinions."

- **The M21-1 Manual** (*Veterans Disability Adjudication Procedures Manual*) is an internal guide used by VA adjudicators when reviewing benefits claims. "The VA consolidates its policy and procedures into one resource known as the M21-1 Manual."[6] According to VA, "The M21–1 is an internal manual used to convey guidance to VA adjudicators."[7] Even though its provisions generally do not have the same binding effect as formal VA regulations or statutes passed by Congress, the M21-1, which is often referred to as the "Bible," is crucial to understanding how claims are processed at the regional office level. In some situations, a failure to follow M21-1 guidelines could possibly serve as the grounds for an appeal.

* * *

---

[2] 38 U.S.C. § 311. Office of General Counsel; (*see also* 38 C.F.R. §14.500. Functions and Responsibilities of the General Counsel)
(§ 311) There is in the Department the Office of the General Counsel. There is at the head of the office a General Counsel, who is appointed by the President, by and with the advice and consent of the Senate. The General Counsel is the chief legal officer of the Department and provides legal assistance to the Secretary concerning the programs and policies of the Department.

[3] 38 U.S.C. § 7104; 38 C.F.R. §§ 14.507, 19.5

[4] *Hatch v. Principi*, 18 Vet.App. 527, 535 (2004), citing *Butts v. Brown*, 5 Vet.App 532, 539 (1993) (en banc).

[5] *Summary of Precedent Opinions of the General Counsel*. 84 Fed. Reg. 13,991-13,997 (24 July 2009). https://www.federalregister.gov/d/2019-06855.

[6] *DAV v. Sec'y of Veterans Affairs*, 859 F.3d 1072, 1074 (Fed. Cir. 2017).

[7] 72 Fed. Reg. 66,218, 66,219 (27 Nov. 2007) federalregister.gov/d/E7-22983.

4. CASE LAW (aka Common Law)

Think Article III. When the judicial branch is called upon to settle disputes, written decisions of the courts are known as *case law*. When a court rules on a particular issue, the new ruling and law it creates is called a *precedent*. If, however, a court adheres to a legally-sound precedent that was already established in a previous case it is called *stare decisis*. Precedent rulings are given by courts in two situations. First, when social attitudes evolve, established precedents are sometimes viewed by the evolving public as "bad" law that must be overturned. For example, in *Brown v. Board of Education* (1954), the U.S. Supreme Court overruled its previous discriminatory ruling in *Plessy v. Ferguson* (1898), and in the process created a new precedent. The second reason for issuing a precedent ruling is when a novel issue is before the court where no precedent exists.

Important cases, like those before the Federal Circuit and the Supreme Court, appear in multiple publications and with different citations.

Example: *Walters v. Nat. Assoc. of Radiation Survivors*, 473 U.S. 305, 105 S.Ct. 3180, 87 L.Ed.2d 220 (1985)

Official citation – Supreme Court

Walters v. Nat. Assoc. of Radiation Survivors	473	U.S.	305
Parties to the case	Volume	US Reports	Page number

Parallel citation – Supreme Court Reporter

105	S.Ct.	3180
Volume	Supreme Court Reporter	Page

Parallel citation – Lawyer's Edition 2nd Series

87	L.Ed.2d	220	1985
Volume	Lawyer's Edition 2nd Series	Page	Decision Year

★ ★

Another case law citation example:

Cushman v. Shinseki, 576 F.3d 1290 (Fed. Cir. 2009)

Cushman v. Shinseki	576	F.3d	1290	Fed. Cir.	2009
Parties	Volume	Federal Reporter 3rd Series	Page	Federal Circuit Court of Appeals	Decision Year

Not all veterans case law comes from Article III courts, however.

★ ★ ★

The U.S. Court of Appeals for Veterans Claims ("CAVC")

The U.S. Court of Appeals for Veterans Claims ("CAVC") reviews decisions of the Board of Veterans Appeals ("BVA") on appeal, and operates in virtually the same manner as other federal courts. CAVC rulings not only guide VA claims examiners, but they can also be cited in claims appeals and legal briefs to argue why the Board's decision was incorrect. Note, the CAVC is organized under Article I of the Constitution, and is considered an administrative court. CAVC judges serve 15-year terms, unlike Article III judges who are appointed for life.

CAVC opinions are considered binding precedent when a panel of three or more judges issue a decision.[8] To prevail on your claim or appeal, it is important to know if CAVC has decided issues that are similar and relevant to your individual claim. Thankfully, Congress requires the CAVC to publish all of its precedent decisions online.[9] (Google search "Court of Appeals for Veterans Claims" or follow the link at https://va-handbook.com)

CAVC assigns a unique case number to each appellate decision.

ex.   *Hickson v. West*, Case. No. 96-1669

CAVC cases are later recorded in a bound series of books called "West's Veterans Appeals Reporter," which assigns each case a volume and page number. The citation that appears in *West's* is the citation most commonly used to cite CAVC cases.

ex.   *Hickson v. West*, 12 Vet.App. 247 (1999)

Hickson v. West	12	Vet.App.	247	1999
Parties	Volume	West's Veterans Appeals Reporter	Page	Decision Year

---

[8] *Frankel v. Derwinski*, 1 Vet.App. 23, 25 (1990) established the criteria for single-judge CAVC orders, "Whether a decision warrants an opinion of the Court or whether it should be summarily decided by [a single judge's] order is, to a great extent, a function of its precedential value."
In order for a single CAVC judge to rule on a BVA decision—as opposed to a panel of three or more judges deciding the case with a precedential decision that establishes new case law—the BVA decision that is being appealed:
(1) must be of relative simplicity;
(2) cannot establish a new rule of law;
(3) cannot alter, modify, criticize, or clarify an existing rule of law;
(4) cannot apply an established rule of law to a novel fact situation;
(5) cannot constitute the only recent, binding precedent on a particular point of law within the power of the Court to decide;
(6) cannot involve a legal issue of continuing public interest; and
(7) the outcome cannot be reasonably debatable.
[9] 38 U.S.C. § 7269

Lastly, decisions of **The Board of Veterans Appeals** (the Board, or "BVA") are not case law or precedent and cannot be cited in your appeal. However, BVA decisions, which are indexed and searchable online, are extremely helpful to understanding how the law is applied to individual VA claims and appeals. BVA decisions regularly cite statutes, regulations, and rulings by the CAVC and federal courts. (Google search "Board of Veterans Appeals Decisions" or follow the link at https://va-handbook.com)

$$\star \; \star \; \star$$

§ 2.2 — Structure of the Department of Veterans Affairs

The U.S. Department of Veterans Affairs is comprised of three main Administrations.

Veterans Benefits Administration—[10]

The Veterans Benefits Administration ("VBA") handles all applications for VA benefits, including registering claims and determining eligibility. With a budget of more than $100 billion annually, VBA is also tasked with administering disability compensation benefits, pensions, VA home loan guarantees, insurance, education, vocational rehabilitation benefits and more.

Veterans Health Administration—[11]

The Veterans Health Administration ("VHA") is one of the world's largest integrated health care systems, providing medical and hospital care to veterans at 167 medical centers and more than 1,400 community-based outpatient clinics and Vet Centers across the country.

---

[10] 38 U.S.C. § 7701
[11] 38 U.S.C. § 7301

National Cemetery Administration—[12]

The National Cemetery Administration ("NCA") oversees a system of 131 national cemeteries and other soldiers' lots and monuments. The NCA is also responsible for providing death benefits like burial headstones and markers for deceased veterans.

★ ★

Two quasi-independent agencies also operate within the VA.

Board of Veterans Appeals—[13]

Every veteran is entitled to one review of their claim on appeal to the Board of Veterans Appeals ("the Board" or "BVA"). BVA is comprised of Veterans Law Judges ("VLJs") who review Regional Office decisions and issue more than 50,000 rulings every year. Decisions of the Board are the final word of the VA (which in some cases are appealable to the U.S. Court of Appeals for Veterans Claims, which operates independently of the VA).

Office of General Counsel—[14]

The Office of General Counsel ("OGC") is responsible for all legal matters within the VA. The OCG, which effectively serves as the "law firm" of the Department, is responsible for helping to implement all laws that are applicable to VA, providing legal opinions that interpret statutes and regulations, and handling all litigation in suits that involve VA employees. The duties of the OCG are defined by statute and regulation.

---

[12] 38 U.S.C. § 2400; C.F.R. Pt. 38
[13] 38 U.S.C. Ch. 71; 38 C.F.R. Pt. 20
[14] 38 U.S.C. § 311; 38 C.F.R. § 14.500

U.S. DEPARTMENT OF VETERANS AFFAIRS

VETERANS HEALTH ADMINISTRATION	NATIONAL CEMETERY ADMINISTRATION	VETERANS BENEFITS ADMINISTRATION
Office of General Counsel	Board of Veterans Appeals	

★ ★ ★

§ 2.3 — VA Claim / Appeals Hierarchy

The VA claims process is uniquely pro-veteran and non-adversarial. *Skoczen v. Shinseki*, 564 F.3d 1319, 1328 (Fed. Cir. 2009)

1. VA Regional Offices—[15]

All disability compensation claims are filed with one of 58 VA regional offices ("VARO" or "RO") around the country. As part of the Veterans Benefits Administration, VA regional office employees are tasked with helping veterans develop their claims by obtaining relevant federal service records and medical evidence.

Non-adversarial benefits claims filed at VAROs are *ex parte*, or one-sided, which means that unlike conventional civilian trials where two opposing sides advance competing versions / theories of the facts, with VA claims only the veteran gets to submit evidence and the VA has a duty to help them substantiate the claim. After a review of the evidentiary record, using, if necessary, the benefit-of-the-doubt standard, VA will issue a decision about the veteran's injury and claim for benefits.

In addition, under the modern appeals system, VAROs conduct higher-level reviews of denied claims on appeal (same evidence), or supplemental claims that include new and relevant evidence. At the VARO level, VA has a duty to assist veterans with developing evidence during original and supplemental claims, but not for higher-level reviews of the record. VARO decisions may be appealed to the Board of Veterans Appeals.

★ ★

---

[15] 38 U.S.C. § 315

2. Board of Veterans Appeals—[16]

The Board of Veterans Appeals ("the Board" or "BVA") conducts *de novo*[17] reviews (without deference to the previous decision) of VARO rating decisions on appeal.[18] The Board must follow all applicable statutes, VA Regulations, and precedent opinions of the Office of General Counsel ("OGC").[19] The BVA is responsible for making the final decision on behalf of the VA.

A veteran may appeal to the Board after (1) a VARO decision, (2) a supplemental claim, or (3) a higher-level review. Veterans have a right to a BVA hearing before a Veterans Law Judge ("VLJ"), either at the Board in Washington, DC, or with a traveling VLJ at the local VARO.[20] Veterans have the right to present testimony and other evidence to the Board.[21] If a hearing is not desired or needed, veterans may instead request judicial review of the record without a hearing. Decisions of the Board may be appealed to the U.S. Court of Appeals for Veterans Claims.

**Note that when a BVA decision is appealed to the Court of Appeals for Veterans Claims, proceedings become adversarial. Forshey v. Principi, 284 F.3d 1335, 1355 (Fed. Cir. 2002)*

★ ★

3. U.S. Court of Appeals for Veterans Claims—[22]

The U.S. Court of Appeals for Veterans Claims ("CAVC") has exclusive limited jurisdiction to review decisions of the Board on appeal. The CAVC, which offers veterans the first level of appellate review conducted outside of the VA (Article I), may only review the record that was before the BVA.[23] Veterans who do not completely prevail at the BVA may appeal

---

[16] 38 U.S.C. Ch. 71

[17] "De novo" means "anew." Black's Law Dictionary (11th ed. 2019)

[18] *Jarrell v. Nicholson*, 20 Vet.App. 326, 329 (2006)

[19] 38 U.S.C. § 7104(c)

[20] 38 C.F.R. §§ 20.705, 14.628(a)(2)(iv-v)

[21] 38 C.F.R. §§ 20.706, 20.710

[22] 38 U.S.C. Ch. 72

[23] 38 U.S.C. § 7266(a)

to the CAVC. CAVC appeals are adversarial.[24] CAVC decisions may in limited circumstances be appealed to the U.S. Court of Appeals for the Federal Circuit.

The CAVC may hold unlawful and set aside or reverse VA's **findings of material fact** that are adverse to the veteran if the finding is "clearly erroneous."[25] Clearly erroneous, as defined by the U.S. Supreme Court, means that a reviewing court "is left with the definite and firm conviction that a mistake has been committed."[26] In *Gilbert v. Derwinski*,[27] the CAVC adopted the Supreme Court's definition of clearly erroneous as applied to veteran's law. Note that a decision by the BVA may be clearly erroneous even if there is evidence to support the BVA's decision.[28] Findings that are favorable to the veteran cannot be reviewed by the CAVC.

The CAVC reviews **questions of law** under *de novo* review, or without deference to the legal positions held by the VA. The Court may hold unlawful and set aside decisions that are "arbitrary, capricious, an abuse of discretion, or otherwise not in accordance with the law."[29]

Lastly, veterans have 120 days to file an appeal with the CAVC. Appeals that are filed after the 120-day deadline are generally only reviewable in

---

[24] *Holland v. Brown*, 9 Vet.App. 324 (1996)

[25] 38 U.S.C. § 7261(a)(4)

[26] *Anderson v. Bessemer City*, 470 U.S. 564, 573 (1985) (citing *United States v. U.S. Gypsum Co.*, 333 U.S. 364, 395 (1948)); *Merchants Nat'l Bank of Mobile v. U.S.*, 7 Cl. Ct. 1, 7 (1984); see *Easley v. Cromartie*, 532 U.S. 234, 242 (2001) ("In applying [the clearly erroneous] standard, we, like any reviewing court, will not reverse a lower court's finding of fact simply because we 'would have decided the case differently.' Rather, a reviewing court must ask whether, 'on the entire evidence,' it is 'left with the definite and firm conviction that a mistake has been committed.'") (citations omitted); accord *Andino v. Nicholson*, 498 F.3d 1370, 1373 n.1 (Fed. Cir. 2007) ("It is not enough that the VA conclude that it would have decided the issue differently had it been analyzing all the evidence to determine whether to grant service connection in the first instance. To be 'clearly erroneous' there must be a definite and firm conviction that a mistake has occurred.") (citations omitted); *Woehlaert v. Nicholson*, 21 Vet.App. 456, 461-62 (2007).

[27] *Gilbert*, 1 Vet.App. 49, 52 (1990)

[28] *Padgett v. Nicholson*, 19 Vet.App. 84 (2005)

[29] 38 U.S.C. § 7261(a)(3)(a); *Butts v. Brown*, 5 Vet.App. 532, 538-40 (1993).

certain circumstances.[30] Reasons for "equitable tolling," or waiving the 120-day deadline in the interest of fairness, might include:

1. Mental illness impacted the veteran's ability to file the appeal, seek assistance of counsel, function and make decisions, or was otherwise directly related to their untimely filing;
2. The veteran accidentally filed their (otherwise timely) appeal at the wrong location; or
3. The veteran relied on inaccurate information from the VA.

Absent compelling circumstances, veterans who fail to file their appeal within the 120-day deadline run the risk of not being heard. The CAVC will generally refuse to hear late appeals where the "failure to file is due to general negligence or procrastination."[31]

★ ★

4. U.S. Court of Appeals for the Federal Circuit—[32]

The U.S. Court of Appeals for the Federal Circuit has exclusive limited jurisdiction to review legal (but not factual) determinations of the CAVC. The Federal Circuit is the first level of appellate review conducted by the judiciary (Article III). In *Flores v. Nicholson*, the court explained:

> Under 38 U.S.C. § 7292, this court has limited jurisdiction over appeals of decisions of the Veterans Court. *Morgan v. Principi*, 327 F.3d 1357, 1359-60 (Fed. Cir. 2003); *Forshey v. Principi*, 284 F.3d 1335, 1338 (Fed. Cir. 2002) (en banc). This court has jurisdiction over appeals from the Veterans Court "with respect to the validity of a decision of [that] Court on a rule of law or of any statute or regulation … or any interpretation thereof (other than a determination as to a factual matter) that was relied on by [that] Court in making the decision." 38 U.S.C. § 7292(a). Except to

---

[30] *Bove v. Shinseki*, 25 Vet.App. 136 (2011); also *Henderson v. Shinseki*, 131 S. Ct. 1197, 1208 (2011)

[31] *Bove*, 25 Vet.App. 136, 140 (2011)

[32] 38 U.S.C. § 7292

the extent that an appeal under this chapter presents a constitutional issue, this court may not "review (A) a challenge to a factual determination, or (B) a challenge to a law or regulation as applied to the facts of a particular case." 38 U.S.C. § 7292(d)(2). See also *Davis v. Principi,* 276 F.3d 1341, 1344 (Fed. Cir. 2002); *Joyner v. McDonald,* 766 F.3d 1393 (Fed. Cir. 2014).[33]

Veterans who want to appeal to the Federal Circuit must do so within 60 days of the CAVC issuing its decision. The Federal Circuit reviews questions of law, as well as CAVC interpretations of law and regulation *de novo,* without deference.

★ ★

5. Supreme Court of the United States—[34]

In very limited circumstances, a veteran dissatisfied with a ruling from the U.S. Court of Appeals for the Federal Circuit may have one final option in appealing to the U.S. Supreme Court. Supreme Court review is extremely rare, however, and generally limited in scope to a single question of law regarding the constitutionality of a statute or regulation. see *Walters v. Nat. Assoc. of Radiation Survivors,* 473 U.S. 305 (1985); *Brown v. Gardner,* 513 U.S. 115 (1994); *Henderson v. Shinseki,* 562 U.S. 428 (2011).

---

[33] *Flores,* 476 F.3d 1379, 1381 (Fed. Cir. 2007)

[34] 38 U.S.C. § 7292(c)

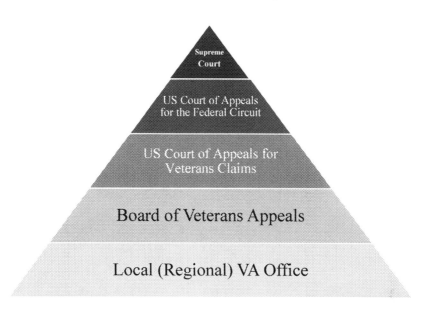

★ ★ ★

§ 2.4 — Strongly and Uniquely Pro-Veteran System

The VA disability claims system is designed to afford veterans every possible opportunity and advantage to substantiate their claim and receive benefits. In fact, veterans benefits are protected property interests under the Fifth Amendment of the U.S. Constitution that are entitled to Procedural Due Process protections.[35]

"A veteran faces no time limit for filing a claim, and once a claim is filed, the VA's process for adjudicating it at the regional office and the Board is *ex parte* and nonadversarial, 38 C.F.R. §§ 3.103(a), 20.700(c)."[36] In addition, "Numerous procedural protections guarantee that the claims process is far less adversarial than general civil litigation. For example, a claimant has wide latitude, compared to general civil litigation, to reopen final claims based on new and [relevant] evidence, thus removing the traditional strictures of *res judicata*. See 38 U.S.C. § 5108."[37] "In such

---

[35] *Cushman v. Shinseki*, 576 F.3d 1290, 1298 (Fed. Cir. 2009)

[36] *Henderson v. Shinseki*, 562 U.S. 428, 431 (2011)

[37] *Skoczen v. Shinseki*, 564 F.3d 1319 (Fed. Cir. 2009)

a beneficial structure there is no room for such adversarial concepts as cross examination, best evidence rule, hearsay evidence exclusion, or strict adherence to burden of proof."[38] "[P]roceedings before the VA are non-adversarial in nature."[39] They are "designed to function throughout with a high degree of informality and solicitude for the claimant."[40]

The VA disability claims system is a "strongly and uniquely pro-claimant system."[41] "[U]niquely pro-claimant principles [underlie] the veterans' benefits dispensation scheme."[42] "VA proceedings operate within a 'strongly and uniquely pro-claimant' system."[43] In *Hodge v. West*, the Federal Circuit described the long tradition of favoring those who served:[44]

> This court and the Supreme Court both have long recognized that the character of the veterans' benefits statutes is strongly and uniquely pro-claimant. See, e.g., *Coffy v. Republic Steel Corp.*, 447 U.S. 191, 196 (1980) (veterans statutes must be liberally construed for the benefit of the returning veteran (citing *Fishgold v. Sullivan Drydock & Repair Corp.*, 328 U.S. 275, 285 (1946); *McKnight v. Gober*, 131 F.3d 1483, 1485 (Fed. Cir. 1997) (noting that, where statute is ambiguous, "interpretive doubt is to be resolved in the veteran's favor" (citing *Brown v. Gardner*, 513 U.S. 115, 118 (1994); Smith, 35

---

[38] *Hodge v. West*, 155 F.3d 1356, 1363 (Fed. Cir. 1998)
[39] *Scott v. McDonald*, 789 F.3d 1375, 1378 (Fed. Cir. 2015)
[40] *Walters v. Nat. Assoc. of Radiation Survivors*, 473 U.S. 305, 311 (1985)
[41] *Hayre v. West Jr.*, 188 F.3d 1327, 1333 (Fed. Cir. 1999)
[42] *Smith v. Brown*, 35 F.3d 1516, 1522 (Fed. Cir. 1994)
[43] *Robinson v. O'Rourke*, 891 F.3d 976 (Fed. Cir. 2018) citing *Hodge v. West*, 155 F.3d 1356 (Fed. Cir. 1998)
[44] Every piece of legislation reviewed by the U.S. Supreme Court has been construed in favor and for the benefit of military veterans.
"The Soldiers' and Sailors' Civil Relief Act is always to be liberally construed to protect those who have been obliged to drop their own affairs to take up the burdens of the nation." *Boone v. Lightner*, 319 U.S. 561 (1943)
"This legislation is to be liberally construed for the benefit of those who left private lift to serve their country in its hour of great need." *Fishgold v. Sullivan Drydock Repair Corp.*, 328 U.S. 275 (1946)
"The statute is to be liberally construed for the benefit of the returning veterans." *Coffy v. Republic Steel Corp.*, 447 U.S. 191 (1980)

F.3d at 1522 (noting the "uniquely pro-claimant principles underlying the veterans' benefits dispensation scheme").

The *Hodge* court aptly described Congress' co-equal role in passing legislation to create a system that would ensure a nonadversarial pro-veteran benefits system:

> Congress itself has recognized and preserved the unique character and structure of the veterans' benefits system. For example, when it passed the Veterans' Judicial Review Act and Veterans' Benefits Improvement Act of 1988, and thus for the first time established judicial review for DVA disputes, Congress emphasized the historically nonadversarial system of awarding benefits to veterans and discussed its intent to maintain the system's unique character:
>
> "Each year, VA processes approximately 5 million claims. In most cases, claimants submit their own applications without assistance. If a claimant desires advice or other help, VA provides specially-trained personnel to answer inquiries and assist in the submission of the claim. VA medical facilities often serve as an important referral source, and the major veterans service organizations also furnish claims assistance by trained specialists at no charge.
>
> Congress has designed and fully intends to maintain a beneficial nonadversarial system of veterans benefits. This is particularly true of service-connected disability compensation where the element of cause and effect has been totally by-passed in favor of a simple temporal relationship between the incurrence of the disability and the period of active duty.
>
> Implicit in such a beneficial system has been an evolution of a completely ex-parte system of adjudication in which Congress expects VA to fully and sympathetically develop the veteran's claim to its optimum before deciding it on the merits. Even then, VA is expected to resolve all issues by giving the claimant the benefit of any reasonable

doubt. In such a beneficial structure there is no room for such adversarial concepts as cross examination, best evidence rule, hearsay evidence exclusion, or strict adherence to burden of proof. H.R. Rep. No. 100-963, at 13 (1988)."

This passage demonstrates that, even in creating judicial review in the veterans context, Congress intended to preserve the historic, pro-claimant system.

Hodge, at 1362-63 (Fed. Cir. 1998)

In *Hesley v. West Jr.*,[45] the Federal Circuit gave additional insight about the pro-veteran system with regards to the VA's duty to assist a veteran in developing a claim:

"[A] low evidentiary threshold is particularly appropriate in the veterans context because in the early stages of the application process, the veteran is almost always unassisted by legal counsel. See 38 U.S.C. § 5904(c)(1) (attorneys and agents prevented from charging for services rendered prior to date of final decision from VA). Since significant if not essential evidence regarding the merits of a claim often resides in the VA's files, it would be fundamentally unfair to erect a steep evidentiary hurdle in front of an unassisted veteran before allowing the veteran to receive assistance from the VA. The low threshold is also appropriate in light of the uniquely pro-claimant nature of the veterans compensation system.

"When a claim for benefits is before the [VA], either at the [regional office] or before the BVA, the relationship between the veteran and the government is nonadversarial and pro-claimant."[46] "The veterans' benefits system has been calibrated with uniquely pro-claimant principles."[47] It is

---

[45] *Hesley*, 212 F.3d 1255, 1262 (Fed. Cir. 2000)
[46] *Jaquay v. Principi*, 304 F.3d 1276, 1282 (Fed. Cir. 2002)
[47] *Nat'l Org. of Veterans Advocates, Inc. v. Affairs*, 710 F.3d 1328, 1330 (Fed. Cir. 2013)

a highly "benevolent nonadversarial veterans system."[48] "Veterans rely on the strongly and uniquely pro-claimant character of the veterans' benefits system."[49]

Veterans Law – Conclusion

The veterans benefits system administered by VA is like no other. As Congress and the Courts (and most Presidential administrations) have made clear, it is a pro-veteran system that is designed function with a great deal of latitude and flexibility to ensure that former service members and their families receive every possible benefit to which they are lawfully entitled. For anyone who wants to file a claim for VA benefits, is important to know the hierarchy of legal authorities, including which VA agencies administer what benefits, and the various forms of appeal and judicial review that give life to veterans law. All original disability claims for service-connected injuries are filed at the nearest VA regional office. Once a claim has been filed, the VARO will communicate with the veteran by sending paper documents via USPS to the veteran's home address. (VA also calls veterans by phone to schedule and remind of appointments). It is important to pay close attention to every correspondence, ideally keeping paper documents together in a binder. If applicable, notify your authorized claims representative who helped file the claim(s) with VA so that they remain informed and in the loop.

If a valid claim has been denied, or the VA examiner awarded a lower rating than is warranted, do not fret. VA began using a modernized appeals process (*see* Chapter 6, Appeals) in February of 2019, which streamlined the appeals process in an effort to improve efficiency and accuracy without disturbing the structure of external appeals to the CAVC or Federal Circuit. The modern appeal system was designed to give veterans greater control over the direction, and ultimately, the success of their claim. Not to mention, new and relevant evidence can be filed at any time with a Supplemental Claim at the VA regional office. Many veterans feel that the VA and its employees have hidden motives to deny their claims, but that is simply not the case.

The point is to know how to properly file your claim, support it with

---

[48] *Forshey v. Principi*, 284 F.3d 1335 (Fed. Cir. 2002)
[49] *DAV v. Sec'y of Veterans Affairs*, 327 F.3d 1339, 1349 (Fed. Cir. 2003)

evidence, and if necessary appeal in the way that best suits your needs. When a VA issues a denial, it does so in writing. All VA decisions give a detailed explanation of what deficiencies exist and what evidence is needed to overcome that deficiency or reach a higher rating. If a claim is denied for lack of evidence, your job is to figure out what evidence is needed, and then obtain it. If the rating is inaccurate, gather new evidence that proves it. The goal is for your claim to be awarded as quickly and accurately as possible, but if it does not happen on the first try, stick with it until your VA rating matches the level of impairment caused by your injuries.

★ ★ ★

Chapter 3

Claims for Disability Compensation

T he vast majority of VA claims are for compensation benefits for disabling illnesses or injuries that stem from active duty military service. Once a veteran establishes service-connection of a current disabling condition, they then qualify for other benefits like VA health care, home loans, vocational rehabilitation, etc. Disability compensation, the military version of worker's comp, is a monthly tax-free payment to injured veterans. In order to receive disability compensation benefits, a veteran must be discharged under "conditions other than dishonorable" and have a current disability that was incurred or aggravated during active duty service. Unlike other benefits, there is no minimum length-of-service requirement for service-connected disability compensation.

★ ★ ★

§ 3.1 — Service-Connected Disability

> Manual M21-1, IV.ii.2.B.1.b. **Satisfying the Current Disability Requirement for SC**

Veterans are entitled to receive VA disability compensation benefits in the form of a monthly tax-free financial payment if they develop a disability as the result of an illness or injury that was incurred or aggravated in the line of duty.

Basic entitlement

Wartime service disability — 38 U.S.C. § 1110
Peacetime service disability — 38 U.S.C. § 1131

> **(§ 1110)** — For disability resulting from personal injury
> suffered or disease contracted in line of duty, or for
> aggravation of a preexisting injury suffered or disease
> contracted in line of duty, in the active military, naval, or
> air service, during a period of war, the United States will
> pay to any veteran thus disabled and who was discharged
> or released under conditions other than dishonorable from
> the period of service in which said injury or disease was
> incurred, or preexisting injury or disease was aggravated,
> compensation as provided in this subchapter, but no
> compensation shall be paid if the disability is a result of
> the veteran's own willful misconduct or abuse of alcohol
> or drugs.

Title 38 veterans disability benefits are Constitutionally protected property interests entitled to Due Process protections under the Fifth Amendment. "Veteran's disability benefits are nondiscretionary, statutorily mandated benefits … such entitlement to benefits is a property interest protected by the Due Process Clause of the Fifth Amendment to the United States Constitution."[1] Therefore, all claims, even those that may eventually be denied, deserve fair notice and an opportunity to be heard— both hallmarks of Procedural Due Process. Claims for service-connected disability compensation benefits are extinguished when a veteran dies.[2]

See 38 C.F.R. § 3.303(a). Principles related to service connection.

★ ★ ★

---

[1] *Cushman v. Shinseki*, 576 F.3d 1290, 1298 (Fed. Cir. 2009)
[2] *Richard ex rel. Richard v. West*, 161 F.3d 719, 721 (Fed. Cir. 1998).

§ 3.2 — Veteran Status[3]

Manual M21-1, III.ii.6.A.1. **Determining Veteran Status**

When VA receives a claim for benefits, a regional office examiner must first determine if the claimant qualifies as a "veteran." Only qualifying veterans may receive VA disability benefits.[4] Under federal law, a veteran is "a person who served in the active military, naval, or air service and who was discharged or released therefrom under conditions other than dishonorable."[5] Thus, in order to be eligible, a former military service member must show that they were discharged or released from active duty service "under conditions other than dishonorable."[6]

Discharge "Under Conditions Other Than Dishonorable" —

Veterans must be discharged from the military "under conditions other than dishonorable" in order to be eligible to receive VA disability benefits. For an in depth discussion on Congress' adoption of the term "Under Conditions Other than Dishonorable," see *Garvey v. Wilkie* (Fed. Cir. 2020). In order to understand the phrase "Other Than Dishonorable," which is unique to VA regulations, it is important to know the different types of discharges received by veterans, how they are given and under what circumstances.

★ ★

5 Types of Discharge

There are five different "characterizations" or types of military discharge. Three are given administratively by a commanding officer and are achieved simply by filing paperwork, while two types of punitive discharges can only be given after a conviction at military trial, called a

---

[3] 38 U.S.C. § 101(2)

[4] *Cropper v. Brown*, 6 Vet.App. 450, 452 (1994)

[5] 38 U.S.C. § 101(2); 38 C.F.R. § 3.1(d)

[6] 38 U.S.C. § 101(18); 38 C.F.R. § 3.12(a)

court-martial. Veterans must be discharged under conditions "other than dishonorable" in order to be eligible to receive VA benefits.[7]

Administrative Discharges—via paperwork

1. Honorable
2. General / Under Honorable Conditions
3. Less (Other) Than Honorable (formerly "Undesirable")

Punitive Discharges—via Courts-Martial conviction

4. Bad-Conduct
5. Dishonorable

HOW DISCHARGE STATUS IMPACTS VA ELIGIBILITY		
ELIGIBLE	MAY BE Eligible	NOT Eligible
Honorable General (Under Honorable Conditions)	Less (Other)-than-Honorable Bad Conduct (SpecCM)	Bad Conduct (GCM) Dishonorable

Honorable & General (Under Honorable Conditions) —

Honorable and General discharges (Under Honorable conditions) are issued administratively by a commanding officer via paperwork with no judicial oversight. A discharge under honorable conditions is binding on the Department of Veterans Affairs as to character of discharge.[8] Veterans with Honorable and General discharges are presumptively eligible to receive VA benefits.

---

[7] 38 C.F.R. § 3.12

[8] Manual M21-1, III.v.1.B.1.b. <u>When DoD's Characterization of Service Is Binding on VA.</u>

Less (Other) Than Honorable, (Undesirable)—[9]

"Less (Other)-Than-Honorable" and "Undesirable" discharges commonly known as "bad paper," are also given administratively, with extremely limited oversight and virtually no due process for the service member. Discharges under less-than or other-than honorable conditions are most often given by officers to enlisted personnel in conjunction with Art. 15 nonjudicial punishment or following a summary court-martial that they conducted in-house.[10] Before the merits of a claim for VA benefits can be reviewed or decided, Veterans with less-than-honorable discharges must first complete a "character of service" review in order to determine eligibility. (*see* Section 3.2.1, Character of Discharge) Recent reports (2016, 2020) from the Veterans Legal Services Clinic at Harvard Law School conducted a review of BVA decisions, which showed extraordinarily high rates of denial for veterans with less-than-honorable discharges who sought compensation and care for their disabling service injuries and conditions. (*see* Section 3.2.2, Unlawful COS/CSD Denials by VA of Veterans with Less-than-Honorable Discharges)

Bad Conduct —

Bad Conduct discharges ("BCD") are given to enlisted service members after a conviction by either a special court-martial or general court-martial. A bad-conduct discharge is "less severe than a dishonorable discharge and is designed as a punishment for bad-conduct rather than as a punishment for serious offenses of either a civilian or military nature."[11] BCDs are also authorized if a servicemember is "convicted repeatedly of minor offenses and whose punitive separation appears to be necessary." *Veterans who have a bad-conduct discharge may be entitled to receive disability compensation benefits if, after COS/CSD review, their service is found to be "honorable for VA purposes" However, BCD veterans are **ineligible to receive VA health care benefits.**

---

[9] Manker, Tyson. "Bad Paper" Discharges Brand Veterans for Life. *The Nation.* Nov. 2019. thenation.com/article/military-veterans-day-discharge/.

[10] 10 U.S.C. §§ 815, 820

[11] R.C.M. 1003(b)(8)(C)

Dishonorable —

Dishonorable discharges are barred from receiving VA benefits under all circumstances, the only exception being clinical insanity at the time of offense. DDs are given to enlisted service members and warrant officers—but not commissioned officers—following a conviction of a serious offense(s) by a general court-martial. Dishonorable discharges are "reserved for those who should be separated under conditions of dishonor, after having been convicted of offenses usually recognized in civilian jurisdictions as felonies, or of offenses of a military nature requiring severe punishment."[12]

★ ★ ★

3 Types of Courts-Martial

There are three types of courts-martial.[13]

1. Summary court-martial—[14]

A summary court-martial is composed of a single commissioned officer to promptly adjudicate minor offenses under a simple procedure. There is no right to counsel at summary court-martial, and as such, limitations apply to the punishment that may be given. The maximum penalty from a summary court-martial is confinement for 30 days, forfeiture of two-thirds pay per month for one month, and reduction to the lowest pay grade. Service members may not be punished with a discharge at summary court-martial, but are often administratively dismissed with a less-than-honorable discharge upon completion of their court-martial punishment.

---

[12] R.C.M. 1003(b)(8)(B)

[13] 10 U.S.C. § 816

[14] 10 U.S.C. § 820

2. Special court-martial—[15]

A special court-martial is more serious that a summary court-martial and may be convened to adjudge all noncapital offenses and certain capital offenses. Special courts-martial are overseen by a military law judge and in some cases may include 4 jurors.[16] Generally, the maximum penalty allowed after conviction by special court-martial is a Bad Conduct Discharge, plus confinement and forfeiture of pay for more than 6 months.

3. General court-martial—[17]

A general court-martial is the most serious type of courts-martial and may only be convened after a grand-jury-like pretrial investigation has been conducted to determine probable cause.[18] General courts-martial are overseen by a military law judge, who can be joined by 8 jurors for noncapital cases, and 12 jurors for death-penalty cases. Because general courts-martial are authorized to impose serious penalties, including Bad Conduct and Dishonorable discharges, and even death, veterans are guaranteed the right to counsel.

★ ★ ★

§ 3.2.1 — Character of Discharge

Manual M21-1, III.v.1.B.1.c. **When a COD Determination Is Necessary**

"A person seeking VA benefits must first establish by a preponderance of the evidence that the service member, upon whose service such benefits are predicated, has attained the status of veteran."[19] If a veteran was given a discharge under less-than-honorable conditions or a bad conduct

---

[15] 10 U.S.C. § 818

[16] 10 U.S.C. § 816(b)(3)

[17] 10 U.S.C. § 818

[18] 10 U.S.C. § 832

[19] *Holmes v. Brown*, 10 Vet.App. 38, 40 (1997)

discharge, they must overcome an additional hurdle known as the character of discharge ("COD") review, or as it has also been called, Character of Service Determination ("CSD"),[20] before VA will address the merits of their claim to be eligible for benefits.

38 C.F.R. § 3.12, the controlling regulation, states:

> (a) If the former service member did not die in service … then … compensation … is payable for claims based on periods of service that were terminated by discharge or release ***under conditions other than dishonorable*** … (emphasis added)

With a large volume of denied claims and little known about how the VA conducts COS/CSD reviews, in 2018 Congress passed a law that requires VA to establish a process for veterans to apply to find out if their discharge status qualifies them for VA benefits.[21] How the statutory addition of 38 U.S.C. § 5303B will impact the existing regulatory COS/CSD review under 38 C.F.R. § 3.12 remains to be seen.

★ ★

DoD Discharge vs. VA Character of Discharge —

In conducting a COD/CSD review[22] VA looks at the totality of a veteran's overall record to determine whether their service should be considered "Honorable for VA/benefits purposes" or "Dishonorable for VA/benefits purposes." **Because the Department of Defense and Department of Veterans Affairs use different standards, it is entirely possible for DoD to label a veteran's service as less-than-honorable that**

---

[20] Swords-to-Plowshares. *VA Character of Service Determinations: An Alternative to Discharge Review.* swords-to-plowshares.org/guides/va-character-of-service-determination-an-alternative-to-discharge-review/.

[21] 38 U.S.C. § 5303B; Pub. L. 115–141, div. J, title II, §259(a)—Mar. 23, 2018, 132 Stat. 828.

[22] Swords-to-Plowshares, National Veterans Legal Services Program, Veterans Legal Clinic at the Legal Services Center of Harvard Law School. *Underserved: How VA Wrongfully Excludes Veterans with Bad Paper.* https://www.swords-to-plowshares.org/research-publications/underserved.

the VA concludes to be "Honorable for VA Purposes"—However, such a finding only impacts VA benefits and has no effect on DoD discharge status, which can only be changed by a military Discharge Review Board (10 U.S.C. § 1553) or Correction Board (10 U.S.C. § 1552), or by Presidential Pardon. VA makes its own determination about a veteran's service, but has no authority to alter a veteran's DoD discharge classification. A veteran's only recourse for DoD discharge upgrade is with the service department.[23]

Manual M21-1, III.v.1.B.1.e. **Overview of the COD Determination Process**

The COD/CSD review is automatically triggered when a veteran without an honorable discharge files a claim for VA benefits. VA will respond in writing with a request for additional information regarding the circumstances of their active duty service and discharge:

> "We have received your claim for benefits based on your military service. Any time a Veteran receives a discharge that is not "Honorable," we have to decide if he/she is eligible for VA benefits. The military has said your service was not "honorable." Therefore, we have to make a decision about your service. As long as we decide that your service was not "dishonorable," you will be eligible for VA benefits."

When that happens, it is then the veteran's responsibility to respond to VA with a statement about their service and circumstances surrounding their less-than-honorable discharge.

★ ★ ★

♣ VA form 21-4138 — **Statement in Support of Claim**

To demonstrate that their service was not "dishonorable" and that they should be found eligible under the law for VA benefits, veterans with less-than-honorable discharges should respond to the COD/CSD letter with an

---

[23] *Spencer v. West*, 13 Vet.App. 376, 380 (2000); *Duro v. Derwinski*, 2 Vet.App. 530, 532 (1992); *Harvey v. Brown*, 6 Vet.App. 416, 424 (1994)

explanation (using the "Statement in Support Claim" VA form 21-4138) that describes the quality of their service and the circumstances surrounding their administrative less-than-honorable discharge.

Veterans with less-than-honorable administrative discharges should make sure to acknowledge their underlying infraction(s), but also help VA to understand that their "misconduct" was not reflective of their entire career, and if applicable, that it was connected and therefore mitigated by a service-connected injury or condition. **Special emphasis should be placed on any mitigating factors that may have impacted the veteran's behavior at the time of discharge, like PTSD from combat or military sexual trauma.** (for example: *veteran's isolated drug use after combat deployment was self-medicating behavior in response to PTSD*) Also, in cases that involve command abuse (which is shockingly common), describe improprieties or wrongdoing committed by members of the veteran's command or other investigating units. Make sure to provide as much information and evidence of mitigating factors, including private PTSD or other diagnoses, to include with the explanation.

Buddy (Statement) Letters —

In addition to a personal statement, veterans are encouraged to submit statements from fellow service members as evidence of their honorable service. These are known as "Buddy Letters." (for example, *see* Section 3.8.1, Combat Stressor - PTSD). In a COD/CSD buddy letter, fellow veterans should highlight the sound quality of service that they witnessed which leads them to believe that their friend's infraction was minor and an isolated incident and not willful or persistent misconduct. It is important to argue and show evidence that the veteran's service was otherwise honorable and meritorious—certainly not "dishonorable"! **Use the terms and phrases from VA regulations in COD/CSD statements and buddy letters (and elsewhere). To the greatest extent possible, COD/CSD letters should stress the following three points:

- Service was honorable (and meritorious)
- Misconduct was minor
- Infraction(s) was not willful or persistent

If VA determines that a veteran's service is **Honorable for VA (benefits) purposes**, then the claim proceeds. If, however, a VA examiner decides that the veteran's service was dishonorable for VA purposes and therefore disqualifying, they must explain how they reached that conclusion. Veterans may appeal a COD/CSD denial.

★ ★ ★

§ 3.2.2 — Unlawful COS/CSD Denials by VA of Veterans with Less-than-Honorable Discharges

In 2016, the Veterans Legal Clinic at Harvard Law School released a damning report about improper COS/CSD denials by the VA, "Underserved: How the VA Wrongfully Excludes Veterans with Bad Paper." The report, written in partnership with the National Veterans Legal Services Program ("NVLSP") and the San Francisco-based veterans service organization, Swords-to-Plowshares, highlights a growing disparity against veterans of the wars in Iraq and Afghanistan who are now being given administrative less-than-honorable discharges at higher rates than any previous generation. The report found that of the hundreds of thousands of post-9/11 veterans with PTSD who were being denied care due to their discharge status, Marines are ten times more likely to be denied VA care than Air Force veterans. The report also found that three of every four veterans with less-than-honorable discharges are denied by the Board of Veterans Appeals due to their discharge status.

In 2020, the veterans legal clinic at Harvard Law School followed up with a second report, "Turned Away: How the VA Unlawfully Denies Health Care to Veterans with Bad Paper Discharges." The report shows that little has changed since 2016. In fact, it called into question VA's ability to properly administer COD/CSD reviews under the law. Documents obtained by the Harvard Law School show that VA employees received inadequate training that erroneously misstates the law and encourages unlawful denials of COD/CSD reviews. In an unknown number of cases, veterans with less-than-honorable discharges were turned away by VA before a COS/CSD was even conducted (this is the exact experience of the author, which unnecessarily caused a 10-year delay in benefits). The "Turned Away" report found of the estimated 550,000 administrative less-than-honorable discharges given since 1980, more than 400,000 veterans with PTSD, TBI and other service-connected conditions are now at risk of being denied care due to improper training of VA adjudicators and claims examiners.

★ ★ ★

§ 3.3 — Bars to Benefits

While less-than-honorable discharges are not necessarily a bar to VA benefits, a veteran with a less-than-honorable discharge is automatically considered to have been discharged under dishonorable conditions under certain circumstances.[24]

In certain circumstances veterans are explicitly barred from receiving VA benefits. There are two types of character of discharge bars to VA benefits: **statutory bars**[25] enacted by Congress, and **regulatory bars**[26] put into place by the executive branch. A veteran may overcome either statutory or regulatory bars if they were clinically insane at the time of the offense that led to their discharge.[27]

★ ★ ★

§ 3.3.1 — Statutory Bars to Benefits[28]

Manual M21-1, III.v.1.B.2. **Statutory Bars to Benefits**

A statutory (legislative/Congressional) bar to benefits exists when the VA determines that a former service member's discharge or release from active duty was under any of the conditions discussed in 38 U.S.C. § 5303

---

[24] 38 U.S.C. § 5303; 38 C.F.R. § 3.12; *Camarena v. Brown*, 6 Vet.App. 565, 567-68 (1994) (finding that 38 C.F.R. § 3.12 does not limit "dishonorable conditions" to only those cases where "dishonorable discharge" was adjudged)

[25] 38 U.S.C. § 5303(a); *see also* 38 C.F.R. § 3.12(c)

[26] 38 C.F.R. § 3.12(d)

[27] 38 C.F.R. § 3.12(b); *see also* 38 U.S.C. § 5303(b); 38 C.F.R. § 3.354(a)

[28] 38 U.S.C. § 5303

and listed in 38 C.F.R. § 3.12(c). Benefits are not payable where a veteran was discharged or released under one of the following conditions:

- Conscientious objector who refused to perform military duty, wear the uniform, or otherwise comply with lawful orders of competent military authorities.[29]
- General-court martial sentence.[30]
- Resignation for the good of the service.[31]
- Desertion.[32]
- Requesting release from service as an alien during a period of hostilities.[33]
- Unauthorized absence without leave (AWOL) for more than 180 days, ***absent compelling circumstances.***[34]

A veteran who was AWOL for a period of more than 180 days may still receive benefits if they "demonstrate[e] to the satisfaction of the Secretary that there are compelling circumstances to warrant such prolonged unauthorized absence."[35]

* * *

§ 3.3.2 — Regulatory Bars to Benefits[36]

Manual M21-1, III.v.1.B.3. **Regulatory Bars to Benefits**

A regulatory (administrative/Executive) bar to benefits exists when the VA determines that a former service member's discharge or release

---

[29] 38 C.F.R. § 3.12(c)(1)
[30] 38 C.F.R. § 3.12(c)(2)
[31] 38 C.F.R. § 3.12(c)(3)
[32] 38 C.F.R. § 3.12(c)(4)
[33] 38 C.F.R. § 3.12(c)(5)
[34] 38 C.F.R. § 3.12(c)(6)
[35] 38 U.S.C. § 5303(a); *see also* 38 C.F.R. § 3.12(c)(6)(i)
[36] 38 C.F.R. § 3.12(d)

was issued under any of the conditions listed in 38 CFR § 3.12(d).[37] In late 2020, VA announced it would update Section 3.12 with a new title, by defining several terms, and by adding a "compelling circumstances exception" for three of the regulatory bars. After the update, 38 C.F.R. § 3.12(d) now reads:

(1) Compelling circumstances exception is **not applicable** for:

    i.   Acceptance of a discharge under other than honorable conditions or its equivalent to escape trial by general court-martial.[38]

    ii.   Mutiny or spying.[39]

(2) Compelling circumstances exception is applicable for:

    i.   Moral turpitude crimes; An offense involving moral turpitude means a willful act that gravely violates accepted moral standards and would be expected to cause harm or loss of a person or property. Minor misconduct, as defined by paragraph (d)(2)(ii) of this section, will not be considered an offense involving moral turpitude.[40]

    ii.   Willful and persistent misconduct.[41]

- Instances of minor misconduct occurring within 2 years or each other;
- An instance of minor misconduct occurring within two years or more serious misconduct;
- Instances of more serious misconduct occurring within 5 years or each other.
- For purposes of this section, minor misconduct is misconduct for which the maximum sentence imposable pursuant to the M.C.M. would not include a dishonorable discharge or confinement for more than one year.

---

[37] In 2020, VA published proposed rule change "Update and Clarify Regulatory Bars to Benefits Based on Character of Discharge." (Aug. 10, 2020). https://www.federalregister.gov/d/2020-14559.

[38] 38 C.F.R. § 3.12(d)(1)(i)

[39] 38 C.F.R. § 3.12(d)(1)(ii)

[40] 38 C.F.R. § 3.12(d)(2)(i)

[41] 38 C.F.R. § 3.12(d)(2)(ii)

iii. Sexual acts involving aggravating circumstances or other factors affecting the performance of duty; Examples include child molestation, prostitution or solicitation of prostitution, sexual acts or conduct accompanied by assault or coercion, and sexual acts or conduct between service members of disparate rank, grade, or status where a service member has taken advantage of his superior rank, grade.[42]

★ ★ ★

§ 3.3.3 — Compelling Circumstances Exception[43]

In late 2020, VA added to Section 3.12 "Regulatory Bars to Benefits" a new paragraph (e), "Compelling Circumstances Exception." The compelling circumstances exception serves as an affirmative legal defense for a discharge that would otherwise cause a veteran to be barred from VA eligibility by regulation, and applies to less-than-honorable discharges that were given for:

- Absence without leave (AWOL) for 180 days or more;
- Moral turpitude offenses;
- Willful and persistent misconduct;
- Sexual acts involving aggravating circumstances or other factors affecting performance of duty.

Under 38 C.F.R. § 3.12(e), VA shall consider a number of factors to determine whether compelling circumstances exist to grant an exception. The compelling factors, which veterans and advocates should base their arguments on, include:

(1) Length and character of service exclusive of the period of prolonged AWOL or misconduct. Service exclusive of the period of prolonged AWOL or misconduct should generally be of such quality and length that it can be characterized as honest, faithful and meritorious and of benefit to the Nation.

---

[42] 38 C.F.R. § 3.12(d)(2)(iii)
[43] 38 C.F.R. § 3.12(e)

(2) Reasons for prolonged AWOL or misconduct. Factors include:

    i.   Mental impairment at the time of prolonged AWOL or misconduct, to include a clinical diagnosis of, or evidence that could later be medically determined to demonstrate existence of, PSTD, depression, bipolar disorder, schizophrenia, substance use disorder, attention deficit hyperactivity disorder (ADHD), impulsive behavior, cognitive disabilities, and co-morbid conditions (i.e. substance use disorder and other mental disorders).

    ii.   Physical health, to include physical trauma and any side effects of medication.

    iii.   Combat-related or overseas-related hardship.

    iv.   Sexual abuse/assault.

    v.   Duress, coercion, or desperation.

    vi.   Family obligations or comparable obligations to third-parties.

    vii.   Age, education, cultural background, and judgmental maturity.

(3) Whether a valid legal defense would have precluded a conviction for AWOL or misconduct under the UCMJ. For purposes of this paragraph, the defense must go to the substantive issue of absence or misconduct rather than to procedures, technicalities, or formalities.

With the "Compelling Circumstances Exception," Veterans and advocates have an opportunity to share additional information with VA about the series of events that led to their less-than-honorable discharge, and why their discharge status should not preclude them from receiving care and benefits for their disabling service-connected illness or injury. In this way, veterans can provide additional context, narrative and perspective about their service and discharge situation.

* * *

Willful and persistent misconduct is the most commonly used bar to deny veterans eligibility for their benefits. According to an analysis by Swords-to-Plowshares, from 1992-2015, an astounding 84.2% of COD/CSD denials made by the Board of Veterans Appeals were cited as willful and persistent misconduct. That is because it is an overly-broad concept that can be used as a catch-all to classify any infractions, no matter how minor, and thus bar veterans from receiving their much-needed benefits. The following example comes from the 2016 Swords-to-Plowshares report, *Underserved* (pp. 24-25):

> J.E. twice deployed to Iraq and, while in service, was diagnosed with Post-Traumatic Stress Disorder. He was cited for talking to his Sergeant while he had a toothpick in his mouth and then discharged after he failed a single drug test. The VA denied him eligibility for basic veteran services on the basis of "willful and persistent" misconduct.

Keep in mind that a discharge upgrade issued by the Boards for Correction of Military/Naval Records (10 U.S.C. § 1552) sets aside all prior bars to VA eligibility.[44] In contrast, a discharge upgrade issued on or after October 8, 1977, by a discharge review board [10 U.S.C. § 1553] sets aside regulatory bars but not statutory bars, provided that: (1) the discharge is upgraded as a result of an individual case review; (2) the discharge is upgraded under uniform published standards and procedures that generally apply to all persons administratively discharged under conditions other than honorable; and (3) such standards are consistent with historical standards for determining honorable service and do not contain any provision for automatically granting or denying an upgraded discharge. Presidential Pardons generally do not restore eligibility for VA benefits.[45] Also, an honorable or general discharge awarded by a post-Vietnam or other special review board does not remove any bar to benefits.

★ ★ ★

§ 3.3.4 — Willful Misconduct

Manual M21-1, III.v.1.D.1. **General Information on Willful Misconduct Determinations**

---

[44] 38 C.F.R. § 3.12(f)
[45] *Robertson v. Shinseki*, 26 Vet.App. 169 (2013)

Tyson Manker

Disabilities stemming from injuries caused by a veteran's own willful misconduct are generally ineligible for most VA benefits, including:

- service-connected disability compensation[46]
- non-service-connected disability pension[47]
- vocational rehabilitation benefits[48]

In addition, if a veteran's death is caused by their own willful misconduct, VA will not consider the death to be service-connected and surviving family members will not qualify for Dependency and Indemnity Compensation ("DIC") survivor benefits.[49] That said, all injuries and deaths that occur during active military service are initially presumed to have been in the line of duty, and not as a result of willful misconduct.[50]

Willful misconduct is defined by VA regulations as "an act involving conscious wrongdoing or known prohibited action" that "involves deliberate or intentional wrongdoing with knowledge of or wanted and reckless disregard of its probable consequences."[51] Mere technical violation of police regulations or ordinances will not per se constitute willful misconduct. Keep in mind that willful misconduct is not "determinative unless it is the proximate cause of injury, disease or death."[52]

Drug and alcohol abuse may be considered willful misconduct depending upon the circumstances. For example, veterans are not eligible to receive benefits for disabilities caused by drug or alcohol abuse.[53] Be aware of the regulations regarding drug and alcohol use and abuse:

"The simple drinking of alcoholic beverage is not of itself willful misconduct. The deliberate drinking of a known poisonous substance or under conditions which would raise a presumption to that effect will be considered

---

[46] 38 U.S.C. §§ 105(a), 1110; 38 C.F.R. § 3.301(a)

[47] 38 U.S.C. § 1521(a); 38 C.F.R. § 3.301(b)

[48] 38 U.S.C. §§ 3102, 3462(a)(1)

[49] 38 U.S.C. § 1310; see *Myore v. Nicholson*, 489 F.3d 1207 (Fed. Cir. 2007)

[50] *Holton and Bryant v. Shinseki*, 557 F.3d 1362, 1366-67 (Fed. Cir. 2009); *Smith v. Derwinski*, 2 Vet.App. 241, 244 (1992)

[51] 38 C.F.R. § 3.1(n)

[52] 38 C.F.R. § 3.1(n)(3)

[53] 38 U.S.C. §§ 105(a), 1110; 38 C.F.R. § 3.301(c)

willful misconduct. If, in the drinking of a beverage to enjoy its intoxicating effects, intoxication results proximately and immediately in disability or death, the disability or death will be considered the result of the person's willful misconduct."[54]

Drug usage.[55] The isolated and infrequent use of drugs by itself will not be considered willful misconduct; however, the progressive and frequent use of drugs to the point of addiction will be considered willful misconduct. Where drugs are used to enjoy or experience their effects and the effects result proximately and immediately in disability or death, such disability or death will be considered the result of the person's willful misconduct.

Line of duty; abuse of alcohol or drugs.[56] An injury or disease incurred during active military, naval, or air service shall not be deemed to have been incurred in line of duty if such injury or disease was a result of the abuse of alcohol or drugs by the person on whose service benefits are claimed. For the purpose of this paragraph, alcohol abuse means the use of alcoholic beverages over time, or such excessive use at any one time, sufficient to cause disability to or death of the user; drug abuse means the use of illegal drugs (including prescription drugs that are illegally or illicitly obtained), the intentional use of prescription or non-prescription drugs for a purpose other than the medically intended use, or the use of substances other than alcohol to enjoy their intoxicating effects.

★ ★ ★

---

[54] 38 C.F.R. § 3.301(c)(2)
[55] 38 C.F.R. § 3.301(c)(3)
[56] 38 C.F.R. § 3.301(d)

§ 3.3.5 — Suicide[57]

Manual M21-1, III.iv.4.O.1.e. **Considering SC for Mental Unsoundness in Suicide**

In the unfortunate event that a veteran takes their own life, an eligible surviving spouse or family member may be eligible for service-connected death benefits. This is generally the case when a veteran with Post-Traumatic Stress Disorder dies from suicide because of their PTSD. Under VA regulations, a veteran's suicide is not considered willful misconduct if the veteran was of "unsound mind" at the time of their death.[58] If a veteran's "unsound mind" was the result of a service-connected injury, like PTSD, then a surviving family member may be eligible for service-connection death benefits.[59]

According to the M21-1, "Whether a person, at the time of suicide, was so unsound mentally that he or she did not realize the consequences of such an act, or was unable to resist such impulse, is a question to be determined in each individual case, based on all available lay and medical evidence pertaining to the individual's mental condition at the time ... **The act of suicide or a bona fide attempt is considered to be evidence of mental unsoundness.** Therefore, where no reasonable adequate motive for suicide is shown by the evidence, the act will be considered to have resulted from mental unsoundness."

The M21-1 further instructs that "In all instances, any reasonable doubt should be resolved favorably to support a finding of [service-connection]." However, "Mental unsoundness by itself without evidence of an underlying psychiatric disability is not a service-connectable disorder. Therefore, when death from suicide has occurred after separation from active duty, service-connection may be granted only in the presence of a service-connectable disability that meets all of the requirements for service-connection."

★ ★ ★

---

[57] 38 C.F.R. § 3.302

[58] 38 C.F.R. § 3.302(a)(2); *Elkins v. Brown*, 8 Vet.App. 391, 397 (1995)

[59] *Sheets v. Derwinski*, 2 Vet.App. 512, 516 (1992)

§ 3.4 — *Requirements for Establishing Service-Connection of a Current Disability*

Manual M21-1, IV.ii.2.B.1. **Determining Direct SC**

38 C.F.R. § 3.303 lays out the general principles of service connection under the authority of 38 U.S.C. § 1110 or § 1131.

38 C.F.R. § 3.303. **Principles Relating to Service Connection**.

> (a) **General**. Service connection ... means that the facts, shown by evidence, establish that a particular illness or injury resulting in disability was incurred coincident with service in the Armed Forces, or if preexisting such service, was aggravated therein. This may be accomplished by affirmatively showing inception or aggravation during service or through the application of statutory presumptions. Each disabling condition shown by a veteran's service records, or for which he seeks a service connection must be considered on the basis of the places, types and circumstances of his service as shown by service records, the official history of each organization in which he served, his medical records and all pertinent medical and lay evidence. Determinations as to service connection will be based on review of the entire evidence of record, with due consideration to the policy of the Department of Veterans Affairs to administer the law under a broad and liberal interpretation consistent with the facts in each individual case.

Therefore, in order to establish a right to compensation for a service-connected disability, a qualifying veteran must show evidence of:

1. A current disability;
2. An illness or injury incurred or aggravated in-service;
3. A link, or nexus, between the current disability and in-service illness or injury shown by the evidence, or:

  a Medical nexus opinion (private doctor/therapist);

  b Chronicity and continuity; or

  c Continuous symptoms since discharge.

See: *Caluza v. Brown*, 7 Vet.App. 498, 506 (1995) *aff'd*, 78 F.3d 604 (Fed. Cir. 1996) (table); *Washington v. Nicholson*, 19 Vet.App. 362, 372 (2005) *citing Caluza*, 7 Vet.App. at 506; *Hickson v. West*, 12 Vet.App. 247, 252 (1999).

  In *Shedden v. Principi*,[60] the U.S. Court of Appeals for the Federal Circuit affirmed these requirements:

> The Court of Appeals for Veterans Claims has correctly noted that in order to establish service-connection veterans must show: (1) the existence of a present disability; (2) in-service incurrence or aggravation of a disease or injury; and (3) a causal relationship between the present disability and the disease or injury incurred or aggravated during service.

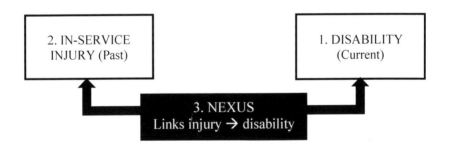

★ ★ ★

---

[60] *Shedden*, 381 F.3d 1163, 1167 (Fed. Cir. 2004); citing *Hansen v. Principi*, 16 Vet.App. 110, 111 (2002); see also: *Holton v. Shinseki*, 557 F.3d 1362, 1366 (Fed. Cir. 2009)

§ 3.4.1 — Current Disability

Manual M21-1, IV.ii.2.B.1.b. **Satisfying the Current Disability Requirement for SC**

To establish service-connection a veteran must show evidence that they currently have a disability. "In the absence of a proof of present disability there can be no valid claim."[61] The requirement of a current disability is "satisfied when a claimant has a disability at the time a claim for VA disability compensation is filed or during the pendency of that claim."[62]

Evidence to show the existence of a current disability might include:

- Diagnosis in Veteran's DoD service medical records
- Private health records held by a physician or hospital
- Letter from private health provider confirming diagnosis
- Letter from family member or close friend describing veteran's disability and persistent and recurrent symptoms
- Statement from veteran describing life impact of disability and persistent and recurrent symptoms

Evidence must be **competent**, or offered from a qualified source. For VA claims, there are two types of evidence: *medical* evidence and *lay* evidence. Both are defined by regulation.

Competent medical evidence—[63]

Manual M21-1, I.1.A.4.d. **Definition: Competent Medical Evidence**

Competent medical evidence is evidence provided by a person who is qualified through education, training, or experience to offer medical diagnoses, statements, or opinions. Competent medical evidence may also

---

[61] *Brammer v. Derwinski*, 3 Vet.App. 223, 225 (1992)

[62] *McClain v. Nicholson*, 21 Vet.App. 319, 321 (2007); *Romanowsky v. Shinseki*, 26 Vet.App 289 (2013)

[63] 38 C.F.R. § 3.159(a)(1)

mean statements conveying sound medical principles found in medical treatises. It would also include statements contained in authoritative writings such as medical and scientific articles and research reports or analyses.

Competent lay evidence—[64]

Manual M21-1, I.1.A.4.e. **Definition: Competent Lay Evidence**

Competent lay evidence is any evidence not requiring that the proponent have specialized education, training, or experience. Lay evidence is competent if it is provided by a person who has knowledge of facts or circumstances and conveys matters that can be observed and described by a lay person. Lay evidence cannot be determined to be not credible merely because it is unaccompanied by contemporaneous medical evidence.[65] However, the lack of contemporaneous medical evidence can be considered and weighed against a veteran's lay statements.

Generally, only certified health professionals with specialized training are qualified to medically *diagnose* a veteran's disability. However, that is not always the case, and in limited situations veterans are considered competent to diagnose their own condition, when: (1) a layperson is competent to identify the medical condition, (2) the layperson is reporting a contemporaneous medical diagnosis, and (3) lay testimony describing symptoms at the time supports a later diagnosis be a medical professional.[66] Since VA is required to give proper weight to all competent evidence, veterans are strongly encouraged to submit both medical *and* lay evidence of their current disability. (Until they were abruptly removed from the VA website in 2020, Disability Benefits Questionnaires were provided by VA to allow private providers to quickly record their diagnosis and document all information that is needed for VA to process their diagnosing information. It is the author's hope and belief that "public facing" DBQs

---

[64] 38 C.F.R. § 3.159(a)(2)

[65] *Buchanan v. Nicholson*, 451 F.3d 1331, 1336-37 (Fed. Cir. 2006)

[66] *Jandreau v. Nicholson*, 492 F.3d 1372, 1377 (Fed. Cir. 2007) (veteran dislocated shoulder in service and was found capable of diagnosing shoulder issues); also: *Barr v. Nicholson*, 21 Vet.App. 303 (2007) (veteran found competent to diagnose own varicose veins, which were clearly visible to all)

will return[67]). Lay statements from veterans, family, and friends should also be included in a letter or on a "Statement in Support of Claim" (VA Form 21-4138).

★ ★ ★

§ 3.4.2 — In-Service Injury

> Manual M21-1, IV.ii.2.B.3. **Determining Service Incurrence of an Injury**

Second, a veteran must show that they suffered an injury while on active duty that caused their current disability. This can be accomplished in several ways, including with official service or treatment records, or by submitting a personal statement about the incident(s), buddy letters, newspaper articles, or statements from friends or family members with knowledge of the event(s). Service injuries may have occurred during official military duties or while on authorized leave, but cannot be the result of a veteran's own willful misconduct or drug / alcohol abuse. In order to corroborate or deny each claim, VA considers the places, types and circumstances of a veteran's service by reviewing their service and medical records, the official history of each unit in which they served, and all relevant medical and lay evidence.

§ 3.4.3 — Nexus / Link

Third, a veteran must show evidence of "service connection" or "a causal relationship between the present disability and the disease or injury incurred or aggravated during service—the so-called 'nexus' requirement.[68] Determinations as to service connection are based on a full review of the entire evidence of record.[69]

To present their case, a veteran can establish that their current disability

---

[67] *See* H.R. 6493 - *Veterans Benefits Fairness and Transparency Act* (introduced 4 April 2020)

[68] *Walker v. Shinseki*, 708 F.3d 1331, 1333 (Fed. Cir. 2013)

[69] 38 C.F.R. § 3.303(a)

had its onset or inception during active duty service with evidence, including (*only* one of the following):

1. Nexus letter (private healthcare provider)
2. Chronicity and Continuity
3. Continuous symptoms

★ ★ ★

1. NEXUS LETTER

Manual M21-1, IV.ii.2.B.1.e. **Establishing Direct SC Under 38 CFR 3.303(a)**

Direct Service-Connection may be established when:

(1) the evidence, or
(2) a medical opinion

shows a nexus between a current disability and an injury, disease, or event in service.

See also: 38 C.F.R. § 3.303(a)—**Principles relating to service connection.**

★ ★ ★

One way to prove that military service caused a current disability is by having the veteran's treating doctor, therapist, or other qualified health professional write what is known as a "nexus letter" with a statement that includes, among other things, their professional opinion about the likeliness of a causal relationship, or link, between the current disability and active duty service. VA examiners will look to verify this nexus during a C&P examination, but generally give great credence to nexus letters from private doctors that are included with the veteran's claim. Unlike chronic conditions that are service-connected through 3.303(b), service connection through § 3.303(a) is not limited to any specific condition.

A nexus opinion letter should describe: the author's credentials; details about their treatment history of the veteran; a statement that they have reviewed the veteran's relevant records, naming each of the pertinent records; and any medical diagnosis given. Most importantly, the physician should include a "nexus statement" giving their opinion about the likelihood that the veteran's current disabling injury was caused by their military service.

A statement describing the causal relationship between the veteran's injury and their service is phrased in terms of likelihood, depending upon the extent of the expert's certainty of opinion based on the evidence. For example: *In my opinion, it is more likely than not that [Veteran's] post-traumatic stress disorder was caused by her combat service in Iraq, which is documented in her military records, and which I have gained insight about during private counseling sessions...* As the CAVC explained in *McLendon v. Nicholson*:[70]

> "[W]hen a nexus between a current disability and an in-service event is "indicated," there must be a medical opinion that provides some nonspeculative determination as to the degree of likelihood that a disability was caused by an in-service disease or incident to constitute sufficient medical evidence on which the Board can render a decision with regard to nexus."

As explained by the CAVC, a medical nexus opinion must give more than a generic passing reference to a veteran's records. Rather, "the Board must be able to conclude that a medical expert has applied valid medical analysis to the significant facts of the particular case in order to reach the conclusion submitted in the medical opinion."[71] Further, "It is the factually accurate, fully articulated, sound reasoning for the conclusion, not the mere fact that the claims file was reviewed, that contributes probative value to a medical opinion."

Keep in mind that the nexus opinion letter or statement is just one piece of evidence that is used to help a veteran apply for, and ultimately receive, VA benefits. A veteran's own statements about the impact that their conditions and disabilities now have on their daily life also holds great value in helping VA to better understand their circumstances. In some cases, private practitioners may be reluctant to write a nexus letter.

---

[70] *McLendon*, 20 Vet.App. 79, 85 (2006)
[71] *Nieves-Rodriguez v. Peake*, 22 Vet.App. 295, 303 (2008)

If so, help them understand how a VA disability claim is processed. You can explain that there is no liability attached to their nexus letter, which remains confidential in the veteran's file, and only helps the veteran get their "foot in the door" to continue their claim for veterans benefits.[72] VA will always conduct its own examinations and ultimately makes its own medical determinations, and in no circumstance would ever contact a private physician about their opinion. Just remember that the health professional who provides a nexus statement about their diagnosis must always include a statement about the likelihood of nexus. That is: it must be at least *as likely as it is not* that a veteran's current disability was caused by an injury, condition or incident that was incurred or experienced during active duty military service.

Key Nexus Phrases:

"AS LIKELY AS IT IS NOT"   50%

"MORE THAN LIKELY"   >50%

"REASONABLE CERTAINTLY / VERY LIKELY"   <100%

"WITHOUT QUESTION"   100%

For a sample NEXUS Opinion Letter, *see* Section 3.8, Post-Traumatic Stress Disorder.

★ ★ ★

2. CHRONICITY (and CONTINUITY)—[73]

> Manual M21-1, IV.ii.2.B.1.c. **Establishing Direct SC Based on Chronicity**

Service-connection is also granted to certain chronic conditions that are due to active duty military service but do not stem from any particular in-service incident or event. In some rare cases, chronic conditions <u>are</u>

---

[72] 38 U.S.C. § 5701
[73] 38 C.F.R. § 3.303(b)

diagnosed while the veteran is on active duty—DoD medical records are the easiest way of proving service-connection of a chronic disease. However, most veterans are not diagnosed with chronic illnesses while on active duty. In fact, most veterans develop chronic service-connected illnesses over time and are not diagnosed until years after they were discharged (i.e. prostate cancer from Agent Orange herbicide exposure). In these cases, service-connection may be possible through what is known as "chronicity and continuity."

The principles of chronicity and continuity discussed under 38 CFR 3.303(b) may be used only to establish service-connection for chronic diseases listed under 38 CFR 3.309(a). Service connection for a disease not listed under § 3.309(a) may not be established on the basis of the chronicity provisions of § 3.303(b).

> (b) **Chronicity and continuity**. With chronic disease shown as such in service (or within the presumptive period under § 3.307) so as to permit a finding of service connection, subsequent manifestations of the same chronic disease at any later date, however remote, are service connected, unless clearly attributable to intercurrent causes. This rule does not mean that any manifestation of joint pain, any abnormality of heart action or heart sounds, any urinary findings of casts, or any cough, in service will permit service connection of arthritis, disease of the heart, nephritis, or pulmonary disease, first shown as a clear-cut clinical entity, at some later date. For the showing of chronic disease in service there is required a combination of manifestations sufficient to identify the disease entity, and sufficient observation to establish chronicity at the time, as distinguished from merely isolated findings or a diagnosis including the word "Chronic." When the disease identity is established (leprosy, tuberculosis, multiple sclerosis, etc.), there is no requirement of evidentiary showing of continuity. Continuity of symptomatology is required only where the condition noted during service (or in the presumptive period) is not, in fact, shown to be chronic or where the diagnosis of chronicity may be legitimately questioned. When the fact of chronicity in

service is not adequately supported, then a showing of continuity after discharge is required to support the claim.

38 C.F.R. § 3.309 — *Disease subject to presumptive service connection.*

(a) **Chronic diseases**. The following diseases shall be granted service connection although not otherwise established as incurred in or aggravated by service if manifested to a compensable degree within the applicable time limits under §3.307 following service in a period of war or following peacetime service on or after January 1, 1947, provided the rebuttable presumption provisions of §3.307 are also satisfied.

- Anemia, primary.
- Arteriosclerosis.
- Arthritis.
- Atrophy, progressive muscular.
- Brain hemorrhage.
- Brain thrombosis.
- Bronchiectasis.
- Calculi of the kidney, bladder, or gallbladder.
- Cardiovascular-renal disease, including hypertension.
- Cirrhosis of the liver.
- Coccidioidomycosis.
- Diabetes mellitus.
- Encephalitis lethargica residuals.
- Endocarditis.
- Endocrinopathies.
- Epilepsies.
- Hansen's disease.
- Hodgkin's disease.
- Leukemia.
- Lupus erythematosus, systemic.
- Myasthenia gravis.
- Myelitis.
- Myocarditis.
- Nephritis.

- Other organic diseases of the nervous system.
- Osteitis deformans (Paget's disease).
- Osteomalacia.
- Palsy, bulbar.
- Paralysis agitans.
- Psychoses.
- Purpura idiopathic, hemorrhagic.
- Raynaud's disease.
- Sarcoidosis.
- Scleroderma.
- Sclerosis, amyotrophic lateral.
- Sclerosis, multiple.
- Syringomyelia.
- Thromboangiitis obliterans (Buerger's disease).
- Tuberculosis, active.
- Tumors, malignant, or of the brain or spinal cord or peripheral nerves
- Ulcers, peptic (gastric or duodenal)

For any disability not listed under 38 C.F.R. § 3.309(a), service-connection must be established with a typical three-element nexus analysis of 38 C.F.R. § 3.303(a).[74]

See also:

38 C.F.R. § 3.307 — *Presumptive service connection for chronic, tropical, or prisoner-of-war related disease, disease associated with exposure to certain herbicide agents, or disease associated with exposure to contaminants in the water supply at Camp Lejeune.*

> (a) **General**. A chronic, tropical, or prisoner of war related disease, a disease associated with exposure to certain herbicide agents, or a disease associated with exposure to contaminants in the water supply at Camp Lejeune listed in §3.309 will be considered to have been incurred in or aggravated by service under the circumstances outlined

---

[74] *Walker v. Shinseki*, 708 F.3d 1331 (Fed. Cir. 2013)

in this section even though there is no evidence of such disease during the period of service. No condition other than one listed in §3.309(a) will be considered chronic.

★ ★ ★

CHRONICITY — *Chronic illness/disease.*

Manual M21-1, IV.ii.2.B.1.c. **Establishing Direct SC Based on Chronicity**

To establish service connection under **38 CFR 3.303(b)** based on the CHRONICITY of a disease that is diagnosed in service while the veteran was on active duty, the evidence must include:

- manifestations sufficient to identify the disease, and
- evidence sufficient to establish the presence of a chronic disability in service (as opposed to an isolated finding of the word "chronic")

When a chronic illness listed under 38 CFR 3.309(a) is shown in service, VA considers all subsequent manifestations of the same chronic illness to be service-connected unless they are clearly due to intercurrent causes. **Once the disease identity is established (leprosy, tuberculosis, multiple sclerosis, etc.), there is no requirement of evidentiary showing of continuity.**

See the following VA Handbook sections for additional information regarding presumptions for chronic illnesses:

§ 3.9.2 — Presumption of Exposure

§ 3.10.2 — Claims for Disability Compensation (Lejeune Water)

★ ★ ★

CONTINUITY — *Continuous chronic symptoms.*

Manual M21-1, IV.ii.2.B.1.d. **Establishing SC
Based on Continuity of Symptoms**

Continuity of symptomatology under **38 CFR 3.303(b)** may only be used to establish service-connection for a chronic disease that is listed under **38 CFR 3.309(a)**. Further, evidence of continuity is only required to establish service-connection for conditions listed under 38 CFR 3.309(a) when the finding of chronicity is in question.

A showing of CONTINUITY for a chronic disability listed under **38 CFR 3.309(a)** is required only if:

- the condition noted during service is NOT chronic, or
- where chronicity may be legitimately questioned.

See:

38 C.F.R. § 3.303(b). Chronicity and continuity.
38 C.F.R. § 3.307(a). Presumptive service connection(s).
38 C.F.R. § 3.309(a). Chronic diseases.

★ ★ ★

3. CONTINUOUS SYMPTOMS

Manual M21-1, IV.ii.2.B.1.f. **Establishing Direct SC Under 38 CFR 3.303(d)**

Lastly, if a veteran's chronic condition was not diagnosed (1) as chronic in service or (2) within a presumptive period, the veteran may, with evidence, show that they suffered symptoms since military service or the presumptive period.

**In fact, service-connection may be granted for *any disease* diagnosed after discharge, when all the evidence, including that pertinent to service, establishes that the disease was incurred in service. Presumptive periods are not intended to limit service connection to diseases so diagnosed when the evidence warrants direct service connection. *The presumptive provisions are intended as liberalizations applicable when the evidence would not warrant service connection without their aid.*

★ ★ ★

§ 3.5 — NEXUS | 5 THEORIES to Establish Service-Connection

In order to be eligible for disability benefits, veterans must show that their current disabling illness or injury was either incurred or aggravated during their active duty military service. This is called establishing "service-connection." Veterans can establish a service-connection nexus in one of five different ways:

1. Direct Service-Connection—[75]

> Manual M21-1, IV.ii.2.B.1.a. **Overview of Direct SC**

Direct service-connection (most common) means that a particular illness or injury was incurred in service. For direct service connection, a veteran must show evidence that their current illness or injury occurred during active duty service.

★ ★

2. Presumptive Service-Connection—[76]

> Manual M21-1, IV.ii.2.B.2.a. **Overview of Presumptive SC**

> Manual M21-1, IV.ii.2.C.3.a. **Presumptive SC Based on Herbicide Exposure**

---

[75] 38 C.F.R. § 3.304
[76] 38 C.F.R. § 3.307

(Common for Vietnam Veterans with Agent Orange exposure) Certain medical conditions are presumed to be caused by military service— injuries caused by Agent Orange exposure in Vietnam, for example. In order to qualify for presumptive service-connection, a veteran must show evidence of a current diagnosis of a qualifying condition, plus qualifying military service. *example.* A Vietnam Veteran who suffers from Diabetes Mellitus Type 2 only needs to show their current diagnoses and proof of qualifying service in the Republic of Vietnam (through medals, buddy statements, and other records). **A nexus letter is not required (but may still be submitted) for presumptive service-connection. (Burn pit exposures are a looming issue that could in time result in certain presumptions for Iraq and Afghanistan veterans)

★ ★

3. Aggravating of a Preexisting Condition—[77]

> Manual M21-1, IV.ii.2.B.4. **Determining In-Service Aggravation of Pre-Service Disability**

Veterans can establish service-connection when there is evidence that a condition that was noted upon their entrance to service was aggravated by active duty service, and not because of the natural progress of the condition. In order to prove aggravation, the injury or condition must have been recorded when the member joined the military. If no injury was documented, a "Presumption of Soundness" applies and the condition is instead considered directly service-connected—unless the VA rebuts the presumption with clear and convincing evidence.

★ ★

---

[77] 38 U.S.C. § 1153; 38 C.F.R. § 3.306

4. Secondary Service-Connection—[78]

Manual M21-1, IV.ii.2.B.5. 5. **Determining
Secondary SC, Including by Aggravation**

Secondary conditions are either caused or aggravated by another service-connected disability. In order for a veteran to establish secondary service-connection for a secondary condition, they must first establish a qualifying service-connected injury or disease. If the service-connected condition then causes a secondary condition, the veteran may file their second diagnosis or evidence of aggravation. *Example*: A Vietnam Veteran with presumptive service-connection for Diabetes develops a painful skin condition. With a doctor's nexus letter stating their medical opinion that the skin condition may have been caused by service-connected Diabetes, the veteran can qualify for secondary service-connection.

★ ★

5. Disabilities Caused by VA Treatment—[79]

Manual M21-1, IV.ii.2.G.1.a. **Basic Criteria for Entitlement
to Compensation Under 38 U.S.C. 1151**

If a veteran is injured at a VA medical facility or during authorized treatment, and the injury or death was caused by recklessness, negligence, lack of proper skill, or error in judgment, and was not reasonably foreseeable, that injury is presumed to be service-connected. *Example*: A veteran underwent surgery at a VA medical hospital, but the surgeon negligently left a small rag in his abdomen, which led to further surgeries and caused severe permanent injuries. Such injuries from VA care are considered service-connected.

★ ★ ★

---

[78] 38 C.F.R. § 3.310
[79] 38 U.S.C. § 1151

§ 3.6 — Burden of Proof

Manual M21-1, III.iii.5.A.2. **Burden of proof and Weighing of Evidence**

"Burden of proof" refers to the veteran's (legal) duty to prove the assertions made by their disability claim, including: (1) qualifying veteran status; (2) in-service injury, condition or incident; (3) current disability. As described by Black's Law Dictionary (11th), the burden of proof includes both the ***burden of production*** and the ***burden of persuasion***. This simply means that veterans must show (produce) evidence and, through their claim, explain (persuade) why the evidence shows a service-connected disability that is entitled to compensation benefits.[80] Veterans have the initial legal burden of proving their veteran status and service-connected disability.

The "Burden of Proof" is a legal duty that shifts from the veteran to the VA like a tennis match —

Imagine a two-player tennis match. One person begins by hitting a ball over a net and onto their opponent's side of the court. When the ball lands (or sometimes before it lands), the other person tries to hit it back over the net. This back-and-forth continues until one player fails to hit the ball back over the net and to their opponent's side, at which point the match (point) ends.

VA claims are like tennis because, like a ball crossing a court, the burden of proof shifts from the veteran to the VA. It is the veteran's job to serve, or file, a claim for benefits. The initial burden of proof (evidence and persuasion) always starts with the veteran. "This means that unless the [veteran] furnishes evidence on each element needed to establish the point at issue, VA must deny his/her claim."[81] However, once a veteran files a claim that makes assertions and includes evidence about their veteran status, in-service injury, and disability, the burden of proof, like a tennis ball, shifts

---

[80] **Burden of production**: the veteran's duty to identify enough substantiating evidence about an issue to have VA decide the issue in the veteran's favor.

Burden of persuasion: the veteran's duty to convince the VA to view the evidence and facts in a way that favors the veteran's claim for benefits.

[81] M21-1, III.iii.5.A.2.a. Responsibilities of VA and Claimants for Securing Evidence.

to the VA. The burden will only shift back to the veteran if VA notifies them of missing evidence that is necessary to substantiate their claim (*see* Section 4.3, Duty: Give Notice about Information Needed to Substantiate a Claim), if additional evidence is needed, such as in a COD/CSD review (*see* Section 3.2.1, Character of Discharge), or if a compensation and pension ("C&P") examination is necessary to decide the claim. (*see* Section 4.5, Duty: Provide Medical Examination/Opinion)

Unlike tennis, though, VA claims are non-adversarial. VA does not submit its own evidence to oppose or disprove a veteran's credible evidence. In fact, veterans and the VA are (supposed to be) playing on the same team—for the veteran! VA has a legal duty to assist the veteran and examine the record evidence to ascertain the truth. (*see* Chapter 4, Duty to Assist). If a veteran qualifies for VA benefits, VA is obligated by law to assist them in the process.

Burden of Proof vs. Standards of proof

The terms "burden of proof" and "standards of proof" have at times been used interchangeably by courts and scholars. Do not be confused. For VA claims, the "burden of proof" refers to the **veteran's legal duty** to produce evidence and persuade the VA about their claim. Meanwhile, "standard of proof" refers to the **degree of confidence held by VA** that a veteran has proven the assertions made by their claim. Standards of proof are used by VA to judge whether or not burdens of proof (production and persuasion) have been met.

Just remember that in VA claims the burden of proof (*production* and *persuasion*) applies to veterans as part of their initial burden to show VA that their evidence and assertions are competent, credible and persuasive. VA in turn reviews the claim and evidence and decides which standard of proof best describes the level of certainty held by VA to decide the claim.

★ ★ ★

§ 3.7 — Standards of Proof

Manual M21-1, III.iv.5.A.1.i – **Standards of evidentiary proof**

"Standards of proof" refer to the various degrees of confidence that VA believes a veteran has proven the assertions made by their claim. VA uses standards of proof to describe how the evidence proves or disproves a disability claim. That includes (1) the "confidence in the evidence," and (2) "degree of persuasion" — both of which relate to the veteran's burden of proof (production and persuasion).

Most people are already familiar with the different standards of proof that are used in the U.S. legal system for different types of civil and criminal cases.

Benefit of the doubt	VA claims	=50%
Preponderance of the evidence	Civil lawsuits	>50%
Clear and convincing evidence	Civil lawsuits	51%-99%
Beyond all reasonable doubt	Criminal cases	100%

The M21-1 Manual defines the standards of proof used to decide VA claims, which are similar to civilian judicial standards.

- **Affirmative evidence to the contrary.** The fact is unlikely; and the evidence against the matter is of greater weight. This standard is the opposite of the "preponderance of the evidence" standard.
- **Relative equipoise.** Evidence must persuade the decision maker that the fact is as likely as not.
- **Preponderance of the evidence.** The greater weight of evidence is that the fact exists. The fact is more likely than not.
- **Clear and convincing evidence.** The fact finder has reasonable certainty of the truth of a fact. This is a higher standard of proof than having to find a fact is more likely than not.
- **Clear and unmistakable evidence.** The evidence must establish the fact without question.

Naturally, the goal for every VA claim is to show evidence that unequivocally proves one's veteran status, in-service injury and current disability. Of course, the best cases *do* have clear and unmistakable evidence, and benefits are promptly awarded. However, it is not necessary for a veteran to prove facts with absolutely certainty and "without question." Rather, a much lower standard of proof is all that is needed.

For veterans, the *minimum* burden of proof needed to prevail on a claim for benefits is called the **benefit of the doubt ("reasonable doubt rule")**. For the reasonable doubt rule to apply, the evidence must persuade the claims examiner that the asserted fact **is as likely true as it is not true**. In terms of percentages, the benefit of the doubt applies when there is an approximately balance of positive and negative evidence, at 50%.

Conversely, in order for VA to deny a claim, a **preponderance of evidence,** or majority of evidence, must be against the veteran's claim and assertion.[82] When a preponderance of the evidence is against the claim, the claim is denied. (When a preponderance of positive evidence favors the veteran, the claim is granted.) This preponderance of negative, or unfavorable evidence, is known as **affirmative evidence to the contrary**. In terms of percentages, affirmative evidence to the contrary means greater than 50% of the evidence is against the veteran. As noted by the M21-1 Manual, affirmative evidence to the contrary "is the opposite of the preponderance standard."

Benefit of the Doubt—[83]

The "benefit of the doubt" is the minimum burden of proof required to prevail on a disability claim. When VA is considering a claim, it will give positive and negative values to different pieces of evidence. When there is an approximate balance of positive and negative evidence, a unique standard—the "Benefit of the Doubt"—applies, and the veteran is entitled to relief.[84] As described by the CAVC, the benefit of the doubt is akin to the Major League Baseball rule that the "tie goes to the runner." When there is a tie between negative and positive evidence, VA should grant the claim, even when uncertainty exists. (VA has a duty to give veterans the benefit of doubt. *see* Section 4.9, Duty: Resolve Questions of Reasonable Doubt in Favor of the Veteran)

---

[82] *Gilbert v. Derwinski*, 1 Vet.App. 49 (1990)
[83] 38 U.S.C. § 5107(b); 38 C.F.R. §§ 3.102, 4.3
[84] *Glbert v. Derwinski*, 1 Vet.App. 49 (1990); M21-1, III.iv.5.A.1.j.

Preponderance of the Evidence —

Manual M21-1, III.v.1.A.2.e. **Evidence Thresholds**

According to the M21-1 Manual, "A preponderance of the evidence exists if the evidence is not in equipoise, which means it is not evenly balanced both for and against the fact or proposition at issue. When there is a fair preponderance of the evidence, one side clearly outweighs the other."

The benefit of the doubt rule is inapplicable when the preponderance, or majority, of evidence is either for or against the claim.[85] "If a fair preponderance of the evidence supports a veteran's claim, the claim will be granted and the rule has no application. Similarly, if a fair preponderance of the evidence is against a veteran's claim, the claim will be denied, and the rule has no application. Where the Board makes a finding of fact adverse to a claimant, it has necessarily concluded that the fact is established by a fair preponderance of the evidence."[86] The preponderance, or greater portion, of evidence must be against the claim for benefits to be denied.[87]

If VA "is persuaded that the preponderant evidence weighs either for or against the veteran's claim, it necessarily has determined that the evidence is not "nearly equal" or "too close to call," and the benefit of the doubt rule therefore has no application. Alternatively, the benefit of the doubt rule may be viewed as shifting the [burden of persuasion] ... onto the VA to prove that the veteran is not entitled to benefits.[88]

★ ★ ★

§ 3.8 — Post-Traumatic Stress Disorder

Manual M21-1, III.iv.4.O.2.b. **Requirements for Establishing
SC for PTSD From In-Service Stressors**

Post-Traumatic Stress Disorder ("PTSD") often occurs when a military service member experiences or witnesses a life-threatening or otherwise

---

[85] *Ortiz v. Principi*, 274 F.3d 1361 (Fed. Cir. 2001)
[86] *Hayes v. Brown*, 5 Vet.App. 60, 69 (1993) citing *Gilbert*, 1 Vet.App. at 55
[87] *Alemany v. Brown*, 9 Vet.App. 518, 519 (1996)
[88] *Ortiz v. Principi*, 274 F.3d 1361, 1365 (Fed. Cir. 2001)

traumatic incident or series of events, like combat or sexual assault. Direct service-connection for PTSD requires three things.

Direct Service-Connection for PTSD—[89]

1. **DIAGNOSIS** — A current medical diagnosis of PTSD;
2. **STRESSOR** — Credible supporting evidence that the claimed in-service stressor actually occurred; and
3. **NEXUS** — Medical evidence of a causal nexus between current symptomatology and a claimed in-service stressor.

See: *Cohen v. Brown*, 10 Vet.App. 128, 138 (1997); *Serv. Women's Action Network v. Sec'y of Veterans Affairs*, 815 F.3d 1369, 1373 (Fed. Cir. 2016). *also* 38 C.F.R. § 4.130, Diagnostic Code (DC) 9411 (Schedule of ratings for mental disorders).

In adjudicating a claim for service connection for PTSD, VA will review evidence of the places, types, and circumstances of a veteran's service, as shown by their military records and all pertinent medical and lay evidence.[90]

1. PTSD DIAGNOSIS

A veteran seeking service-connection for PTSD must first show a current medical diagnosis of PTSD.[91] VA considers certain private health care providers to be qualified to diagnose PTSD for VA benefit purposes, including: psychiatrists, psychologist therapists, licensed clinical social workers (L.C.S.W.), nurse practitioners, clinical nurse specialists, and physician assistants.

Although Disability Benefits Questionnaires have been removed from the VA's "public-facing" website, VA must still accept DBQs that are submitted along with all applications for disability benefits.

A veteran seeking service-connection for PTSD is encouraged when possible to have their private physician document the disability on

---

[89] 38 C.F.R. § 3.304(f)
[90] *Hayes v. Brown*, 5 Vet.App. 60, 66 (1993)
[91] 38 C.F.R. § 3.304(f)

a Disability Benefits Questionnaire PTSD review form. (VA Form 21-0960P-3). ****VA Form 21-0960P-3 is technically intended for appeals for higher PTSD ratings, but can and should be included with original claims when possible. PTSD DBQs allow private practitioners to communicate their diagnosis, treatment history and professional opinions to VA for uniform and efficient processing.** Find all DBQs at https://va-handbook/resources/dbqs.

2. IN-SERVICE STRESSOR

Once a current PTSD diagnosis is established, the veteran must show "credible supporting evidence" that the claimed in-service stressor(s) actually occurred.[92] Whether or not the record of evidence shows the occurrence of an in-service stressor is a question of fact that is determined by a VA claim processor (while the question of whether a veteran has PTSD is a question for a medical professional during a C&P examination).

Some PTSD claims can establish in-service stressor with lay testimony alone —

In certain circumstances, a veteran's lay statement is sufficient on its own to establish the occurrence of in-service PTSD stressors. This relaxed evidentiary standard applies to the following in-service stressors: (1) In-Service Diagnosis of PTSD; (2) Combat; (3) Fear of Hostile Military or Terrorist Activity; (4) POW.

Manual M21-1, IV.ii.1.D.3.a. **When a Veteran's Lay Testimony Alone May Establish an In-Service Stressor**

---

1. **In-Service PTSD Diagnosis.**[93] If the evidence establishes a diagnosis of posttraumatic stress disorder during service and the claimed stressor is related to that service…

---

[92] 38 C.F.R. § 3.304(f)
[93] 38 C.F.R. § 3.304(f)(1)

2. **Combat.**[94] If the evidence establishes that the veteran engaged in combat with the enemy and the claimed stressor is related to that combat…

3. **Fear of Hostile Activity.**[95] If a stressor claimed by a veteran is related to the veteran's fear of hostile military or terrorist activity…

4. **POW.**[96] If the evidence establishes that the veteran was a prisoner-of-war … and the claimed stressor is related to that prisoner-of-war experience…

VA "allows a veteran's lay testimony alone to constitute the credible supporting evidence required for stressors related to combat in which the veteran engaged, a veteran's fear of hostile military or terrorist activity, or a veteran's experience being a prisoner of war. 38 C.F.R. § 3.304(f) (2)-(4).'"[97] "If none of these exceptions apply, then the veteran's statements alone will not be sufficient to establish an in-service stressor, but must be corroborated by credible supporting evidence.'"[98]

★ ★ ★

PTSD claims based on Sexual Assault require additional evidence

5. **Sexual Assault PTSD Stressor.**[99] If a posttraumatic stress disorder claim is based on in-service personal assault, evidence from sources other than the veteran's service records may corroborate the veteran's account of the stressor incident …

While combat veterans, POWS, and veterans exposed to hostile or terrorist activity may establish the occurrence of an in-service stressor with lay testimony alone, non-combat veterans, including survivors, must

---

[94] 38 C.F.R. § 3.304(f)(2)

[95] 38 C.F.R. § 3.304(f)(3)

[96] 38 C.F.R. § 3.304(f)(4)

[97] *Serv. Women's Action Network v. Sec'y of Veterans Affairs*, 815 F.3d 1369, 1373 (Fed. Cir. 2016)

[98] *Dizoglio v. Brown*, 9 Vet.App. 163, 166 (1996); *Moreau v. Brown*, 9 Vet.App. 389, 394-95 (1996); also *Cohen v. Brown*, 10 Vet.App 128, 146-47 (1997)

[99] 38 C.F.R. § 3.304(f)(5)

show other credible evidence of an in-service stressor beyond a personal statement.[100] (*see* Section 5.4.2, File Claim for Service-Connected PTSD caused by Sexual Assault)

3. NEXUS

Lastly, a veteran must show "a link, established by medical evidence, between current symptoms and an in-service stressor."[101] One way to accomplish this is having the veteran's psychiatrist, psychologist, counselor or therapist draft a "nexus letter" or statement that gives their professional opinion that the veteran's PTSD was caused by in-service stressors that were experienced on active duty. Nexus letters (example below) are strongly recommended (but not required) to be included with disability claims.

★ ★

SAMPLE (Direct SC) NEXUS LETTER - PTSD

Date
Veteran Name / Social Security Number

Subj: (Veteran's) Post-Traumatic Stress Disorder from Military Service

To Whom It May Concern:

I am Dr. _____. My credentials are included. I am writing a letter for (Veteran) to assist him/her in establishing a claim with the Department of Veterans Affairs for Post-Traumatic Stress Disorder.

I have reviewed (Veteran's) service and medical records, including her DD214, Post Deployment Health Assessment, and (list other records). I have also reviewed and have noted the circumstances and events of her military service. which includes two combat deployments to Afghanistan, as indicated by her awards and medals, between the years 2006 and 2009.

(Veteran) has been a patient under my care since (date), during which

---

[100] *Doran v. Brown*, 6 Vet.App. 283, 290 (1996)
[101] 38 C.F.R. § 3.304(f)

time I have diagnosed her with Post-Traumatic Stress Disorder. (provide a short explanation of diagnosis, including list of key standard criterion for injury) discuss DSM-IV criterion, PTSD DBQ axis, etc.

After a review of the aforementioned relevant records and multiple consultations/examinations of [veteran], it is my opinion that [veteran's] Post-Traumatic Stress Disorder [choose one] is "as likely as not" – "more than likely" – "very likely" – is "due to" her military service, specifically her combat experiences while deployed to Iraq.

My opinion is based on my knowledge of current medical literature, in addition to a full review of [veteran's] military service and medical records, as well as routine therapy sessions with [Veteran] over the past year, from [date] to [date].

Signed,

_____ (include professional credentials)

★ ★ ★

§ 3.8.1 — Combat – Stressor

> Manual M21-1, IV.ii.2.B.3.d. **Considering Evidence for Combat-Related Disabilities**

> Manual M21-1, III.iv.4.O.4.b. **Determining Combat Service**

When a veteran's PTSD stressor is related to combat, a lower burden of proving an in-service stressor applies. To prove stressors of combat PTSD, the veteran's lay testimony or statements are accepted as conclusive evidence of the occurrence of the claimed stressor. No additional corroborative evidence is required, as long as the claimed stressor is "consistent with the circumstances, conditions, or hardships of the veteran's service" and there exists no clear "evidence to the contrary."[102] Combat service is can be confirmed by a veteran's DD214 that shows combat medals, ribbons, or other combat awards. However, other records may also corroborate combat service when a DD214 is missing certain items, which is common. If no

---

[102] 38 U.S.C. § 1154(b); 38 C.F.R. § 3.304(f)(2)

official records exist of individual firefights and combat missions, and the veteran's records are missing combat awards, try to obtain buddy letters from fellow platoon members who are VA service-connected for their combat injuries. **Always include a statement from the veteran about their combat service and the stressful incidents that they experienced.

"Section 1154 makes it abundantly clear that special considerations attend he cases of combat veterans."[103] This lower threshold is necessary for combat veterans because individual skirmishes are often undocumented. "Section 1154(b) provides a factual basis upon which a determination can be made that a particular disease or injury was aggravated or incurred in service."[104]

> **38 U.S.C. § 1154(b).** In the case of any veteran who engaged in combat with the enemy in active service with a military, naval, or air organization of the United States during a period of war, campaign, or expedition, the Secretary shall accept as sufficient proof of service-connection of any disease or injury alleged to have been incurred in or aggravated by such service satisfactory lay or other evidence of service incurrence or aggravation of such injury or disease, if consistent with the circumstances, conditions, or hardships of such service, notwithstanding the fact that there is no official record of such incurrence or aggravation in such service, and, to that end, shall resolve every reasonable doubt in favor of the veteran. Service-connection of such injury or disease may be rebutted by clear and convincing evidence to the contrary. The reasons for granting or denying service-connection in each case shall be recorded in full.
>
> **38 C.F.R. § 3.304(d) — Combat.** Satisfactory lay or other evidence that an injury or disease was incurred or aggravated in combat will be accepted as sufficient proof of service connection if the evidence is consistent with the circumstances, conditions or hardships of such service

---

[103] *Jensen v. Brown*, 19 F.3d 1413, 1416 (Fed. Cir. 1994)
[104] *Cohen v. Brown*, 10 Vet.App. 128 (1997)

even though there is no official record of such incurrence or aggravation.

38 C.F.R. § 3.304(f)(2). If the evidence establishes that the veteran engaged in combat with the enemy and the claimed stressor is related to that combat, in the absence of clear and convincing evidence to the contrary, and provided that the claimed stressor is consistent with the circumstances, conditions, or hardships of the veteran's service, the veteran's lay testimony alone may establish the occurrence of the claimed in-service stressor.

According to the M21-1 Manual, **Engaging in combat with the enemy** means personal participation in events constituting an actual fight or encounter with a military foe or hostile unit or instrumentality. It includes presence during such events either as a:

- combatant, or
- service member performing duty in support of combatants, such as providing medical care to the wounded.

Manual M21-1, IV.ii.1.D.3.d. **Definition: Engaging in Combat With the Enemy**

Manual M21-1, IV.ii.1.D.3.f. **Individual Decorations as Evidence of Combat Participation**

Claims examiners look at the following records for *primary evidence* to determine whether claims of combat service and PTSD stressors are supported by the evidence:

- Service personnel and pay records
- Military occupation evidence
- Hazard pay records
- Military performance reports
- Verification of combat/hostile fire/imminent danger pay
- Unit and organization history
- After action reports (AARs)
- Radio and deck logs, ship histories, muster rolls

- Command chronologies and war diaries,
- Monthly summaries and morning reports.

★ ★ ★

♣ VA Form 21-0781 — **Statement in Support of Claim for Service-Connection for PTSD**

A veteran's personal statement about the traumatic in-service stressor(s) is **required** for establishing service-connection for PTSD. As a general rule, the more details a veteran can provide about the stressful incidents, the better. Veterans should use **VA Form 21-0781** to describe one or more traumatic events that they experienced, including vivid details of their experience. (*see* Section 5.4.1 — File Claim for Service-Connected PTSD) While PTSD may result from one stressfully traumatic incident, additional forms may be used to describe further incidents. VA Form 21-0781 explains:

> List the stressful incident or incidents that occurred in service that you feel contributed to your current condition. For each incident, provide a description of what happened, the date, the geographic location, your unit assignment and dates of assignment, and the full names and unit assignments of you know of who were killed or injured during the incident. Please provide dates within at least a 60-day range and do not use nicknames. It is important that you complete the form in detail and be as specific as possible so that research of military records can be thoroughly conducted. If more space is needed, attach a separate sheet, indicating the item number to which the answers apply. (*Instructions*, Form 21-0781)

Buddy Letters (Statements) —

Manual M21-1, IV.ii.1.D.1.e. **Accepting Buddy Statements of a Fellow Veteran as Corroboration of a Claimed In-Service Stressor**

For additional credible evidence of in-service stressors, veterans can include with their claim statements from other veterans who served in the same military unit and have firsthand knowledge of shared experiences. Testimonials can be extremely helpful in establishing facts that are necessary to corroborate claims. Veterans who write "Buddy Letters" should also submit their DD214 to enable VA examiners to verify their service.

**On September 11, 2020, just prior to VA Handbook's publication, VA published notice in the Federal Register that the Agency will begin collecting "buddy statements" on a new standardized VA Form, 21-10210 Lay/Witness Statements.*[105]

♣   VA Form 21-10210 — **Lay/Witness Statement**

★ ★ ★

SAMPLE BUDDY LETTER

Date
Name: Veteran submitting claim
Social Security Number: Veteran submitting claim

Subj: Buddy Letter for (Veteran)

To Whom It May Concern:

My name is _____. I served with (Veteran) from 2006-2009 as a (military occupational specialty) with (military unit). I was honorably discharged in 2011. VA rates me 100% disabled from my PTSD.

I am writing to share my combat experiences with [Veteran] to help with her claim for PTSD. In 2007, we were both deployed to Iraq, where on numerous occasions we took direct fire from enemy forces. On August 22 while on patrol in Karbala, [Veteran] chased after an insurgent into a compound and used her rifle to provide suppressive fire, allowing her team to close width towards the location. During this encounter, which I participated in, [Veteran] was credited with killing 2 enemy fighters.

[Veteran] was also present when our section leader Staff Sergeant Smith

---

[105] *Agency Information Collection Activity: Lay/Witness Statement.* 85 Fed. Reg. 56, 290 (11 Sept. 2020) www.federalregister.gov/d/2020-20054.

was shot while on patrol on September 19, 2006. At the time, [Veteran] was the closest nearby team member and she immediately responded by firing several rounds at the sniper's position before dragging Smith to safety. Unfortunately, Smith died from his injuries.

This statement is true and correct to the best of my knowledge.

Sincerely,
Buddy name
Final rank, branch
Social security number
Phone, address, email

★ ★ ★

§ 3.8.2 — Fear of Hostile Activity – PTSD Stressor

> Manual M21-1, III.iv.4.O.4.d. **Establishing a Stressor Related to the Fear of Hostile Military or Terrorist Activity**

Veterans may develop PTSD while deployed to a war zone, even if they do not engage in combat. In order to establish the occurrence of an in-service stressor due to a veteran's fear of hostile military or terrorist activity under § 3.304(f)(3), the veteran's lay testimony as to the existence of the stressor is adequate if three conditions are satisfied:

(1) a VA psychiatrist or psychologist confirms that the claimed stressor is adequate to support a diagnosis of PSTD and that the veteran's symptoms are related to the claimed stressor;
(2) the VA psychiatrist or psychologist's findings are not contradicted by clear and convincing evidence; and
(3) the claimed stressor is consistent with the places, types, and circumstances of the veteran's service.

Sanchez-Navarro v. McDonald, 774 F.3d 1380, 1384 (Fed. Cir. 2014)

> **"Fear of hostile military or terrorist activity"** means that a veteran experienced, witnessed, or was confronted with an event or circumstance that involved actual or

threatened death or serious injury, or a threat to the physical integrity of the veteran or others, such as from an actual or potential improvised explosive device; vehicle-imbedded explosive device; incoming artillery, rocket, or mortar fire; grenade; small arms fire, including suspected sniper fire; or attack upon friendly military aircraft, and the veteran's response to the event or circumstance involved a psychological or psycho-physiological state of fear, helplessness, or horror.[106]

According to the M21-1 Manual, examples of exposure to hostile military or terrorist activity include presence at events involving:

- actual or potential improvised explosive devices (IEDs)
- vehicle-embedded explosive devices
- incoming artillery, rocket, or mortar fire
- small arms fire, including suspected sniper fire, or
- attacks upon friendly aircraft.

Manual M21-1, IV.ii.1.D.3.e. **Definition: Fear of Hostile Military or Terrorist Activity**

★ ★ ★

§ 3.8.3 — Sexual Assault – PTSD Stressor

Manual M21-1, IV.ii.1.D.5.b. **Developing Claims of SC Based on In-Service Personal Trauma**

Disability compensation is not given for military sexual trauma ("MST"), but for conditions resulting from MST, such as PTSD. Veterans who have PTSD from MST are entitled to compensation, even in cases where there is no contemporaneous record of the attack. VA provides MST coordinators at all local regional offices, both male and female, who, if needed, can assist with MST applications. The VA MST phone number is (800) 827-1000. Online: benefits.va.gov/benefits/mstcoordinators.asp.

---

[106] 38 C.F.R. § 3.304 (f)(3)

Counseling and treatment for sexual trauma—[107]

Section 1720D, which requires VA to provide care and services to veterans who experienced psychological trauma, defines MST as trauma caused from one of the following events:

- Psychological trauma from a physical assault of a sexual nature;
- Battery of a sexual nature;
- Sexual harassment that occurred while the veteran was serving on:
  o Active Duty
  o Active duty for training
  o Inactive duty training

VA uses the general term "military sexual trauma" to refer to these different traumas.[108] A 2018 VA Office of the Inspector General report describes the difficult nature of MST claims:

> VA is aware that because of the nature of military sexual trauma (MST) stressors, it is often difficult for a victim to report or document the event when it occurs. Reasons for not reporting that are unique to the military include reluctance to submit a report when the perpetrator is a superior officer, concerns about negative implications for performance reports, worries about punishment for collateral misconduct, and the perception of an unresponsive military chain of command. As a result, if the MST leads to posttraumatic stress disorder (PTSD), it is often difficult for victims of MST to produce the required evidence to support the occurrence of the reported assault.[109]

Despite the difficulties that are sometimes associated with obtaining evidence, for claims involving sexual assault or MST a veteran's lay

---

[107] 38 U.S.C. § 1720D

[108] *see* VHA Directive 1115, "Military Sexual Trauma Program" (May 8, 2018)

[109] Office of the Inspector General Department of Veterans Affairs. *Denied Posttraumatic Stress Disorder Claims Related to Military Sexual Trauma.* Report #17-05248-241. 21 Aug. 2018.

testimony alone is not considered sufficient to establish the occurrence of the alleged stressor.[110] Claims for PTSD from MST must provide some corroborative evidence which substantiates or verifies the veteran's testimony or statements as to the occurrence of the claimed stressor.[111]

However, "VA may not treat a claimant's failure to report an alleged sexual assault to military authorities as pertinent evidence that the sexual assault did not occur."[112]

"[U]nder 38 C.F.R. § 3.304(f)(5), medical opinion evidence may be submitted for use in determining whether the occurrence of a stressor is corroborated.[113]

Sexual Assault PTSD Stressor—[114]

If a posttraumatic stress disorder claim is based on in-service personal assault, evidence from sources other than the veteran's service records may corroborate the veteran's account of the stressor incident. Examples of such evidence include, but are not limited to: records from law enforcement authorities, rape crisis centers, mental health counseling centers, hospitals, or physicians; pregnancy tests or tests for sexually transmitted diseases; and statements from family members, roommates, fellow service members, or clergy. Evidence of behavior changes following the claimed assault is one type of relevant evidence that may be found in these sources. Examples of behavior changes that may constitute credible evidence of the stressor include, but are not limited to: a request for a transfer to another military duty assignment; deterioration in work performance; substance abuse; episodes of depression, panic attacks, or anxiety without an identifiable cause; or unexplained economic or social behavior changes. VA will not deny a posttraumatic stress disorder claim that is based on in-service personal assault without first advising the claimant that evidence from sources other than the veteran's service records or evidence of behavior changes

---

[110] *Moreau v. Brown*, 9 Vet.App. 389, 395 (1996); *Dizoglio v. Brown*, 9 Vet.App. 163, 166 (1996)
[111] *West (Carlton) v. Brown*, 7 Vet.App. 70, 76 (1994); *Zarycki v. Brown*, 6 Vet. App. 91, 98 (1993)
[112] *Az v. Shinseki*, 731 F.3d 1303 (Fed. Cir. 2013)
[113] *Menegassi v. Shinseki*, 638 F.3d 1379, 1382 (Fed. Cir. 2011)
[114] 38 C.F.R. § 3.304(f)(5)

may constitute credible supporting evidence of the stressor and allowing him or her the opportunity to furnish this type of evidence or advise VA of potential sources of such evidence. VA may submit any evidence that it receives to an appropriate medical or mental health professional for an opinion as to whether it indicates that a personal assault occurred.

"Section 3.304(f)(5) enumerates several categories of corroborating evidence that may be used in cases where, as here, a PTSD claim is based on "in-service personal assault.""[115]

♣ VA Form 21-0781a — **Statement in Support of Claim for Service-Connection for PTSD Secondary to Personal Assault**

Although more than a personal statement is required to corroborate a sexual assault, veterans should still share as much evidence about the traumatic event as possible by providing a statement using VA Form 21-0781a. Corroborating evidence, defined by 38 C.F.R. § 3.304(f)(5), can help substantiate the occurrence of a sexual assault in-service stressor. That includes:

Description. Veterans should provide as much descriptive information about the incident as possible, including all potential sources that may help to corroborate their harassment or assault.

Reports. If the veteran reported the incident to military or civilian law enforcement authorities or sought help from a rape crisis center, counseling facility, or other health clinic, provide the names and addresses of the facilities that were visited. As with treatment records, veterans can submit the records with their application or authorize VA to obtain them.

Treatment. If the veteran received treatment for sexual assault, they can either submit the private records themselves or authorize VA to obtain them by using VA Form 21-4142, "Authorization and Consent to Release Information to the Department of Veterans Affairs" and Form 21-4142a,

---

[115] *Viale v. Wilkie* (Fed. Cir. 2018) *nonprecedential opinion;* also *Kays v. Snyder*, 846 F.3d 1208, 1211 (Fed. Cir. 2017) (quoting 38 C.F.R. § 3.304(f);
Serv. Women's Action Network v. Sec'y of Veterans Affairs, 815 F.3d 1369, 1373 (Fed. Cir. 2016) ("[W]hen the stressor is related to an in-service personal assault, . . . the veteran is required to provide corroborating evidence to substantiate the occurrence of the stressor.")

"General Release for Medical Provider Information to the Department of Veterans Affairs." If needed, use multiple authorization forms.

Contemporaneous Conversations. If the veteran confided in friends, family members, chaplains, clergy, or fellow service members, have these individuals prepare a statement concerning their knowledge of the incident. In addition, when available include copies of personal diary or journal entries about the incident.

Behavioral Changes. A veteran who was sexually assaulted should also tell VA about any behavioral changes that they experienced after the assault. These may include:

- breakup of a primary relationship
- sudden requests for a change in duty assignment
- increased use of leave without an apparent reason
- sudden changes in performance and performance evaluations
- episodes of depression, panic attacks, or anxiety
- increased or decreased use of prescription medications
- increased use of over-the-counter medications
- substance abuse such as alcohol or drugs
- increased disregard for military or civilian authority
- obsessive behavior such as overeating or undereating
- pregnancy tests around the time of the incident
- tests for HIV or sexually transmitted diseases
- unexplained economic or social behavior changes

★ ★ ★

Improper MST Claim Denials by VA —

In 2018, the VA Office of the Inspector General found that VA had improperly denied thousands of MST-related PTSD claims.[116] The report, "Denied Posttraumatic Stress Disorder Claims Related to Military Sexual Trauma," found that nearly half of the 12,000 claims filed in the previous year "were not properly processed following VBA policy ... [which may]

---

[116] Office of the Inspector General Department of Veterans Affairs. *Denied Posttraumatic Stress Disorder Claims Related to Military Sexual Trauma*. Report #17-05248-241. 21 Aug. 2018.

have resulted in the denial of benefits to potential victims of MST who could have been entitled to receive them." The report found that:

- Medical examinations and opinions were not requested, even when sufficient evidence existed for a claim (28 percent of cases)
- Failures to gather the necessary records (13 percent of cases)
- MST coordinators did not contact veterans as required, and employees failed to use the required language to determine if a report was filed, and failed to obtain reports (11 percent of cases)
- Claims adjudicators used insufficient and contradictory medical evidence to deny claims (10 percent of cases)

Due to VA's documented failures to properly adjudicate PSTD-MST claims, veterans are permitted to refile claims that were previously denied for reconsideration. As such, a veteran who was denied for PSTD-MST is encouraged to reapply for *de novo* review, without regard to the previous decision. Because of the history of improper MST denials, veterans and advocates should pay close attention to VARO ratings decisions regarding PSTD-MST claims and be prepared to appeal an erroneous denial.

★ ★ ★

§ 3.9 —Agent Orange Herbicide Exposure

Manual M21-1, IV.ii.1.H.1. **Processing of Herbicide Claims**

During the Vietnam War, the Department of Defense ("DoD") used military aircraft to spray millions of gallons of toxic herbicide chemicals onto the jungles, and consequently, U.S. troops, below. These poisonous herbicides were manufactured pursuant to government contracts by U.S. corporations like DOW Chemical Company[117] and Monsanto,[118] who were

---

[117] "Agent Orange." *DOW Chemical Company.* web.archive.org/web/20200327172228/https://corporate.dow.com/en-us/about/legal/issues/agent-orange.html.

[118] "Agent Orange: Background on Monsanto's Involvement." *Monsanto.* web.archive.org/web/20200327172842/https://monsanto.com/company/media/statements/agent-orange-background/.

later sued by Vietnam Veterans and accused of knowingly concealing the dangers that herbicides posed to military service members.[119]

Under 38 C.F.R. 3.307(a)(6)(i), **herbicide agent** means a harmful defoliant chemical, such as Agent Orange, used in support of U.S. and allied military operations in the Republic of Vietnam during the period beginning on January 9, 1962, and ending on May 7, 1975, that contained the following components:

- 2,4,5-T and its contaminant, TCDD (dioxin)
- 2,4-D
- cacodylic acid, and
- picloram.

> Manual M21-1, IV.ii.2.C.3.b. **Definition: Herbicide Agent**

Operation Ranch Hand —

"**Agent Orange** was one of several chemically-similar herbicides used by the United States government during the Vietnam War in connection with "Operation Ranch Hand," the code name for the military's efforts to defoliate various areas in Vietnam."[120] "Between 1961 and 1971, herbicide mixtures — nicknamed by the colored identification band painted on their 208-litre storage barrels — were used by the United States ... to defoliate forests and mangroves, to clear perimeters of military installations and to destroy "unfriendly" crops, as a tactic for decreasing enemy armed forces protective cover and food supplies."[121] Known as "rainbow herbicides," each chemical formula was given a color name: Agents Pink, Green,

---

[119] For a complete history of Agent Orange use and subsequent litigation, see: *In re* "Agent Orange" Prod. Liab. Litig., 373 F.Supp.2d 7, 2005 WL 729177 (E.D.N.Y. 2005).

[120] *In re* "Agent Orange" Prod. Liab. Litig., 517 F.3d 76 (2nd Cir. 2008)

[121] *In re* "Agent Orange" Prod. Liab. Litig., 373 F.Supp.2d 7, 2005 WL 729177 (E.D.N.Y. 2005)

Purple, Orange, Orange II, White, Blue (powder and liquid).[122] The most widely-used herbicide was Agent Orange (45,677,937 liters sprayed). For simplicity, this Handbook refers to all Vietnam-era herbicides collectively as "Agent Orange."

Ever since Vietnam Veterans first began filing VA disability claims for herbicide-related exposures in 1977, the number one claim filed by Vietnam Veterans (other than PTSD) has been for diseases and conditions that were caused by Agent Orange.

Despite the now-obvious proven connection between DoD defoliants, disability, and death, VA for many years denied thousands of disability and health care claims filed by sick and dying Vietnam Veterans. As awareness about the toxic herbicide grew, in 1984 Congress passed the Veterans' Dioxin and Radiation Exposure Compensation Standards Act.[123] "Section 5 of that Act directed the VA to prescribe regulations establishing guidelines and standards for resolving claims for benefits based on exposure during service in the Republic of Vietnam during the Vietnam era to a herbicide containing dioxin."[124]

Agent Orange Act of 1991—[125]

Seven years later in 1991, Congress passed the Agent Orange Act, which established a comprehensive framework for herbicide-based claims, and granted Vietnam Veterans presumptive service-connection for a greater number of Agent Orange-related diseases and conditions. Today, VA regulations recognize two separate presumptions related to Agent Orange herbicide exposure. First, (1) VA presumes *causation*: that certain diseases were caused by exposure to Agent Orange and other toxic herbicides. Second, (2) VA presumes *exposure*: that military service in certain places at certain times exposed veterans to Agent Orange. As such,

---

[122] Stellman, Jeanne M., et al., The Extent and Patterns of Usage of Agent Orange and Other Herbicides in Vietnam, 422 *NATURE* 681 (2003). https://web.archive.org/web/20191224120046/https://epiville.ccnmtl.columbia.edu/assets/pdfs/Stellman3.pdf

[123] Pub. L. 98-542—Oct. 24, 1984, 98 Stat. 2725

[124] *Haas v. Peake*, 525 F. 3d 1168 (Fed. Cir. 2008)

[125] Pub. L. 102-4—Feb. 6, 1991 105 Stat. 11

---

service-connection for qualifying diseases may granted even when there is no clear record of herbicide exposure during service.

As with all other claims for service-connection, veterans suffering from issues related to Agent Orange herbicide exposure must show the three factors outlined by the Federal Circuit in *Shedden v. Principi*[126], starting with a current disability.

1. Current disability,
2. In-service exposure to Agent Orange (presumptive or actual)
3. Nexus - causation of current disability by Agent Orange exposure.

However, if a veteran suffers from a current disability that is presumed to have been caused by herbicide exposure, VA will presume that the second requirement (in-service exposure) third requirement (causation) are satisfied so long as the veteran can prove qualifying service in Vietnam, Korea, or in the Air Force. Disabling diseases that are presumed to have been caused by herbicide exposure are defined by regulation.[127] Likewise, service that qualifies for the presumption of exposure is also defined by VA regulation.[128]

Manual M21-1, IV.ii.1.H - **Developing Claims for Service Connection (SC) Based on Herbicide Exposure**

★ ★ ★

§ 3.9.1 — Presumption of Causation

VA applies a **Presumption of Causation** to certain diseases that are presumed to have been caused by exposure to Agent Orange and other deadly herbicides. When a Vietnam-era veteran who suffers from a "presumptive-herbicide" disease files a claim for disability benefits with proof of their current disability, no nexus medical opinion is necessary — the veteran must only show proof of their exposure to Agent Orange (*see* Section 3.9.2, Presumption of Exposure). The full list of diseases and

---

[126] *Shedden*, 381 F.3d at 1167 (Fed. Cir. 2004)
[127] 38 C.F.R. § 3.309(e)
[128] 38 C.F.R. § 3.307(a)(6)(iii-v)

conditions that are presumed to have been caused by herbicide exposure appears at 38 C.F.R. § 3.309(e).

Cancers Associate with Agent Orange Exposure—[129]

- **Hodgkin's disease**: A type of cancer that causes your lymph nodes, liver, and spleen to get bigger and your red blood cells to decrease (called anemia)
- **Multiple myeloma**: A type of cancer that affects your plasma cells (white blood cells made in your bone marrow that help to fight infection)
- **Non-Hodgkin's lymphoma**: A group of cancers that affect the lymph glands and other lymphatic tissue (a part of your immune system that helps to fight infection and illness)
- **Prostate cancer**: Cancer of the prostate (the gland in men that helps to make semen)
- **All chronic B-cell leukemias**: A type of cancer that affects your white blood cells (cells in your body's immune system that help to fight off illnesses and infections)
- **Respiratory cancers**: cancers of the organs involved in breathing (including the lungs, larynx, trachea, and bronchus)
- **Soft-tissue sarcoma**: Different types of cancers in body tissues such as muscle, fat, blood and lymph vessels, and connective tissues.

Other Illnesses Associated with Agent Orange—[130]

- **AL amyloidosis**: A rare illness that happens when an abnormal protein (called amyloid) builds up in your body's tissues, nerves, or organs (like your heart, kidneys, or liver) and causes damage over time.
- **Chloracne** (or other acneform disease): A skin condition that happens soon after contact with chemicals and looks like acne often seen in teenagers. Under VA rating regulations, it must be at least 10% disabling within one year of contact with herbicides.

---

[129] 38 C.F.R. § 3.309(e)
[130] 38 C.F.R. § 3.309(e)

- **Type 2 diabetes** (Type II diabetes mellitus or adult-onset diabetes): An illness that happens when your body is unable to properly use insulin (a hormone that turns blood glucose, or sugar, into energy), leading to high blood sugar levels.
- **Ischemic heart disease**: A type of heart disease that happens when your heart doesn't get enough blood (and the oxygen the blood carries). It often causes chest pain or discomfort.
- **Parkinson's disease**: An illness of the nervous system (the network of nerves and fibers that send messages between your brain and spinal cord and other areas of your body) that affects your muscles and movement-and gets worse over time.
- **Early-onset peripheral neuropathy**: An illness of the nervous system that causes numbness, tingling, and weakness. Under VA rating regulations, it must be at least 10% disabling within one year of contact with herbicides.
- **Porphyria cutanea tarda**: A rare illness that can make your liver stop working the way it should and can cause your skin to thin and blister when you're out in the sun. Under VA rating regulations, it must be at least 10% disabling within one year of contact with herbicides.

★ ★ ★

§ 3.9.2 — Presumption of Exposure

Manual M21-1, IV.ii.2.C.3.d. **Presuming Exposure to an Herbicide Agent**

VA applies a **Presumption of Exposure** to toxic herbicides to certain veterans who served in specific places at times. The qualifications for presumptions of exposure appear at 38 C.F.R. § 3.307(a)(6).

38 C.F.R. § 3.307(a)(6)(iii-v). **Presumptive service-connection for exposure to herbicide agents.**

1. the Republic of Vietnam between January 9, 1962 - May 7, 1975.
2. in or near the Korean DMZ between April 1, 1968 - August 31, 1971.

3. members of the Air Force (and AF reserves) who regularly and repeatedly operated, maintained, or served onboard C-123 aircraft that were known to have been used to spray an herbicide agent.

The **Presumption of Exposure** applies to all veterans who served (1) in Vietnam between January 9, 1962 and May 7, 1975; (2) near the Korean DMZ between September 1, 1967 and August 31, 1971; and (3) as members of the Air Force who routinely entered military C-123 airplanes that were once used to transport and spray herbicide. If a disabled veteran can prove that they served in one of these three qualifying places during a qualifying period, they "shall be presumed to have been exposed during such service to an herbicide agent."[131]

1. Presumption of Exposure, Service in Vietnam—[132]

All Vietnam Veterans are eligible to receive a presumption of exposure to Agent Orange regardless of whether they served at sea or on the mainland. That is because service in Vietnam, for the purposes of Agent Orange exposure, is defined as "the Republic of Vietnam," to include "service in the waters offshore and service in other locations if the conditions of service involved duty or visitation in the Republic of Vietnam." 38 C.F.R. § 3.307(a)(6)(iii). This definition always included land forces, but now also includes naval veterans who served aboard vessels and ships that operated on inland waterways or within 12 nautical miles of the coast.

2. Presumption of Exposure, Korea—[133]

> Manual M21-1, IV.ii.1.H.3. – **Developing Claims Based on Herbicide Exposure on the Korean DMZ**

Beyond Vietnam, Agent Orange was also used as a defoliant along the demilitarized zone the separates North Korea from South Korea. As described in the Federal Register, "The Korean demilitarized zone (DMZ) is a strip of land running across the Korean Peninsula that separates North Korea from South Korea and serves as a buffer zone between the two

---

[131] 38 C.F.R. § 3.307(a)(6)(iii)

[132] 38 U.S.C. § 1116

[133] 38 U.S.C. §§ 1116B, 1821

countries. The DMZ cuts the Korean Peninsula roughly in half following the geographic 38th parallel north latitude and is approximately 155 miles long and 2.5 miles wide. It became a de facto border following World War II as the demarcation line between the northern Soviet-controlled Democratic People's Republic of Korea and the southern United Nations-controlled Republic of Korea. When an attacking North Korean military force crossed the DMZ on June 25, 1950, United States and United Nations troops came to the aid of South Korea and the Korean War commenced. A ceasefire agreement was signed on July 27, 1953, which established the current DMZ buffer zone between North and South Korea. No peace treaty was ever signed and the two Koreas remain technically at war. The United States established a permanent contingent of troops on the DMZ to support South Korea."[134]

Further, "DoD has advised that herbicides were not applied within the DMZ, but were applied in some adjacent areas. Specifically, DoD has reported that herbicides were applied between April 1968 and July 1969 along a strip of land 151 miles long and up to 350 yards wide along the southern edge of the DMZ north of the civilian control line. The herbicide agents were applied through hand spraying and hand distribution of pelletized herbicides. There was no aerial spraying. DoD also has provided VA a list of the military units that are currently known to have operated in that area during the period that herbicides were applied."

Units Acknowledged by DoD and VA as having performed missions near the DMZ during the period herbicides were used.

DoD and VA have acknowledged that certain units performed missions in or near the Korean DMW during the period when herbicides were used. Veterans who can show that they served in one of the following units will be presumed to have been exposed to herbicides while in Korea. (If a veteran's unit is not included, "VA will develop further evidence to verify that assertion.") "Because DoD and VA may recognize additional units in the future based on additional information or evidence, we will not list the units in the regulation." The most up-to-date listing of Korea DMZ units can be found in the M21-1 Manual (Online at: va-handbook.com/m21-1/)

---

[134] *Herbicide Exposure and Veterans with Covered Service in Korea.* 76 Fed. Reg. 36,640, 36,641 (24 July 2009). www.federalregister.gov/d/E9-17035.

- Combat Brigades of the 2nd and 7th Infantry Divisions:
  - o 1st Battalion, 9th Infantry | 2nd Battalion, 9th Infantry
  - o 1st Battalion, 17th Infantry | 2nd Battalion, 17th Infantry
  - o 1st Battalion, 23rd Infantry | 2nd Battalion, 23rd Infantry | 3rd Battalion, 23rd Infantry
  - o 1st Battalion, 31st Infantry | 2nd Battalion, 31st Infantry
  - o 1st Battalion, 32nd Infantry | 2nd Battalion, 32nd Infantry | 3rd Battalion, 32nd Infantry
  - o 1st Battalion, 38th Infantry | 2nd Battalion, 38th Infantry
  - o 4th Battalion, 7th Cavalry
  - o 2nd Battalion, 10th Cavalry
  - o 1st Battalion, 72nd Armor | 2nd Battalion, 72nd Armor
  - o 1st Battalion, 12th Artillery
  - o 1st Battalion, 15th Artillery
  - o 7th Battalion, 17th Artillery
  - o 6th Battalion, 37th Artillery
  - o 5th Battalion, 38th Artillery

3. Agent Orange Presumptions based on contact with C-123 Aircraft

> Manual M21-1, IV.ii.1.H.2. -- Developing Claims Based on Exposure to Agent Orange for Select Air Force Personnel Through Contact With Contaminated C-123 Aircraft Used in the RVN as Part of ORH

Thousands of Air Force veterans were also exposed to Agent Orange herbicides when they worked and trained in C-123 aircraft that had been used to transport and spray chemicals during the Vietnam War. In a 2009 report published by the Institute of Medicine ("IOM") (now the National Academy of Medicine, "NAM"), samples taken from C-123 aircraft found that "residual chemicals from the Agent Orange (AO) and other herbicides that were sprayed in Vietnam remained on the interior of some of the aircraft."[135] In addition, the IOM concluded that service members who were exposed to Agent Orange residues experienced adverse health outcomes.

---

[135] Institute of Medicine. *Post-Vietnam Dioxin Exposure in Agent Orange-Contaminated C-123 Aircraft.* Washington, DC: The National Academies Press. 2015. nap.edu/catalog/18848/post-vietnam-dioxin-exposure-in-agent-orange-contaminated-c-123-aircraft.

As a result, on June 19, 2015, VA issued new rules to extend Agent Orange presumptions to Air Force veterans who had developed diseases as a result of herbicide exposure from C-123 aircraft.[136] This presumption appears at 38 C.F.R. § 3.307(a)(6)(v). Under § 3.307(a)(6)(v), Air Force veterans who "operated, maintained, or served onboard C-123 aircraft known to have been used to spray an herbicide agent during the Vietnam era shall be **presumed to have been exposed** during such service to an herbicide agent." In addition to the presumption of exposure, C-123 veterans who develop any of the diseases identified by 38 C.F.R. § 3.307(e) are also entitled to a presumption that they were exposed to herbicide and became disabled during "active" air service as defined by 38 U.S.C. § 101(24)(B) and (C).

★ ★ ★

§ 3.9.3 —Actual Exposure (Agent Orange)

> Manual M21-1, IV.ii.2.C.3.h. **Considering Direct SC When Entitlement to Presumption Does Not Exist**

If a veteran who suffers from a disease or condition presumptively caused by Agent Orange is unable to prove that they served in Vietnam or Korea during the covered periods of time, and thus do not qualify for presumption of exposure, they may instead prove *actual* exposure to Agent Orange, although this is more difficult to prove in an absence of corroborating evidence.

★ ★ ★

§ 3.9.4 — Blue Water Navy Veterans

The 1991 Agent Orange Act empowered Vietnam Veterans to receive and VA to distribute disability benefits and compensation for illnesses

---

[136] Presumption of Herbicide Exposure and Presumption of Disability During Service for Reservists Presumed Exposed to Herbicide. *Interim final rule.* 80 Fed. Reg. 35,246 (19 June 2015); *Final rule.* 83 Fed. Reg. 53,179 (22 Oct. 2018); codified at 38 C.F.R. § 3.307(a)(6)(v).

presumed to have been caused by herbicide exposure. However, in 2002 the VA limited the scope of eligible veterans to only those who could show "boots on the ground." Boots on the ground included veterans who physically served on land in Vietnam or in the inland waterways ("Brown Water") of Vietnam, but excluded those who served on a ship or other naval vessel off the coast of Vietnam. These sailors and marines became known as "Blue Water Navy" veterans. In 2008, the U.S. Court of Appeals for the Federal Circuit upheld this restrictive interpretation in *Haas v. Peake*, 525 F.3d 1168.

That all changed in 2019, when that same court reversed its previous decision and issued an en banc decision in *Procopio v. Wilkie*.[137] *Procopio* overruled *Haas* and effectively loosened VA's restrictive interpretation of service in Vietnam to also include oceanic naval service. In its opinion, the court held that the presumption of exposure created by the Agent Orange Act of 1991 was clearly meant to also include naval service on board ships that operated within the territorial waters of Vietnam. "When the Agent Orange Act was passed in 1991, the "Republic of Vietnam" included both its landmass and its 12 nautical mile territorial sea," the court found. "By using the formal term "Republic of Vietnam," Congress unambiguously referred, consistent with that backdrop, to both its landmass and its territorial sea … Congress has spoken directly to the question of whether those who served in the 12 nautical mile territorial sea of the "Republic of Vietnam" are entitled to § 1116's presumption if they meet the section's other requirements. They are."[138] Within months of the *Procopio* decision, Congress passed the Blue Water Navy Vietnam Veteran Act of 2019, which codified the court's ruling.

§ 3.9.4.1 — Blue Water Navy Veterans Act of 2019

The Blue Water Navy Vietnam Veterans Act of 2019 was signed into law on June 25, 2019, and went into effect on January 1, 2020.[139] The law established several major changes for herbicide-related disabilities incurred during naval service in Vietnam, and revisions to the VA home loan program.

---

[137] *Procopio v. Wilkie*, 913 F.3d 1371 (Fed. Cir. 2019)
[138] *Procopio*, 913 F.3d at 1375-77
[139] Pub. L. 116-23—June 25, 2019, 133 Stat. 966

> **M21-1, IV.ii.2.C.3.m. Impact of PL 116-23 on the Definition of RVN Service**

- Extends the **presumption of exposure** to veterans who served in the offshore waters of the Republic of Vietnam between January 9, 1962 and May 7, 1975.[140]
- Extends the **presumption of exposure** to veterans who served in or near the Korean Demilitarized Zone (DMZ) between September 1, 1967, and August 31, 1971.[141]
- Extends benefits to children with spina bifida whose parent was exposed to herbicide in Thailand.[142]

and

- VA home loans. Increases loan access to Purple Heart recipients and Native American veterans; removes "conforming loan limit" restrictions so that veterans may now receive no-down payment loans virtually everywhere regardless of local home prices.

The 2019 law defines the precise nautical limits of the Republic of Vietnam with latitudinal and longitudinal coordinates that form the national boundaries of Vietnam.[143] It directs "the Secretary [to] treat a location as being offshore of Vietnam if the location is not more than 12 nautical miles seaward of a line commencing on the southwestern demarcation line of the waters of Vietnam and Cambodia and intersecting" a series of specific geographic coordinates. Those include:

"Points Geographic Names	Latitude North	Longitude East
At Hon Nhan Island, Tho Chu Archipelago KienGiang Province	9°15.0′	103°27.0′
At Hon Da Island southeast of Hon Khoai Island Minh Hai Province	8°22.8′	104°52.4′

---

[140] *see* 38 U.S.C. § 1116A
[141] *see* 38 U.S.C. § 1116B
[142] *see* 38 U.S.C. § 1822
[143] 38 U.S.C. § 1116A(d)

At Tai Lon Islet, Con Dao Islet in Con Dao-Vung Toa Special Sector	8°37.8′	106°37.5′
At Bong Lai Islet, Con Dao Islet	8°38.9′	106°40.3′
At Bay Canh Islet, Con Dao Islet	8°39.7′	106°42.1′
At Hon Hai Islet (Phu Qui group of islands) Thuan Hai Province	9°58.0′	109°5.0′
At Hon Doi Islet, Thuan Hai Province	12°39.0′	109°28.0′
At Dai Lanh point, Phu Khanh Province	12°53.8′	109°27.2′
At Ong Can Islet, Phu Khanh Province	13°54.0′	109°21.0′
At Ly Son Islet, Nghia Binh Province	15°23.1′	109° 9.0′
At Con Co Island, Binh Tri Thien Province	17°10.0′	107°20.6′

★ ★

§ 3.9.4.2 — VA "Ship List"

Since October 2019, VA has maintained "Ship List" of the *Navy and Coast Guard Ships Associated with Service in Vietnam and Exposure to Herbicide Agents.*[144] Veterans who served on a qualifying vessel are entitled to Agent Orange Presumptions of *Exposure* and *Causation*. The Ship List "is intended to provide VA regional offices with a resource for determining whether a particular US Navy or Coast Guard Veteran of the Vietnam era is eligible for the presumption of Agent Orange herbicide exposure based on operations of the Veteran's ship."

Veterans and advocates should determine whether or not their unit or vessel has been included on the *Ship List*, and for substantiating evidence of their service aboard a qualifying vessel. Ship categories include:

---

[144] U.S. Department of Veterans Affairs. "Ship List." 28 Oct. 2019. https://web.archive.org/web/20200111133130/https://www.va.gov/shiplist-agent-orange.pdf. "Inland waterways include rivers, canals, estuaries, and deltas."

I. **Ships operating primarily or exclusively on Vietnam's inland waterways.** This category includes smaller naval vessels involved with patrolling and interdicting enemy activity on the inland waterways of Vietnam. It also includes ships supplying and supporting those operations. Examples of such vessels include swift boats, river patrol boats, and LSTs [landing ship, tank]. The inland waterways are often referred to as "brown waters" because of their muddy color and the naval vessels operating on them are referred to as the Brown Water Navy and/or the Mobile Riverine Force. All Veterans who served aboard these vessels are eligible for the presumption of Agent Orange exposure because their primary service was on the inland waterways of Vietnam.

II. **Ships operating temporarily on Vietnam's inland waterways.** This category includes large ocean-going ships that operated primarily on Vietnam's offshore waters for gunfire support of ground operations and interdiction of enemy vessels travelling along coastal waters. It also includes ships supplying and supporting these operations. Examples of such vessels include destroyers, cruisers, and cargo ships. The deep offshore waters are often referred to as "blue waters" and naval vessels operating on them are referred to as the Blue Water Navy. Ships in this category entered Vietnam's inland waterways temporarily as part of their gunfire, interdiction, or support missions. All Veterans who served aboard these vessels at the time of entry into Vietnam's inland waterways are eligible for the presumption of Agent Orange exposure.

III. **Ships that docked to shore or pier in Vietnam.** This category includes large ocean-going ships of the Blue Water Navy that entered an open water harbor and docked to a pier or otherwise docked to the shore of Vietnam. As a result of this docking, it is assumed that crewmembers had the opportunity to go ashore for a work detail or for liberty leave. Therefore, any Veteran aboard the ship at the time of docking will be eligible for the presumption of exposure if that Veteran provides a lay statement of personally going ashore.

IV. **Ships operating on Vietnam's close coastal waters for extended periods with evidence that crew members went ashore.** This category includes large ocean-going ships of the Blue Water Navy that conducted a variety of missions along the close coastal waters of Vietnam for extended periods of time. Documentary evidence has been obtained for all ships in this category showing that some crewmembers actually went ashore. Examples of such vessels include hospital ships, harbor repair ships, mine sweepers, and seaplane tenders. Also included are combat ships, such as destroyers, when evidence shows that crewmembers went ashore. Because shore activity of some crewmembers has been documented, any Veteran aboard the ship at the time of documented shore activity will be eligible for the presumption of exposure if that Veteran provides a lay statement of personally going ashore.

V. **Ships operating on Vietnam's close coastal waters for extended periods with evidence that smaller craft from the ship regularly delivered supplies or troops ashore**. This category includes large ocean-going ships of the Blue Water Navy that conducted supply missions to Vietnam or transported troops into and out of the country through use of smaller landing craft housed within the mother ship. Examples of such vessels include attack cargo ships, amphibious attack transports, and landing ship docks. The smaller landing vessels within these ships required a crew of from 3 to 14, depending on size, as they ferried supplies or troops to and from shore. Although official documents show that some crewmembers went ashore with the landing craft, they do not generally provide the names of these crewmembers. Additionally, many of these ships are listed for extended time frames because they routinely travelled back and forth between the US and Vietnam, and between Vietnam and other Asian Pacific ports, as they delivered supplies and troops to Vietnam. Therefore, military records should be checked to ensure that the Veteran was aboard when the ship was in Vietnamese waters (as shown by a PIES O34 request). Any Veteran aboard the mother ship during the time frame of offshore Vietnam landing craft activity will be eligible for the presumption of exposure if that Veteran provides a lay statement of personally going ashore with the landing craft.

§ 3.9.4.3 — Retroactive Effective Date of Benefits for Blue Water Veterans[145]

Because blue water navy veterans were unlawfully denied benefits for decades, the Blue Water Navy Vietnam Veteran Act of 2019 included a provision that allows for some veterans and their surviving family members to receive retroactive back pay for Agent Orange disability claims that were previously denied. If veterans or their survivors filed disability claims that VA denied between September 25, 1985 and January 1, 2020, they may refile that same disability claim under § 1116A, and if successful receive retroactive back pay to the date of the original claim. For many veterans and survivors, this would amount to a sizeable lump sum payment of back benefits—in some cases up to 35 years of benefits payments.

Veterans can prove that they served in Vietnam in a number of ways, starting with official service, personnel and medical treatment records. Obvious evidence also includes Vietnam service medals and combat ribbons that appear on a veteran's DD214. Original orders are also helpful, but sometimes difficult to obtain. Any kind of relevant evidence can be provided, including photographs from Vietnam, news articles, letters, and other documentation that can show a veteran served in Vietnam during a qualifying period of time. As always, veterans are encouraged to submit a statement in support of their claim that outlines what they can recall about their service before and during their deployment to Vietnam. Buddy letters from fellow service members describing and corroborating overseas service are also recommended.

§ 3.9.5 — Lawsuits against Agent Orange Manufacturers

Before VA recognized disability claims for diseases caused by Agent Orange exposure, veterans and their families had to take various alternative actions to achieve justice and obtain compensation for their injuries. One strategy involved filing regular and class-action lawsuits against private corporations that contracted with the U.S. government to produce and supply Agent Orange herbicides during the war. Vietnam Veterans filed hundreds of lawsuits against the chemical companies that manufactured Agent Orange for concealing the toxic and deadly effects of the herbicide

---

[145] 38 U.S.C. § 1116A(c)

to humans. The first generation of suits filed by Vietnam Veterans and their families commenced in the late 1970s and ultimately concluded with the creation of a settlement fund. The second generation of lawsuits began in the 2000s and ended in 2009, when the U.S. Supreme Court declined to review a Court of Appeals ruling against the veterans and their families.

A. First Generation of lawsuits by Vietnam Veterans against Agent Orange Manufacturers, resulting in a Settlement Fund (now closed)

Soon after the Fall of Saigon in 1975, which marked the end of the Vietnam War, as early as 1978 veterans began filing lawsuits in state and federal courts against chemical companies for injuries that they believed were attributable to Agent Orange exposure. In 1984, over 600 different cases were consolidated into one class-action settlement in the U.S. District Court in the Eastern District of New York. The case was described as "one of the most complex litigations ever brought."[146] "After five years of numerous motions and extensive discovery a tentative settlement was reached on the eve of trial." In return for dropping the lawsuits, the chemical companies that manufactured Agent Orange herbicides agreed to contribute up to $180 million for a compensation fund. Eligible veterans were each given around $2,700, and in return, the chemical companies were not forced to admit liability for their involvement in the war.[147]

B. Second Generation of lawsuits by Vietnam Veteran against Agent Orange Manufacturers (now final)

Only veterans who became ill prior to January 17, 1995, were able to file claims and participate in the original 1995 settlement fund. For all other veterans whose symptoms did not appear until later, the depleted settlement fund offered no compensation.

When a group of Vietnam Veterans who became ill after 1995 attempted to file a new lawsuit, in 2003 the U.S. Supreme Court affirmed

[146] *In re* "Agent Orange" Prod. Liab. Litig., 597 F. Supp. 740 (E.D.N.Y. 1984)
[147] Berman, Harvey P. "The Agent Orange Veteran Payment Program." 53 Law and Contemporary Problems 49-60 (Fall 1990). https://scholarship.law.duke.edu/lcp/vol53/iss4/7/.

a lower court's ruling that it would be unfair to deny them the opportunity to present their claim.[148] This allowed the group of poisoned, ill Vietnam Veterans a chance to prove their case in federal court. Unfortunately, the District Court dismissed the lawsuit in 2004.[149] In 2008, the U.S. Court of Appeals for the Second Circuit affirmed the ruling.[150] And in 2009 the U.S. Supreme Court refused to hear the case, making the decision final.[151] After that decision, Vietnam Veterans no longer have standing to bring suit in federal court against chemical companies that produced Agent Orange-style herbicides.

* * *

§ 3.10 — Claims for Diseases Associated with Exposure to Contaminated Drinking Water at Camp Lejeune

In 1982, it was discovered that the water supply facilities that provided drinking water to the U.S. Marine Corps Base Camp Lejeune, in North Carolina, were contaminated with toxic industrial solvents. For decades, these tainted systems delivered poisonous water to enlisted-family housing, barracks for unmarried service personnel, base administrative offices, schools, recreational areas, and even the base hospital.[152] As a result, service members and their families who were stationed at Camp Lejeune between 1953 and 1987, as well as civilian contractors, were potentially exposed to dangerous cancer-causing carcinogens benzene, vinyl chloride, trichloroethylene ("TCE"), tetrachloroethylene ("PCE"), and dichloroethylene ("DCE").

In 2006, in its annual legislation to fund the military, Congress mandated that the Navy enter into an agreement with the National Academy

---

[148] *Dow Chem. Co. v. Stephenson*, 539 U.S. 111 (2003)

[149] *Isaacson v. Dow Chem. Co. (In re "Agent Orange" Prod. Liab. Litig.)*, 344 F. Supp. 2d 873 (E.D.N.Y. 2004)

[150] *In re "Agent Orange" Prod. Liab. Litig.*, 517 F.3d 76 (2nd Cir. 2008)

[151] *Isaacson v. Dow Chem. Co.*, 129 S. Ct. 1523, 555 U.S. 1218 (2009)

[152] U.S. National Research Council, Committee on Contaminated Drinking Water at Camp Lejeune. Contaminated Water Supplies at Camp Lejeune: Assessing Potential Health Effects. Washington (DC): National Academies Press (US); 2009. https://www.ncbi.nlm.nih.gov/books/NBK215298/.

of Sciences ("NAS") to study and determine whether certain illnesses and health conditions were caused by contaminated water supplies at Camp Lejeune.[153] A subsequent partnership between the Navy and the National Research Council ("NRC") resulted in the creation of the "Committee on Contaminated Drinking Water at Camp Lejeune" which convened hearings, consulted victims and experts, and studied the issue. In 2009, the committee released the first of several public reports, "Contaminated Water Supplies at Camp Lejeune: Assessing Potential Health Effects." However, benefits for these diseases were not made available until 2012.

> **Manual M21-1, IV.ii.2.C.6.a. Presumptive SC Based on Exposure to Contaminated Water Supply on the Marine Corps Base at Camp Lejeune, North Carolina**

★ ★ ★

§ 3.10.1 — Claims for Medical Care (Lejeune Water)

- **Honoring America's Veterans and Caring for Camp Lejeune Families Act of 2012—[154]**

On August 6, 2012, the Honoring America's Veterans and Caring for Camp Lejeune Families Act was signed into law.[155] The law guarantees VA medical care for veterans and family members who served on active duty or resided at Camp Lejeune for thirty (30) days or more between Jan. 1, 1957 and Dec. 31, 1987 eligible for VA medical care for fifteen (15) different health conditions. Those illnesses include:

(i)   Esophageal cancer.
(ii)   Lung cancer.
(iii)   Breast cancer.
(iv)   Bladder cancer.
(v)   Kidney cancer.
(vi)   Leukemia.

---

[153] Public Law 109–364, Oct. 17, 2006, 120 Stat. 2143; Sec. 318
[154] 38 U.S.C. § 1710(F)
[155] Public Law 112–154, Aug. 6, 2012, 126 Stat. 1165

(vii) Multiple myeloma.

(viii) Myelodysplastic syndromes.

(ix)   Renal toxicity.

(x)   Hepatic steatosis.

(xi)   Female infertility.

(xii) Miscarriage.

(xiii) Scleroderma.

(xiv) Neurobehavioral effects.

(xv)   Non-Hodgkin's lymphoma.

Family members of service members who lived at Camp Lejeune for more than thirty days can apply to VA for reimbursement for medical expenses for any presumptive condition.[156] Family members can apply for reimbursement of medical expenses by contacting VA or using VA Form 10-10068.

♣   VA Form 10-10068 — **Camp Lejeune Family Member Program Application**

For family members seeking reimbursement for treatment of any of the medical conditions listed at 38 U.S.C. § 1710(F), VA recommends that the following items are provided to corroborate and prove their claim:

- Documentation showing dependent relationship to a veteran who served at Camp Lejeune, such as marriage license or birth certificate.
- Documentation showing you lived on the base for 30 days or more between Aug. 1, 1953 and Dec. 31, 1987 such as copies of orders or base housing records.
- You paid health care expenses for a covered condition respective to the following date ranges.

When evidence is not submitted, VA will use all relevant evidence from internal sources and the Department of Defense (DoD) to support your application. *Without evidence, it may take VA longer to review your application.*

---

[156] 38 U.S.C. § 1787. Health care of family members of veterans stationed at Camp Lejeune, North Carolina

♣   VA Form 10-10068b — **Camp Lejeune Family Member Program Treating Physician Report**

Qualifying family members are encouraged to include with their application for reimbursement of medical expenses a report of their treating physician. Much like a Disability Benefits Questionnaire (DBQ), VA Form 10-10068b gives the family member and their doctor(s) a standardized way to submit private medical information that is relevant to the claim.

★ ★ ★

§ 3.10.2 — Claims for Disability Compensation (Lejeune Water)

In 2014, the Centers for Disease Control ("CDC") released an additional report that found service members and their families stationed at Camp Lejeune had higher rates of kidney cancer, liver cancer, esophageal cancer, cervical cancer, multiple myeloma, Hodgkin lymphoma, and ALS, than marines and sailors stationed at Marine Corps Camp Pendleton in California.[157]

As a result, in September 2016, VA announced it would amend 38 C.F.R. §§ 3.307 and 3.309 to establish presumptive service connection for certain diseases associated with contaminants present in the base water supply at U.S. Marine Corps Base Camp Lejeune, North Carolina, from August 1, 1953 to December 31, 1987. The final rule, "Diseases Associated With Exposure to Contaminants in the Water Supply at Camp Lejeune," went into effect on March 14, 2017.[158] The new rule amended 38 C.F.R. § 3.307 to establish **Presumptions of Exposure** to contaminants in the water supply at Camp Lejeune. In addition, 38 C.F.R. § 3.309 was amended to include eight conditions that are subject to **Presumptions of Causation** from contaminated water exposure at Camp Lejeune.

---

[157] Bove, F.J., *et al.* Evaluation of mortality among marines and navy personnel exposed to contaminated drinking water at USMC base Camp Lejeune: a retrospective cohort study. Environ Health 13, 10 (2014). https://doi.org/10.1186/1476-069X-13-10.

[158] 82 Fed. Reg. 4173 (17 March 2017) federalregister.gov/d/2017-00499.

1. Presumption of Exposure—[159]

A veteran who spent more than 30 days at Camp Lejeune between 1953 and 1987 is presumed to have been exposed to toxins in the drinking water. The requirements for a veteran to receive the presumption of exposure to contaminated water at Camp Lejeune appear at 38 C.F.R. § 3.307(a)(7):

> A veteran, or former reservist or member of the National Guard, who had no less than 30 days (consecutive or nonconsecutive) of service at Camp Lejeune during the period beginning on August 1, 1953, and ending on December 31, 1987, shall be presumed to have been exposed during such service to the contaminants in the water supply, unless there is affirmative evidence to establish that the individua was not exposed to contaminants in the water supply during that service.

2. Presumption of Causation—[160]

Veterans who were exposed to contaminated water at Camp Lejeune and who now suffer from certain injuries are entitled to a presumption that their injuries were caused by the toxic water. Eight conditions that are presumed to be caused by toxic water at Camp Lejeune appear at 38 C.F.R. § 3.309(f), and include:

(1) Kidney cancer.
(2) Liver cancer.
(3) Non-Hodgkin's lymphoma.
(4) Adult leukemia.
(5) Multiple myeloma.
(6) Parkinson's disease.
(7) Aplastic anemia and other myelodysplastic syndromes.
(8) Bladder cancer.

---

[159] 38 C.F.R. § 3.307(a)(7)
[160] 38 C.F.R. § 3.309(f)

Veterans can file claims for VA disability compensation and/or healthcare benefits for illnesses caused by toxic water at Camp Lejeune in the same manner as Vietnam veterans who were exposed to Agent Orange herbicides. Both are entitled to legal presumptions: a presumption of exposure and presumption of causation. If Camp Lejeune veterans are currently suffering from an qualifying illness, all they have to show is proof of that illness and that they served at Camp Lejeune for more than thirty days. No proof of nexus is required.

★ ★ ★

§ 3.11 — Most Common Service-Connected Injuries

According to the most recent data released by VA, heading into 2019-2020 there are nearly five million veterans with service-connected injuries and conditions.[161] The most commonly rated disabilities are:

1. Tinnitus
2. Hearing Loss
3. Post-Traumatic Stress Disorder
4. Scars
5. Limitation of flexion, knee
6. Lumbosacral or cervical strain
7. Paralysis of the sciatic nerve
8. Limitation of motion of the ankle
9. Migraine Headaches
10. Degenerative Arthritis of the Spine

Note that in 2018, the Federal Circuit ruled that "pain" itself was a compensable injury for disability compensation benefits.[162] The court held that "'disability' in § 1110 refers to the functional impairment of earning capacity, not the underlying cause of said disability." Further, "pain is an impairment because it diminishes the body's ability to function, and that

---

[161] Veterans Benefits Administration. Dept. of Veterans Affairs. Annual Benefits Reports are published online every year. <benefits.va.gov/REPORTS/abr/>

[162] *Saunders v. Wilkie*, 886 F.3d 1356 (Fed. Cir. 2018)

pain need not be diagnosed as connected to a current underlying condition to function as an impairment."

* * *

§ 3.12 — Disability "Ratings"

If VA receives a claim for benefits, performs a C&P exam, and after reviewing the evidence determines that a former servicemember has a disabling illness or injury that was caused or aggravated during their active duty service, VA will assign a "rating" percentage between 0-100 percent based upon the severity of the injury and its overall impact on the veteran's employability. i.e. 10, 20, 30, 40, 50, 60, 70, 80, 90, or 100 percent. If more than one service-connected disability is claimed and diagnosed, a rating percentage is assigned to each injury and then combined for an overall disability rating, which establishes the level of benefits. This disability system is required by Congressional statute.[163]

> The Secretary shall adopt and apply a schedule of ratings of reductions in earning capacity from specific injuries or combination of injuries. The ratings shall be based, as far as practicable, upon the average impairments of earning capacity resulting from such injuries in civil occupations. The schedule shall be constructed so as to provide ten grades of disability and no more, upon which payments of compensation shall be based, namely, 10 percent, 20 percent, 30 percent, 40 percent, 50 percent, 60 percent, 70 percent, 80 percent, 90 percent, and total, 100 percent. The Secretary shall from time to time readjust this schedule of ratings in accordance with experience. However, in no event shall such a readjustment in the rating schedule cause a veteran's disability rating in effect on the effective date of the readjustment to be reduced unless an improvement in the veteran's disability is shown to have occurred.

---

[163] 38 U.S.C. § 1155

Combined Ratings Table—[164]

When a veteran has more than one service-connected disability, VA uses a "Combined Ratings Table" to calculate their overall disability rating. The table appears at 38 C.F.R. § 4.25 and is replicated in part below.

	10	20	30	40	50	60	70	80	90
19	27	35	43	51	60	68	76	84	92
20	28	36	44	52	60	68	76	84	92
21	29	27	45	53	61	68	76	84	92
22	30	38	45	53	61	68	77	84	92
23	31	38	46	54	62	69	77	85	92
24	32	39	47	54	62	70	77	85	92
25	33	40	48	55	63	70	78	85	93
26	33	41	48	56	63	70	78	85	93
27	34	42	49	56	64	71	78	85	93
28	35	42	50	57	64	71	78	86	93
29	36	43	50	57	65	72	79	86	93
30	37	44	51	58	65	72	79	86	93
31	38	45	52	59	66	72	79	86	93
32	39	46	52	59	66	73	80	86	93
33	40	46	53	60	67	73	80	87	93
34	41	47	54	60	67	74	80	87	93
35	42	48	55	61	68	74	81	87	94
36	42	49	55	62	68	74	81	87	94
37	43	50	56	62	69	75	81	87	94
38	44	50	57	63	69	75	81	88	94
39	45	51	57	63	70	76	82	88	94
40	46	52	58	64	70	76	82	88	94
Cont.	↓	↓	↓	↓	↓	↓	↓	↓	

[164] 38 C.F.R. § 4.25

Tyson Manker

How to use the combined ratings table — aka "VA Math"

Veterans often refer to the process of using the Combined Ratings Table (CRT) as "VA Math" because the formula often defies common mathematical logic. The following rules apply when using the CRT:

1. Arrange your rated disabilities in order from most severe to least severe.
2. Locate your highest disability rating in the left column.
3. Find your next highest disability rating in the top row.
4. The number in the space where the column and row intersect will represent the combined value of the two disabilities.
5. Round to the nearest 10%.
6. For three or more disabilities, continue the same process: use the combined value in the left column with the next disability on the top row, until all disabilities have been combined.

For example, if a Veteran has an illness/injury rated at 40 percent disabling and another disability rated at 20 percent, the combined value is 52 percent, which must be converted to the nearest degree divisible by 10, which is 50 percent. Thus, 40% + 20% = 50%.

Benefit of the Doubt (degree of disability)

When after careful consideration of all evidence, a reasonable doubt arises regarding the degree of disability such doubt will be resolved in favor of the injured veteran.[165]

★ ★ ★

§ 3.13 — Effective Dates[166]

Manual M21-1, III.iv.5.C. **Effective Dates**

---

[165] 38 C.F.R. § 4.3
[166] 38 U.S.C. § 5100

The "Effective Date" of an award of compensation (or other benefits like pension or dependency and indemnity compensation) based on an **original claim** or **supplemental claim** is the date of receipt of the claim or the date entitlement arose, whichever is later.[167] Even if a veteran requests Higher-Level Review, or files a Supplemental Claim or Notice of Disagreement, so long as the claim was "continuously pursued," the effective date will remain the date the claim was filed or entitlement arose.[168]

If a claim is filed within one year of discharge from active duty, the effective date will be the first day after discharge.[169]

For **supplemental claims** received more than one year after the date on which the agency of original jurisdiction or BVA issued its decision, the effective date will be the date the supplemental claim was received by VA.[170]

★ ★ ★

§ 3.14 — Individual Unemployability (IU)[171]

> Manual M21-1, IV.ii.2.F. – **Compensation based on Individual Unemployability (IU)**

When a veteran with an overall VA rating of less than 100 percent cannot find or maintain "substantially gainful employment" due to their service-connected illness or injury, they are considered "Unemployable," and as such, they may qualify for an important benefit called "Individual Unemployability" ("IU" – sometimes called Total Disability based on Individual Unemployability, or "TD/IU"). The TD/IU benefit allows veterans with no or limited income to receive benefits at the 100 percent level, even if their combined service-connected disabilities are rated at less than 100 percent. For example, an unemployable veteran rated at 70 percent disabled due to PTSD may receive TD/IU, and their monthly compensation

---

[167] 38 C.F.R. § 3.400

[168] 38 U.S.C. § 5100(a)(2)

[169] 38 U.S.C. § 5100(b)(1)

[170] 38 U.S.C. § 5100(a)(3)

[171] 38 C.F.R. § 4.16

will double from approximately $1,500 to $3,000, if their PTSD makes them unable to find and maintain a job.[172]

> Total disability ratings for compensation may be assigned, where the schedular rating is less than total, when the disabled person is, in the judgment of the rating agency, unable to secure or follow a substantially gainful occupation as a result of service-connected disabilities ... 38 C.F.R. § 4.16(a).
>
> It is the established policy of the Department of Veterans Affairs that all veterans who are unable to secure and follow a **substantially gainful occupation** by reason of service-connected disabilities shall be rated totally disabled ... 38 C.F.R. § 4.16(b).

A request for a total disability evaluation on the basis of unemployability, whether expressly raised by the Veteran or reasonably raised by the record, **is not a separate claim for benefits**. Rather, the IU claim involves an attempt to obtain an appropriate rating for a disability or disabilities, either as part of the initial adjudication of a claim or as a part of a claim for increased compensation if the disability upon which IU is based has already been found to be service-connected. In that sense, a TD/IU claim cannot be freestanding, but must be attached as part of an original claim or reevaluation of service-connected disability for the purpose of a higher rating.

In order to receive Individual Unemployability (TD/IU) benefits, a veteran must:

1. Be unemployable (unable to find and maintain substantially gainful employment) as a result of one or more service-connected disabilities; (odd jobs are considered "marginal" employment and do not impact TD/IU eligibility)
2. And either:
   a. Meet the Schedular requirements of § 4.16(a)
      i. One disability that is rated at 60 percent or higher; or

---

[172] *see* 38 C.F.R. § 4.16 - Total disability ratings for compensation based on unemployability of the individual.

ii. Multiple disabilities, with one disability rated at 40 percent or higher, and a total disability rating of 70 percent or more.

b. Have an extra-schedular evaluation under § 4.16(b)

Manual M21-1, IV.ii.2.F.1.a – **Establishing Entitlement to TDIU**

All TD/IU claims must submit a VA Form 21-8940.
All TD/IU claims must submit a VA Form 21-8940.
All TD/IU claims must submit a VA Form 21-8940.

♣ VA Form 21-8940 — **Veteran's Application for Increased Compensation Based on Unemployability**

"**A substantially complete VA Form 21-8940 is required to establish entitlement to TD/IU** because it gathers relevant and indispensable information regarding a veteran's disabilities and employment and educational histories. The form concludes with a series of sworn certification statements, and in endorsing it, a Veteran attests to their employment status, and signals understanding of the TD/IU benefit's incompatibility with substantially gainful work."[173]

"A properly signed and executed VA Form 21-8940 enables VA to gather the information necessary to determine the Veteran's entitlement to IU and recover IU compensation that is later discovered to have been awarded on fraudulent terms."

"Substantially Gainful Employment"

Manual M21-1, IV.ii.2.F.1.e. **Definition:**
Substantially Gainful Employment:

Until recently, there was no standard legal definition of the term "Substantially Gainful Employment" for veteran TD/IU claims. For many years the Court of Appeals for Veterans Claims refrained from defining the phrase, and routinely issued rulings that instead asked the VA to develop its own regulatory definition. As early as 1991, the CAVC noted that "[s]

---

[173] M21-1, IV.ii.2.F.2.c. Requirement for VA Form 21-8940.

ubstantially gainful employment' is a term of art which ... has no concrete definition." The Court left "the development of such a definition to the [VA] Secretary and urge[d] that he establish a clear definition of this term."[174] Many times since, the Court has reminded the VA that "there is a need for the Secretary to clarify the regulations concerning unemployability."[175] In 2016, the Court again declined to define "substantially gainful employment" "without first allowing VA to take a position on the matter," noting that "[i] t is VA's responsibility to define the terms contained within its regulation and the Court encourages it to do so."[176]

"VA is aware of the problems created by the lack of defined terms in § 4.16(b)," the Court said in 2019.[177] Calls for reform were not only limited to the Veterans Court. The U.S. Government Accountability Office (GAO) and its predecessor, the General Accounting Office, both issued reports about the need for concrete standards for TD/IU claims. As early as 1987, the GAO warned that failing to define the term "Substantially Gainful Employment" could lead to inconsistent outcomes and give "the appearance of arbitrary and inequitable decision making."[178] In June 2015, the GAO again investigated VA's TDIU analysis, concluding that "VA's procedures do not ensure that [TDIU] benefit decisions are well-supported."[179]

"RAY v. WILKIE" Factors[180]

In 2019, the U.S. Court of Appeals for Veterans Claims issued its own guidelines for interpreting the phrase "substantial gainful employment" for unemployed veterans with service-connected illness and injuries. In *Ray v. Wilkie*, the CAVC ruled that "substantial gainful employment" has

---

[174] *Ferraro v. Derwinski*, 1 Vet.App. 326, 333 (1991)

[175] *Moore v. Derwinski*, 1 Vet.App. 356, 359 (1991)

[176] *Ortiz-Valles v. McDonald*, 28 Vet.App. 65, 72 (2016)

[177] *Ray v. Wilkie*, 31 Vet.App. 58 (2019)

[178] U.S. General Accounting Office, Improving the Integrity of VA's Unemployability Compensation Program, at 18, 42 (Sept. 21, 1987) https://www.gao.gov/products/134197.

[179] U.S. Government Accountability Office, VA Can Better Ensure Unemployability Decisions Are Well Supported, GAO-15-464 (June 2, 2015) https://www.gao.gov/products/GAO-15-464.

[180] *Ray v. Wilkie*, 31 Vet.App. 58 (2019)

two components: (1) an economic component; and (2) a non-economic component. "The economic component simply means an occupation earning more than marginal income (outside of a protected environment) as determined by the U.S. Department of Commerce as the poverty threshold for one person." The second, non-economic component focuses on the veteran's ability (or inability) to secure and maintain employment.

As established by the CAVC in *Ray v. Wilkie*, VA must look at certain factors when deciding whether a veteran can "secure and follow a substantially gainful occupation" for TD/IU purposes. These factors now appear in the M21-1.[181] "In determining whether a Veteran has the ability to secure and follow a substantially gainful occupation, attention must be given to whether the Veteran has the ability to perform the types of activities required by the occupation at issue."

- The veteran's history[182], education[183], skill, and training[184]

Manual M21-1, IV.ii.2.F.1.i. **Vocational and Educational History in IU Determinations**

- Whether the veteran has the physical ability (both exertional and non-exertional) to perform the type of activities (e.g. sedentary, light, medium, heavy, or very heavy) required by the occupation at issue. Factors that may be relevant include, but are not limited to, the veteran's limitations, if any, concerning:

  o Lifting
  o Bending
  o Sitting
  o Standing
  o Walking
  o Climbing
  o Grasping
  o Typing
  o Reaching

---

[181] M21-1, IV.ii.2.F.1.j. Limitation of Ability in IU Determinations.
[182] M21-1, IV.ii.2.F.4.e. Considering Occupational History in IU Claims
[183] M21-1, IV.ii.2.F.4.d. Considering Educational History in IU Claims.
[184] *Pederson v. McDonald*, 27 Vet.App. 276, 286 (2015) (en banc).

o   Auditory and visual limitations

- Whether the veteran has the mental ability to perform the activities required by the occupation at issue. Factors that may be relevant include, but are not limited to, the veteran's limitations, if any, concerning:

    o   Memory
    o   Concentration
    o   Ability to adapt to change
    o   Ability to handle work-place stress
    o   Ability to get along with co-workers
    o   Ability to demonstrate reliability and productivity

M21-1, IV.ii.2.F.1.j. Limitation of Ability in IU Determinations

---

As the Court in *Ray v. Wilkie* noted, the above factors are not a "checklist" and that "discussion of any factor is only necessary if the evidence raises it."[185] The M21-1 also states, "The examples are not all-inclusive. Consider any factor that results in impairment of the Veteran's ability to perform work-related activities." Thus, veterans and advocates should develop their arguments for TD/IU eligibility based upon whatever factors (which may or may not be listed) apply to their own claim.

★ ★ ★

Additional Individual Unemployability (TD/IU) Factors

In addition to the TD/IU considerations of the CAVC in *Ray v. Wilkie*, VA must consider other factors when determining a veteran's eligibility for Individual Unemployability benefits.

- When there is evidence that a veteran has received social security benefits from the Social Security Administration (SSA), VA must

---

[185] see *Dela Cruz v. Principi*, 15 Vet.App. 143, 149 (2001); *Schafrath v. Derwinski*, 1 Vet.App. 589, 593 (1991).

obtain and consider complete copies of SSA decision (awards and denials) and any supporting medical records.[186]

- When considering a claim for TD/IU Individual Unemployability, VA may not base its determination solely on a veteran's:[187]
  o Age
  o Non-service-connected (NSC) disabilities
  o Long work career
  o Voluntary withdrawal from the labor market
  o High education level
  o Availability of jobs

Manual M21-1, IV.ii.2.F.4.c. **Factors Not Affecting IU Determinations**

- VA must take into account any medication that a veteran is taking to treat their service-connected disabilities, and assess any effect or side effect of the medication on a veteran's employability.[188]
- When a veteran suffers from service-connected and non-service-connected disabilities, the VA may be unable to determine whether the veteran's unemployability is caused by his non-service-connected disabilities or by his service-connected disabilities. If that is the case, then "benefit of the doubt" doctrine found in 38 U.S.C. § 5107(b) may apply.[189]

TD/IU applications will be denied if the VA determines that the veteran:

- is not precluded from securing or following substantially gainful employment by reason of service-connected disabilities;

---

[186] M21-1, IV.ii.2.F.2.k. When to Obtain SSA Records in IU Claims. See also: *Baker v. West*, 11 Vet.App. 163, 169 (1998); *Cohen v. Brown*, 10 Vet.App. 128, 151 (1997); *Hayes v. Brown*, 9 Vet.App. 73-74 (1996); *Lind v. Brown*, 3 Vet.App. 493, 494 (1992); *Murincsak v. Derwinski*, 2 Vet.App. 363, 370-72 (1992); *Masors v. Derwinski*, 2 Vet.App. 182, 187-88 (1992)
[187] *Gleicher v. Derwinski*, 2 Vet.App. 26 (1991)
[188] See *Moyer v. Derwinski*, 2 Vet.App. 289 (1992) ("narcotics for pain … [caused veteran to miss] so many work days")
[189] *Fluharty v. Derwinski*, 2 Vet.App. 409, 413 (1992)

- is gainfully employed; or
- has failed to cooperate with development of the TD/IU petition, such as failing to return a completed VA Form 21-8940 when requested.

★ ★ ★

Chapter 4

VA's Duty to Assist

Veterans disability benefits are not awarded automatically. They must be applied for, or "claimed." Under the law, it is a veteran's responsibility to file a "claim" for VA benefits.[1] However, once a veteran files a claim for benefits, the VA has a legal "duty to assist" them with the claim. In fact, multiple distinct duties are triggered that require VA to take various actions to complete and substantiate the claim. The multi-faceted duty to assist is defined across various statutes, regulations, and judicial rulings, but starts with the Veterans Claims Assistance Act of 2000.

Veterans Claims Assistance Act of 2000—[2]

> Manual M21-1, I.1.A.1. **Description of PL 106-475, Veterans Claims Assistance Act of 2000, and its Impact on 38 U.S.C. 5102, 5103, and 5103A**

The Veterans Claims Assistance Act of 2000 ("VCAA") was enacted on November 9, 2000. The VCAA:

- redefined the Department of Veterans Affairs' (VA's) duty to assist veterans in obtaining evidence necessary to substantiate a claim

---

[1] *see* 38 U.S.C. §§ 5101(a), 5107(a); *Cromer v. Nicholson*, 455 F.3d 1346, 1350 (Fed. Cir. 2006)

[2] Pub. L. 106–475— Nov. 9, 2000, 114 Stat. 2096. For a complete history of the of the VCAA, see "The Veterans Claims Assistance Act of 2000: Ten Years Later." T.T. Griffin and T.D. Jones. Vet. Law Review, vol. 3, 2011. pp. 284-381

- eliminated the requirement from *Morton v. West*, 13 Vet.App 205 (1999), that a veteran must submit a well-grounded claim before VA can assist in developing the claim, and
- mandated specific notice requirements regarding information that is necessary to substantiate a claim.

The statutory duty to assist legally compels VA to locate and obtain medical records, provide a medical examination, and take other actions to help a veteran successfully develop their disability claim. That duty ends once a ratings decision has been issued by a VA Regional Office—the agency of original jurisdiction for disability claims. If a veteran files a supplemental claim with new evidence, the duty to assist reattaches.

All-in-all, VA is tasked with at least ten distinct responsibilities with regards to assisting eligible veterans and military family members with claims for benefits. The ten elements of VA's duty to assist include:

VA Duty to Assist – Ten Elements —

1. Duty to provide free forms and information
2. Duty to give notice, incomplete claims
3. Duty to give notice, evidence needed to substantiate a claim
4. Duty to obtain records to substantiate a claim
5. Duty to provide (C&P) medical examination or opinion
6. Duty to liberally read pro se filings, sympathetically and fully develop claims
7. Duty to infer all possible claims and maximize benefits
8. Duty to consider the entire record of evidence
9. Duty to resolve reasonable doubt in favor of the veteran
10. Duty to give notice of decision regarding benefits

★ ★ ★

§ 4.1 — Duty: Provide Free Forms and Information

M21-1, III.ii.2.B.1.b. **Requirements for a Complete Claim Received on or After March 24, 2015**

VA is required to provide veterans with free information and standardized forms to apply for benefits.[3] In fact, standardized VA forms are now required for all claims for benefits. All standardized forms are available on the VA website, VA.GOV (/find-forms). When a veteran communicates their intent to file a claim for disability compensation benefits but does not use a standardized VA form, VA will send the veteran an application (VA form 21-526EZ) with an explanation about what information is needed to complete the claim.[4]

Furnishing Forms—[5]

> Upon request made by any person claiming or applying for, or expressing an intent to claim or apply for, a benefit under the laws administered by the Secretary, the Secretary shall furnish such person, free of all expense, all instructions and forms necessary to apply for that benefit.

"Section 5102 requires the Secretary, upon request by a veteran seeking benefits, to furnish to that person all instructions and forms necessary to apply for the benefit."[6] Some of the most commonly used VA forms include:

- 21-0966: Intent to File a Claim
- 21-526EZ: Application for Disability Compensation and Related Compensation Benefits
- 21-4138: Statement in Support of Claim
- 21-22: Appointment of Veterans Service Organization as Claimant's Representative
- 21-22a: Appointment of Individual as Claimant's Representative
- 21-0960P-3: Review Post-Traumatic Stress Disorder (PTSD) Disability Benefits Questionnaire
- 21-0781: Statement in Support of Claim for Service Connection for Post-Traumatic Stress Disorder (PTSD)

---

[3] 38 C.F.R. § 3.150
[4] 38 C.F.R. § 3.155; M21-1, III.ii.2.B.1.b. Requirements for a Complete Claim Received on or After March 24, 2015.
[5] 38 U.S.C. § 5102(a)
[6] *Rankin v. Lull* (W.D. Mich., 2017)

- <u>21-0781a</u>: Statement in Support of Claim for Service-Connection for PTSD Secondary to Personal Assault
- <u>10-10EZ</u>: Application for Health Benefits
- <u>20-0995</u>: Supplemental Claim
- <u>20-0996</u>: Higher-Level Review appeal
- <u>10182</u>: Board Appeal (Notice of Disagreement)
- <u>21P-534EZ</u>: Application for DIC, Survivor Pension, and/or accrued benefits

Disability Benefits Questionnaires (DBQs) —

Disability Benefits Questionnaires ("DBQs") are standardized VA forms that help streamline the claims process by organizing all of the necessary information about a service-connected illness or injury to successfully establish a claim. DBQs are used by VA clinicians when performing disability examinations, or Compensation and Pension ("C&P") exams. VA uses more than 70 different DBQs for establishing disability claims. Each uses standardized language and check boxes to streamline the information intake process and ensure timely and accurate ratings decisions.

DBQs were originally developed in 2010 to give veterans an improved method to submit medical evidence from their **PRIVATE PHYSICIANS** to support their disability claims. For the last ten years, as recently as April 2020, DBQs were available for download from the VA website for use by private physicians and therapists. However, on April 2, 2020, VA abruptly announced without warning that "public facing" DBQs would no longer be made available for download on the VA website. As such, **at the time of this VA Handbook's publication, DBQs are not currently available for download on the VA website**.

**HOWEVER, even though VA has removed DBQs from its website, VA must still accept all relevant evidence, including any DBQ, that is submitted with any claim for disability compensation benefits. After all, DBQs are nothing more than forms that organize all relevant service, diagnosing and treatment information required by VA regulations. Luckily, the author of this VA Handbook downloaded all DBQs before they were removed and uploaded them to the VA-Handbook website. All DBQs can be viewed and downloaded at va-handbook.com.[7]

VIEW & DOWNLOAD DBQs
va-handbook.com/resources/dbqs

Because the VA currently has removed most of its helpful information on DBQs, I have provided internet archive links to these pages. Because DBQs are indeed so helpful, it is the author's hope that VA will eventually restore them to the VA website to improve access for all sick and injured veterans.[8]

- **DQB Webinar**
  youtu.be/Ij3kmGLYndo

  If YouTube link has been removed, the Department of Veterans Affairs DBQ training video also available at: https://va-handbook.com/wp-content/uploads/2020/06/Disability-Benefits-Questionnaire-DBQ-Webinar.mp4.

- **The Advantages of Using Disability Benefits Questionnaires (DBQs)**
  youtu.be/0jx2Ako_TRQ

  If YouTube link has been removed, the Department of Veterans Affairs "Advantages of Using DBQs" video is also available at: https://va-handbook.com/wp-content/uploads/2020/09/the-advantages-of-using-disability-benefits-questionnaires.mp4.

- **DBQ Frequently Asked Questions**
  https://web.archive.org/web/20190316002030/benefits.va.gov/compensation/dbq_FAQs.asp.

---

[7] https://va-handbook.com/resources/dbqs/
[8] See H.R. 6493 - *Veterans Benefits Fairness and Transparency Act* (introduced 4 April 2020) – directs VA to restore public-facing DBQs to VA website.

- **DBQ list by symptom**
  https://web.archive.org/web/20190227124537/https://www.
  benefits.va.gov/compensation/dbq_ListBySymptom.asp.

- **DBQ list by form name**
  https://web.archive.org/web/20190227011018/benefits.va.gov/
  compensation/dbq_ListByDBQFormName.asp.

★ ★ ★

§ 4.2 — Duty: Give Notice of Incomplete Claims

Manual M21-1, I.1.B.1.g. **Notification Requirements for an Incomplete Application**

When a veteran files a claim for benefits, VA must determine if their application is complete.[9] A substantially complete claim for service-connected disability compensation is one that identifies the benefit sought and the service-connected medical condition(s) on which it is based. If the claim lacks this or other required information it is "incomplete" and VA has a duty to inform the veteran in writing what additional evidence is needed to complete the application.[10] This duty to give notice also applies when a veteran files an "Intent to File."[11] Veterans have one year to respond with the requested information.

Notice of Incomplete Applications—[12]

(b) If a claimant's application for a benefit under the laws administered by the Secretary is incomplete, the Secretary shall notify the claimant

---

[9] *see* 38 C.F.R. §§ 3.159(b)(2), 3.160; M21-1, I.1.B.1.b. Reviewing for Substantially Complete Applications.

[10] 38 C.F.R. § 3.155(c)

[11] 38 C.F.R. § 3.155(b)(3)

[12] 38 U.S.C. § 5102

and the claimant's representative, if any, of the information necessary to complete the application.

★ ★ ★

§ 4.3 — Duty: Give Notice about Information Needed to Substantiate a Claim

> Manual M21-1, I.1.B.1.a. **VA's Duty to Notify Claimants of Necessary Information or Evidence**

As provided by the Veterans Claims Assistance Act ("VCAA") of 2000, upon receipt of a substantially complete application, VA must notify the veteran of any information and medical or lay evidence needed to substantiate, or prove, their claim. "The primary purpose behind the Veterans Claims Assistance Act of 2000 was to ensure that all information necessary to making a determination on a claim is obtained by or presented to VA early on in the decision-making process—that is, prior to the initial adjudication of the claim."[13]

Required Information and Evidence—[14]

(1) the Secretary shall provide to the claimant and the claimant's representative, if any, by the most effective means available … **notice of any information**, and any medical or lay evidence, not previously provided to the Secretary that is necessary to substantiate the claim …

This is known as a *Section 5103 Notice* (previously a VCAA notice).[15] The Section 5103 notice is intended "to require that the VA provide affirmative notification to the claimant prior to the initial decision in the

---

[13] *Locklear v. Nicholson*, 20 Vet.App. 410 (2006)

[14] 38 U.S.C. § 5103(a); 38 C.F.R. § 3.159(b)(1)

[15] M21-1, I.1.A.1.c. Amendment to 38 U.S.C. 5103. "VA traditionally referred to the required notice in 38 U.S.C. 5103 as a "VCAA Notice." However, because of amendments to the law since the Veterans Claims Assistance Act (VCAA) of 2000, the term "Section 5103 notice" has replaced VCAA Notice…"

case as to the evidence that is needed and who shall be responsible for providing it."[16]

Both the statute, 38 U.S.C. § 5103(a), and the regulation, 38 C.F.R. § 3.159, require VA to notify a veteran of any missing information and evidence (1) that is necessary to substantiate the claim; (2) that VA will assist the veteran in obtaining; and (3) that the veteran is expected to provide.[17]

Section 5103 notices should be provided prior to an initial decision on a claim by the VARO.[18] "Section 5103(a) does not apply to proceedings that take place after the VARO's final decision."[19] Although section 5103 does not require VA to fully evaluate the available evidence, at least "some cognitive review of the claim must be made prior to providing the notice." Thus, "a boilerplate notice letter might not suffice."[20] Where the issue involves the character of discharge [38 C.F.R. § 3.12], proper notice must inform the former service members of the evidence needed to establish veteran status.[21]

Once a Section 5103 notice is received, the veteran has up to one year to respond with the necessary substantiating evidence in order to maintain the "effective date" of the claim.[22] As long as the claim is constantly pursued, and communications with VA are never broken, if the claim is decided in the veteran's favor, they will receive a lump sum payment of monthly benefits from the earliest effective date—the date the claim (or intent to file) was filed. *When possible, veterans who receive a 5103 notice should attempt to provide the necessary evidence and information to VA as soon as possible.*

★ ★ ★

---

[16] *Mayfield v. Nicholson*, 444 F.3d 1328, 1333 (Fed. Cir. 2006)

[17] *Quartuccio v. Principi*, 16 Vet.App. 183, 187 (2002); *Charles v. Principi*, 16 Vet.App. 370, 373-74 (2002)

[18] *Pelegrini v. Principi*, 18 Vet.App. 112 (2004)

[19] *Wilson v. Mansfield*, 506 F.3d 1055, 1059 (Fed. Cir. 2007) citing *Hartman v. Nicholson*, 484 F.3d 1311, 1314-15 (Fed. Cir. 2007); see also: 38 C.F.R. § 3.159(b)(3)

[20] *Locklear v. Nicholson*, 20 Vet.App. 410 (2006)

[21] *Dennis v. Nicholson*, 21 Vet.App. 18 (2007)

[22] 38 U.S.C. § 5103(b)

§ 4.4 — Duty: Obtain Records to Substantiate a Claim

> Manual M21-1, I.1.C. – **Duty to Assist with Obtaining Medical Records and a Medical Examination or Opinion**

VA has a duty to search for and obtain relevant records that could help prove or substantiate a veteran's claim. VA's duty to assist in obtaining records begins upon receipt of the substantially complete *original* or *supplemental* claim and ends when VA issues a final decision on the claim. VA's duty to obtain relevant records includes both public and private records.

Duty To Assist—[23]

(a)(1) The Secretary shall make reasonable efforts to assist ... in obtaining evidence necessary to substantiate the claimant's claim for a benefit under a law administered by the Secretary.

Veterans are not required to prove the existence of a particular record to trigger the VA's duty to assist. "Section 5103A does not allow the VA to avoid the duty to assist in obtaining records based on a mere belief that the likelihood of finding a record substantiating a veteran's claim is "low" or "extremely low." Rather, the applicable standard is whether "no reasonable possibility exists that such assistance would aid in substantiating the claim."[24]

VA must attempt to obtain records that are relevant to the claim. "Relevant records for the purpose of § 5103A are those records that relate to the injury for which the claimant is seeking benefits and have a reasonable possibility of helping to substantiate the veteran's claim."[25] Keep in mind, however, that "the duty to assist is not boundless in its scope."

***Whenever possible, a veteran should gather their own military service and medical treatment records prior to filing a claim, to be included as evidence with the claim, rather than relying on VA to try and locate them. VA's duty to obtain records prevents VA from ignoring claims, and compels the Secretary to take action to locate records and ascertain*

---

[23] 38 U.S.C. § 5103A; 38 C.F.R. § 3.159(c)
[24] *Jones v. Wilkie*, 918 F.3d 922 (Fed. Cir. 2019)
[25] *Golz v. Shinseki*, 590 F.3d 1317, 1321 (Fed. Cir. 2010)

Tyson Manker

whether evidence is authentic, credible, and persuasive. Never, however, assume that VA will successfully locate your military records or your private treatment records. Only if and when a veteran cannot find or obtain their records should they file a disability claim with no evidence and rely entirely on the VA examination and record review.

**Always request military and other records prior to filing a claim for benefits.

Before filing a claim for benefits a veteran should always request their Official Military Personnel File ("OMPF") by submitting a Standard Form 180 ("SF 180"). This is important for a few reasons. First, a veteran's OMPF contains evidence about their service to corroborate a disability or other benefits claim. It should hold all of the veteran's service records, their medical treatment records, and importantly, the veteran's DD214 discharge document. The DD214 is the final record that shows the length of a veteran's time in service, their type of discharge, medals, ribbons, awards and more. This vital document is how a veteran proves their veteran status, and determines what standard of review they will receive. If, for example, they have a purple heart, combat action ribbon/medal, or POW medal, as combat veterans a lay statement about an in-service incident is sufficient to prove their claim. Soon after a claim is filed, VA will likewise request the veteran's records for review to determine whether the claim is supported by evidence and should be granted. It is extremely important to have access to the full record when developing any claim. *While some veterans may have copies of some of their of their service records, all are encouraged to request their official military personnel file containing their entire DoD record before filing any claim.*

★ ★ ★

Public records—[26]

Manual M21-1, I.1.C.1.a. **VA's Duty to Obtain Federal Records**

---

[26] 38 U.S.C. § 5103A(c)

> **Manual M21-1, I.1.C.1.e. Claimant Cooperation With the Duty to Assist in Obtaining Federal Records**

VA's duty to assist includes a duty to make reasonable efforts to obtain public records held by the federal government that could be relevant to substantiating a veteran's claim, that the veteran identifies and authorizes VA to obtain.[27] Public records include those held by the (1) Defense Department, (2) Department of Veterans Affairs (3) Labor Department, (4) Social Security Administration, and (5) Public Health Service. In turn, the veteran has a corresponding duty to cooperate and provide the necessary information to locate the sought-after federal records.

In order to fulfill its duty to assist in obtaining public records that are held by a federal department or agency, VA must make as many record requests as are necessary, until they are obtained or it becomes clear the record does not exist or is not in the possession of the custodian.[28]

> **Manual M21-1, I.1.C.1.c. Definition: Reasonable Efforts to Obtain Federal Records**

DoD Service Records —

> **Manual M21-1, I.1.C.1.c. Definition: Reasonable Efforts to Obtain Federal Records**

VA has a duty to obtain all relevant Defense Department records generated during a veteran's active military service.

Service records[29] include:

- **DoD Service Treatment Records ("STRs") —**
  Medical and dental care outside of a medical treatment facility that the veteran received during active service, including mental health care.

---

[27] 38 U.S.C. § 5103A(c)(1)(C)

[28] 38 C.F.R. § 3.159(c)(2); *Gagne v. McDonald*, 27 Vet.App. 397 (2015)

[29] M21-1, III.iii.2.A.1.General Information on Service Records.

- **DoD Medical/Clinical Records —**
  Care received at a medical treatment facility ("MTF").

- **DoD Personnel Records —**
  Administrative records that show the date and type of enlistment; duty stations and assignments; training, qualifications, performance, awards and decorations; disciplinary and personnel items; date and type of separation including DD214.

★ ★

Veterans Affairs Records —

VA will make as many requests as are necessary to obtain relevant records that are held by VA medical facilities. Such records are in constructive possession of the agency, and must be obtained if relevant to deciding the claim.[30] VA will only assist in obtaining records that have a reasonable possibility of helping substantiate a claim.[31]

★ ★

Social Security Administration Records —

Manual M21-1, III.iii.3.A.1. **General Overview of VA Requests for Information from SSA**

Included in duty to assist is the responsibility of VA to obtain any relevant records from the Social Security Administration.[32] After obtaining relevant SSA records VA must weigh and give them appropriate consideration in its determination to award or deny a total disability rating.[33]

★ ★

---

[30] *Bell v. Derwinski*, 2 Vet.App. 611 (1992)
[31] 38 U.S.C. § 5103A(a)(2); *Swisher v. Wilkie* (Fed. Cir. 2019)
[32] *Voerth v. West*, 13 Vet.App. 117, 121 (1999)
[33] *Murincsak v. Derwinski*, 2 Vet.App. 363, 370 (1992)

Lost or Missing Records - alternate records —

Records are sometimes missing from a veteran's file, or in some cases were destroyed. Notably, for example, in 1973 a massive fire at the National Personnel Records Center in St. Louis destroyed over 20 million records, including 80% of Army records from 1912-1960. In such cases where public records are lost or destroyed, VA has a *"heightened"* duty to assist in locating alternate records. "This duty is heightened in a case such as this where service medals are destroyed and includes the obligation to search for alternate medical records."[34]

Lost or Missing Records – heightened duty to explain —

When VA is unable to locate a veteran's records, VA must advise the veteran to submit alternative forms of information and assist them in obtaining sufficient evidence from alternative sources.[35] Just because records are lost or missing does not mean that a claim will be granted. "In cases involving lost records, the Board has a heightened duty to explain its findings."[36]

★ ★ ★

Private records—[37]

Manual M21-1, I.1.C.2.a. **VA's Duty to Obtain Relevant Non-Federal or Private Records**

Private medical and treatment records can be supplied by the veteran[38] (recommended), or the veteran can rely on VA to locate and obtain them. Claims that include substantiating medical records are generally decided

---

[34] *Cueva v. Principi*, 3 Vet.App. 542, 548 (1992); *Russo v. Brown*, 9 Vet.App. 46, 51 (1996)
[35] *Dixon v. Derwinski*, 3 Vet.App. 261 (1992)
[36] *Cromer v. Nicholson*, 455 F.3d 1346, 1351 (Fed. Cir. 2006); citing *O'Hare v. Derwinski*, 1 Vet.App. 365, 367 (1991)
[37] 38 U.S.C. § 5103A(b)
[38] 38 U.S.C. § 5103A(b)(4)(A)

more quickly, because they eliminate the step of VA trying to obtain evidence.

When a veteran asks VA to help locate their private medical records, VA must make at least two (2) requests, an initial request and a follow-up. If, after two attempts, VA has not obtained the records it will inform the veteran of what attempts were made and that the claim will be proceed, but that evidence found later may be submitted.[39] Ultimately, it is the veteran's responsibility to provide VA with relevant medical records or information about where to locate relevant medical records that could substantiate their claim.

Veterans have a corresponding obligation to cooperate with VA in locating records for their claim.[40] They must provide enough information to identify the records, and if necessary granting authorization to permit the release of information to VA. "The duty to assist … is not a one-way street"[41] "Corresponding to VA's duty to assist the veteran in obtaining information is a duty on the part of the veteran to cooperate with VA in developing a claim. VA's duty must be understood as a duty to assist the veteran in developing a claim, rather than a duty on the part of VA to develop the entire claim with the veteran performing a passive role."[42]

**A veteran should only submit authorization and release forms if private records are not included with their claim and they wish the VA to locate them. *If private records are included with the claim, do not ask VA to locate them.* If a veteran wants VA to help locate private records, they should complete the following two authorization release forms:

♣ VA Form 21-4142 — **Authorization to Disclose Information to the Department of Veterans Affairs**

♣ VA Form 21-4142a — **General Release for Medical Provider Information to the Department of Veterans Affairs**

Manual M21-1, III.iii.1.D.1.b. **VA Forms 21-4142 and 21-4142a**

★ ★

---

[39] 38 C.F.R. § 3.159(e)

[40] 38 C.F.R. § 3.159(c)(1)&(2)

[41] *Wamhoff v. Brown*, 8 Vet.App. 517, 522 (1996)

[42] *Turk v. Peake*, 21 Vet.App. 565, 568 (2008)

Appeals Modernization Act —

The Veterans Appeals Improvement and Modernization Act of 2017 ("AMA") restructured the claims appeals process, which modified the duty to obtain relevant records to apply only in original and supplemental claims. When a veteran requests a higher-level review (of the same evidence) or appeals to the Board of Veterans Appeals, VA's duty to obtain records no longer applies. The duty reattaches when a claim is remanded by the BVA to the regional office for re-adjudication of a duty to assist error.

No Duty to Help Obtain Records—[43]

VA has no duty to help obtain records when there is no reasonable possibility that the sought after records would help substantiate the claim. In addition, VA has no duty to assist with records when:

(1) The claimant's ineligibility for the benefit sought because of lack of qualifying service, lack of veteran status, or other lack of eligibility;

(2) A claim is inherently incredible or clearly lacks merit; and

(3) An application requests a benefit to which the claimant is not entitled as a matter of law.

> Manual M21-1, I.1.C.1.d. **Concluding Federal Records Do Not Exist or Further Efforts Would be Futile**

★ ★ ★

§ 4.5 — Duty: Provide Medical Examination/Opinion

> Manual M21-1, I.1.C.3. **Assisting With Obtaining a Medical Examination or Opinion**

VA has a duty to provide a medical examination or opinion when it is necessary to decide a claim. "That duty includes providing an examination

---

[43] 38 U.S.C. § 5103A(a)(2); 38 C.F.R. § 3.159(d)

that is adequate for [disability] rating purposes."[44] The medical assessment, called the Compensation and Pension, or "C & P" Exam, is performed by a VA doctor at the closest Veterans Health Administration ("VHA") facility or office, or if necessary, by a contracted third-party provider.

Medical Examinations for Claims—[45]

(1) In the case of a claim for disability compensation, the assistance provided by the Secretary ... shall include providing a medical examination or obtaining a medical opinion when such an examination or opinion is necessary to make a decision on the claim.

Exam Must be Necessary—[46]

VA must provide a medical examination when it is necessary to deciding a claim. A medical examination is considered necessary if the following four elements are present:

(1) competent evidence of a current disability or persistent or recurrent symptoms of a disability, and
(2) evidence establishing that an event, injury, or disease occurred in service or establishing certain diseases manifesting during an applicable presumptive period for which the veteran qualifies,
(3) an indication that the disability or persistent or recurrent symptoms of a disability may be associated with the veteran's service or with a different service-connected disability, but
(4) insufficient competent medical evidence on file for the VA Secretary to make a decision on the claim.

McLendon v. Nicholson, 20 Vet.App. 79, 81 (2006); see also: *Waters v. Shinseki*, 601 F.3d 1274, 1277 (Fed. Cir. 2010); *Paralyzed Veterans of Am. v. Sec'y of Veterans Affairs*, 345 F.3d 1334, 1355-57 (Fed. Cir. 2003); *Wells v. Principi*, 326 F.3d 1381, 1384 (Fed. Cir. 2003).

---

[44] *Stefl v. Nicholson*, 21 Vet.App. 120, 123 (2007)
[45] 38 U.S.C. § 5103A(d); 38 C.F.R. § 3.159(c)(4)
[46] 38 U.S.C. § 5103A(d)(2)(A-C)

> Manual M21-1, I.1.C.3.b. **Regulatory Standard for Finding an Examination or Medical Opinion Necessary**

Low Threshold —

The second requirement that the evidence of record "indicate" that the claimed disability or symptoms "may be" associated with the established event, disease or injury is a low threshold.[47] Veterans are always strongly encouraged to provide a detailed statement about their service, including whatever event may have caused their current disability, as well as current and persistent symptoms of their service-connected disability. A lay statement about these things, while not conclusive as to the existence of a current disability, will help to establish the factors to prove that a medical examination is necessary to prove a claim.

Note that no medical evaluation will be administered if the record contains enough evidence for VA to make a decision about the claim.[48] This sometimes occurs, for example, when a veteran seeks a higher rating reevaluation with new evidence that is sufficient for VA to make a decision without an additional examination.

Factor of Time —

When a veteran claims an injury has worsened since their last VA exam, and the last examination is too remote to constitute a contemporaneous examination, a new examination is required.[49]

PTSD Examination —

When a veteran files a claim for PTSD, VA will provide a mental health examination to determine the severity of the disability. The veteran will receive advance notice of the date, time and location of their scheduled appointment, which will take place at a local VA hospital, a VA office on a DoD installation, or with a private psychologist. PTSD interviews generally last around one hour.

---

[47] *Locklear v. Nicholson*, 20 Vet.App. 410 (2006)

[48] 38 U.S.C. § 5103A(d)(2)(C)

[49] *Snuffer v. Gober*, 10 Vet.App. 400 (1997); *Green v. Derwinski*, 1 Vet.App. 121 (1991)

Veterans should expect to talk to a psychologist about their current symptoms and disability, as well as the stressful events from their military service that caused their PTSD. Veterans need to be open and honest about their struggles, which can sometimes be difficult to discuss with a complete stranger. The important thing to keep in mind is that the C&P examiner should see the veteran as they normally are. No additional effort to impress should be made—as would be the case with a job interview. The C&P is not a job interview, but rather an assessment of the veteran's PTSD and the impact it has on their life. C&P doctors ultimately make a determination about the level of social and occupational impairment caused by the veteran's PTSD.

Individual Unemployability – TD/IU—[50]

For veterans who may be eligible for Individual Unemployability ("TD/IU"), VA is not required to provide an additional medical examination/opinion to determine the extent to which one or more disabilities have on a veteran's ability to maintain gainful employment.[51] Once a C&P medical examiner rates a veteran's disability, it is the responsibility of the regional office claims examiner to determine eligibility for TDIU unemployability benefits.[52] As such, TDIU is not considered on its own, but as an inherent part of each disability claim.

★ ★ ★

§ 4.6 — Duty: Liberally Read Pro Se Filings, and Fully and Sympathetically Develop Claims

Manual M21-1, III.ii.2.B.1.m. **Considering Unclaimed Theories of SC**

Disabled veterans are not expected to be claims experts, but VA is. As part of its duty to assist, VA must go the extra mile and show great leniency to veterans who file their claims without assistance, which is called ***pro se.***

---

[50] 38 C.F.R. § 4.16

[51] *Geib v. Shinseki*, 733 F.3d 1350, 1353-54 (2013); also *Floore v. Shinseki*, 26 Vet.App. 376 (2013)

[52] *Sanchez-Navarro v. McDonald*, 774 F.3d 1380 (Fed. Cir. 2014)

(Latin for "on one's own behalf") "Pro se filings must be read liberally."[53] VA regional offices and the BVA have "a special obligation to read pro se filings liberally."[54] In *Harris v. Shinseki*[55], the Federal Circuit explained the VA's duty to liberally read, and fully and sympathetically develop, pro se claims:

> Our previous decisions have made clear that pro se filings must be **read liberally**. In *Roberson v. Principi*, 251 F.3d 1378, 1384 (Fed. Cir. 2001), we held that the VA has a duty to fully develop any filing made by a pro se veteran by **determining all potential claims** raised by the evidence. We reiterated this requirement in *Szemraj v. Principi*, 357 F.3d 1370, 1373 (Fed. Cir. 2004), when we stated that the VA must **generously construe** a pro se veteran's filing to discern all possible claims raised by the evidence. Finally, in *Moody v. Principi*, 360 F.3d 1306, 1310 (Fed. Cir. 2004), we held that any ambiguity in a pro se filing that could be construed as an informal claim must be **resolved in the veteran's favor**.
>
> The duty articulated in *Moody*, *Szemraj*, and *Roberson* stems from the "uniquely pro-claimant" character of the veterans' benefits system and requires VA "to **fully and sympathetically develop the veteran's claim** to its optimum before deciding it on the merits." *Roberson*, 251 F.3d at 1384 (citing *Hodge v. West*, 155 F.3d 1356, 1362 (Fed. Cir. 1998).

In 2019 the Federal Circuit reiterated, "The lesson of our cases is that, while a pro se claimant's "claim must identify the benefit sought," the identification need not be explicit in the claim-stating documents, but can also be found indirectly through examination of evidence to which those documents themselves point when sympathetically read."[56] VA has "an

---

[53] *Shea v. Wilkie*, 926 F.3d 1362, 1367 (Fed. Cir. 2019)
[54] *Robinson v. Shinseki*, 557 F.3d 1355, 1358-59 (Fed. Cir. 2009)
[55] *Harris*, 704 F.3d 946 (Fed. Cir. 2013)
[56] *Shea v. Wilkie*, 926 F.3d 1362, 1368 (Fed. Cir. 2019)

obligation to "fully and sympathetically develop the veteran's claim to its optimum before deciding it on the merits."[57]

Manual M21-1, III.iv.6.B.1.c. **Definition and Example: Issues Within Scope**

**The duty to liberally read a claim for benefits also applies to direct appeals filed by accredited attorneys before the Board of Veterans Appeals. *Note, however, that the duty to read liberally does not extend to CUE appeals filed by accredited attorneys.*

In 2009, the Federal Circuit in *Robinson v. Shinseki* ruled that the BVA has an obligation to liberally read <u>all direct appeals,</u> including those filed by an accredited attorney. "We hold that the Board must read such filings liberally because this obligation is expressly imposed by the VA's own regulations."[58]

Robinson v. Peake, 21 Vet.App. 545 (2008); *Bingham v. Principi*, 18 Vet.App. 470 (2004); *Roebuck v. Nicholson*, 20 Vet.App. 307, 313 (2006).

Read pro se filings liberally, including:

- Direct appeals of VARO decisions to the BVA
- CUE appeals

Read attorney filings liberally, including:

- Direct appeals

DO NOT read liberally CUE appeals filed by accredited attorney.

★ ★ ★

---

[57] *McGee v. Peake*, 511 F.3d 1352, 1357 (Fed. Cir. 2008); also *Comer v. Peake*, 552 F.3d 1362, 1368-1369 (Fed. Cir. 2009) ("A liberal and sympathetic reading of appeal submissions is necessary because a pro se veteran may lack a complete understanding of the subtle differences in various forms of VA disability benefits and of the sometimes arcane terminology used to describe those benefits."

[58] *Robinson v. Shinseki*, 557 F.3d 1355 (Fed. Cir. 2009)

§ 4.7 — Duty: Infer all Claims and Maximize Benefits

> Manual M21-1, IV.ii.2.F.2.o. **Developing Reasonably Raised Claims of IU**

When making a rating decision, VA is required to grant the highest award of benefits and the highest disability rating possible based on the available evidence. In fact, a presumption that the veteran is applying for the maximum benefit possible attaches to every claim.

Procedural due process and appellate rights—[59]

> Every claimant has the right to written notice of the decision made on his or her claim, the right to a hearing, and the right of representation. Proceedings before VA are ex parte in nature, and **it is the obligation of VA** to assist a claimant in developing the facts pertinent to the claim and **to render a decision which grants every benefit that can be supported in law** while protecting the interests of the Government …

VA has a "well-established duty to maximize a claimant's benefits."[60] "On a claim for an original or an increased rating, the claimant will generally be presumed to be seeking the maximum benefit allowed by law and regulation, and it follows that such a claim remains in controversy where less than the maximum available benefit is awarded."[61] VA has a duty to consider every benefit to which that claimant may be entitled.[62] "The Secretary is required to maximize benefits."[63]

"Proceedings before VA are *ex parte* [one-sided] in nature, and it is the obligation of VA to assist a claimant in developing the facts pertinent to the claim and to render a decision which grants every benefit that can be supported in law while protecting the interests of the Government."[64]

In that regard, VA has a duty to identify all ancillary, or secondary,

---

[59] 38 C.F.R. § 3.103(a)

[60] *Buie v. Shinseki*, 24 Vet.App. 242, 250 (2011)

[61] *AB v. Brown*, 6 Vet.App. 35, 38 (1993)

[62] *Akles v. Derwinski*, 1 Vet.App. 118 (1991)

[63] *Bradley v. Peake*, 22 Vet.App. 280 (2008)

[64] 38 C.F.R. § 3.103

benefits to which the veteran may be entitled, even if not specifically identified by the veteran. The CAVC has described these as "inferred claims."[65] VA must review claims in liberal manner to identify and adjudicate all reasonably-raised claims (known as a *sympathetic reading*) and when VA fails to adjudicate a reasonably-raised claim, that claim remains pending.[66]

Once "inferred claims" have been identified, if they are determined to be "inextricably intertwined" with any of the issues certified for appeal, they must be considered simultaneously.[67]

Individual Unemployability (TD/IU)

The Federal Circuit ruled that entitlement to TD/IU is raised in every disability claim where a veteran: (1) submits evidence of a medical disability; (2) makes a claim for the highest rating possible; and (3) submits evidence of unemployability.[68] Thus, evidence of unemployability that is submitted during the course of a claim ultimately serves as an informal claim for TDIU. For many veterans who receive combined ratings of less than one-hundred percent, but who are unable to procure gainful employment due to their service-connected injuries, TD/IU should be pursued to ensure the veteran receives maximum benefits until they secure gainful employment or receive a higher total rating. (*see* Section 3.14, Individual Unemployability (IU))

Manual M21-1, IV.ii.2.F.2.o. **Developing Reasonably Raised Claims of IU**

Rice v. Shinseki, 22 Vet.App. 447 (2009) (quoting *Comer v. Peake*, 552 F.3d 1362 (Fed. Cir. 2009) (a claim for "TDIU benefits is not a free-standing claim that must be plead with specificity; it is impliedly raised

---

[65] *Akles v. Derwinski*, 1 Vet.App. 118 (1991)

[66] *Norris v. West*, 12 Vet.App. 413 (1999)

[67] *Harris v. Derwinski*, 1 Vet.App. 180 (1991); also *Norris v. West*, 12 Vet.App. 413, 417 (1999) (the BVA must "review the claim, supporting documents, and oral testimony in a liberal manner to identify and adjudicate all reasonably-raised claims")

[68] *Roberson v. Principi*, 251 F.3d 1378 (Fed. Cir. 2001); also: *Jackson v. Shinseki*, 587 F.3d 1106, 1109 (2009) (holding that an inferred claim for a TD/IU is raised as part of an increased rating claim only when the Roberson requirements are met).

whenever a ... veteran, who presents cogent evidence of unemployability seeks a higher disability rating.")

* * *

§ 4.8 — Duty: Consider the Entire Record of Evidence[69]

VA and the Board of Veterans Appeals are required to consider the entire record of evidence, as well as applicable laws and regulations, when making a decision about a veteran's claim for benefits. If, for example, VA fails to acknowledge a relevant piece of evidence submitted by a veteran, or fails to explain how it considered certain evidence, that failure could serve as the basis of appeal.

Manual M21-1, III.iv.5.A.1. **Guidelines for Evaluating Evidence**

* * *

§ 4.9 — Duty: Resolve Questions of Reasonable Doubt in Favor of the Veteran

Manual M21-1, III.iv.5.A.1.j. **Reasonable Doubt Rule**

As part of the "uniquely pro-claimant principles underlying the veterans' benefits dispensation scheme,"[70] when there is an approximate balance of positive and negative evidence regarding any material issue of a claim, VA is required to give the veteran the benefit of the doubt, and rule on the issue-at-hand in the veteran's favor.[71] VA regulations also require VA examiners to award the higher of two disability ratings when reasonable doubt about the extent of a veteran's disability.[72]

---

[69] 38 U.S.C. § 7104

[70] *Smith v. Brown*, 35 F.3d 1516, 1522 (Fed. Cir. 1994)

[71] 38 U.S.C. § 5107(b); 38 C.F.R. § 3.102; (for a discussion of the benefit of the doubt standard of proof, see also *Gilbert v. Derwinski*, 1 Vet.App. 49, 53 (1990))

[72] 38 C.F.R. § 4.3

Benefit of the Doubt—[73]

> The Secretary shall consider all information and lay and
> medical evidence of record in a case before the Secretary
> with respect to benefits under laws administered by
> the Secretary. When there is an approximate balance
> of positive and negative evidence regarding any issue
> material to the determination of a matter, the Secretary
> shall give the benefit of the doubt to the claimant.

Reasonable Doubt—[74]

> When, after careful consideration of all procurable and
> assembled data, a reasonable doubt arises regarding
> service origin, the degree of disability, or any other point,
> such doubt will be resolved in favor of the claimant. By
> reasonable doubt is meant one which exists because of an
> approximate balance of positive and negative evidence
> which does not satisfactorily prove or disprove the
> claim. It is a substantial doubt and one within the range
> of probability as distinguished from pure speculation or
> remote possibility. It is not a means of reconciling actual
> conflict or a contradiction in the evidence. Mere suspicion
> or doubt as to the truth of any statements submitted …
> is not justifiable basis for denying the application of the
> reasonable doubt doctrine if the entire, complete record
> otherwise warrants invoking this doctrine …

In *Capellan v. Peake*[75], the Federal Circuit explained, "The "benefit
of the doubt" statute, 38 U.S.C. § 5107(b), and the analogous "reasonable
doubt" regulation, 38 C.F.R. § 3.102, apply to all material issues relating to
a claim, including verification of military service. See *Kelly v. Nicholson*,
463 F.3d 1349, 1354 (Fed. Cir. 2006) (stating that 38 U.S.C. § 5107(b)
"applies not only to decisions relating to the overall merits of a claim, but
by its plain language it applies to all decisions determining any material

---

[73] 38 U.S.C. § 5107(b)

[74] 38 C.F.R. § 3.102

[75] *Capellan*, 539 F.3d 1373, 1383 (Fed. Cir. 2008)

issue relating to a claim") ... Both the statute and the regulation explicitly require the consideration of all evidence submitted by the claimant."

In *Donnellan v Shinseki*[76], the CAVC further described the benefit of the doubt rule:

> The "benefit of the doubt" standard applies when the positive and negative evidence regarding the merits of a veteran's claim for benefits are in approximate balance. When such equipoise exists, the veteran must prevail on the merits of his claim. Therefore, a veteran need only demonstrate that there is an approximate balance of evidence in order to prevail on his claim. A claim for veterans benefits may only be denied when the preponderance of evidence is against a claim.

Of course, the benefit of the doubt rule is inapplicable when the preponderance, or majority, of evidence is against the claim.[77] "If a fair preponderance of the evidence supports a veteran's claim, the claim will be granted and the rule has no application. Similarly, if a fair preponderance of the evidence is against a veteran's claim, the claim will be denied, and the rule has no application. Where the Board makes a finding of fact adverse to a claimant, it has necessarily concluded that the fact is established by a fair preponderance of the evidence."[78]

If VA "is persuaded that the preponderant evidence weighs either for or against the veteran's claim, it necessarily has determined that the evidence is not "nearly equal" or "too close to call," and the benefit of the doubt rule therefore has no application. Alternatively, the benefit of the doubt rule may be viewed as shifting the [burden of persuasion] ... onto the VA to prove that the veteran is not entitled to benefits.[79]

---

[76] *Donnellan*, 24 Vet.App. 167, 175 (2010)

[77] *Ortiz v. Principi*, 274 F.3d 1361 (Fed. Cir. 2001)

[78] *Hayes v. Brown*, 5 Vet.App. 60, 69 (1993) citing *Gilbert*, 1 Vet.App. at 55

[79] *Ortiz v. Principi*, 274 F.3d 1361, 1365 (Fed. Cir. 2001)

Resolution of Reasonable Doubt—[80]

> It is the defined and consistently applied policy of the Department of Veterans Affairs to administer the law under a broad interpretation, consistent, however, with the facts shown in every case. When after careful consideration of all procurable and assembled data, a reasonable doubt arises regarding the degree of disability such doubt will be resolved in favor of the claimant …

Manual M21-1, III.v.1.A.2.f. **Application of the Reasonable-Doubt Rule**

★ ★ ★

§ 4.10 — Duty: Notice Of Decision Regarding Benefits[81]

Manual M21-1, III.v.2.B.1.b. **Decision Notice Requirements**

When a veteran files a claim for benefits, VA has an obligation to obtain records, give medical exams when necessary, and lastly, issue a decision about the claim. When a rating decision has been made, VA must notify the veteran about that decision. By statute, the notice must include an explanation of how to appeal the decision, and what evidence is needed.

(1) Identification of the issues adjudicated.
(2) A summary of the evidence considered by the Secretary.
(3) A summary of the applicable laws and regulations.
(4) Identification of findings favorable to the claimant.
(5) In the case of a denial, identification of elements not satisfied leading to the denial.
(6) An explanation of how to obtain or access evidence used in making the decision.
(7) If applicable, identification of the criteria that must be satisfied to grant service connection or the next higher level of compensation.

---

[80] 38 C.F.R. § 4.3
[81] 38 U.S.C. § 5104; 38 C.F.R. § 3.103(a)

Thus, decisional documents are like roadmaps that explain how to reach a favorable decision or higher rating for a service-connected condition.

> Manual M21-1, III.v.2.B.1.a. **Notifying a Claimant or Beneficiary of a Potentially Adverse Decision**

> Manual M21-1, III.iv.2.B.5.b. **Requirement to Notify Claimant of Favorable Findings**

> Manual M21-1, I.1.A.3.e. **PL 115-55 and Duty to Provide Decision Notice**

★ ★ ★

Conclusion

The veterans benefits system really is unique in its mission and purpose to serve those who served. Although for many veterans it may not seem like it, the VA disability claims process is designed to be a nonadversarial pro-veteran system, and the VA is mandated by law to work with, not against, those who apply for benefits. VA exists to serve veterans, which means making sure that veterans and their families receive every benefit to which they are entitled by law. For advocates, it is important to conduct a thorough review of not only a veteran's service records, but also of their claims history, in order to fully assess a veteran's current situation and assist in future claims and appeals. Always check to make sure that VA followed the correct procedure at every step of the process.

★ ★ ★

Chapter 5

How to File a Claim for VA Disability Benefits

I n order to receive disability benefits, a veteran must file a "claim" for benefits with the VA. Once a fully developed claim has been received, a VA claims adjudicator will review the veteran's military file, including relevant service and medical records, and along with the claim and any submitted evidence to determine if a medical examination is necessary to decide the claim. If an examination is needed, one will be scheduled, and the VA will write and call the veteran to make the arrangements. Once an exam is scheduled, VA is good at sending appointment reminders, which veterans should opt to receive in all forms, i.e. text, phone, email, USPS mail. If a rating decision can be made based upon the existing record, then no examination will be scheduled.

Proper Prior Planning Prevents Piss Poor Performance. Veterans and advocates who take the time to learn and understand the claims process will achieve better results. Most importantly, keep in mind that it is a relatively simple process: you are just filing a few forms to describe your service and disability, and if needed, attend an examination for each claim.

Filing a Claim for VA Disability Benefits — 4 Basic Steps

1. Gather records
   a. Obtain federal and private medical records
   b. Appoint VA claims representative (optional)
   c. File "Intent to file" (optional)

2. File claim(s)
3. Claim review by VA
   a. VA may request additional evidence
   b. Compensation & Pension exam (scheduled only if necessary to decide the claim)
   c. C & P exam performed
4. VA issues decision

★ ★ ★

§ 5.1 — Gather Records

Before all else, veterans should first gather together all of their service and medical records, including records that are held by the federal government, as well as any relevant private medical records. Doing so will save time and help the VA make its decision more quickly.[1] Due to privacy laws, hospitals and other private providers will only release confidential treatment records to the veteran or an authorized individual. Rules protecting privacy also apply to records held by either the individual service branches or the National Personnel Records Center ("NPRC") of the National Archives and Records Administration ("NARA"), which may be only released to a veteran or if deceased, the veteran's next-of-kin.

VA Forms **21-4142** and **21-4142a** are used in conjunction with each other and both forms must be completed in order to obtain private treatment records. (*see* Section 5.1.2, Gather private medical / other records)

§ 5.1.1 — How to request a Veteran's military personnel and medical records

A veteran applying for VA disability benefits should always request their complete DoD service record, including their DD214 discharge certificate, medical records, and Official Military Personnel File ("OMPF"). This is important for several reasons. First, these records contain documentary

---

[1] "When Veterans, Servicemembers and survivors provide all required evidence at the same time they submit a claim AND certify that they have no more evidence, VA can issue a decision faster." See "Filing an FDC." https://web.archive.org/web/20200916190522/https://www.benefits.va.gov/compensation/

evidence of their active duty service, including any medical treatments, and should be examined for helpful (and not-so-helpful) information that might help corroborate an in-service injury or event for a disability claim. In the case that key items are missing from a veteran's DD214 that are necessary to corroborate a claim, i.e. missing combat or overseas service awards, this issue should first be resolved if possible with a DoD records correction board prior to filing the claim with VA. Once a claim is filed, VA (on its own) will access the veteran's service personnel and medical treatment records to determine whether evidence supports granting or denying the claim. As such, it is important for a veteran to have their full record of service, and as mentioned, resolve any issues that might hamper or delay their claim. In some cases, veterans will already be in possession of their personnel and medical records, having retained documents and records from their time in service.

Veterans may submit their Service Treatment Records (STRs) or treatment records from a VA medical facility. However, doing so is optional, as VA already has access to these records.

♣ Request Pertaining to Military Records
— Standard Form 180

A veteran or authorized person may use **Standard Form 180 ("SF 180")** to request a veteran's military records, by either fax or standard mail. Use of the SF180 is not required, however, and a written request that describes what information is sought will be considered sufficient. Written requests for service records should include: the veteran's name while in service; social security number; branch of service; dates of service; last held rank; and if known, the veteran's date and place of birth.

Veterans can request the different records of their service as identified on the SF 180: (1) DD214 certificate of release or discharge from active duty—given to veterans since 1950; (2) medical records, including service treatment records; and (3) other records, like the veteran's Official Military Personnel File. When making a request, make sure to identify the record sought.

Veterans should make sure to SIGN and DATE their records request, and make at least three copies, including one for their personal records. In some cases, a veteran's personnel and medical records will be held at a different locations, and multiple requests will be necessary. Where a claims officer, attorney or other representative is assisting a veteran in obtaining their military records, have the veteran sign the SF 180 to authorize the release of records to the representative.

eBenefits Account — VA.gov —

Veterans can also create a free online "eBenefits" account to submit evidence, manage their status with VA, monitor a claim, add or change their authorized claims representative, and more.

Personnel and medical files can be requested for most post-9/11 veterans through eBenefits. Even if not used for this purpose, all veterans who apply for disability benefits are highly advised to create an eBenefits account. (www.ebenefits.va.gov/) Once a regular account is created, a veteran can request a "premium" account, which is also free, to unlock all user options for the site. To upgrade to a premium eBenefits account, veterans should visit the closest VA Regional Office or Vet Center with one government-issued photo ID (driver's license, ID, passport) one secondary form of identification (birth certificate, social security card), and a copy of their DD214. As always, you will sign a form that the VA will provide. A premium account will be granted once a veteran's identity has been confirmed. Once service-connection is awarded, a veteran can also create a "myHeatheVet" account for health care to track medical appointments, refill prescriptions, and more. (www.myhealth.va.gov/)

eVetRecs Account — Archives.gov — (records requests)

NARA offers an online service to request military records called eVetRecs (vetrecs.archives.gov) which can be launched from its online website. This service allows a veteran to submit an electronic records request after entering basic identifying information, but still requires the veteran to print and sign a signature page that must be mailed or faxed. As such, this step does not appear to be advantageous over a SF 180 on its own, but may prove most valuable in cases of hard-to-find records.

Where are your records located?—

The location of a veteran's personnel records—i.e. DD214, OMPF— and medical treatment records depends on their branch and dates of service and discharge. Veterans should refer to the chart of addresses on page 2 of the SF 180 to find the correct address to match with their service and the type of record sought. *Be prepared to make multiple requests to obtain the full record.*

Service Medical Records —

VA stores DoD the service medical treatment records of most veterans who were discharged after 1994. Each of the military services began the practice of forwarding service member medical records to the VA at that time. If a veteran's medical records are stored elsewhere, VA will notify the requester upon receipt of a SF 180 medical record request. The mailing address for DoD medical records held by VA is:

Department of Veterans Affairs
Records Management Center
P.O. Box 5020
St. Louis, MO 63155

OMPF — Personnel Records —

Veterans can request a digital PDF version of their OMPF (and DD214) through eBenefits, as mentioned above, or by submitting a SF 180 to the appropriate address listed on page 2 of the SF 180. Veterans should make sure to specifically request their full OMPF in writing.

DD214 — Personnel Records —

A copy of a veteran's DD214 discharge certificate should be located in their OMPF. Veterans can also request a copy of their DD214 directly from their service branch. To request a copy of a veteran's DD214, submit a SF 180 and mail or fax to the appropriate service branch listed on page 2 of the SF 180. Be sure to identify the sought after record—full OMPF or DD214 discharge certificate.

§ 5.1.2 — Gather private medical / other records

In addition to military service records held by the federal government, veterans should gather medical records of any hospitalizations, health care or treatment that they received from a private provider for their service-connected disability. According to VA guidelines, "The Department of Veterans Affairs encourages all veterans to submit their private medical records for consideration during the processing of their benefits claim. **VA values evidence from your private treatment providers because they are familiar with your medical history, often over a long period of time.** VA appreciates the trusted and special relationship between private treatment providers and their Veteran/patients."

Private Medical Records. Where applicable, veterans should talk with their private healthcare provider and explain that they want to file a claim for VA benefits. If necessary, complete the healthcare provider's release of information form to obtain private records. Include private medical records with the claim.

VA Forms 21-4142 and 21-4142(a). Another way to gather private medical evidence, which VA now prefers, is for veterans to authorize their private healthcare provider to release their confidential medical history to VA. For this, veterans must complete VA Form 21-4142, *Authorization to Disclose Information to the Department of Veterans Affairs* <u>and</u> VA For 21-4142a, *General Release for Medical Provider Information to the Department of Veterans Affairs.* VA Forms 21-4142 and 21-4142a are used in conjunction with each other and both forms must be completed in order to obtain treatment records. Once both forms are submitted with a claim, VA will attempt to obtain the veteran's private medical records.

In addition, Veterans can also submit other relevant records that can help substantiate their disability claim. For example, disabled veterans can provide documentation of their inability to maintain gainful employment (i.e. IRS tax records) due to their disability. In addition, veterans with PTSD may submit any relevant law enforcement arrest records or criminal convictions related to their mental health issues. That includes participation in a Veterans Treatment Court program designed to help veterans with

PTSD avoid criminal conviction for offenses stemming from and mitigated by their service-connected PTSD.

★ ★ ★

§ 5.2 — Appoint Representative

Veterans who would like to be represented for free by an accredited Veterans Service Officer ("VSO" or claims officer) who can help file their claims should seek out a local veterans service organization. VSOs work for either State Departments of Veterans Affairs that offer free county-level VSO officers who help veterans to file their claims, or one of the national Veterans Service Organizations (also "VSOs") who maintain offices with trained service officers ready to assist in every state. i.e. VFW, American Legion, Disabled American Veterans.

Before an accredited individual or service organization can legally communicate with VA on a veteran's behalf, the veteran must first file a power of attorney granting them that authority. For this, a veteran should submit the proper authorization form:

> ♣ VA Form 21-22 — **Appointment of Veterans Service Organization as Claimant's Representative**

or

> ♣ VA Form 21-22a — **Appointment of Individual as Claimant's Representative**

★ ★ ★

§ 5.3 — "Intent to File" Claim[2]

Veterans are entitled to receive disability compensation benefits starting on the date that they establish eligibility. For claims filed more than one year after discharge, eligibility starts on the date the claim was filed.

---

[2] 38 C.F.R. § 3.155(b)

Veterans have the option of filing what is known as a "Fully Developed Claim." In some instances, however, where a veteran needs additional time to gather evidence to develop their claim, they should consider filing VA Form 21-0966, *Intent to File a Claim for Compensation and/or Pension and/or DIC.*[3]

♣ VA Form 21-0966 — **Intent to File a Claim for Compensation, and/or Pension, or Survivors Pension, and/or DIC**

The "Intent to File" ("ITF") is a simple one-page form that essentially "locks" the veteran's effective date (*see* Section 3.13, Effective Dates) for up to one year, giving them an additional 12 months to obtain additional substantiating evidence. A veteran's ITF should check the box identifying the general benefit sought (1) disability compensation; (2) pension; or (3) survivor's dependency and indemnity compensation ("DIC"). Veterans do not need to include medical evidence or identify the specific benefit that is sought with their intent to file. Unless the veteran has all of their necessary evidence and records and is ready to file a Fully Developed Claim ("FDC"), veterans are encouraged to file an ITF is to lock their claim date and maximize benefits.

An "intent to file" under § 3.155(b)(1)(i-iii) can be filed in one of three ways:

1. Online.
2. By submitting a VA standard form (VA 21–0966) in either paper (mail or fax) or electronic form.
3. By communicating verbally with certain designated VA personnel "either in person or by telephone," who are authorized to document the claimant's intent.

So long as a completed application is filed within one year of the submission, the VA will deem the effective date of the claim to be the date the "intent to file" submission was received.[4]

★ ★ ★

---

[3] 38 C.F.R. § 3.155(b)

[4] *Veterans Justice Grp., LLC v. Sec'y of Veterans Affairs*, 818 F.3d 1336, 1343 (Fed. Cir. 2016)

§ 5.4 — File Claim for Disability Compensation Benefits

To file an original claim for disability compensation benefits, a veteran must complete a VA Form 21-526EZ, "Application for Disability Compensation and Compensation Related Benefits." *Be sure to include DBQs and other relevant medical evidence with your claim.* This is the general application used by VA to intake new applications for disability benefits, and how a veteran makes a formal claim of entitlement to compensation for service-connected disability.

♣ VA Form 21-526EZ — **Application for Disability Compensation and Compensation Related Benefits**

VA currently offers two methods of applying for disability compensation benefits, depending upon whether or not the veteran has submitted all of the necessary evidence to decide the claim. The two methods of filing a claim are:

(1) Fully Developed Claim ("FDC") program; or
(2) Standard claim process.

In BOX 1 (Page 8) of their application for benefits (VA Form 21-526EZ), veterans should identify which method they are applying under. When a veteran chooses FDC review, they are telling VA that the claim includes all of the necessary evidence, so VA won't need to obtain evidence and can review the claim and issue a rating decision more quickly. **Participation in the FDC Program is optional**. If a veteran files a claim in the FDC Program and it is determined that other records exist and VA needs the records to decide the claim, then VA will simply remove the claim from the FDC Program and process it in the Standard Claim Process.

Manual M21-1, III.i.3.A.1. **Overview of the FDC Program**

Manual M21-1, III.i.3.B.1. **Intake Process for Fully Developed Claims**

It is extremely important for veterans and advocates to make sure that the veteran's identifying and contact information is accurate (VA Form 21-526EZ, Section I, Page 8). VA uses the given home address to send all correspondences regarding the claim, information about examinations, and the ratings decision itself. Veterans should make sure to provide VA with their up-to-date contact information, and be sure to update any changes right away. Section IV on Page 9 is where a veteran lists their current disabilities. Only list current disabilities and do not exaggerate or attempt to fill this entire space with information. With most disabilities, the approximate date disability began or worsened will be sometime during active duty service. Exact dates are not required, estimations should suffice. Simply list each disability by name (i.e. PTSD, TBI, tinnitus, etc.). In Section VII on Page 11, veterans can share their checking or savings account information with VA for VA to make direct deposits once a rating decision is made and benefits are awarded. **The application must include a copy of a voided check from the listed bank account. Direct deposit information is only needed with the original claim, and can be changed online later with an eBenefits account.

⋆ ⋆

§ 5.4.1 — File Claim for Service-Connected PTSD

Veterans with PTSD must establish three things in order to become service-connected for their PTSD and qualify for compensation and health care benefits: (1) current PTSD diagnosis; (2) in-service PTSD stressors; and (3) a link, or nexus between the in-service stressor and current PTSD.[5]

To establish a PTSD claim, a veteran should submit the following documents and completed VA forms:

1. Diagnosis: Private health and medical records (21-0960P-3)
2. In-service stressors: 21-0781, 21-0781a
3. Nexus: Nexus opinion letter

⋆ ⋆

1. DIAGNOSIS

When a veteran is diagnosed with PTSD after they are discharged from active duty, they can show a post-service PTSD diagnosis in one of three ways:

---

[5] 38 C.F.R. §§ 3.304(f), 4.125

(1) Private PTSD medical records;

(2) VA Form 21-0960-3, *Review Post-Traumatic Stress Disorder DBQ*; or

(3) Authorize VA to obtain private PTSD records.

Private PTSD Records. Veterans should talk with their private psychologist/therapist and explain that they want to file a claim for VA benefits. If necessary, complete the healthcare provider's release of information form to obtain private records. Include private PTSD records with the claim.

VA Form 21-0960P-3. In addition, veterans can ask their psychologist/ therapist to complete VA Form 21-0960-3, *Review Post-Traumatic Stress Disorder DBQ*. VA Form 21-0960P-3 can be used by private healthcare professionals to diagnose and document the extent of a veteran's PTSD. Although the form is generally intended for supplemental claims for higher ratings, veterans are still encouraged to have their private physician complete a PSTD review DBQ to include with their original claim application for PTSD compensation. VA must give the information it contains the proper value in making its decision.

♣ VA Form 21-0960P-3 — **Review Post-Traumatic Stress Disorder (PTSD) Disability Benefits Questionnaire**—[6]

VA Forms 21-4142 and 21-4142(a). Lastly, VA now prefers veterans to authorize the release their confidential civilian PTSD medical history to VA. For this, veterans must complete VA Form 21-4142, *Authorization to Disclose Information to the Department of Veterans Affairs* and VA For 21-4142a, *General Release for Medical Provider Information to the Department of Veterans Affairs*. VA Forms 21-4142 and 21-4142a are used in conjunction with each other and both forms must be completed in order to obtain treatment records. Once both forms are submitted with a claim, VA will attempt to obtain the veteran's private PTSD records.

---

[6] Although the VA announced it was removing "public facing" Disability Benefit Questionnaires from its public website, DBQs can still be used to submit medical information and other evidence. All DBQs can be found at and downloaded from the VA Handbook website: https://va-handbook.com/resources/dbqs/

2. IN-SERVICE STRESSOR(S)

♣ VA Form 21-0781 — **Statement in Support of Claim for Service Connection for Post-Traumatic Stress Disorder (PTSD)**

Veterans who are filing a claim for PTSD are REQUIRED to provide a written statement about the in-service stressors, called "stressful incidents," that they survived, which can be documented on VA Form 21-0781, *Statement in Support of Claim for Service Connection for Post-Traumatic Stress Disorder (PTSD)*. As is discussed in Section 3.8, Post-Traumatic Stress Disorder, in certain circumstances, veterans can establish the occurrence of in-service stressors with their testimony alone. This is accomplished with VA Form 21-0718. Section II of VA Form 21-0781 allows veterans to describe two separate in-service stressors, or stressful incidents. Veterans can include additional stressors on another form if desired. Some veterans may have experienced a number of stressful incidents, but ultimately only one stressor incident can lead to disabling PTSD.

Having to recall or relive stressful incidents can be stressful in and of itself. However, this step is extremely important because putting uncomfortable details into writing will help the VA adjudicator who is reviewing the claim to better understand the gravity of the incidents that the veteran experienced while on active duty.

In Section II, a veteran should identify the approximate time and location of each stressful incident, as well as the unit that they were serving in at the time. Importantly, in boxes 8e and 11e, "Description of the Incident," a veteran should provide as much detail as possible about each incident. When applicable, identify fellow troops who were killed or injured. Enemy and civilian casualties should also be noted. Veterans are encouraged to consult with their records to ensure that dates, locations and unit affiliations are as accurate as possible. The veteran should also describe how current symptoms of PTSD have impacted their life since the incidents. Statements can either be typed by a VSO or hand written by the veteran, and should be made to fit within the provided space—long narratives about personal histories are not recommended. In the space provided, give a brief statement detailing the traumatic events, and describe how the events led to PTSD today.

3. NEXUS (*see* Section 3.4.3, Nexus / Link)

★ ★ ★

§ 5.4.2 — File Claim for Service-Connected PTSD caused by Sexual Assault

Manual M21-1, III.iv.4.O.3.a. **General Information on Personal Trauma**

Like any PTSD claim, having to recount the details of a sexual assault or harassment is an upsetting thing for a survivor, but doing so is necessary to helping a VA claims examiner corroborate and approve the claim. To file a PTSD claim, an MST survivor should include a written statement about what happened, giving as much detailed information about the time and location of the assault, as well as the identity of the attacker, if known. This and additional corroborating information should be provided with a veteran's statement on VA Form 21-0781a, "Statement in Support of Claim for Service-Connection for PTSD Secondary to Personal Assault."

♣ VA Form 21-0781a — **Statement in Support of Claim for Service-Connection for PTSD Secondary to Personal Assault**

Although more than a personal statement is needed to corroborate a sexual assault, veterans should still share as much evidence about the traumatic event as possible by providing a statement using VA Form 21-0781a. Corroborating evidence, defined by 38 C.F.R. § 3.304(f)(5), can help substantiate the occurrence of a sexual assault in-service stressor:

Description. Veterans should provide as much descriptive information about the incident as possible, including all potential sources that may help to corroborate their attack. **Reports.** If the veteran reported the incident to military or civilian law enforcement authorities or sought help from a rape crisis center, counseling facility, or other health clinic, provide the names and addresses of the facilities that were visited. As with treatment records, veterans can submit the records with their application or authorize VA to obtain them. **Treatment.** If the veteran received treatment for sexual assault, they can either submit the private records themselves or authorize

VA to obtain them by using VA Form 21-4142, "Authorization and Consent to Release Information to the Department of Veterans Affairs" and Form 21-4142a, "General Release for Medical Provider Information to the Department of Veterans Affairs." If needed, use multiple authorization forms. **Contemporaneous Conversations**. If the veteran confided in friends, family members, chaplains, clergy, or fellow service members, have these individuals prepare a statement concerning their knowledge of the incident. In addition, when available include copies of personal diary or journal entries about the incident. **Behavioral Changes.** A veteran who was sexually assaulted should also tell VA about any behavioral changes that they experienced after the assault. For a full explanation of PTSD MST claims, *see* Section 3.8.3, Sexual Assault – PTSD Stressor.

> Manual M21-1, III.iv.4.O.3.b. **Importance of Obtaining and Analyzing Available Evidence of Personal Trauma**

> Manual M21-1, III.iv.4.O.3.c. **Alternative Sources of Evidence of In-Service Personal Trauma**

> Manual M21-1, III.iv.4.O.3.d. **Evidence That May Constitute a Marker of Personal Trauma**

> Manual M21-1, III.iv.4.O.3.e. **Interpretation of Behavioral Changes as Markers of Personal Trauma**

★ ★ ★

**Relationship between VA regulations and DBQS

—VA Form 21-0960P-3 (Box 4a) compared to **38 C.F.R. § 4.130**

PTSD ratings criteria defined by 38 C.F.R. § 4.130 appear as corresponding checkboxes in Box 4A of the PTSD review disability benefits questionnaire, one (1) of which must be selected by the veteran's psychologist, psychiatrist, or therapist. VA will use the level of disability that is identified as a baseline for establishing a rating. In the absence of clear and contrary evidence VA must give weight but not deference to level of disability indicated by the veteran's private provider. The rubric below shows the relationship between the VA regulation and corresponding DBQ.

38 CFR § 4.130

GENERAL RATING FORMULA FOR MENTAL DISORDERS

	Rating
Total occupational and social impairment, due to such symptoms as: gross impairment in thought processes or communication; persistent delusions or hallucinations; grossly inappropriate behavior; persistent danger of hurting self or others; intermittent inability to perform activities of daily living (including maintenance of minimal personal hygiene); disorientation to time or place; memory loss for names of close relatives, own occupation, or own name.	100
Occupational and social impairment, with deficiencies in most areas, such as work, school, family relations, judgment, thinking, or mood, due to such symptoms as: suicidal ideation; obsessional rituals which interfere with routine activities; speech intermittently illogical, obscure, or irrelevant; near-continuous panic or depression affecting the ability to function independently, appropriately and effectively; impaired impulse control (such as unprovoked irritability with periods of violence); spatial disorientation; neglect of personal appearance and hygiene; difficulty in adapting to stressful circumstances (including work or a worklike setting); inability to establish and maintain effective relationships.	70
Occupational and social impairment with reduced reliability and productivity due to such symptoms as: flattened affect; circumstantial, circumlocutory, or stereotyped speech; panic attacks more than once a week; difficulty in understanding complex commands; impairment of short- and long-term memory (e.g., retention of only highly learned material, forgetting to complete tasks); impaired judgment; impaired abstract thinking; disturbances of motivation and mood; difficulty in establishing and maintaining effective work and social relationships.	50
Occupational and social impairment with occasional decrease in work efficiency and intermittent periods of inability to perform occupational tasks (although generally functioning satisfactorily, with routine behavior, self-care, and conversation normal), due to such symptoms as: depressed mood, anxiety, suspiciousness, panic attacks (weekly or less often), chronic sleep impairment, mild memory loss (such as forgetting names, directions, recent events).	30
Occupational and social impairment due to mild or transient symptoms which decrease work efficiency and ability to perform occupational tasks only during periods of significant stress, or symptoms controlled by continuous medication.	10
A mental condition has been formally diagnosed, but symptoms are not severe enough either to interfere with occupational and social functioning or to require continuous medication.	0

VA FORM 21-0960P-3

SECTION IV - OCCUPATIONAL AND SOCIAL IMPAIRMENT

4A. WHICH OF THE FOLLOWING BEST SUMMARIZES THE VETERAN'S LEVEL OF OCCUPATIONAL AND SOCIAL IMPAIRMENT WITH REGARDS TO ALL MENTAL DIAGNOSES? *(Check only one)*

☐ NO MENTAL DISORDER DIAGNOSIS

☐ A MENTAL CONDITION HAS BEEN FORMALLY DIAGNOSED, BUT SYMPTOMS ARE NOT SEVERE ENOUGH EITHER TO INTERFERE WITH OCCUPATIONAL AND SOCIAL FUNCTIONING OR TO REQUIRE CONTINUOUS MEDICATION

☐ OCCUPATIONAL AND SOCIAL IMPAIRMENT DUE TO MILD OR TRANSIENT SYMPTOMS WHICH DECREASE WORK EFFICIENCY AND ABILITY TO PERFORM OCCUPATIONAL TASKS ONLY DURING PERIODS OF SIGNIFICANT STRESS, OR SYMPTOMS CONTROLLED BY MEDICATION

☐ OCCUPATIONAL AND SOCIAL IMPAIRMENT WITH OCCASIONAL DECREASE IN WORK EFFICIENCY AND INTERMITTENT PERIODS OF INABILITY TO PERFORM OCCUPATIONAL TASKS, ALTHOUGH GENERALLY FUNCTIONING SATISFACTORILY, WITH NORMAL ROUTINE BEHAVIOR, SELF-CARE AND CONVERSATION

☐ OCCUPATIONAL AND SOCIAL IMPAIRMENT WITH REDUCED RELIABILITY AND PRODUCTIVITY

☐ OCCUPATIONAL AND SOCIAL IMPAIRMENT WITH DEFICIENCIES IN MOST AREAS, SUCH AS WORK, SCHOOL, FAMILY RELATIONS, JUDGMENT, THINKING, AND/OR MOOD

☐ TOTAL OCCUPATIONAL AND SOCIAL IMPAIRMENT

Disability Benefits Questionnaires (DBQs) are VA forms that organize all of the necessary information required for diagnosing service-connected injuries as defined by VA regulations. This chart for shows how different ratings for Post-Traumatic Stress Disorder (PTSD), as defined by VA regulation 38 C.F.R. § 4.130, appear on the Disability Benefits Questionnaire, VA-Form 21-0960P-3.

★ ★ ★

§ 5.5 — File Claim for Health Care Benefits

Veterans will generally also want to apply for Health Care Benefits at the same time or shortly after they apply for Compensation Benefits, using VA Form 10-10EZ. While compensation is a financial benefit awarded each month by the VBA for employment handicaps, health care services and treatment is an entirely separate benefit offered by the Veterans Health Administration ("VHA"). The level of coverage of care and prescription drug coverage depends on the level of a veteran's service-connected disability. Veterans rated 100% totally disabled, for example, receive free health care and prescriptions for most ailments, including non-service related injuries and conditions. From there, different tiers represent priority levels assigned to the veteran's health care status.

♣ VA Form 10-10EZ — **Application for Health Benefits**

★ ★ ★

§ 5.6 — Initial Claim Review

Once a VA Regional Office has received a substantially complete claim, a claims adjudicator will examine the entire record to ensure that the applicant meets basic eligibility requirements, including veteran status and length of service. It is the veteran's responsibility to respond to any requests for information during this time.

§ 5.6.1 — Character of Discharge Review

Veterans who received less-than-honorable discharges must overcome an additional hurdle in order to be eligible to receive VA benefits. A Character of Discharge review (also known as "Character of Service Determination") requires veterans to explain why they did not receive an Honorable discharge, and why their service should not be considered dishonorable for VA purposes. 38 C.F.R. § 3.12. Due to this extra step, veterans with less-than-honorable discharges who apply for disability benefits are not eligible to file a fully developed claim for expedited review, and instead receive standard review. For a full explanation of COD/CSD review, *see* Section 3.2.1, Character of Discharge.

§ 5.6.2 — Compensation & Pension Examination

As part of its duty to assist, for claims where the record proves insufficient to make a rating decision, VA must provide a medical examination and opinion, free of charge. The C&P exam is an inspection, not intended as treatment, that generally lasts one hour or less. The purpose of the C&P exam is for a VA medical representative to diagnose, on behalf of VA, the veteran's current disabling injury or condition. Veterans should arrive before their scheduled examination, but should not make any additional effort to dress up or otherwise "impress" their C&P examiner. In fact, the purpose of the examination is for the VA examiner to make a medical assessment about the veteran's level of disability, and how that disability impacts a veteran's daily activities and functioning. As a result, veterans should act as they normally would during their examination, making sure to describe to the examiner how their service-connected disability has negatively impacted their private life and employment. For a full explanation of the C&P exam, see Section 4.5, Duty: Provide Medical Examination/Opinion

★ ★ ★

§ 5.7 — VA Issues Rating Decision

Once the VA has received the C&P examination report and the record is complete, a claims adjudicator at the VA regional office will examine the full record. If they determine that the veteran has a condition that was caused or aggravated during their service, VA will assign the disability a "rating" in terms of percentage between 0-100 percent based upon the severity of the injury and its overall impact on the veteran's employability. If more than one disability is found, a schedule rating is assigned to each injury and then combined for an overall disability rating, which establishes the level of benefits. A set calculation (commonly known as "VA Math") employs a "Combined Ratings Table" rubric to determine the overall rating. (*see* Section 3.12, Disability "Ratings")

VA will sent its rating decision to the veteran by USPS mail, which the veteran may accept or appeal. (*see* Chapter 6, Appeals)

★ ★ ★

§ 5.8 — Finality of Decisions

When a VA regional office issues a ratings decision on an original disability claim, the veteran has the option of accepting the decision if it is accurate, or challenging the decision by filing an appeal in the modernized appeals system. A VARO disability rating decision becomes final if the veteran does not file an appeal within one year of the decision.[7] After the decision becomes final, a veteran may only reopen their claim in one of two ways:

1. Clear and unmistakable error ("CUE")
2. New evidence (Supplemental Claim)

§ 5.8.1 — Clear and unmistakable error ("CUE")[8]

Manual M21-1, III.iv.2.B.4. **Clear and Unmistakable Error**

CUEs are errors that are undebatable.[9] Disability rating decisions of the VARO (§5109A) and the BVA (§7111) that contain clear and unmistakable error ("CUE") may be appealed at any time — there is no statute of limitations for CUE. When CUE is shown in the previous decision and an appeal is granted, the effective date of the benefit award becomes the date of the original claim, and backpay is due.[10] When the courts review a BVA decision that does not involve CUE, their review is limited to determining whether the Board's conclusions were arbitrary, capricious, an abuse of discretion, or otherwise not in accordance with law and whether it was supported by an adequate statement of reasons or bases.[11]

---

[7] 38 U.S.C. § 7105(c)

[8] 38 U.S.C. §§ 5109A; 7111

[9] *Russell v. Principi*, 3 Vet.App. 310 (1992)

[10] *Flash v. Brown*, 8 Vet.App. 332, 340 (1995)

[11] *Eddy v. Brown*, 9 Vet.App. 52, 57 (1996)

Clear and unmistakable error—[12]

> A clear and unmistakable error is a very specific and rare kind of error. It is the kind of error, of fact or of law, that when called to the attention of later reviewers compels the conclusion, to which reasonable minds could not differ, that the result would have been manifestly different but for the error. If it is not absolutely clear that a different result would have ensued, the error complained of cannot be clear and unmistakable. Generally, either the correct facts, as they were known at the time, were not before VA, or the statutory and regulatory provisions extant at the time were incorrectly applied.

See: 38 C.F.R. § 20.1403; *Thompson v. Derwinski*, 1 Vet.App. 251, 253 (1991); *Porter v. Brown*, 5 Vet.App. 233, 235-36 (1993); *Luallen v. Brown*, 8 Vet.App. 92, 95 (1995); *Baldwin v. West*, 13 Vet.App. 1, 5 (1999); *King v. Shinseki*, 26 Vet.App. 433, 441 (2014); *Glover v. West*, 185 F.3d 1328 (Fed. Cir. 1999); *Cook v. Principi*, 318 F.3d 1334 (Fed. Cir. 2003).

As defined by regulation, in order to establish CUE it must be shown that (1) either the facts known at the time of the decision being attacked on the basis of CUE were not before the adjudicator or the law then in effect was incorrectly applied; (2) an error occurred based on the record and the law that existed at the time; and (3) had the error not been made, the outcome would have been manifestly different.[13]

♣ VA Form 10182 — **Notice of Disagreement**

★ ★ ★

---

[12] 38 CFR § 3.105(a)(1)(i)

[13] 38 C.F.R. §§ 3.105(a)(1)(i), 20.1403(c); *Bouton v. Peake*, 23 Vet.App. 70 (2008)

§ 5.8.2 — Supplemental claims with new evidence[14]

Unlike CUE appeals that allege a previous decision was erroneous, supplemental claims are based on new evidence that either show the existence of a disabling injury or that the condition has worsened. All disability ratings decisions, including final decisions that are more than one-year old, may be reopened at any time with **new and relevant evidence** that shows the disability has worsened since it was last adjudicated by VA. As with clear and unmistakable error review, there is no statute of limitations on filing a supplemental claim with new evidence. However, unlike CUE, if a favorable rating is granted on a reopened claim due to new evidence, the effective date of the claim will be the date that the supplemental claim was filed with new evidence, and not the date of the original claim. For more information, *see* Section 6.2.1, "Supplemental Claims."

♣ VA Form 20-0995 — **Supplemental Claim**

★ ★ ★

Favorable findings; binding nature of—[15]

Findings that are favorable to a veteran are final and binding on all subsequent VA adjudicators, unless clear and convincing ("CAC") evidence rebuts that favorable finding. This includes favorable ratings decisions, as well as affirmative factual determinations about a veteran's service history or the existence or nature of their disability.

★ ★ ★

---

[14] 38 U.S.C. §§ 5108, 5104C(b); 38 C.F.R. § 3.2501
[15] 38 U.S.C. § 5104A; 38 CFR § 3.104

Chapter 6

Appeals

V eterans have the "full right to representation in all stages of an appeal by a recognized organization, attorney, agent, or other authorized person."[1] In fact, VA strongly encourages veterans to consider enlisting the help of an accredited individual when filing an appeal.[2]

Prior to 2019, VA claims appeals were unnecessarily complicated and inefficient. Under the old system, veterans faced an outdated labyrinth of processes. Appeals took anywhere from three to seven years to resolve. To improve the unacceptable situation, in 2017 Congress enacted the Veterans Appeals Improvement and Modernization Act ("AMA").[3] Accordingly, VA issued a final rule with new regulations and the AMA went into effect on February 19, 2019.[4] All claims filed after February 19, 2019 are automatically classified as "modern" claims, while those filed before the new system went into effect are considered "legacy" claims. Veterans have the option of appealing legacy claims to the modern system.

★ ★ ★

---

[1] 38 C.F.R. § 20.5 - Rule 5. Right to representation.

[2] U.S. Dept. of Veterans Affairs, Board of Veterans Appeals, VA Pamphlet 01-00-1, "Understanding the Appeals Process." (2000) *available at*: https://va-handbook.com/understanding-the-appeals-process-bva/

[3] Pub. L. 115–55—Aug. 23, 2017, 131 Stat. 1105

[4] *VA Claims and Appeals Modernization*. 84 Fed. Reg. 138 (1 Jan. 2019) https://www.federalregister.gov/d/2018-28350.

§ 6.1 — Modern Review System

The AMA implemented a "modernized review system" to simplify the appeals process.[5] It eliminated unnecessary steps like the "Statement of the Case," which took on average 300 days to do little more than reiterate the VARO decision and a boilerplate list of statutes and regulations. Now, VARO ratings decision contain all of this information from the start (38 U.S.C. § 5104), and veterans have three options for appeal.

When a VA Regional Office (the agency of original jurisdiction) denies a disability claim or issues an inaccurate low rating, a veteran has up to one year to file an appeal for either Higher-Level Review[6] by a senior claims adjuster or file a Notice of Disagreement[7] with the Board of Veterans Appeals. These traditional appeals, which challenge the accuracy of a regional office decision by requesting appellate review for error, are different from supplemental claims[8] that don't allege error but are instead based on "new and relevant" substantiating evidence. Supplemental claims can be filed with the VA regional office at any time once new and relevant evidence is obtained.

New and Relevant Evidence—[9]

The AMA introduced a new standard of evidence for supplemental claims. Instead of "new and material" evidence (old standard), now evidence offered with supplemental claims must be "new and relevant."[10] There is no difference between the old term (material) and new term (relevant).

★ ★ ★

---

[5] 38 C.F.R. § 19.2(b)
[6] 38 C.F.R. § 3.2601
[7] 38 C.F.R. § 20.202
[8] 38 C.F.R. § 3.2501
[9] 38 C.F.R. § 3.2501(a)(1)
[10] 38 U.S.C. § 101(35)

§ 6.2 — How to appeal a claim[11]

The AMA created three distinct avenues for appeal, which are found at 38 U.S.C. § 5104C:

(1) **Supplemental Claim** [VARO]
   – within one year of decision, or at any time

(2) **Higher-Level Review** [VARO]
   – within one year of decision

(3) **Notice of Disagreement** [BVA]
   – within one year of decision

   a. Direct Review
   b. Evidence Submission Review
   c. Hearing with a Veterans Law Judge

★ ★ ★

§ 6.2.1 — Supplemental claim[12]

Supplemental Claims are for veterans who have new and relevant evidence to support a claim that was previously decided. When a veteran files a supplemental claim with their VA regional office, the duty to assist reattaches and if necessary VA must help gather records and otherwise develop the claim. When a veteran seeks a higher rating of a service-connected injury, a supplemental claim should include evidence that their disabling condition has worsened. Veterans may file supplemental claims with new evidence (preceded if necessary with an "Intent to File") at any time, but only "continuously pursued" claims are eligible for payment of benefits from the original effective date.[13] For supplemental claims filed more than one year after a ratings decision, the new effective date will be

---

[11] 38 C.F.R. § 3.2500
[12] 38 U.S.C. § 5108
[13] 38 U.S.C. § 5110; 38 C.F.R. § 3.2501

the date that the supplemental claim was filed. VBA's goal for completing Supplemental Claims is an average of 125 days.

♣   VA Form 20-0995 — **Supplemental Claim**

★ ★ ★

§ 6.2.2 — Higher-level review[14]

Higher-Level Review is for veterans who want an experienced senior claims adjudicator at the regional office level to perform an expedited review of a prior rating decision based upon the same evidence. The higher-level review is conducted *de novo*, or without regard to the previous determination. As such, it is an entirely new review. Veterans must appeal for a Higher-Level Review within one year of a rating decision before the decision becomes final. Veterans concerned about bias have the option of requesting a higher-level review at a different regional office. VBA's goal for completing Supplemental Claims is an average of 125 days.

♣   VA Form 20-0996 — **Higher-Level Review**

★ ★ ★

§ 6.2.3 — Notice of Disagreement[15]

Veterans may also appeal to the Board of Veterans Appeals by filing a *Notice of Disagreement*, VA Form 10182. The NOD must indicate which of three review options with the BVA they would like to utilize: (1) direct review; (2) evidence submission review; or, (3) a hearing with a veterans law judge.

♣   VA Form 10182 — **NOD**

★ ★

---

[14] 38 U.S.C. §§5104B; 38 C.F.R. § 3.2601; *also* 38 U.S.C. §5109B
[15] 38 U.S.C. § 7105; 38 C.F.R. § 20.201

§ 6.2.3.1 Direct Review[16]

Direct Review is for veterans who do not want a Board hearing, and who do not need to submit any additional evidence in support of their appeal. Under direct review a Veterans Law Judge ("VLJ") will review the existing record for errors. Direct review is appropriate when you believe the VARO made the wrong decision by ignoring key evidence or misapplying the law. The Board's goal for completing Direct Review appeals is 365 days.

★ ★

§ 6.2.3.2 Evidence Submission Review[17]

Evidence Submission Review is for veterans who have additional evidence in support of their appeal, but do not want a Board hearing. In evidence submission review, a Veterans Law Judge will review the existing record and also the new substantiating evidence submitted with the appeal. Veterans have 90 days after filing their NOD to submit new evidence. Evidence Submission Review appeals are expected to take longer than one year.

★ ★

§ 6.2.3.3 Hearing with a Veterans Law Judge[18]

As a final option, veterans can request a *Hearing with a Veterans Law Judge* where they can submit additional evidence, including testimony, in support of their appeal. A date will be scheduled for the hearing, at which time new substantiating evidence may be presented. Evidence may also be provided within 90 days after the hearing. Due to the resources involved and number of appeals, hearings are expected to take longer than one year.

If the Board denies your claim and you believe the decision was wrongly decided contrary to the law or the evidence, you can appeal to

---

[16] 38 U.S.C. § 7105(b)(3)(C); 38 C.F.R. § 20.301
[17] 38 U.S.C. § 7105(b)(3)(B); 38 C.F.R. § 20.303
[18] 38 U.S.C. § 7105(b)(3)(A); 38 C.F.R. § 20.302

the CAVC. Alternatively, a supplementary claim with new and relevant evidence may be filed at any time, which automatically reopens the claim.

★ ★ ★

If the Board of Veterans Appeals denies an appeal, veterans who feel they were wrongfully denied may appeal the claim further, starting with the U.S. Court of Appeals for Veterans Claims.

U.S. Court of Appeals for Veterans Claims—[19]

The *U.S. Court of Appeals for Veterans Claims* ("CAVC") has exclusive jurisdiction to review BVA decisions. CAVC is for veterans who feel the BVA improperly denied their claim by wrongly interpreting a statute or regulation, or by ruling against the evidence or the law. Veterans have 120 days to appeal a BVA decision to the CAVC.

The CAVC is strictly a court of review—no new evidence may be presented. It may only settle questions of law or interpret constitutional, statutory, and regulatory provisions. CAVC has the power to set aside BVA decisions that are arbitrary, capricious, an abuse of discretion, or otherwise not in accordance with the law.

Claims and appeals before the VA are *ex parte*, or one-sided, and non-adversarial. However, **once claims are appealed to the U.S. Court of Appeals for Veterans Claims, proceedings become adversarial.**[20]

★ ★

U.S. Court of Appeals for the Federal Circuit—[21]

The *U.S. Court of Appeals for the Federal Circuit* ("Federal Circuit") has exclusive limited jurisdiction to hear appeals of CAVC decisions. The Court may not review factual determinations or challenges to how a law or regulation was applied to the facts of a particular claim. Rather, the Court may only review disputes about the validity or interpretation of any

---

[19] 38 U.S.C. Ch. 72
[20] *Forshey v. Principi*, 284 F.3d 1335 (Fed. Cir. 2002)
[21] 38 U.S.C. § 7292

statute, regulation, or constitutional provision—a rather narrow, limited jurisdiction.

★ ★

U.S. Supreme Court—[22]

The *U.S. Supreme Court* may in limited circumstances grant a "writ of certiorari" to review final decisions of the Court of Appeals for the Federal Circuit. However, this narrow jurisdiction is limited to significant precedential questions of law and is rarely granted.

★ ★ ★

---

[22] 38 U.S.C. § 7292(c)

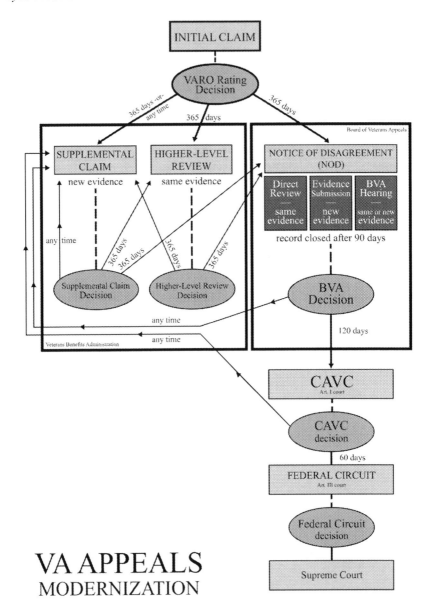

VA APPEALS
MODERNIZATION

The Veterans Appeals Improvement and Modernization Act ("AMA") of 2017 created three distinct avenues of appealing denied claims or inaccurate ratings. The modernized appeals structure was intended to give veterans and advocates greater control to choose the path of appeal that best matches with their needs. Keep in mind that Supplemental Claims with New and Relevant evidence can be submitted at any time.

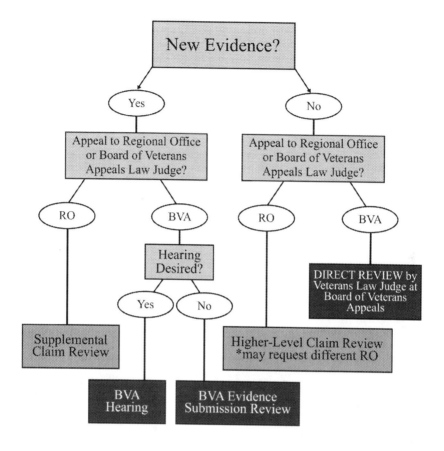

Appeals strategies are guided by the available evidence. In moving forward, veterans and advocates must determine: Whether or not new and relevant evidence exists; whether a Regional Office appeal is appropriate, as opposed to an appeal to the Board of Veterans Appeals; whether a review of the record is adequate, or if a hearing is preferred.

★ ★ ★

§ 6.3 — Legacy Claims & Appeals

In addition to implementing a new appeals system, the 2017 Appeals Modernization Act required that the VA develop a comprehensive plan for processing of all the claims and appeals that were filed before the law went into effect, called "legacy claims / appeals."[23] Accordingly, VA regulations classify claims in one of two ways, based on if they were decided before or after the effective date of the AMA. Again, all original claims filed on or after February 19, 2019, automatically fall into the modernized review system, including requests to reopen finally adjudicated claims and for revision based on clear and unmistakable error.

Legacy claims are all of the claims that were decided prior to February 19, 2019.[24] *Legacy appeals* are ongoing appeals of legacy claims where the veteran has not elected to participate in the modernized review system.[25]

Veterans with a pending legacy appeal may choose to either (1) continue their legacy appeal in the legacy appeals system by filing a Notice of Disagreement with the BVA followed by a Substantive Appeal, or (2) elect to have their claim reviewed in the modernized review system.[26] Veterans who want to transfer their legacy appeal to the new system must respond within 60 days to the opt-in notice provided with either the Statement of the Case ("SOC") or Supplemental Statement of the Case ("SSOC") by filing an appeal with their preferred type of review.

The appeal form for each type of modern review, (1) Supplemental Claim, (2) Higher-Level Review, and (3) Notice of Disagreement with the BVA, includes a section for the veteran to indicate if they are appealing one or more issues from the legacy appeals process. The section reads:

> Check the SOC/SSOC Opt in box if any issue listed below is being withdrawn from the legacy appeals process. **?** Opt In from SOC/SSOC

★ ★ ★

Rapid Appeals Modernization Program ("RAMP") — (closed)

As part of its plan to process legacy claims while simultaneously transitioning to the new system, between the AMA's 2017 enactment and 2019 implementation, VA offered some veterans with legacy appeals the chance to opt-in to the modernized review system early. The Rapid Appeals Modernization Program ("RAMP") allowed veterans to replace their

[23] Pub. L. 115–55, §§3–6, 131 Stat. 1116–1127.
[24] 38 C.F.R. § 3.2400(b)
[25] 38 CFR § 19.2(c)
[26] 38 C.F.R. § 19.2(b); also 38 C.F.R. § 3.2400(a)(2) & (c)

legacy appeal with the new system. RAMP was discontinued in February 2019 when the appeals law went into full effect, and is now *obsolete.[27]

★ ★ ★

§ 6.4 — Requesting your claims folder (C-file)

VA maintains a paper file called a claims folder (also known as a claims file or "C-file") for every veteran and qualifying family member who files a claim for benefits. C-files contain a veteran's active duty service and treatment records, applications for benefits, appointments of claims representatives forms, correspondences with the veteran, C&P exam requests and reports, and more. VA claims adjudicators base their decisions on the records contained in the C-file. **When a claim is denied, it is extremely important for veterans and advocates to know what records and evidence the VA relied on to make its decision—these records are contained in the C-file.** Proceeding on appeal without a C-file is like going into battle totally blind and is highly ill-advised.

Veterans Benefits Management System (VBMS) —

The VA operates its own web-based information technology ("IT") platform called the Veterans Benefits Management System ("VBMS") which it uses to process all claims for benefits.[28] VBMS is essentially a giant database that gives claims adjudicators easy access to records and information in order to make a decision on a claim. VBMS was first deployed nationwide to all VA Regional Offices in 2012 as part of modernizing efforts to move towards paperless claims processing (for VA adjudicators), eliminate the backlog of claims, and allow for quicker, more

---

[27] Dept. of Veterans Affairs. *VA's Rapid Appeals Modernization Program to end ahead of implementation of new Veteran appeals law.* [release] (14 Feb. 2019) https://web.archive.org/web/20200830162018/https://www.va.gov/opa/pressrel/pressrelease.cfm?id=5203.

[28] Dept. of Veterans Affairs. *VA hits milestone with Electronic Claims Processing Program.* 9 March 2017. [VA blog] https://web.archive.org/web/20181128110814/https://www.blogs.va.gov/VAntage/35749/va-hits-milestone-electronic-claims-processing-program/; see M21-1 III.ii.3.B.1.d. Establishing Claims in VBMS.

accurate and uniform claims processing.[29] In additional to a physical paper file folders, veterans' C-files are also stored electronically in the VBMS system. As such, C-files are accessible through VBMS. While there is no legal right to remote VBMS access[30], accredited VSO service officers/ advocates, attorneys and claims agents may request VBMS access on behalf of veterans that they represent.

★ ★ ★

3 Ways of Requesting a Veteran's C-file —

Veterans and duly appointed claims representatives are permitted by VA regulation to view a veteran's C-file.[31] All requests for copies of C-file records must be made in writing.[32]

1. Veteran may request their own C-file

Veterans may request their own C-file in paper or electronic PDF form either in-person at their VA Regional Office or by USPS mail. There is no duplication fee for veterans who request a copy of their own records.[33]

- **In-Person at VA Regional Office ("Veteran Waiting")**

Manual M21-1, III.ii.4.C.2.a. **Definition: Veteran-Waiting Case**

A veteran may visit their VA Regional Office in-person to view and copy their paper claims folder/C-file. VA calls this a "Veteran-waiting case" because the veteran is literally waiting in the office for the file, and a priority is placed on the request. In-person C-file requests can be made by veterans who file their own claims, as well as veterans who are represented

---

[29] Dept. of Veterans Affairs. *Department of Veterans Affairs Strategic Plan to Eliminate the Compensation Claims Backlog.* http://va-handbook.com/ va-strategic-plan-to-eliminate-the-compensation-claims-backlog/.

[30] *Green v. McDonald*, 28 Vet.App. 281, 282-83 (2016)

[31] 38 C.F.R. § 1.525. Inspection of records by or disclosure of information to recognized representatives of organizations and recognized attorneys.

[32] 38 C.F.R. § 1.526(a)

[33] 38 C.F.R. § 1.526(i)(2)

by accredited VSO claims advocates that have offices located within the VA Regional Office.

Veterans who make in-person C-file requests may be accompanied by one other person. However, a signed authorization form (or letter) granting disclosure of the records in the presence of the accompanying person is required. Also, "One VA official must be present at all times during the review of the record in order to ensure the integrity of the record."[34]

Keep in mind that veterans who wish to view their C-file records in-person still need to inform VA of their request. According to internal VA guidelines:

> When an individual elects to gain access to his or her records in person, that individual will be advised of a time, location, and the personal identification requirements for the granting of access.[35]

As such, to avoid delay and confusion veterans are advised to plan ahead and contact their VSO representative, if applicable, or their VA Regional Office about their desire to request to view their C-file and other records. Of course, walk-ins are facilitated, but could result in avoidable delays.

Manual M21-1, III.ii.4.C.2.b. Delivery of a Paper Claims Folder in a Veteran-Waiting Case

---

- **By USPS Mail**

  ♣ VA Form 3288 — *Request For and Consent to Release Information From Individual's Records*

Veterans can also request a copy of their C-file by mail using VA Form 3288, *Request For and Consent to Release Information From Individual's Records.* In the "Information Requested" section, veterans can request their C-file by stating the following:

I hereby request a copy of all of the records, files and documents that

---

[34] VA Handbook 6300.4 (19 Aug. 2013) Procedures for Processing Requests for Records Subject to the Privacy Act.

[35] VA Handbook 6300.4, § 3(d)(3)

are contained in my VA claims folder ("C-file") including all records contained in my paper claims folder, as well as all temporary and electronic claims files stored by VA computer systems. Please send me these records in [paper / PDF] form.

Once complete, mail (or fax) the finished VA Form 3288 to the closest VA Regional Office. If no response is received, veterans may consider contacting their U.S. Senators and Representative for assistance. VA is generally extremely responsive to Members of Congress who submit inquiries on behalf of veteran constituents.

★ ★

2. VSO service officers may review/request C-file

Veterans Service Organizations ("VSOs") such as the Veterans of Foreign Wars ("VFW"), American Veterans ("AMVETS"), Vietnam Veterans of America ("VVA"), Military Order of the Purple Heart ("MOPH"), Paralyzed Veterans of America ("PVA"), Disabled Veterans of America ("DVA"), Wounded Warrior Project ("WWP"), and all State Departments of Veterans Affairs maintain offices in the largest VA Regional Offices in every state.[36] Veterans who live in larger cities thus enjoy the convenience of having access to VSO claims advocates (called "service officers") inside their VA Regional Office—with the ability to request in-office delivery of a veteran's C-file.

- **VSO Access to VBMS Electronic PDF C-file**

Accredited Veterans Service Organization service officers may access a veteran's electronic C-file through VBMS. To grant VSO access, a veteran must first submit the necessary signed authorization form, which is stored in the veteran's claims folder: VA Form 21-22, *Appointment of Veterans Service Organization as Claimant's Representative.*

---

[36] U.S. Department of Veterans Affairs. *VSOs at Regional Benefit Offices.* Accredited Representatives. https://web.archive.org/web/20200831150100/https://www.benefits.va.gov/vso/varo.asp.

- **VSO Access to Paper Folder C-file**

Manual M21-1, III.ii.4.C.2.c. **Request for a Paper
Claims Folder by a Service Organization**

In addition, VSOs with offices inside a VA Regional Office can also request for the veteran's paper claims folder to be physically delivered to the VSO office. When a VSO requests in-office delivery of a veteran's paper folder C-file, as long as the veteran has a signed VA Form 21-22 on file, the C-file will be delivered to the VSO office. If a veteran is presently waiting for the C-file/folder, VA will expedite the request.[37]

Manual M21-1, III.ii.4.C.1.b. **Delivery of Paper
Claims Folders to Service Organizations**

★ ★

3. Duly Appointed Attorneys and Claims Agents

- **In-Person at VA Regional Office**

Accredited attorneys and claims agents may request in-person access to a veteran's paper claims folder or electronic C-file at the appropriate VA Regional Office.[38] As with VSO service officers, attorneys and claims agents must have specific authorization from the veteran with a signed VA Form 21-22a, *Appointment of Individual as Claimant's Representative.* As long as the attorney/claims agent has been authorized by the veteran, they may view the C-file at a designated location within VA the Regional Office. The U.S. Court of Appeals for Veterans Claims ("CAVC") has ruled that there is no recognized legal right to remote VBMS access for private practitioners.[39]

---

[37] M21-1, III.ii.4.C.2.b. <u>Delivery of a Paper Claims Folder in a Veteran-Waiting Case.</u>

[38] 38 C.F.R. § 1.525

[39] *Green v. McDonald*, 28 Vet.App. 281, 282-83 (2016)

Tyson Manker

- **Remote Access to VBMS Electronic PDF C-file**

Attorneys and claims agents may still request and receive remote VBMS access to view their veteran clients' C-files, monitor claims, view appointment schedules, and more. Only accredited attorneys and claims agents who have been properly designated by one or more veterans to represent them in their claim (or appeal) may receive remote access to VBMS.

**Although legal interns, law students, and paralegals are permitted in some circumstances to assist in the preparation, presentation and prosecution of a claim for benefits (*see* 38 C.F.R. § 14.629(c)(3)), only accredited attorneys and claims agents may access VBMS and other VA information systems.[40]

In order to access VBMS online, all accredited attorneys and claims agents must first be issued a Personal Identification Verification ("PIV") badge. VA only issues PIV badges to individuals who are:

1. Accredited by VA's Office of General Counsel ("OGC") to represent Veterans as a claims agent, attorney, or employee of a Veterans Service Organization; and
2. Designated by one or more veterans to represent him or her in pursuing a claim or appeal for VA benefits.

The security requirements for VBA systems access are:

- Fingerprinting (favorable outcome);
- Office of Personnel Management (OPM) background investigation (initiated);
- Completed information security training;
- Completed Optional Form (OF) - 306, Declaration of Federal Employment, and
- Signed Rules of Behavior (ROB).

---

[40] *Individuals Accredited by the Department of Veterans Affairs Using Veterans Benefits Administration Information Technology Systems To Access VBA Records Relevant to a Claim While Representing a Claimant Before the Agency.* 85 Fed. Reg. 9435 (2 Feb. 2020) https://www.federalregister.gov/d/2020-03196.

Upon successful adjudication of the background investigation and issuance of a PIV badge, VA will grant access to the VA network and to the Veterans Benefits Management System ("VBMS"). An individual granted access to VBMS will have a user role of "POA" and will be associated with the electronic records of veterans he or she represents. To request remote access, accredited representatives should submit to their assigned Change Management Agent ("CMA") at the closest regional office:

♣ OF-306, **Declaration of Federal Employment**;

and

♣ VA Form 20-0344, **Annual Certification of Veterans Status and Veteran-Relatives.**

★ ★

• **By USPS Mail**

Duly appointed attorneys and claims agents may also mail a request for a paper or digital PDF copy of a veteran's C-file. Written requests should be sent to VA's Claims Intake Center in Janesville, Wisconsin. (see Sample Attorney/Claims Agent C-file request below). Attorneys and agents should be sure to include mandatory authorization forms signed by the veteran with their request.

★ ★ ★

SAMPLE ATTORNEY/CLAIMS AGENT C-FILE REQUEST

Department of Veterans Affairs
Claims Intake Center
P.O. Box 4444
Janesville, WI 53547-4444

Re: Susan Veteran
VA Claim Number: 55 555 5555

Tyson Manker

Dear Sir or Ma'am:

This is a request for records under the Privacy Act, 5 U.S.C. § 552a, and 38 C.F.R. §§ 1.525, 1.526, and 1.577 on behalf of Susan Veteran. I am Mrs. Veteran's duly appointed representative. On September 1, 2020, Mrs. Veteran authorized the release of her Department of VA records by executing VA Form 21-22a, a copy of which is attached.

Therefore, I request a copy of all records and documents contained in Mrs. Veteran's VA claims file, including any and all paper and electronic claims folders and eFolders. I hereby request these records [in paper form / electronically in PDF form].

Please send Mrs. Veteran's claims file records to me within twenty business days at 123 Main Street, City, State, Zip.

Sincerely,
Signed

★ ★ ★

SAMPLE BVA DECISION

The following is a February 28, 2019 Board of Veterans Appeals decision out of the Roanoke, VA Regional Office. Like all BVA decisions, it can be found online by searching the Board decision database with the case citation number: 19114940.

BVA database: https://www.index.va.gov/search/va/bva.jsp
(link to BVA database also found at va-handbook.com)

Citation Nr: 19114940
Decision Date: 02/28/19
DOCKET NO. 15-35 571A

ORDER

The claim of entitlement for service connection for malignant skin neoplasms (hereinafter referred to as skin cancer) is dismissed.

The claim of entitlement to an evaluation of 70 percent, but no higher, for posttraumatic stress order (PTSD) is granted.

The claim of entitlement of total a disability rating based on individual unemployability due to service connected disabilities (TDIU) is granted.

FINDINGS OF FACT

1. In the Appellate Brief submitted by the Veteran's counsel, prior to promulgation of a decision in the appeal, the Board received notification from the Veteran that a withdrawal of the appeal for skin cancer is requested.
2. During the entire period on appeal, the Veteran's PTSD has been associated with symptoms of such severity as to result in occupational and social impairment with deficiencies in most areas; the evidence has not reflected symptoms of such severity as to result in total occupational and social impairment at any time during the pendency of the appeal.
3. The combination of the Veteran's disabilities precluded him from maintaining substantially gainful employment.

CONCLUSIONS OF LAW

(1) The criteria for withdrawal of an issue on appeal by the Veteran have been met. 38 U.S.C. § 7105(b)(2), (d)(5) (2012); 38 C.F.R. §20.204 (2018).

(2) The criteria to establish entitlement to an evaluation in excess of 70 percent, but no higher, for PTSD have been met. 38 U.S.C. §§ 1155, 5107 (2012); 38 C.F.R. §§ 4.1, 4.2, 4.7, 4.130, Diagnostic Code (DC) 9411 (2018).

(3) The criteria to establish a claim of entitlement to TDIU have been met. 38 U.S.C. §§ 1114, 1155, 5107 (2012); 38 C.F.R. §§ 3.340, 3.341, 4.1, 4.2, 4.3, 4.16(a) (2018).

Reasons and Bases For Findings and Conclusions

The Veteran had honorable active duty service with the United States Army from October 1964 to July 1966. The Veteran had active duty service in the Republic of Vietnam and was awarded a Combat Infantry Badge, the Vietnam Service Medal, and the National Defense Medal.

These matters are before the Board of Veteran's Appeals (Board) from an April 2011 rating decision of the Department of Veterans Affairs (VA) Regional Office (RO) in Roanoke, Virginia, which granted service connection for PTSD at 50 percent disabling effective April 15, 2011.

The Board notes that the Veteran has, through counsel, submitted a brief in lieu of having a Board hearing that was scheduled for October 4, 2018. See Appellate Brief dated November 12, 2018.

While the issue of TDIU was on appeal, the Veteran's Substantive Appeal, Form 9, clearly limited the issues before the Board to only the claim for an increased rating for PTSD. Nonetheless, as a TDIU is inherently part of a claim for an increased rating, and the Veteran's representative indicated a belief in a November 2018 statement that this issue was still on appeal, the Board will proceed to adjudicate the issue of entitlement to TDIU benefits as well.

Entitlement to service connection for skin cancer

The Board may dismiss any appeal which fails to allege specific error of fact or law in the determination being appealed. 38 U.S.C. § 7105. An appeal may be withdrawn as to any or all issues involved in the appeal at any time before the Board promulgates a decision. 38 C.F.R. § 20.204.

Withdrawal may be made by the veteran or by his or her authorized representative. 38 C.F.R. § 20.204. In the present case, the Veteran's counsel submitted an Appellate Brief on November 12, 2018, which included a statement specifically withdrawing the issue of skin cancer and did not wish to pursue an appeal with respect to that issue.

The Board finds that this written statement constitutes an explicit and unambiguous withdrawal of the issue of entitlement to service connection for skin cancer. Again, the Veteran is represented by counsel and, thus, the Board finds that the withdrawal was done with a full understanding of the consequences of such action. *DeLisio v. Shinseki*, 25 Vet.App. 45, 57 (2011); 38 C.F.R. § 20.204 (2017); see also *Acree v. O'Rourke*, 891 F.3d 1009 (2018).

Hence, there remain no allegations of fact or law for appellate consideration with respect to the claim of service connection for a skin cancer. Under these circumstances, the issue is no longer within the Board's jurisdiction. See *Hamilton v. Brown*, 4 Vet.App. 528 (1993) (en banc) aff'd, 39 F.3d 1574 (Fed. Cir. 1994) (holding that the Board is without the authority to proceed on an issue if the claimant indicates that consideration of that issue should cease).

Accordingly, there remain no allegations of errors of fact or law for appellate consideration. As such, the Board does not have jurisdiction to review the appeal for skin cancer and it is dismissed.

Entitlement to an evaluation of 70%, but no higher, for PTSD

The Veteran and his counsel contend that the Veteran is entitled to an increased rating of 70 percent for the entire period on appeal.

Disability ratings are determined by applying the criteria set forth in VA's Schedule for Rating Disabilities. The percentage ratings are based on the average impairment of earning capacity and individual disabilities are assigned separate diagnostic codes (DCs). 38 U.S.C. § 1155; 38 C.F.R. § 4.1.

When there is a question between two evaluations, the higher evaluation will be assigned if the disability picture more nearly approximates the criteria required for that rating. 38 C.F.R. § 4.7. Any reasonable doubt regarding a degree of disability will be resolved in favor of the Veteran. 38 C.F.R. § 4.3.

The VA must consider all favorable lay evidence of record. 38 U.S.C. § 5107(b). Lay testimony is competent to establish the presence of observable symptomatology, where the determination is not medical in nature and is capable of lay observation and does not require specialized educations, training, or experience. See *Barr v. Nicholson*, 21 Vet.App. 303 (2007); 38 C.F.R. § 3.159 (2018).

When all the evidence is assembled, if there is a balance between positive and negative competent evidence then the issues shall be resolved in favor of the Veteran. 38 U.S.C. § 5107(b); 38 C.F.R. § 3.102 (2018).

Pursuant to *AB v. Brown*, 6 Vet.App. 35, (1993), the claimant will generally be presumed to be seeking the maximum benefit allowed by law and regulation, and it follows that such a claim remains in controversy where less than the maximum available benefit is awarded. The Veteran and counsel are contending that he is entitled to an increased rating of 70 percent. Through this opinion the Veteran is being granted an evaluation for his PTSD at 70 percent disabling, but no higher.

However, the award of an increased evaluation for PTSD at 100 percent disabling, is the maximum benefit available for the entire period on appeal.

Therefore, the Board finds that the maximum benefit has not been awarded and the Board will focus on the Veteran's lack of entitlement to a 100 percent disability rating for PTSD.

The Veteran was previously rated at 50 percent disabling for his PTSD. The next higher rating of 70 percent requires:

Occupational and social impairment, with deficiencies in most areas, such as work, school, family relations, judgment, thinking, or mood, due to such symptoms as: suicidal ideation; obsessional rituals which interfere with routine activities; speech intermittently illogical, obscure, or irrelevant; near-continuous panic or depression affecting the ability to function independently, appropriately and effectively; impaired impulse control (such as unprovoked irritability with periods of violence); spatial disorientation; neglect of personal appearance and hygiene; difficulty in adapting to stressful circumstances (including work or a worklike setting); inability to establish and maintain effective relationships. 38 C.F.R.§ 4.130, DC 9411.

Through this opinion the Veteran has been granted an increased rating to 70 percent disabling for his PTSD. The next highest rating is a 100 percent disabling, requires:

Total occupational and social impairment, due to such symptoms as: gross impairment in thought processes or communication; persistent delusions or hallucinations; grossly inappropriate behavior; persistent danger of hurting self or others; intermittent inability to perform activities of daily living (including maintenance of minimal personal hygiene); disorientation to time or place; memory loss for names of close relatives, own occupation, or own name. Id.

The Veteran was being treated at the Vet Center of West Virginia for PTSD and was provided with clinical update summaries by his treating medical practitioner. These summaries indicated that the Veteran's PTSD manifested as occupational and social deficiencies in most areas since the beginning of his treatment at the Vet Center.

The initial clinical update of March 2011 noted symptoms of memory impairment, sleep impairment, nightmares, irritability, angry outbursts, anxiety, memory loss, concentration problems, depression, emotional numbing, and flashbacks. The Veteran is only noted as having social and occupational impairment, but not at what level, but his PTSD was noted as chronic and severe, with recurrent major depression. This initial evaluation of the Veteran, does not clearly indicate the level of occupational and social impairment of the Veteran.

However, the clinical update summary of November 2011 indicated clearly that the Veteran exhibited occupational and social impairment with deficiencies in most areas. The summary indicated that the Veteran had few friends and relied on his long-term wife heavily for support. The summary indicated as well that the Veteran's diagnosis "basically remains unchanged since my last clinical summary update", from March 2011.

The clinical update summaries of the Veteran in March 2013 and May 2014 indicated symptoms reported by the Veteran's wife of severe mood swings, continuous anxiety and depression, outbursts of anger, restlessness, intrusive thoughts, difficulty concentrating, chronically depressed, memory impairment, panic attacks twice a week, problems adapting to stressful circumstances which result with behavior of avoidance and isolation. The Veteran was found to have difficulty establishing and maintaining effective relationships, with few friends and again relying heavily on his wife. A discussion of inpatient treatment was indicated in the March 2013 summary due to the level of severity of PTSD symptoms and the as indicated, the Veteran's functioning had worsened in the May 2014 update.

The clinical update summaries of September 2015 and November 2017 indicated symptoms of the Veteran's chronic and severe PTSD as occupational and social impairment with deficiencies in most areas. The mental health practitioner of the Veteran noted his inability to establish and maintain effective relationships, found issues with spatial distortion, and neglect of his personal hygiene without the instance of his wife.

The summary from September 2015 indicated the Veteran was awaiting trial for an assault and that his PTSD symptoms combined with his other medical problems made it impossible for him to hold any occupation. The summary from November 2017 indicated that the Veteran's functioning had grown increasingly worse in the last 5 years but basically remained unchanged since his last summary in 2015. The Veteran was noted as having fewer hobbies due to his physical limitations and few friends.

The Board finds the clinical update summaries of March 2011, November 2011, March 2013, May 2014, September 2015, and November 2017 to be competent, credible, and of significant probative weight. The summaries are based off the regular treatment of the Veteran and regular exposure of the treating mental health practitioner to the Veteran over the span of six years and continuing. This allowed the mental health practitioner to provide a fuller and clearer picture of the Veteran's severity, frequency, and duration of symptoms.

The Veteran's initial VA examination in May 2011 noted that the Veteran had been diagnosed with PTSD and Major Depression by the Veteran's mental health practitioner. The VA examiner noted symptoms of impairment in social, occupational, or other important areas of functioning. The Veteran was also found to have disturbances of motivation and mood with obsessional rituals which interfere with routine activities, and homicidal ideations, with indications of an attempted assault of a neighbor in November 2010. The Veteran indicated that he had weapons for every vehicle and every room. The Veteran also indicated that he went to church six times per year, went out to eat once per month with his wife, and went camping alone once per year. The Veteran was found to have occupational and social impairment with occasional decrease in work efficiency.

The next VA examination for PTSD was in October 2014, which indicated that the Veteran was living with his wife; that his granddaughter and her husband were also living with them. The VA examiner noted that their relationship was good, and his relationship with his two daughters was also good. It was noted that the Veteran's main friend had passed away five years ago and he went to church sometimes, with only one hobby of motorcycle riding when his hips allowed him to ride. The Veteran noted that he no longer fished, no longer went camping, and had sold his livestock. The VA examiner noted that the Veteran had gotten into a physical fight with a stranger in spring 2014 during a traffic issue, but no charges were filed. The Veteran was found to be occupationally and socially impaired with reduced reliability and productivity.

The VA examination of November 2016 noted the Veteran's symptoms of disturbances of mood and motivation and difficulty establishing and maintaining effective work and social relationships. Since the last VA examination, the Veteran was also charged with assaulting his granddaughter's boyfriend in 2015, however the charges were dropped. The Veteran was found to be occupationally and socially impaired with reduced reliability and productivity.

The VA examinations of May 2011, October 2014, and November 2016, are found to be competent and credible. However, when viewing all of the evidence of record in its totality, the Board finds that these examinations carry less probative weight, as the Veteran's mental health practitioner from the Vet Center provided regular and consistent clinical update summaries as discussed above that provided a fuller picture due to the Veteran's consistent treatment with the same mental health practitioner. This regular treatment allowed this practitioner more time to get to know the Veteran and gauge the Veteran's full disability picture.

The Veteran received a private psychological evaluation in November 2018, which found that the Veteran was occupationally and socially impaired with deficiencies in most areas. The Veteran's symptoms were noted as depressed mood, suspiciousness, sleep impairment, memory loss, impaired abstract thinking, disturbances of mood and motivation, difficulty in establishing and maintaining effective work and social relationships, impaired impulse control, suicidal ideations, and difficulty adapting to stress. The Veteran was noted as still being marred and their relationship being "better than ever" and having two children who "are doing well".

The Board finds the private psychological evaluation to be competent, credible, with some probative weight. The evaluator went through the criteria for PTSD and had an extensive interview with the Veteran to be able to provide a clear picture of the Veteran's severity of his disability, but does not provide the same level of detail as the Veteran's mental health practitioner.

The Veteran's lay statements in his treatment records of his flashbacks, nightmares, and issues with his anger, and other symptoms are found to be competent and credible as they are consistent and clearly observable symptoms, with significant probative weight. The Veteran's daughter's statement also indicated memory problems and suffering severally from PTSD, with daily struggles. These statements are found to be competent and credible, with some probative weight as there are no specifics regarding the Veteran's symptoms except for his memory issues, nightmares, and emotional sensitivity, but no indications of when or how often these occurred.

The Board finds that the Veteran is not entitled to the highest rating of 100 percent for his PTSD, however, as his symptoms are not of such severity as to have resulted in total occupational and social impairment. He has been married to the same person for over 50 years in which he described the last three years as having been better than ever. The Veteran has a large family of 2 children, 4 grandchildren, and 3 great-grandchildren, as of November 2016. The Veteran has a friend with whom he visits the country store for coffee and has done some altruistic work with Veterans. He also spends time with his grandson watching dirt track racing. See VA examination November 2016 and private psychological evaluation November 2018.

The Board finds that the Veteran's disability picture more closely manifested as 70 percent disabling throughout the entire appeal period with noted symptoms of obsessional rituals which interfere with routine activities, continuous depression affecting the ability to function independently, impaired impulse control, difficulty adapting to stressful circumstances, and inability to establish and maintain effective relationships. The Veteran's assaulting people, homicidal ideations, paranoia, and weapons in every room and vehicle more closely resemble a 70 percent rating for his PTSD.

The Board notes that the Veteran continues his individual and group therapy, as of November 2018.

When there is an approximate balance between positive and negative evidence the benefit of the doubt doctrine must apply in favor of the Veteran. But when the preponderance of the evidence weighs against the claims of the Veteran the claim will be denied on the merits. When the preponderance of the evidence weights for the claims of the Veteran the claim will be granted on its merits.

As indicated in this opinion, the Veteran is receiving only a partial grant of a 70 percent increased rating, but no higher. The remainder of the Veteran's claim for a 100 percent rating is denied. The evidence before the Board here indicated that the Veteran's claims must be partially granted and partially denied, and the benefit of the doubt doctrine is inapplicable. 38 U.S.C. § 5107; *Gilbert v. Derwinski*, 1 Vet.App. 49 (1990).

Therefore, the Veteran's PTSD is entitled to an increased evaluation of 70 percent, but no higher, for the entire period on appeal.

Entitlement to a TDIU

The Board notes that the record of the Veteran indicated that a claim for TDIU was initially filed in May 2013, was denied by a rating decision in January 2014, was then re-opened in the rating decision of December 2014 and denied again. TDIU was included in the Statement of the Case issued in September 2015 which was denied for lack of meeting the schedular criteria. However, the request to re-open the claim of TDIU was filed in October 2016, and the issue was reopened in a rating decision of February 2017 and denied again. The Veteran filed a Notice of Disagreement (NOD) in March 2017, and while not specifically noted in his substantive appeal, as previously discussed, the Board finds that this issue is properly before the Board for appellate consideration.

The Veteran contends that he is entitled to an evaluation of TDIU; however, even if he did not, the claim is reasonably raised by the record. See *Rice v Shinseki*, 11 Vet.App. 447 (2009); see also *Moore v. Shinseki*, 555 F.3d 1369, 1373 (Fed. Cir. 2009).

Entitlement to a TDIU requires the presence of impairment so severe that it is impossible for the average person to follow a substantially gainful occupation. See 38 U.S.C. § 1155; 38 C.F.R. §§ 3.340, 3.341, 4.16. In reaching such a determination, the central inquiry is "whether the Veteran's service-connected disabilities alone are of sufficient severity to produce unemployability." See *Hatlestead v. Brown*, 5 Vet.App. 524, 529 (1993). Consideration may be given to the Veteran's level of education, special training and previous work experience in arriving at a conclusion, but not to age or to the impairment caused by nonservice-connected disabilities. See 38 C.F.R. §§ 3.341, 4.16, 4.19 (2018).

Where the schedular rating is less than total, a total disability rating for compensation purposes may be assigned when the disabled person is unable to secure or follow a substantially gainful occupation as a result of service-connected disabilities, provided that, if there is only one such disability, this disability shall be ratable at 60 percent or more, or if there are two or more disabilities, there shall be at least one ratable at 40 percent or more, and sufficient additional disability to bring the combined rating to 70 percent or more. 38 C.F.R. §§ 3.340, 3.341, 4.16(a).

The Board notes that with this opinion the Veteran's PTSD is rated at 70 percent disabling effective the entire period on appeal, which would allow him to meet the schedular criteria of TDIU.

The Veteran was already service connected for PTSD at 50 percent disabling, effective as of April 2011. With the Veteran's PTSD rating of 50 percent, the diabetes mellitus type II rated at 20 percent, peripheral neuropathy left lower extremity associated with diabetes mellitus type II rated at 20 percent, strongyloidiasis rated at 10 percent, peripheral neuropathy right lower extremity associated with diabetes mellitus type II rated at 10 percent, tinnitus associated with bilateral hearing loss rated at 10 percent, malaria rated at 0 percent, and bilateral hearing loss rated at 10 percent, he meets the schedular criteria for TDIU. 38 C.F.R. § 4.16(a).

Accordingly, the remaining issue is whether the Veteran's service-connected PTSD and his other service-connect disabilities listed above precluded the Veteran from securing and following a substantially gainful occupation. See 38 C.F.R. § 4.16(b). The fact that a veteran is unemployed or has difficulty finding employment does not alone warrant assignment of a TDIU, as a high rating itself establishes that his disability makes it difficult for him to obtain and maintain employment. *Van Hoose v. Brown*, 4 Vet.App. 361, 363 (1993).

The Board notes that the Veteran's last employment was as a truck driver from 1987 to 2007, the Board notes that he did have part-time truck driving work from October 2012 to March 2013. The Veteran had previous training as a truck driver. His employment as a truck driver required driving large vehicles and allowed him to be alone with little interaction with the public and co-workers. The Veteran has had difficulty with social interactions and regularly avoided leaving his home, he also has had physical altercations in the past, one due to a situation in traffic while he was driving in 2010. The Veteran dropped out of school after 10th grade, did not get his General Education Diploma (GED), and has had no further vocational training.

The issues of employment and employability are addressed in the clinical updates of the Veteran's therapeutic care from his mental health practitioner, the May 2014 psychiatric evaluation, the VA examinations of the Veteran, the medical treatment records of the Veteran on his individual and group therapy submitted in November 2011, and throughout the records of the Veteran.

There are consistent statements made throughout the Veteran's medical records on his inability to secure and maintain employment such as in March 2015 when the mental health practitioner noted that the Veteran's dispatcher and terminal manager at work said he was a ticking time bomb and would explode any moment. See Buddy Statement submitted November 2015.

The clinical updates of the Veteran's mental health practitioner in November 2011 and March 2013 indicated he would benefit from in-patient care. The May 2014 clinical update indicated that the Veteran's impairment had worsened since his last clinical update in March 2013.

The psychiatric evaluation of May 2014 indicated that the Veteran did not appear to be able to tolerate much stress or handle any gainful employment. In the clinical update of September 2015, it was indicated that due to the Veteran's PTSD symptoms combined with his other medical problems make it "impossible for him to hold down any occupation." In the clinical update of November 2017, the mental health practitioner indicated that the Veteran was not able to work due to his PTSD, that his medication alone impaired his concentration and focus, which affected his ability for any type of gainful employment. This was confirmed by Dr. D., a psychiatrist who also evaluated the Veteran in May 2014 agreeing that the Veteran was unable to maintain gainful employment.

The VA examiner of November 2016 opined that a job requiring the veteran to be interacting with large numbers of people or exposed to large crowds would likely pose a problem. The VA examiner however indicated that he would likely be able to function adequately at a job that did not require contact with people.

The Veteran received a private Vocational Evaluation in October 2018 which indicated that the Veteran was not able to perform any type of substantial gainful occupation at any exertional level. The evaluation took into consideration his memory issues, his impulse control, his inability to stand or walk for a long period of time, his limited education, his inability to remain in a stationary position of either sitting or standing for longer than twenty to thirty minutes before changing positions, and considered his other service-connected disabilities. The evaluator indicated that the vocational limitations were severe and that he was not employable in any occupation.

Although it is conceivable that there may be some occupations that the Veteran could have performed with accommodations, the totality of the evidence supports a finding that his service-connected PTSD and other service-connected disabilities rendered him unable to obtain and maintain a substantially gainful occupation when his educational and work background are taken into consideration.

The Board finds that the evidence is at least in equipoise as to whether the Veteran's PTSD rendered him unemployable. The VA examiners and the Veteran's regular mental health practitioner did not clearly conclude that the Veteran's PTSD resulted in total occupational impairment until September 2015; however, this does not preclude a finding that PTSD substantially affects employment. The evidence of record shows that the Veteran's PTSD symptoms had a significant effect on his ability to work. Given the impairment produced by his PTSD, it appears that the Veteran would not have been capable of more than marginal employment in any type of work setting. See *Ortiz-Valles v. McDonald*, 28 Vet.App. 65, 72 (2016).

Thus, the Board will resolve reasonable doubt in the Veteran's favor and find that he was unable to secure or follow a substantially gainful occupation as a result of his service-connected PTSD for the entire period on appeal. 38 U.S.C. § 5107, 38 C.F.R. § 4.16. Therefore, entitlement to a TDIU is warranted.

[end]

★ ★ ★

Chapter 7

Help Filing a Claim

Many veterans file and appeal their own claims. However, millions more (including the author) choose to enlist help from an accredited claims representative. Generally, veterans and qualifying family members have three options to assist with the filing of a VA claim:

1. Veterans Service Organization (**FREE**)[1]
2. Attorney
3. Claims Agent

Veterans Service Organizations like VFW, AMVETS, DAV and American Legion employ thousands of claims representatives (called "claims officers" or "service officers") whose sole purpose is to help veterans file VA claims at no cost to the veteran. In addition, nearly all State Departments of Veterans Affairs, and many local governments also provide accredited claims representatives free of charge. When it comes to identifying benefits and collecting all of the evidence necessary to prevail on a claim, few people are more capable or dedicated to veterans they serve than experienced claim representatives/advocates (many are themselves veterans).

Attorneys and **Claims Agents** can also help file claims, but are forbidden by law from charging a fee for their services before an Agency of Original Jurisdiction ("AOJ") has issued an original ratings decision.

---

[1] 38 C.F.R. §14.636(b). (VSOs and VSO service officers are "not permitted to receive fees")

Thus, *if an attorney helps a veteran file their **original claim**, it must be pro bono, free of charge.* As a result, most lawyers and non-lawyer agents begin representing veterans with their claims only after a decision or denial has been rendered, on appeal. Of course, legal representation is also more common at the Court of Appeals for Veterans Claims, where attorneys are authorized to charge reasonable fees for their services, which are in some cases reimbursable under the Equal Access to Justice Act ("EAJA"). *see* Section 7.6.3, EAJA Fees)

★ ★ ★

§ 7.1 — Accreditation[2]

Manual M21-1, I.3.C.3.b. **Checking Accreditation**

In order to represent veterans before the VA, VA requires all individuals to be "accredited," which means they have received special training and have the necessary competency and skills to assist veterans with their claims.[3] As VA regulations make clear, the ultimate goal of accreditation is "to ensure that claimants for Department of Veterans Affairs (VA) benefits have responsible, qualified representation in the preparation, presentation, and prosecution of claims for veterans' benefits."[4] Guidelines for accreditation eligibility are set by the VA Secretary through the Office of General Counsel.[5] For more information on VA accreditation, Google search "VA Accreditation" or visit VA's accreditation website va.gov/ogc/accred_faqs.asp.

★ ★ ★

---

[2] 38 C.F.R. § 14.627(a); https://www.va.gov/ogc/accreditation.asp
[3] 38 U.S.C. § 5901; 38 C.F.R. § 14.629
[4] 38 C.F.R. § 14.626; 38 U.S.C. § 5904(a)(1)
[5] 38 U.S.C. § 5904

§ 7.2 — Veterans Service Organization Representation[6]

National Veterans Service Organizations ("VSOs") offer a variety of services for veterans and have VA-accredited representatives who **help file VA disability claims for free**. In fact, VSOs and their accredited service officers are prohibited by law from charging a fee for any of their services. In some cases, veterans may already be a member of the VSO that they authorize to represent them. However, membership is not required, and all VSOs offer free claims representation to non-members. According to VA, the following national VSOs have been "recognized" and are qualified to provide free assistance with claims for VA disability and other benefits:

African American PTSD Association
American Legion
American Red Cross
AMVETS
American Ex-Prisoners of War, Inc.
American GI Forum, National Veterans Outreach Program
Armed Forces Services Corporation
Army and Navy Union, USA
Associates of Vietnam Veterans of America
Blinded Veterans Association
Catholic War Veterans of the U.S.A.
Disabled American Veterans
Fleet Reserve Association
Gold Star Wives of America, Inc.
Italian American War Veterans of the United States, Inc.
Jewish War Veterans of the United States
Legion of Valor of the United States of America, Inc.
Marine Corps League
Military Officers Association of America (MOAA)
Military Order of the Purple Heart
National Amputation Foundation, Inc.
National Association of County Veterans Service Officers, Inc,
National Association for Black Veterans, Inc.
National Veterans Legal Services Program

---

[6] 38 C.F.R. § 14.628(a)

National Veterans Organization of America
Navy Mutual Aid Association
Paralyzed Veterans of America, Inc.
Polish Legion of American Veterans, U.S.A.
Swords to Plowshares, Veterans Rights Organization, Inc.
The Retired Enlisted Association
The Veterans Assistance Foundation, Inc.
The Veterans of the Vietnam War, Inc.
The Veterans Coalition
United Spanish War Veterans of the United States
United Spinal Association, Inc.
Veterans of Foreign Wars of the United States
Veterans of World War I of the U.S.A., Inc.
Vietnam Era Veterans Association
Vietnam Veterans of America
West Virginia Department of Veterans Assistance
Wounded Warrior Project

VA accredits individual members of recognized veterans service organizations who receive special training to represent veterans with claims before the VA. Before a VSO service officer can legally assist with a claim, the organization must file a VA Form 21, *Application for Accreditation as Service Organization Representative*, for each person it wants to be accredited as a representative of the organization

Individuals employed by a Veterans Service Organization who want to apply for accreditation, use VA Form 21.

♣ VA Form 21 — **Application for Accreditation as Service Organization Representative**

By filing a VA Form 21, Veterans Service Organizations must certify that each applicant[7]:

1. Is of good character and reputation and has demonstrated an ability to represent claimants before the VA;

---

[7] 38 C.F.R. § 14.629(a)

2. Is either a member in good standing or a paid employee of such organization working not less than 1,000 hours annually; is accredited and functioning as a representative of another recognized organization; or, in the case of a county veterans' service officer or tribal veterans' service officer recommended by a recognized State organization, meets the following criteria:

    i. Is a paid employee of the county or tribal government working for it not less than 1,000 hours annually;

    ii. Has successfully completed a course of training and an examination which have been approved by the appropriate District Chief Counsel; and

    iii. Will receive either regular supervision and monitoring or annual training to assure continued qualification as a representative in the claim process; and

    iv. Is not employed in any civil or military department or agency of the United States.

Once a VSO representative is accredited, they need authorization from each veteran that they assist. To grant such authorization, veterans must execute and submit VA Form 21-22.[8] Once VA receives the veteran's authorization, the VSO representative may advise and assist the veteran, access their electronic claim file history, and otherwise file documents and advocate on their behalf.

Veterans who want to appoint a VSO as their authorized claim representative use VA Form 21-22.

    ♣ VA Form 21-22—**Appointment of Veterans Service Organization as Claimant's Representative**

★ ★ ★

§ 7.3 — State Dept. of Veterans Affairs Representation[9]

All states have a Department (or equivalent) of Veterans Affairs and most states employ accredited claims representatives to help veterans and

---

[8] 38 C.F.R. § 14.629(a)

[9] 38 C.F.R. § 14.628(b)(1)

their dependents to file claims for benefits. In the author's home state of Illinois, for example, the Illinois Department of Veterans Affairs employs a number of VA claims officers across the state. These representatives generally work in offices that are shared with other state government agencies that administer public services. Some claims representatives are responsible for multiple counties and may travel with limited hours. For veterans who wish to utilize their public claims representative, find the local State-level VA office. Local public VA offices generally operate M-F 9am-5pm, but hours are days of availability may vary. For example, some State Department of Veterans Affairs representatives offer walk-ins from 9-12noon with scheduled appointments in the afternoon. The following states offer local and county-level accredited claims officers to help veterans file their claims for free.

Alabama
American Samoa
Arizona
Arkansas
California
Colorado
Connecticut
Delaware
Florida
Georgia
Guam
Hawaii
Idaho
Illinois
Iowa
Kansas
Kentucky
Louisiana
Maine
Maryland
Massachusetts
Michigan
Minnesota
Mississippi

Missouri
Montana
Nebraska
Nevada
New Hampshire
New Jersey
New Mexico
New York
North Carolina
North Dakota
Northern Mariana Islands
Ohio
Oklahoma
Oregon
Pennsylvania
Puerto Rico
Rhode Island
South Carolina
South Dakota
Tennessee
Texas
Utah
Vermont
Virginia
Virgin Islands
Washington
West Virginia
Wisconsin
Wyoming

★ ★ ★

§ 7.4 — Representation by Attorneys

Attorneys can represent veterans at any point in the disability claims process, however, they are prohibited by law from charging a fee for "services provided before the date on which a claimant is provided notice of the agency of original jurisdiction's initial decision."[10] Thus, while members of the bar can file claims *pro bono*, at no charge, the majority of attorneys generally do not get involved with VA claims after the VARO has issued a denial or insufficient rating.

Attorney | Accreditation Requirements —

Only attorneys who have been accredited by VA may assist, advise and otherwise represent veterans with their claims for VA benefits.[11] In order to receive accreditation, attorneys must apply to the Office of General Counsel ("OGC") by submitting:

1. Certificate of good standing to their State bar;
2. 3 hours of qualifying continuing legal education[12] (CLE) requirements during the first 12-month period following the date of initial accreditation by VA;
3. An additional 3 hours of continuing legal education no later than 3 years from the date of accreditation, and 3 hours of continuing legal education every 2 years thereafter.[13]

Attorneys and claims agents who want to apply for accreditation, use VA Form 21A.

> ♣ VA Form 21A — **Application for Accreditation as a Claims Agent or Attorney**

Once an attorney is accredited, they must have authorization from each veteran that they assist. To grant such authorization, veterans must execute and submit VA Form 21-22a, *Appointment of Attorney or Agent as*

---

[10] 38 U.S.C. § 5904(c)(1)

[11] 38 C.F.R. § 14.629(b)

[12] 38 C.F.R. § 14.629(b)(1)(iii). (To qualify ... a CLE course must be approved for a minimum of 3 hours of CLE credit by any State bar association and, at a minimum, must cover the following topics: representation before VA, claims procedures, basic eligibility for VA benefits, right to appeal, disability compensation (38 U.S.C. Chapter 11), dependency and indemnity compensation (38 U.S.C. Chapter 13), and pension (38 U.S.C. Chapter 15))

[13] 38 C.F.R. § 14.629(b)(1)(iv)

Claimant's Representative.[14] Once VA receives the veteran's authorization, the attorney may advise and assist the veteran, access their electronic claim file history, and otherwise file documents and advocate on their behalf.

<u>Veterans who want to appoint an attorney to represent them before the VA, use VA Form 21-22a.</u>

♣ VA Form 21A — **Appointment of Individual as Claimant's Representative**

> Manual M21-1, I.3.C.3.a. **Processing Required Based on Receipt of VA Form 21-22a**

★ ★ ★

§ 7.5 — Representation by Claims Agents

VA also permits authorized non-attorney "claims agents" with specialized training to assist and represent veterans with their claims for benefits. However, unlike licensed attorneys, who attend three years of law school followed by a two-day state administered bar examination, claims agents receive significantly less training. Thus, the process for claims agents to apply for accreditation is slightly different.

Claims Agent | Accreditation Requirements —

Only agents who have been accredited by VA may assist, advise and otherwise represent veterans with their claims for VA benefits.[15] In order to

---

[14] 38 C.F.R. § 14.629(c)(1)
[15] 38 C.F.R. § 14.629(b)

become accredited, claims agents must pass a written exam.[16] In addition, agents, like attorneys, must complete:

1. 3 hours of qualifying continuing legal education (CLE)[17] requirements during the first 12-month period following the date of initial accreditation by VA;

2. An additional 3 hours of continuing legal education no later than 3 years from the date of accreditation, and 3 hours of continuing legal education every 2 years thereafter.[18]

Claims agents who want to apply for accreditation, use VA form 21A.

> ♣ VA Form 21A — **Application for Accreditation**
> **as a Claims Agent or Attorney**

Veterans who want to appoint an attorney to represent them before the VA, use VA Form 21-22a.

> ♣ VA Form 21A — **Appointment of Individual**
> **as Claimant's Representative**

★ ★ ★

---

[16] 38 C.F.R. 14.629(b)(6). ("applicants for accreditation as a claims agent must achieve a score of 75 percent or more on a written examination administered by VA as a prerequisite to accreditation. No applicant shall be allowed to sit for the examination more than twice in any 6-month period")

[17] 38 C.F.R. § 14.629(b)(1)(iii). (In order to qualify ... a CLE course must be approved for a minimum of 3 hours of CLE credit by any State bar association and, at a minimum, must cover the following topics: representation before VA, claims procedures, basic eligibility for VA benefits, right to appeal, disability compensation (38 U.S.C. Chapter 11), dependency and indemnity compensation (38 U.S.C. Chapter 13), and pension (38 U.S.C. Chapter 15))

[18] 38 C.F.R. § 14.629(b)(1)(iv)

§ 7.6 — Fee Agreement (Contract)[19]

Before attorneys and claims agents can legally represent veterans before the VA they must first enter into a written contract, signed by both parties, that outlines the basic terms of their fee agreement. A copy of the written agreement must be filed with the VA before an attorney may proceed.[20]

Manual M21-1, I.3.C.3.c. Checking a Fee Agreement

To be valid, a fee agreement must be in writing and must contain:

1. The name of the veteran (or claimant);
2. (if applicable) The name of any disinterested third-party payer, and the relationship between the third-party payer and the veteran, claimant, or appellant;
3. The applicable VA file number; and
4. The specific terms under which the amount to be paid for the services of the attorney or agent will be determined

In addition, "fee agreements must also clearly specify if VA is to pay the agent or attorney directly out of past due benefits. A "direct-pay fee agreement" is a fee agreement between the claimant or appellant and an agent or attorney providing for payment of fees out of past-due benefits awarded directly to an agent or attorney."[21] When a direct-pay fee agreement directs the VA to pay the agent or attorney directly from past-due benefits, the total fee may not exceed twenty (20) percent of the past-due benefits awarded.[22] A copy of a direct-pay fee agreement must be filed with the agency of original jurisdiction (generally the VARO) within 30 days of its execution. A copy of any fee agreement that is not a direct-pay fee agreement must be filed with the Office of the General Counsel within 30 days of its execution.[23]

---

[19] 38 C.F.R. § 14.636(g)(2)

[20] 38 U.S.C. § 5904(c)(2)

[21] 38 C.F.R. § 14.636(g)(2)

[22] 38 U.S.C. § 5904(d)(1); 38 C.F.R. § 14.636(h)(1)(i)

[23] 38 C.F.R. § 14.636(g)(3)

Manual M21-1, I.3.C.1.c. **Definition: Direct Pay Fee Agreement**

Manual M21-1, I.3.C.1.d. **Additional Requirements** **for Direct Pay Fee Agreements**

Manual M21-1, I.3.C.1.e. **Fee Amount Permitted for Direct Payment of Fees**

Manual M21-1, I.3.C.1.f. **When a Direct Pay Fee Agreement Must Be Filed**

★ ★ ★

§ 7.7 — Fees[24]

VA regulations identify the circumstances under which attorneys and authorized claims agents may charge a fee for their services.[25] With regards to the amount charged, all fees "must be reasonable."[26]

Reasonable fees[27] are generally:

Fees which do not exceed 20 percent of any past-due benefits awarded ... shall be presumed to be reasonable if the agent or attorney provided representation that continued through the date of the decision awarding benefits.

Fees which exceed 331/3 percent of any past-due benefits awarded shall be presumed to be unreasonable. These presumptions may be

---

[24] For more than a century, from the Civil War until 1988, attorneys and claims agents were only permitted by law to charge veterans $10 for helping to file a disability claim. The Supreme Court, in *Walters v. Radiation Survivors*, 473 U.S. 305 (1985), discussed the ten-dollar fee at length. The fee cap, raised from $5 to $10 in 1864 where it remained for over 100 years, was originally put into place as a well-intended provision "to prevent the numerous frauds committed by pension agents." bit.ly/cg-37-2-2101.

[25] 38 C.F.R. § 14.636(c)

[26] 38 C.F.R. § 14.636(e)

[27] 38 C.F.R. § 14.636(f)

rebutted through an examination of the factors in paragraph (e) of this section establishing that there is clear and convincing evidence that a fee which does not exceed 20 percent of any past-due benefits awarded is not reasonable or that a fee which exceeds 331/3 percent is reasonable in a specific circumstance.

The mandatory fee agreement must identify the method of compensation. Fees may be based on a fixed fee, hourly rate, a percentage of benefits recovered, or a combination of such bases.[28] Factors that are considered when determining whether fees are reasonable include:

1. The extent and type of services the representative performed;
2. The complexity of the case;
3. The level of skill and competence required of the representative in giving the services;
4. The amount of time the representative spent on the case;
5. The results the representative achieved, including the amount of any benefits recovered;
6. The level of review to which the claim was taken and the level of the review at which the representative was retained;
7. Rates charged by other representatives for similar services;
8. Whether, and to what extent, the payment of fees is contingent upon the results achieved; and
9. If applicable, the reasons why an agent or attorney was discharged or withdrew from representation before the date of the decision awarding benefits.

★ ★

§ 7.7.1 — When Fees May Be Charged[29]

Attorneys and claims agents are prohibited by law from charging a fee for preparing and presenting a claim for benefits before an agency of original jurisdiction (generally the VARO) has rendered a decision.[30] Attorneys and

---

[28] 38 C.F.R. § 14.636(e)
[29] 38 C.F.R. § 14.636(c)
[30] 38 C.F.R. § 14.636(c)(1)(i)

claims agents are, however, permitted to charge a consultation fee for research and labor performed prior to the filing of a claim. According to the VA Office of General Counsel[31]:

Attorneys may charge veterans for pre-filing consultation without violation the fees limitation. [This might include] review of records, research, counseling, and any other assistance that a potential VA claimant might need short of actually preparing and presenting a specific claim for benefits. We are not aware of anything in the law governing representation of veterans that would prohibit attorneys from charging fees for this kind of pre-filing consultation.

In addition, restrictions on when an attorney or claims agent can charge a fee do not apply to payments made by "disinterested third-parties" such as friends or family of the veteran, as well as fees or a salary paid by a government agency or veterans service organization.[32]

★ ★

Review of Unreasonable Fees —

Veterans and claimants (or the OCG on its own motion) can challenge the reasonableness of a fee charged by a claims agent or attorney. No specific form is required so long as the fee review request is made in writing and identifies the veteran, VA claim number, attorney, and includes an explanation as to why the fee is thought to be unreasonable. When a veteran challenges the reasonableness of a fee, they must notify their attorney.

Manual M21-1, I.3.C.8.a. **What Is a Reasonableness Review**

★ ★

---

[31] U.S. Dept. of Veterans Affairs, Office of General Counsel. Letter from Tim McCain to Rep. Lane Evans. 24 May 2004. https://va-handbook.com/ogc-mcclain-evans-letter/.
[32] 38 C.F.R. § 14.636(d)(2)

§ 7.7.2 — CAVC | Fees and Fee Agreements

Fees and fee agreements for representation before the U.S. Court of Appeals for Veterans Claims (and the U.S. Court of Appeals for the Federal Circuit) have their own rules. As with representation before the VA, agents and attorneys must file a copy of their fee agreement with the CAVC under all circumstances, including pro bono representation.[33] Fees must be *reasonable*; Excessive fees may be reduced by the court.[34] While the term "reasonable" is not defined by statute or regulation, the CAVC has found contingency fees of twenty (20) and thirty percent to be reasonable and enforceable.[35]

Veterans can agree to pay attorneys and claims agents with any combination of the following methods:

- Flat fee
- Retainer/Hourly rate
- Contingency fee paid from past-due benefits (20% maximum)
- Equal Access to Justice Act fees (paid by VA)

★ ★

§ 7.7.3 — Equal Access to Justice Act Fees[36]

> Manual M21-1, I.3.C.5.i. **Handling Cases Involving EAJA Fees**

In the United States, litigants in civil lawsuits generally pay their own costs and attorney's fees. However, under the Equal Access to Justice Act of 1980 ("EAJA"), the CAVC and Federal Circuit may award reasonable attorney's fees to veterans who prevail (the "prevailing party") in cases where the VA's position was not "substantially justified." When a veteran

---

[33] 38 U.S.C. § 7263(c); U.S. Vet. App. Rules. 46(b)(1)(A)

[34] 38 U.S.C. § 7263(d)

[35] *In the Matter of the Fee Agreement of Vernon*, 8 Vet.App. 457, 459 (1996); *Carpenter v. Principi*, 15 Vet.App. 64 (2001) (*en banc*), *reconsideration denied*, 16 Vet.App. 102 (2002), *appeal dismissed for lack of jurisdiction*, 327 F.3d 1371 (Fed. Cir. 2003) (overruled on other grounds by *Ravin v. Wilkie*, 31 Vet.App. 104 (2019)

[36] 28 U.S.C. § 2412, et. seq.

prevails in an EAJA case, the VA (the "losing party") must cover their fees and costs. Thus, Equal Access to Justice Act fees are payments that a court has ordered VA to pay to an attorney for successful representation before the court.

Veterans (and counsel) who seek EAJA fees have the burden of demonstrating that they are the "prevailing party." In order to be the "prevailing party" the veteran must succeed "on any significant issue in litigation which achieve[d] some of the benefit ... sought in bringing suit."[37] Success does not require victory on every claim or issue. Rather, the veteran is generally considered a prevailing party where the CAVC either reverses the BVA decision on appeal, or vacates the BVA decision "predicated on an administrative error" for remand and further proceedings.[38]

Prevailing Party on Remand | 3-Part Test

In *Dover v. McDonald*[39], the U.S. Court of Appeals for the Federal Circuit, established a 3-part test to determine when a veteran who secures a remand from CAVC to the BVA is a "prevailing party" for the purposes of EAJA fees. A veteran is the "prevailing party" on remand if:

1. The remand was necessitated by administrative error
2. The remanding court does not retain jurisdiction
3. The remand order calls for further agency proceedings, which leaves open the *possibility* of a favorable decision.

$$\star\ \star\ \star$$

---

[37] *Shalala v. Schaefer*, 509 U.S. 292, 302 (1993)
[38] *Swiney v. Gober*, 14 Vet.App. 65, 68-70 (2000); *Stillwell v. Brown*, 6 Vet.App. 291 (1994); also *Vaughn v. Principi*, 336 F.3d 1351 (Fed. Cir. 2003)
[39] *Dover*, 818 F.3d 1316, 1319 (Fed. Cir. 2016)

Chapter 8

Other Benefits for Veterans and Dependents

In order to qualify for VA benefits, veterans must demonstrate eligibility and entitlement. The general focus of this VA Handbook (Chapters 1-7) is on establishing eligibility and entitlement for *disability compensation* benefits, which is a monthly monetary payment made by the VA's Veterans Benefits Administration ("VBA") to a veteran as compensation for unemployability caused by their service-connected disability. Not all veterans have service-connected injuries, however, and certain benefits do not require veterans to have a disability. These other benefits, in addition to service-connected disability benefits, cover not only the remainder of a veteran's natural life, but also their death, with death, memorial, and DIC benefits available to family members after their loved one passes. Federal benefits that are available to veterans and qualifying family members include, but are not limited to:

Life Benefits

- VA Educational benefits
    - o Vietnam VEAP
    - o Montgomery GI Bill
    - o Post 9/11 GI Bill
- Vocational Rehabilitation and Employment
- Dependent Education Assistance
- VA home loan
- Pension

Death Benefits

- Dependency and Indemnity Compensation death benefits
- Burial and Memorial benefits

★ ★ ★

§ 8.1 — VA Education Benefits

VA offers education benefits through a number of programs, the most generous of which covers the costs of secondary education tuition, supplies and living expenses for veterans—in limited circumstances, dependent family members who meet basic service eligibility requirements may also qualify for education benefits. Ever since the 1944 Servicemen's Readjustment Act created the first education benefit program for veterans, a number of revisions and additions have been made to "the GI Bill." These updates are reflected by the various education programs administered by VA, each more generous and inclusive than its predecessor.

A BRIEF HISTORY OF VA EDUCATIONAL BENEFITS & LEGISLATION to 2008—[1]

Most recently, the "Harry W. Colmery Veterans Educational Assistance Act" of 2017 modified the Post-9/11 GI Bill to eliminate the 15-year use-it-or-lose-it provision, among other changes, to create the largest eligibility pool in history.[2] The 2017 law also expanded eligibility to purple heart recipients who were wounded after September 11, 2001, regardless of the length of their active duty service, and gave credit to time served for reservists who were previously overlooked. Service members are now given the ability to transfer their VA education benefits to a qualifying spouse or child. In order to apply for GI Bill educational benefits, a veteran can either apply through their regional VA office, or most schools who receive GI Bill students have a dedicated veterans service officer who

---

[1] Congressional Research Service. "A Brief History of Veterans' Education Benefits and Their Value." (25 June 2008) web.archive.org/web/20200806100727/ https://fas.org/sgp/crs/misc/RL34549.pdf

[2] Public Law 115–48, Aug. 16, 2017, 131 Stat. 973

can help any potential student veteran to apply. To apply for VA education benefits, complete and submit VA Form 22-1990, making sure to identify which education benefit is being sought.

♣   VA Form 22-1990 — **Application for VA Education Benefits**

♣   VA Form 22-1990E — **Application for Family Member to Use Transferred Benefits**

VA Form 22-1990, *Application for VA Education Benefits,* asks claimants to identify which education benefit they are seeking. *See*: Page 1, Part II. The primary education benefits available to former service members are:

- Chapter 32 / Section 1601 – Vietnam Era VEAP
- Chapter 30 – Montgomery GI Bill
- Chapter 33 – Post-9/11 GI Bill

In addition, VA offers education benefits for reservists, disabled veterans, and the children and spouses of totally disabled veterans and veterans killed in the line of duty.

- Chapter 1607 – Reservists Education Assistance Program
- Chapter 31 – Vocational Rehabilitation & Employment
- Chapter 35 – Dependents Education Assistance Program

★ ★

§ 8.1.1 — Vietnam Era VEAP[3]

The Post-Vietnam Era Veteran's Educational Assistance Program ("VEAP") is a limited education benefit for former service members who entered active military service between December 31, 1976 and July 1, 1985, who made contributions of $25 to $2,700, and who served for a minimum period of at least 181 days. VEAP was created by the "Veterans'

---

[3] 38 U.S.C. §§ 3201-3243; 38 C.F.R. §§ 21.5001-21.5296. https://www.va.gov/education/other-va-education-benefits/veap/

Education and Employment Assistance Act of 1976" as a way to "provide educational assistance" and "assist young men and women in obtaining an education they might not otherwise be able to afford," and "promote and assist the all-volunteer military ... by attracting qualified men and women to serve in the Armed Forces."[4] Because VEAP is an older program and most VEAP-eligible veterans are also entitled to more generous VA education benefits, like the Post-9/11 GI Bill, VEAP will eventually be phased out of existence.

In order to be eligible for VEAP educational benefits, a veteran must be discharged under conditions other than dishonorable (see Section 3.2.1, Character of Discharge), and either serve for at least 181 days of active duty or be discharged for a service-connected disability.[5] The maximum entitlement under VEAP is $8,100, which includes a 2-to-1 government match for every dollar contributed, up to $2,700, equal to 27 monthly payments of $300 for full-time students. VEAP must be used within 10 years of discharge, or VA will issue a refund to any veteran for the amount they contributed to the program. *See*: VA Form 22-5281; VA Pamphlet 22-79-1, revised December 2001.

♣ VA Form 22-5281 — **Application for Refund of Educational Contributions**

Currently, there is no opportunity for VEAP (Chapter 32) participants to convert to the Montgomery GI Bill-Active Duty (Chapter 30). The last opportunity to do so was in 2001.

★ ★

§ 8.1.2 — Montgomery GI Bill[6]

The All Volunteer Force Education Program, better known as the Montgomery GI Bill ("MGIB"), is an education benefit for service members who entered active duty service on or after June 30, 1985. The MGIB was

---

[4] Pub. L. 94–502, title IV, § 404—Oct. 15, 1976, 90 Stat. 2393, § 1601.

[5] 38 C.F.R. § 21.5040

[6] 38 U.S.C. §§ 3001-3036; 38 C.F.R. §§ 21.7000-21.7320. https://www.va.gov/education/about-gi-bill-benefits/

created by the "Veterans Educational Assistance Act of 1985" to "assist in the readjustment of members of the Armed Forces to civilian life after their separation from military service," "to restore lost educational opportunities to those service men and women," and "to extend the benefits of a higher education to qualifying men and women who might not otherwise be able to afford such an education."[7]

In order to be eligible for MGIB educational benefits, a veteran must have obtained a high school diploma or equivalent, serve for minimum of 24-36 months and receive an honorable discharge. 38 C.F.R. § 21.7042. In addition, in order to receive MGIB educational benefits service members are required to contribute $1,200 while on active duty—generally $100/month for the first year of service.

★ ★

§ 8.1.3 — Post-9/11 GI Bill[8]

The Post-9/11 GI Bill was created by Congress in 2008 to modernize and expand upon the Montgomery GI Bill. The newer, Post-9/11 GI Bill no longer requires service members to make financial contributions while they are on active duty service, and, unlike the MGIB, offers stipends for housing and fees as well as books and tuition. The Post-9/11 GI Bill was created by the "Post-9/11 Veterans' Educational Assistance Act," which passed as Title V of the Supplemental Appropriations Act, 2008.[9] Through the Act, Congress found that military service was "especially arduous for the members of the Armed Forces since September 11, 2001," but that the current MGIB was "outmoded" and needed improvement. Since 2008, the Post-9/11 GI Bill has been amended every year, including most recently, on August 16, 2017, with the passage of the *Harry W. Colmery Veterans Educational Assistance Act of 2017*, also known as the "Forever GI Bill." Among other things, the Forever GI Bill amendment removed the time limitation on the use of benefits and expanded eligibility.

In order to be eligible to receive the full range of benefits under the Post-9/11 GI Bill, a veteran must serve after September 11, 2001, for at least

---

[7] Pub. L. 98–525, title VII, § 702(a)(1)—Oct. 19, 1984, 98 Stat. 2553.

[8] https://www.va.gov/education/about-gi-bill-benefits/post-9-11/

[9] Public Law 110–252, June 30, 2008, 122 Stat. 2357

36 months of continuous active duty and receive an honorable discharge.[10] Alternatively, any veteran who serves at least 30 days and is discharged because of a service-connected disability may be eligible for full benefits.[11] For veterans who serve more than 90 days but less than 36 months, tuition, fees, and stipends are determined by the length of service.[12]

Total Amount of Aggregate Duty	Percentage of Maximum Benefit
Purple Heart recipients	100
GySgt John David Fry Scholarship recipients	100
36 months or greater of active duty service	100
At least 30 days of active duty service and discharged for service-connected disability	100
30-36 months of active duty service	90
24-30 months of active duty service	80
18-24 months of active duty service	70
12-18 months of active duty service	60
6-12 months of active duty service	50
90 days to 6 months of active duty service	40

★ ★ ★

§ 8.2 — Vocational Rehabilitation and Employment

> Manual M21-1, III.i.2.C.1. **Vocational Rehabilitation and Employment (VR&E) Claims**

---

[10] 38 U.S.C. § 3311(b)(1)

[11] 38 U.S.C. § 3311(b)(2)

[12] 38 U.S.C. § 3311(b)(3)-(8); 38 C.F.R. § 21.9520

Vocational Rehabilitation and Employment[13] ("VR&E"), known to most veterans as "Voc Rehab," is a benefit for disabled veterans who suffer some level of employment handicap due to their service-connected disability. The purpose of Voc Rehab is to "to provide for all services and assistance necessary to enable veterans with service-connected disabilities to achieve maximum independence in daily living and, to the maximum extent feasible, to become employable and to obtain and maintain suitable employment." In some cases, that may include covering the costs of college or a university to obtain an advanced degree.[14] Former U.S. Senator Jim Webb (R-VA), for example, utilized the Vocational Rehab program to attend Georgetown Law School and become a lawyer. "Because I had been wounded and was on a Voc Rehab program, I was able to go to Georgetown Law School ... They paid my tuition, they bought my books, and they paid a monthly stipend," Webb recalled during a 2007 Senate VA Committee hearing.[15]

Eligibility for VR&E benefits

> Manual M21-1, IX.i.1.A. **Vocational Rehabilitation and Employment (VR&E) Eligibility**

In order to be eligible for VR&E benefits, a veteran must have at least one service-connected disability that is rated at 20 percent or greater, which contributes to an employment handicap, or one disability rated at 10 percent that contributes to a serious employment handicap.[16] *Serious employment handicap* is defined by statute as "a significant impairment, resulting in substantial part from a service-connected disability rated at 10 percent or more, of a veteran's ability to prepare for, obtain, or retain employment consistent with such veteran's abilities, aptitudes, and interests."[17] Similarly, *Employment handicap* means an "impairment, resulting in substantial part from a disability ... of a veteran's ability to prepare for, obtain, or

[13] 38 U.S.C. § 3100; 38 C.F.R. § 21.1(a)
[14] 38 U.S.C. § 3101(3); 38 C.F.R. § 21.35(k)(3)
[15] December 5, 2007. S. Hrg. 110-536 – Hearing on Nomination of James B. Peake to be Secretary of the Department of Veterans Affairs. https://www.govinfo.gov/app/details/CHRG-110shrg40524.
[16] 38 U.S.C. § 3102; 38 C.F.R. § 21.40
[17] 38 U.S.C. § 3101(7); *also* 38 C.F.R. § 21.35(g)

retain employment consistent with such veteran's abilities, aptitudes, and interests."[18] The duty to assist applies to claims for Voc Rehab benefits.[19]

The process of applying for and receiving VR&E benefits is slightly different than other benefits. To begin, a veteran must first file a claim for VR&E benefits with VA Form 28-1900. Once the claim is received, VA will assign a Vocational Rehabilitation Counselor ("VRC") to the claim.[20] The VRC will contact the veteran and set up an appointment to interview the veteran to better understand their needs and determine eligibility. During the meeting(s), the VRC will conduct a one-on-one interview to assess the disabled veteran's skills, abilities, and interests. Most importantly, the VRC will make a determination about whether the veteran's service-connected disability poses an employment handicap or serious employment handicap. If the VRC determines that the disabled veteran suffers from an employment handicap or serious employment handicap, they will work with the veteran to develop a VR&E plan that sets out vocational goals, as well as independent living goals and timelines.[21] In cases where Voc Rehab covers the costs of higher education, student veterans are required to submit their grades to their VRC at the end of each semester and notify their VRC of any major changes or disruptions to their class work or personal life.

Disabled veterans who pursue their trade certification, bachelors or other advanced degrees through Voc Rehab are strongly encouraged to confidentially communicate their disability to the school office of disability services, even if special accommodations are not sought. This is advised because in the case that medical or personal emergencies may arise in connection with a service-connected disability, it is easier to notify faculty and staff when the disability is already documented on file. Generally, registering a disability like PTSD, TBI, anxiety, hearing impairment, or any other service-connected condition with a college disability services office only requires privately filing a copy of the veteran's VA rating. Some schools may have their own intake forms, as well. In addition to registering service-connected disabilities with the school disability office or equivalent, student veterans who are attending school through Voc

---

[18] 38 U.S.C. § 3101(1); *also* 38 C.F.R. § 21.35(a)

[19] 38 C.F.R. § 21.33

[20] 38 C.F.R. § 21.35(k)(7)

[21] 38 C.F.R. § 21.35(h)

Rehab are also encouraged to share information about their condition with their professors/instructors so that they may be apprised in case of medical or personal emergencies.

♣ VA Form 28-1900 — **Application for Vocational Rehabilitation for Claimants with Service-Connected Disabilities**

* * *

§ 8.3 — Dependent Education Assistance (DEA)[22]

Manual M21-1, III.iii.6.C.1.a. **Who Is Eligible for DEA**

Dependent Education Assistance ("DEA") is an educational benefit available to the spouse and children of veterans who are killed while on active duty or due to a service-connected disability, or who are rated by VA as 100% totally and permanently disabled.[23] Congress created DEA "for the purpose of providing opportunities for education to children whose education would otherwise be impeded or interrupted by reason of the disability or death of a parent from a disease or injury incurred or aggravated in the Armed Forces."[24] DEA offers eligible, surviving spouses and their children up to forty-eight months of education and living expenses at a public college or university. To apply for DEA education benefits, eligible individuals use VA form 22-5490.

♣ VA form 22-5490 — **Dependents Application for VA Education Benefits**

Manual M21-1, III.iii.6.C.2.a. **Initial Actions for Determining Eligibility for Education Benefits**

* * *

---

[22] https://www.va.gov/education/survivor-dependent-benefits/
[23] 38 U.S.C. Chapter 35; 38 C.F.R. § 21.3001-3344
[24] 38 U.S.C. § 3500

§ 8.4 — VA Home Loan

Manual M21-1, IX.i.5.A.1. **Basics of the VA Home Loan Program**

One of the most popular and widely-used VA benefits is the VA home loan guaranty benefit. Created in 1944 by the Servicemen's Readjustment Act, the VA home loan is not a direct loan from the federal government. Rather, it is a special benefit created just for veterans and surviving spouses, where the federal government acts as a guaranty, or co-signer, for the repayment of a portion of a veteran's personal residential home loan in case of default. As a result, veterans who secure private loans with a VA home loan guaranty are generally able to obtain more favorable terms to finance the purchase of a home with no money down. The amount of residential home loan that a veteran can be approved for depends on a number of factors, including the amount of available entitlement, location of the property for purchase, and the credit and income of the veteran, among other considerations.

Eligibility for VA home loan guaranty

Active duty troops who have served more than 90 days are eligible for the VA home loan. Surviving spouses of veterans killed while on active duty or from a service-connected disability are also eligible. All veterans who were discharged from the military due to service-connected disabilities are eligible without regard to minimum length of time in service. The same applies to veterans who have received a disability rating from VA for their service-connected disabilities.

For non-disabled veterans, minimum length-of-service requirements apply. All veterans who entered the service after September 7, 1980 (enlisted) and October 17, 1981 (officer) must have served for a minimum of twenty-four months, or 181 days of activation for members of the reserve forces. For older veterans who served during the WWII, Korea, or Vietnam Wars, ninety days of service is generally required. For all remaining veterans who served during a time of peace, the minimum length of service required is 181 days. In addition, veterans must have been discharged under conditions other than dishonorable. (*see* Section 3.2.1, Character of Discharge) Honorable discharges can be presented as a certificate of eligibility ("COE") for VA home loan. Alternately, Veterans can also apply for a COE online at eBenefits.va.gov, which can be presented to a bank or lender as proof of benefit eligibility. Before VA will actually guaranty a veteran's home loan, once an application is made VA will send someone to conduct a physical inspection of the property to ensure against defects and other issues that may impact the habitability of the property, and also to determine the reasonable value of the home.

♣ VA form 26-1880 — **Request for a Certificate of Eligibility**

♣ VA form 26-1817 — **Request for Determination of Loan Guaranty Eligibility – Unmarried Surviving Spouses**

★ ★ ★

§ 8.5 — Veterans and Survivors Pension[25]

Pension benefits, like disability compensation benefits, are financial payments paid each month to qualifying wartime veterans. However, unlike compensation benefits, which do not consider a veteran's income or net worth and are paid for service-connected disability, pension benefits are only payable to veterans who are permanently and totally disabled due to non-service-connected disabilities, and who meet certain minimum income and net worth requirements set by Congress. Survivors pensions, like veterans pensions, are paid to the surviving spouse or dependent children of a deceased wartime veteran.

♣ VA Form 21P-527EZ — **Application for Veterans Pension**

♣ VA Form 21P-527 — **Income, Asset, and Employment Statement**

♣ VA Form 21P-534 — **Application for Dependency and Indemnity Compensation, Survivors Pensions, and Accrued Benefits by a Surviving Spouse or Child (Including Death Compensation if Applicable)**

---

[25] 38 U.S.C. §§ 1521, 1541; 38 C.F.R. §§ 3.3, 3.342, 3.454, 3.460

♣   VA Form 21P-534EZ — **Application for DIC,
Survivors Pension, and/or Accrued Benefits**

> Manual M21-1, V.i.1.1.a. **Definition: Pension**

★ ★ ★

§ 8.6 — Dependency and Indemnity Compensation[26]

> Manual M21-1, IV.iii.1.A.2.a. **Definition: DIC**

> Manual M21-1, IV.iii.1.B.1.e. **Evidence Required
> to Determine Entitlement to DIC**

Dependency and Indemnity Compensation ("DIC") is a tax-free monthly benefit paid to an eligible surviving spouse, child, or parents because of a veteran's service-connected death. DIC benefits are generally payable: (1) if a service member dies or is killed while serving on active duty; (2) if a veteran's death is principally or contributorily caused by a service-connected or compensable injury; (3) if at the time of death the veteran was receiving or entitled to receive total disability compensation benefits (schedular 100% rating or TDIU); or (4) if the veteran's death was the result of carelessness, negligence, lack of proper skill, or other instance of fault on the part of VA medical personnel.

(1) Death in service (line of duty) — § 1310
(2) Death from service-connected disability — § 1310
(3) Death while entitled to total disability benefits — § 1318
(4) Death from VA negligence — § 1151

Qualifying family members may still be eligible to receive DIC benefits even if the deceased veteran never filed a claim for disability benefits during their lifetime, or if they did attempt to file disability claims

---

[26] *Darby v. Brown*, 10 Vet.App. 243, 245 (1997); 38 U.S.C. §§ 101(14), 1310, 1318, 1151; 38 C.F.R. § 3.5

but their claims were denied service-connection. As with other claims, the "benefit of the doubt" rule applies to DIC claims.[27]

Death in Service —

> Manual M21-1, IV.iii.1.B.3.a. **Determining**
> **Whether an In-Service Death Is SC**

When a service member dies or is killed while serving on active duty, their death is presumed to have been incurred in the line of duty and DIC benefits are awarded unless the death was caused by their own willful misconduct.[28] Death in service while in the line of duty entitles surviving family members to DIC benefits.[29] In addition, veterans who die or are killed in the line of duty are also entitled to service-connected death benefits.[30]

Death due to Service-Connected Disability —

> Manual M21-1, IV.iii.2.A.1.a. **Considering the**
> **Reasonable Probability of SC Death**

"Upon the death of a veteran due to a service-connected disability, [their] surviving spouse may receive DIC."[31] DIC benefits may be awarded to eligible surviving family members when a veteran's service-connected disability is either the **principal** or **contributory** cause of their death.[32] Under VA regulations, a service-connected disability is considered a *principal* cause of death when that disability, "singly or jointly with some other condition, was the immediate or underlying cause of death or was etiologically related thereto."[33] In order to be considered a *contributory* cause of death, the disability must have "contributed substantially or materially" to death, "combined to cause death," or "aided or lent

---

[27] 38 U.S.C. § 5107(b)

[28] 38 U.S.C. § 105(a); *Myore v. Nicholson*, 489 F.3d 1207 (Fed. Cir. 2007)

[29] 38 U.S.C. § 1310

[30] 38 U.S.C. § 2307

[31] *Hanna v. Brown*, 6 Vet.App. 507, 510 (1994)

[32] 38 C.F.R. § 3.312(a)

[33] 38 C.F.R. § 3.312(b)

assistance to the production of death."[34] For a service-connected disability to constitute a contributory cause, it is not sufficient to show that it casually shared in producing death, but rather it must be shown that there was a causal connection.[35] As with line of duty death, veterans who die from their service-connected disabilities and who meet the criteria of § 1310 are also entitled to service-connected death benefits.[36]

In some cases, a veteran may already be receiving VA compensation benefits for one or more service-connected disabilities at the time of their death. When that is the case, family members need only to establish that the veteran's death was caused by their disability, either principally or contributorily, or that one of the three total disability exceptions applies (below). However, if the veteran never filed a claim for disability benefits, or if VA denied their claim during their lifetime, family members can still apply for DIC benefits and receive *de novo* review, but must establish (1) service-connection for the disabilities, and then (2) causation of death from disability. In order to establish service-connection, a surviving dependent must follow the process of a disability compensation claim and prove that the deceased veteran suffered from a service-connected disability at the time of their death. Once a veteran's disability recognized as service-connected by VA, it must then be shown to be a principal or contributory factor in the veteran's death. As with disability claims, surviving family members can bolster their claims with private medical opinions about the veteran's cause of death, and also about the veteran's service-connected disability as a primary or contributing factor of death. VA may also be asked to provide a medical opinion about a veteran's death if doing so is necessary to substantiate the claim.[37]

Exceptions to Death in Service & from Disability —

Congress has provided three exceptions to the requirement of death while on active duty service, from VA negligence, or as a cause or contributing factor in death.[38] These exceptions apply to veterans with VA

[34] 38 C.F.R. § 3.312(c); *Lathan v. Brown*, 7 Vet.App. 359 (1995)
[35] *Schoonover v. Derwinski*, 3 Vet.App. 166, 168-69 (1992); *Ventigan v. Brown*, 9 Vet.App. 34, 36 (1996)
[36] 38 U.S.C. § 2307
[37] 38 U.S.C. § 5103A(a)(1)
[38] 38 U.S.C. § 1318(b); *see also*: 38 C.F.R. § 3.22(a)(2)

disability ratings, who have been examined by VA and determined to be disabled from a service-connected injury or condition.

(1) the disability was continuously rated totally disabling for a period of 10 or more years immediately preceding death;

(2) the disability was continuously rated totally disabling for a period of not less than five years from the date of such veteran's discharge or other release from active duty; or

(3) the veteran was a former prisoner of war and the disability was continuously rated totally disabling for a period of not less than one year immediately preceding death.

"Ten-Year Rule" for DIC Benefits—[39]

The first exception to the DIC requirement of death on active duty, from VA negligence, or from a service-connected disability exists where the deceased veteran was either rated by VA as 100% totally disabled or receiving TDIU unemployability benefits for a continuous period of ten years preceding their death.[40] If a deceased veteran received total disability benefits at the 100% level, whether through schedular ratings or TDIU, their surviving dependents may qualify for DIC benefits regardless of their cause of death—even if their death is not connected in any way to their service-connected disability. For example, if a veteran with a combined overall rating of 90% who received TDIU benefits at the 100% level died from unrelated causes on March 3, 2021, an eligible surviving family member would qualify for DIC under § 1318(b)(1) if TDIU benefit eligibility was assigned on March 3, 2011, or earlier.

"Five-Year Rule" for DIC Benefits—[41]

Similar to the "ten-year rule," a second exception known as the "five-year rule" exists when a veteran has been rated at 100% totally disabled or TDIU benefits for no less than five years from their discharge until their death. 38 C.F.R. § 3.22(2)(ii). The five-year rule applies when a veteran

---

[39] 38 U.S.C. § 1318(b)(1)

[40] 38 C.F.R. §§ 3.22(a)(2)(i); 3.22(c); *Tarver v. Shinseki*, 557 F.3d 1371, 1373 (Fed. Cir. 2009)

[41] 38 U.S.C. § 1318(b)(2)

leaves active duty military service with either a 100% schedular rating or TDIU, which is maintained continuously until their death more than five years later.

"POW One-Year Rule" for DIC Benefits—[42]

The third exception for DIC benefits exists for former prisoners of war ("POWs") who received TDIU benefits or were rated 100% totally disabled by VA for at least one year prior to their death. If a deceased former POW rated at 100% disabled does not qualify under the "ten-year rule" or "five-year rule," their surviving dependents may qualify for DIC benefits under the "POW one-year rule."[43]

Spouse > Children > Parents

Federal law assigns the top priority for DIC benefits to surviving spouses.[44] If, however, a veteran is divorced with children, in the absence of an eligible surviving spouse, the veteran's child(ren) (not the former spouse) will qualify for DIC benefits.[45] Where a deceased veteran leaves no children or eligible surviving spouse, the veteran's parents may qualify for DIC benefits.[46] Surviving spouses, children and parents may apply for DIC benefits upon the death of their loved one or at any time thereafter. There is no statute of limitations for filing DIC benefits. However, the effective start date of any DIC benefit award, if filed more than one year after the veteran's death, will be the date the DIC claim (or intent to file) was filed.[47]

Eligible family members may file a claim for DIC benefits in the same manner that disabled veterans apply for compensation and pension benefits. If additional time is needed to gather documents following a veteran's death, claimants should immediately notify VA of their intent to file a claim for DIC benefits by filing an intent to file VA Form 21-0966, and checking "Box 13" with "Survivors Pensions and/or Dependency and Indemnity Compensation (DIC)." If, however, all documentation has been

---

[42] 38 U.S.C. § 1318(b)(3)

[43] 38 C.F.R. § 3.22(2)(iii)

[44] 38 U.S.C. § 1311

[45] 38 U.S.C. § 1313

[46] 38 U.S.C. § 1315

[47] 38 U.S.C. § 5110(a).

gathered and additional time is not needed, skip the intent to file and submit a full application for DIC and other survivors benefits. Make sure to file the correct form: for surviving spouses and children, VA form 21P-534 or 21P-534EZ; for eligible parents, VA form 21P-535.

♣   VA Form 21-0966 — **Intent to File a Claim for Compensation and/or Pension and/or Survivors Pension and/or DIC**

♣   VA Form 21P-534 — **Application for Dependency and Indemnity Compensation, Survivors Pensions, and Accrued Benefits by a Surviving Spouse or Child (Including Death Compensation if Applicable)**

♣   VA Form 21P-534EZ — **Application for DIC, Survivors Pension, and/or Accrued Benefits**

♣   VA Form 21P-535 — **Application for Dependency and Indemnity Compensation by Parent(s) (Including Accrued Benefits and Death Compensation when Applicable)**

* * *

§ 8.7 — Burial and Memorial Death benefits[48]

Manual M21-1, VII.1.A.1.l. **Definition: Types of Burial Benefits**

The Veterans Benefits Administration ("VBA") provides the following five burial benefits to qualifying individuals:

1. Burial allowance based on service-connected death
2. Burial allowance based on non-service-connected death
3. Burial allowance for veteran who died while hospitalized by VA
4. Burial plot or interment allowance
5. Reimbursement for transportation of remains

* *

---

[48] 38 C.F.R. § 3.1700

1. **Burial allowance based on service-connected death**—[49]

**Manual M21-1, VII.1.B.2.a. General Eligibility
for the SC Burial Allowance**

Service-connected burial allowance is payable when:

a. A veteran dies as a result of one or more service-connected disabilities;

b. A veteran is rated totally disabled (100 percent) due to service-connected disability at the time of death, excluding a total disability rating based on Individual Unemployability;

c. Dependency and Indemnity Compensation is awarded.

★ ★

2. **Burial allowance for non-service-connected death**—[50]

**Manual M21-1, VII.1.B.3.a. General Eligibility
Criteria for NSC Burial Allowance**

Eligibility for non-service-connected burial allowance exists if the veteran:

a. was receiving pension or compensation at the time of death;

b. was receiving military retired pay in lieu of compensation at the time of death;

c. had a claim pending at the time of death and has been found entitled to compensation or pension from a date prior to the date of death, or

d. has no family or friends who claim the Veteran's body and there are insufficient resources to cover burial and funeral expenses.

★ ★

---

[49] 38 C.F.R. § 3.1704
[50] 38 C.F.R. § 3.1705

3. **Burial allowance for veteran who died while hospitalized by VA**—[51]

Manual M21-1, VII.1.B.4.a. **General Eligibility Criteria for VA Hospitalization Death Burial Allowance**

Eligibility for the VA hospitalization death burial allowance exists if the veteran:

a. Was hospitalized by VA at the time of death; or
b. Died while:
    i. hospitalized under VA contract at a non-VA facility
    ii. traveling, under proper authorization and at VA expense, to or from a specified place for the purpose of examination, treatment, or care, or
    iii. a patient at an approved State Veterans' home.

★ ★

4. **Burial plot or interment allowance**—[52]

Manual M21-1, VII.1.B.5.a. **General Eligibility for Plot or Interment Allowance**

For any veteran who is eligible for burial in a national cemetery under the provisions of 38 U.S.C. § 2402, VBA may pay the plot or interment allowance for any cemetery.

★ ★

---

[51] 38 C.F.R. § 3.1706
[52] 38 C.F.R. § 3.1707

5. **Reimbursement for transportation of remains—**[53]

> Manual M21-1, VII.1.B.6.a. **Transportation Reimbursement**
> **for Burial in a National Cemetery**

VBA will reimburse the costs incurred to transport a veteran's remains for burial in a national cemetery if the veteran:

a. Died as the result of an service-connected disability
b. Was receiving service-connected disability compensation on the date of death
c. Would have been receiving service-connected disability compensation on the date of death but for the receipt of military retired pay or VA pension
d. Is later determined by VA to have been entitled to service-connected disability compensation from a date before the Veteran's death, or
e. Remains are unclaimed.

To apply for burial benefits, surviving family members use VA Form 21P-530, *Application for Burial Benefits*. Be sure to attach a certificate of death with the application, and if transportation costs are being claimed, include receipts.

♣ VA Form 21P-530 — **Application for Burial Benefits**

★ ★

Additional Burial and Memorial Benefits

In addition, VA's National Cemetery Administration ("NCA") processes claims for:

---

[53] 38 C.F.R. § 3.1709

1. Headstones and Markers—[54]

VA will furnish a government headstone or marker for all veterans who are buried in a national or state cemetery, or eligible for burial in a national cemetery but buried elsewhere. To apply for a U.S. Government headstone or marker for a deceased veteran, surviving family members use VA Form 40-1330, *Claim for Standard Government Headstone or Marker.*

♣ VA Form 40-1330 — **Claim for Standard Government Headstone or Marker**

★ ★

2. Burial flags—[55]

A burial flag may be issued to the next-of-kin, close friend or associate of the deceased Veteran. To apply for a burial flag, surviving family members use VA Form 21P-530, *Application for Burial Benefits.* Be sure to attach a certificate of death with the application, and if transportation costs are being claimed, include receipts.

♣ VA Form 27-2008 — **Application for United States Flag for Burial Purposes**

★ ★ ★

---

[54] 38 U.S.C. § 2306; 38 C.F.R. § 38.630; *also* 38 C.F.R. § 38.633; *see* Manual M21-1, VII.1.D.3. Burial Headstones and Markers.
[55] 38 U.S.C. § 2301; 38 C.F.R. § 1.10; *see* Manual M21-1, VII.1.D.2. Burial Flags.

Forms Appendix

21-526EZ. Application for Disability Compensation and Related Compensation Benefits (12 pages)...278

21-0966. Intent to File a Claim (1 page) 290

20-0995. Supplemental Claim (4 pages).................................291

20-0996. Higher-Level Review (4 pages) 295

10182. Notice of Disagreement (BVA Appeal) (3 pages) 299

21-4138. Statement in Support of Claim (2 pages)............................... 302

21-22. Appointment of Veterans Service Organization as Claimant's Representative (4 pages) 304

21-22a. Appointment of Individual as Claimant's Representative (3 pages) 308

21-0960P-3. Review Post-Traumatic Stress Disorder (PTSD) Disability Benefits Questionnaire (6 pages) 310

21-0781. Statement in Support of Claim for Service Connection for Post-Traumatic Stress Disorder (PTSD) (3 pages)...........................316

10-10EZ. Application for Health Benefits (5 pages) 319

Search all VA Forms online at https://www.va.gov/find-forms/.

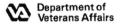

Department of Veterans Affairs

NOTICE TO VETERAN/SERVICE MEMBER OF EVIDENCE NECESSARY TO SUBSTANTIATE A CLAIM FOR VETERANS DISABILITY COMPENSATION AND RELATED COMPENSATION BENEFITS

This notice provides information regarding the evidence necessary to substantiate a claim for:

Disability Service Connection	Special Monthly Compensation
Compensation Claims Submitted Prior to Discharge	Benefits Based on a Veteran's Seriously Disabled Child
Compensation under 38 U.S.C. 1151	Increased Disability Compensation
Automobile Allowance/Adaptive Equipment	Individual Unemployability
Secondary Service Compensation	Specially Adapted Housing/Special Home Adaptation
Temporary Total Disability Rating	

When to Use this Form

Use this notice and the attached application to submit a claim for veterans' disability compensation and related compensation benefits. This notice informs you of the evidence necessary to decide your claim. After you submit your claim on the attached application you *will not* receive an initial letter regarding your claim. You *do not* need to submit another application.

If you are filing a claim for increased disability compensation or disagree with an evaluation decided more than one year ago ...	please complete and submit VA Form 21-526EZ, *Application for Disability Compensation and Related Compensation Benefits.*
If you disagree with an evaluation decided within the past year and have new and relevant evidence *OR* If you are filing a supplemental claim (a claim after an initial claim for the same or similar benefit on the same or similar basis was previously decided) ...	please complete and submit VA Form 20-0995, *Decision Review Request: Supplemental Claim***

** You may also file a request for higher-level review or appeal to the Board of Veterans' Appeals. For additional information on all of these different options, please visit https://benefits.va.gov/benefits/appeals.asp.

Want to apply electronically? You can apply online at www.va.gov. If you sign in or create an account at www.va.gov, we can prefill parts of your application and save your work in progress. You can also upload all your supporting documents with your claim, and submit it through the Fully Developed Claims (FDC) program, then track claim status online. Get Started at https://www.va.gov/disability/how-to-file-claim/.

NOTE: You may wish to contact an accredited veterans service officer (VSO) to assist you with your application. For a list of accredited veterans service organizations go to https://www.va.gov/vso/. You may also contact your state office of veterans affairs at https://www.va.gov/statedva.htm, should you need further assistance with the application process.

Want your claim processed faster? The FDC Program is the **fastest** way to get your claim processed without any risk to participate! To participate in making a claim for veterans disability compensation or related compensation benefits, submit your claim in accordance with the "FDC Program" shown on the following information pages 2 through 7. If you are making a claim for veterans non service-connected pension benefits, use VA Form 21P-527EZ, *Application for Pension.* If you are making a claim for survivor benefits, use VA Form 21P-534EZ, *Application for DIC, Death Pension, and/or Accrued Benefits.* VA forms are available at www.va.gov/vaforms. A separate expedited claims processing program available for current active duty Servicemembers is explained on page 5 under *Compensation Claims Submitted Prior to Discharge*

NOTE: Participation in the FDC Program is optional and will not affect the benefits to which you are entitled. If you file a claim in the FDC Program and it is determined that other records exist and VA needs the records to decide your claim, then VA will simply remove the claim from the FDC Program and process it in the Standard Claim Process. If you wish to file your claim in the FDC Program, see FDC Program (Optional Expedited Process) on page 2 . If you wish to file your claim under the process in which VA traditionally processes claims, see Standard Claim Process on page 2.

SUBMITTING A CLAIM

When submitting a claim(s) for **Veterans Disability Compensation and Related Compensation Benefits** the following information tells you what you need to do and what VA will do during the FDC Program (Optional Expedited Process) or the Standard Claim Process:

1. **HOW TO SUBMIT A CLAIM**

    Submit your claim on a VA Form 21-526EZ, *Application for Disability Compensation and Related Compensation Benefits* (Attached). Make sure you complete and sign your application.

2. **WHAT YOU NEED TO DO**

    The table on page 2 describes the information and evidence you need to submit based on whether you wish to have your claim considered in the FDC Program (Optional Expedited Process) or in the Standard Claim Process. You will need to indicate how you want your claim to be processed by checking the appropriate box in Item 1, on page 8 of this form.

FDC Program (Optional Expedited Process)	Standard Claim Process
You must: • Submit all relevant private treatment records, if they exist • Identify any relevant treatment records available at a Federal Facility, such as a VA medical center • Identify the location and sufficient information to obtain your National Guard and Reserve personnel and service treatment records *(if applicable)* If your claim involves a disability that you had before entering service and that was made worse by service, please provide any information or evidence in your possession regarding the health condition that existed before your entry into service. **NOTE:** If you decide to submit your claim through the FDC Program, please indicate FDC in Item 1 of the application on page 8.	If you know of evidence not in your possession and want VA to try to get it for you: **You must:** • Complete and sign VA Form 21-4142, *Authorization to Disclose Information to the Department of Veterans Affairs (VA)* and VA Form 21-4142a, *General Release for Medical Provider Information to the Department of Veterans Affairs (VA)*, identifying any private medical records you wish VA to request for you • Give VA enough information about other relevant evidence so that we can request it from the person or agency that has it If the holder of the evidence declines to give it to VA, asks for a fee to provide it, or otherwise cannot get the evidence, VA will notify you and provide you with an opportunity to submit the information or evidence. *It is your responsibility to make sure we receive all requested records that are not in the possession of a Federal department or agency.* If your claim involves a disability that you had before entering service and that was made worse by service, please provide any information or evidence in your possession regarding the health condition that existed before your entry into service.
You must: • Send the information and evidence *along* with your claim If you submit additional information or evidence *after* you submit your "fully developed" claim, then VA will remove the claim from the FDC Program (Optional Expedited Process) and process it in the Standard Claim Process. If we decide your claim before one year from the date we receive the claim, you will still have the remainder of the one-year period to submit additional information or evidence necessary to support the claim.	**You are strongly encouraged to:** • Send any information or evidence as soon as you can **You have up to one** year from the date we receive the claim to submit the information and evidence necessary to support your claim. If within **30** days, you do not provide any evidence or do not provide us with the information needed to assist you with obtaining evidence, we may decide your claim prior to the expiration of the one year period. If we decide the claim before one year from the date we receive the claim, you will still have the remainder of the one year period to submit additional information or evidence necessary to support the claim.
If any of the special circumstances in the table below titled *"Special Circumstances"* applies to you; **You must:** • Send the information and evidence identified in the *"Special Circumstances"* table below at the same time as your claim	If any of the special circumstances in the table below titled *"Special Circumstances"* applies to you; **You are strongly encouraged to:** • Send the information and evidence identified in the *"Special Circumstances"* table below at the same time as your claim. If you do not submit the needed information or evidence with your claim but it is needed to make a decision, VA will request it from you.

SPECIAL CIRCUMSTANCES

Under the special circumstances shown below, you *must* also submit along with your claim the following:

- **If you were treated at a Veterans Center**, submit a completed VA Form 21-4142, *Authorization to Disclose Information to the Department of Veterans Affairs (VA)*
- **If claiming dependents**, submit a completed VA Form 21-686c, *Application Request to Add and/or Remove Dependents*. If claiming a child in school between the ages of 18 and 23; also submit a completed VA Form 21-674, *Request for Approval of School Attendance*. If claiming benefits for a seriously disabled (helpless) child, also submit all, relevant, private medical treatment records pertaining to the child's pertinent disabilities
- **If claiming Individual Unemployability**, submit a completed VA Form 21-8940, *Veteran's Application for Increased Compensation Based on Unemployability*
- **If claiming Post-Traumatic Stress Disorder (PTSD)**, submit a completed VA Form 21-0781, *Statement in Support of Claim for Service Connection for Post-Traumatic Stress Disorder*, or if claiming PTSD based on personal assault, submit a completed VA Form 21-0781a, *Statement in Support of Claim for Service Connection for Post-Traumatic Stress Disorder Secondary to Personal Assault*

SPECIAL CIRCUMSTANCES (Continued)

Under the special circumstances shown below, you must also submit along with your claim the following:

- **If claiming Specially Adapted Housing or Special Home Adaptation**, submit a completed VA Form 26-4555, *Application in Acquiring Specially Adapted Housing or Special Home Adaptation Grant*

- **If claiming Auto Allowance**, submit a completed VA Form 21-4502, *Application for Automobile or Other Conveyance and Adaptive Equipment*

- **If claiming additional benefits because you or your spouse require Aid and Attendance**, submit a completed VA Form 21-2680, *Examination for Housebound Status or Permanent Need for Regular Aid and Attendance*, or if claiming Aid and Attendance based on nursing home attendance, a VA Form 21-0779, *Request for Nursing Home Information in Connection with Claim for Aid and Attendance*

NOTE: VA forms are available online at www.va.gov/vaforms.

3. HOW VA WILL HELP YOU OBTAIN EVIDENCE FOR YOUR CLAIM

The table below describes the information and evidence VA will assist you in obtaining based on whether you wish to have your claim considered in the FDC Program (Optional Expedited Process) or in the Standard Claim Process.

FDC Program (Optional Expedited Process)	Standard Claim Process
VA will:	VA will:
• Retrieve relevant records from a Federal facility, such as a VA medical center, that you adequately identify and authorized VA to obtain • Provide a medical examination for you, or get a medical opinion, if we determine it is necessary to decide your claim	• Retrieve relevant records from a Federal facility, such as a VA medical center, that you adequately identify and authorized VA to obtain • Provide a medical examination for you, or get a medical opinion, if we determine it is necessary to decide your claim • Make every reasonable effort to obtain relevant records not held by a Federal facility that you adequately identify and authorize VA to obtain. These may include records from State or local governments and privately held evidence and information you tell us about, such as a private doctor or hospital records from current or former employers

4. WHERE TO SEND INFORMATION AND EVIDENCE

You may send your application and any evidence in support of your claim by using any of the following methods shown in the table below.

MAIL TO	FAX TO	ONLINE
Department of Veterans Affairs **Evidence Intake Center** **PO Box 4444** **Janesville, WI 53547-4444**	**844-531-7818 (Toll Free)** *OR* **For Foreign Claims 248-524-4260**	www.va.gov

5. WHAT THE EVIDENCE MUST SHOW TO SUPPORT YOUR CLAIM

The table below provides a guide to the evidence tables showing what evidence you must provide to support your claim.

If you are claiming...	See the evidence table titled...
You have a disability that was caused or aggravated by your service	Disability Service Connection
Your service connected disability caused or aggravated an additional disability	Secondary Service Connection
Your service connected disability has worsened	Increased Disability Compensation
Compensation and you are a service person who is about to be discharged	Compensation Claims Submitted Prior to Discharge
Your service connected disability caused you to be hospitalized or to undergo surgery or other treatment	Temporary Total Disability Rating
Your service connected disability(ies) prevents you from getting or keeping substantial employment	Individual Unemployability
You have a disability caused or aggravated by VA medical treatment, vocational rehabilitation, or compensated work therapy	Compensation Under 38 U.S.C. 1151
Your service connected disability (ies) causes you to be in need of aid and attendance or to be confined to your residence	Special Monthly Compensation
Adapting and/or purchasing a residence	Special Adapted Housing or Special Home Adaptation
Adapting and/or purchasing a vehicle	Auto Allowance
A Severely Disabled Spouse	Special Monthly Compensation
A Severely Disabled Child	Helpless Child

EVIDENCE TABLES

Disability Service Connection

To support a claim for **service connection**, the evidence must show:

- You had an injury in service, or a disease that began in or was made permanently worse during service, or there was an event in service that caused an injury or disease; **AND**
- You have a current physical or mental disability. This may be shown by medical evidence or by lay evidence of persistent and recurrent symptoms of disability that are visible or observable; **AND**
- A relationship exists between your current disability and an injury, disease, symptoms, or event in service. This may be shown by medical records or medical opinions or, in certain cases, by lay evidence.

However, under certain circumstances, VA may presume that certain current disabilities were caused by service, even if there is no specific evidence proving this in your particular claim. The cause of a disability is presumed for the following veterans who have certain diseases:

- Former prisoners of war;
- Veterans who have certain chronic or tropical diseases that become evident within a specific period of time after discharge from service;
- Veterans who were exposed to ionizing radiation, mustard gas, or Lewisite while in service;
- Veterans who were exposed to certain herbicides, such as by serving in Vietnam; or
- Veterans who served at Camp Lejeune for no less than 30 days (consecutive or nonconsecutive) between August 1, 1953 and December 31, 1987; or
- Veterans who served in the Southwest Asia theater of operations during the Gulf War.

To support a claim for **service connection based upon a period of** *active* **duty for training**, the evidence must show:

- You were disabled during active duty for training due to disease or injury incurred or aggravated in the line of duty; **AND**
- You have a current physical or mental disability. This may be shown by medical evidence or by lay evidence of persistent and recurrent symptoms of disability that are visible or observable; **AND**
- There is a relationship between your current disability and the disease or injury incurred or aggravated during active duty for training. This may be shown by medical records or medical opinions or, in certain cases, by lay evidence.

To support a claim for **service connection based upon a period of** *inactive* **duty training**, the evidence must show:

- You were disabled during inactive duty training due to an injury incurred or aggravated in the line of duty or an acute myocardial infarction, cardiac arrest, or cerebrovascular accident during inactive duty training; **AND**
- You have a current physical or mental disability. This may be shown by medical evidence or by lay evidence of persistent and recurrent symptoms of disability that are visible or observable; **AND**
- There is a relationship between your current disability and your inactive duty training. This may be shown by medical records or medical opinions or, in certain cases, by lay evidence.

In order to file a **supplemental claim**, you must submit or identify new and relevant evidence.

- To qualify as new, the evidence must not have been part of the evidentiary record at the time of the prior decision.
- In order to be considered relevant, the additional evidence must tend to prove or disprove a matter at issue in the claim.

Secondary Service Connection

To support a claim for **compensation based upon an additional disability** that was caused or aggravated by a service-connected disability, the evidence must show:

- You currently have a physical or mental disability shown by medical evidence or by lay evidence of persistent and recurrent symptoms of disability that are visible or observable, in addition to your service-connected disability; **AND**
- Your service-connected disability either caused or aggravated your additional disability. This may be shown by medical records or medical opinions or, in certain cases, by lay evidence. However, VA may presume service-connection for cardiovascular disease developing in a claimant with certain service-connected amputation(s) of one or both lower extremities.

Increased Disability Compensation

If VA previously granted service connection for your disability and you are seeking an **increased evaluation** of your service-connected disability, we need medical or lay evidence to show a worsening or increase in severity and the effect that worsening or increase has on your ability to work.

281

EVIDENCE TABLES (Continued)

Compensation Claims Submitted Prior to Discharge

Under the Benefits Delivery at Discharge (BDD) program you can submit a disability claim 90 to 180 days prior to your anticipated separation date from active duty. Claims are accepted from active duty Servicemembers, including reservists serving on active duty in an Active Guard Reserve (AGR) role under 10 U.S.C. and full-time National Guard members serving in an AGR role under 32 U.S.C.

BDD program participants can have their VA medical examinations conducted while they are still on active duty. You are encouraged to file your claim as close to the 180 day mark as possible to ensure your examinations can be scheduled and completed prior to your discharge from active duty. The BDD program requires that Servicemembers be available to report for examinations for 45 days following submission of a disability claim. Claims and additional contentions received with less than 90 days remaining on active duty, claim types that are excluded from the BDD program, or where the Servicemember is unable to report for an examination within the BDD required time frame will be processed under the standard VA claims process, the Fully Developed Claim (FDC) program or any other qualifying program.

BDD Program Criteria for Claim(s) for Disability Compensation and Related Compensation Benefits Submitted Prior to Separation from Active Duty:

- **be within 90 to 180 days of discharge;**
- **be available to report for examinations for 45 days following the submission of a disability claim;**
- **provide an anticipated release from active duty date,** *and*
- **complete a VA Form 21-526EZ,** *Application for Disability Compensation and Related Compensation Benefits*

Temporary Total Disability Rating

In order to support a claim for **a temporary total disability rating due to hospitalization,** the evidence must show:
- You were treated for more than 21 days for a service-connected disability at a VA or other approved hospital; **OR**
- You underwent hospital observation at VA expense for a service-connected disability for more than 21 days.

In order to support a claim for a temporary total disability rating due to surgical or other treatment performed by a VA or other approved hospital or outpatient facility, the evidence must show:
- The surgery or treatment was for a service-connected disability; **AND**
- The surgery required convalescence of at least one month; **OR**
- The surgery resulted in severe postoperative residuals, such as incompletely healed surgical wounds, stumps of recent amputations, therapeutic immobilizations, house confinement, or the required use of a wheelchair or crutches; **OR**
- One major joint or more was immobilized by a cast without surgery.

Individual Unemployability

In order to support a claim for **a total disability rating based on individual unemployability,** the evidence must show:
- That your service-connected disability or disabilities are sufficient, without regard to other factors, to prevent you from performing the mental and/or physical tasks required to get or keep substantially gainful employment; **AND**
- Generally, you meet certain disability percentage requirements as specified in 38 Code of Federal Regulations 4.16 (i.e. one disability ratable at 60 percent or more, **OR** more than one disability with one disability ratable at 40 percent or more and a combined rating of 70 percent or more).

In order to support a claim for **an extra-scheduler evaluation based on exceptional circumstances,** the evidence must show:
- That your service-connected disability or disabilities present such an exceptional or unusual disability picture, due to such factors as marked interference with employment or frequent periods of hospitalization, that application of the regular scheduler standards is impractical.

Compensation Under 38 U.S.C. 1151

In order to support a claim for **compensation under 38 U.S.C. 1151,** the evidence must show that, as a result of VA hospitalization, medical or surgical treatment, examination, or training, you have:
- An additional disability or disabilities; **OR**
- An aggravation of an existing injury or disease; **AND**
- The disability was the direct result of VA fault such as carelessness, negligence, lack of proper skill, or error in judgment, or not a reasonably expected result or complication of the VA care or treatment; **OR**
- The direct result of participation in a VA Vocational Rehabilitation and Employment or compensated work therapy program.

EVIDENCE TABLES (Continued)

Special Monthly Compensation

In order to support a claim for **increased benefits based on the need for aid and attendance**, the evidence must show that, due to your service-connected disability or disabilities:

- You require the aid of another person in order to perform personal functions required in everyday living, such as bathing, feeding, dressing yourself, attending to the wants of nature, adjusting prosthetic devices, or protecting yourself from the hazards of your daily environment (38 Code of Federal Regulation 3.352(a)); **OR**
- You are bedridden, in that your disability or disabilities requires that you remain in bed apart from any prescribed course of convalescence or treatment (38 Code of Federal Regulation 3.352(a)).

In order to support a claim for **increased benefits based on an additional disability or being housebound**, the evidence must show:

- You have a single service-connected disability evaluated as 100 percent disabling **AND** an additional service-connected disability, or disabilities, evaluated as 60 percent or more disabling, **OR**
- You have a single service-connected disability evaluated as 100 percent disabling **AND**, due solely to your service-connected disability or disabilities, you are permanently and substantially confined to your immediate premises.

In order to support a claim for **increased benefits based on your spouse's need for aid and attendance**, per the provisions of 38 C.F.R. § 3.351(c), the evidence must show:

- Your spouse is blind or so nearly blind as to have corrected visual acuity of 5/200 or less, in both eyes, or concentric contraction of the visual field to 5 degrees or less; **OR**
- Your spouse is a patient in a nursing home because of mental or physical incapacity; **OR**
- Your spouse requires the aid of another person in order to perform personal functions required in everyday living, such as bathing, feeding, dressing, attending to the wants of nature, adjusting prosthetic devices, or protecting him or her from the hazards of his or her daily environment (See 38 C.F.R. § 3.352(a) for complete explanation).

IMPORTANT: For additional benefits to be payable for a spouse, the veteran must be entitled to compensation and evaluated as 30 percent or more disabling.

Specially Adapted Housing or Special Home Adaptation

To support your claim for **specially adapted housing (SAH)**, the evidence must show you are a:

- Veteran entitled to compensation under 38 U.S.C. Chapter 11 for a permanent and totally disabling qualifying condition; **OR**
- Servicemember on active duty who has a permanent and totally disabling qualifying condition incurred or aggravated in the line of duty.

To support that you have a **qualifying condition for SAH** the evidence must show:

- Amyotrophic lateral sclerosis (ALS); **OR**
- Loss (amputation) or loss of use of:
  - *both* lower extremities; **OR**
  - *one* lower extremity **and** *one* upper extremity affecting balance **or** propulsion; **OR**
  - *one* lower extremity **plus** residuals of organic disease or injury affecting balance or propulsion creating a need for regular, constant use of a wheelchair, braces, crutches or canes as a normal mode of getting around (although getting around by other methods may occasionally be possible); **OR**
- Loss or loss of use of *both* upper extremities precluding use of the arms at or above the elbow; **OR**
- Permanent but not total disability due to blindness in *both* eyes, (having central visual acuity of 20/200 or less in the better eye with the use of a standard correcting lens); **OR**
- A severe burn injury, meaning full thickness or sub-dermal burns that have resulted in contractures with limitation of motion of:
  - *two* **or** more extremities; **OR**
  - *at least one* extremity **and** the trunk.

To support your claim for **SAH** the evidence may alternatively show you are a:

- Veteran who served and became permanently disabled from a qualifying condition on or after September 11, 2001; **OR**
- Servicemember on active duty who was permanently disabled in the line of duty from a qualifying condition on or after the same date.

To support that you have a **qualifying condition under the alternative service criteria** the evidence must show:

- Loss (amputation) or loss of use of:
  - *one or more* lower extremities, severely affecting the functions of balance or propulsion and creating a need for regular, constant use of a wheelchair, braces, crutches or canes as a normal mode of getting around (although getting around by other methods may occasionally be possible).

To support your claim for a **special home adaptation (SHA) grant** the evidence must show you are a:

- Veteran entitled to compensation under 38 U.S.C. Chapter 11 for a qualifying condition; **OR**
- Servicemember on active duty who has a qualifying condition incurred or aggravated in the line of duty.

283

EVIDENCE TABLES (Continued)

Specially Adapted Housing or Special Home Adaptation (Continued)

To support that you have a **qualifying condition for SHA** the evidence must show:

- the loss, or permanent loss of use, of at least a foot or a hand; **OR**

- Permanent **and** total disability from loss, **or** loss of use, of *both* hands; **OR**

- Permanent **and** total disability from a severe burn injury meaning:

  - deep partial thickness burns that have resulted in contractures with limitation of motion of *two or more* extremities **or** of *at least one* extremity **and** the trunk; **OR**

  - full thickness **or** sub-dermal burns that have resulted in contracture(s) with limitation of motion of *one or more* extremities **or** the trunk; **OR**

  - residuals of inhalation injury (including, but not limited to, pulmonary fibrosis, asthma, and chronic obstructive pulmonary disease).

Auto Allowance

To support a claim for **automobile allowance or adaptive equipment**, the evidence must show that you have a service-connected disability resulting in:

(1) the loss, or permanent loss of use, of at least a foot or a hand; **OR**

(2) permanent impairment of vision of both eyes, resulting in:

    (a) vision of 20/200 or less in the better eye with corrective glasses; **OR**

    (b) vision of 20/200 or better, if there is a severe defect in your peripheral vision; **OR**

(3) deep partial thickness or full thickness burns resulting in scar formation that cause contractures and limit motion of one or more extremities of the trunk and preclude effective operation of an automobile; **OR**

(4) amyotrophic lateral sclerosis (ALS).

NOTE - You may be entitled to *only* adaptive equipment if you have ankylosis ("freezing") of at least one knee or one hip due to service-connected disability. Medical evidence, including a VA examination, will show these things. VA will provide an examination if it determines that one is necessary.

Helpless Child

To support a claim for **benefits based on a veteran's child being helpless**, the evidence must show that the child, before his or her 18th birthday, became permanently incapable of self-support due to a mental or physical disability.

IMPORTANT: For additional benefits to be payable for a child, the veteran must be entitled to compensation and evaluated as 30 percent or more disabling.

HOW VA DETERMINES THE EFFECTIVE DATE.

If we grant your claim, the beginning date of your entitlement or increased entitlement to benefits will generally be based on the following factors.

- When we received your claim. **OR**
- When the evidence shows a level of disability that supports a certain rating under the rating schedule

If VA received your claim prior to or within one year of your separation from the military, entitlement will be from the day following the date of your separation as long as the disability was present at that time.

HOW VA DETERMINES THE DISABILITY RATING.

When we find disabilities to be service-connected, we assign a disability rating. That rating can be changed if there are changes in your condition. Depending on the disability involved, we will assign a rating from 0 percent to as much as 100 percent. VA uses a schedule for evaluating disabilities that is published as title 38, Code of Federal Regulations, Part 4. In rare cases, we can assign a disability level other than the levels found in the schedule for a specific condition if your impairment is not adequately covered by the schedule.

We consider evidence of the following in determining disability rating:

- Nature and symptoms of the condition;
- Severity and duration of the symptoms; **AND**
- Impact of the condition and symptoms on employment.

Examples of evidence that you should tell us about or give to us that may affect how we assign a disability evaluation include the following:

- Information about on-going treatment records, including VA or other Federal treatment records, you have not previously told us about;
- Social Security determinations;
- Statements from employers as to job performance, lost time, or other information regarding how your condition(s) affect your ability to work; **OR**
- Statements discussing your disability symptoms from people who have witnessed how the symptoms affect you.

For more information on the FDC Program, visit our web site at http://benefits.va.gov/transformation/fastclaims/.

For more information on VA benefits, visit our web site at www.va.gov, contact us at https://iris.custhelp.va.gov, or call us toll-free at 1-800-827-1000. If you use a Telecommunications Device for the Deaf (TDD), the Federal relay number is 711. VA forms are available at www.va.gov/vaforms.

IMPORTANT: If you wish to make a claim for **veterans non service-connected pension benefits** because you have little or no income, use VA Form 21P-527EZ, *Application for Pension*. VA forms are available at www.va.gov/vaforms. If you cannot access this form, write the word **"Pension"** in Item 16, or at the top of the attached application and VA will send you the form.

OMB Control No. 2900-0747
Respondent Burden: 25 minutes
Expiration Date: 09/30/2022

Department of Veterans Affairs

APPLICATION FOR DISABILITY COMPENSATION AND RELATED COMPENSATION BENEFITS

| VA DATE STAMP (DO NOT WRITE IN THIS SPACE) |

IMPORTANT: Please read the Privacy Act and Respondent Burden on page 12 before completing the form.

1. SELECT THE TYPE OF CLAIM PROGRAM/PROCESS *(Check the appropriate box) (See instruction pages 1-3 for definitions of the Fully Developed Claim (FDC) Program (Optional Expedited Process) or the Standard Claim Process. (See instruction page 5 for the definition of a Benefits Delivery at Discharge (BDD) Program Claim)*

- ○ FULLY DEVELOPED CLAIM (FDC) PROGRAM   ○ STANDARD CLAIM PROCESS
- ○ IDES (Select this option *only* if you have been referred to the IDES Program by your Military Service Department)
- ○ BDD Program Claim (Select this option *only* if you meet the criteria for the BDD Program specified on Instruction Page 5)

NOTE: You may *either* complete the form online or by hand. If completed by hand, print the information requested in ink, neatly, and legibly to expedite processing of the form.

SECTION I: IDENTIFICATION AND CLAIM INFORMATION
(If claim is not an original claim, only Section I, IV, and a signature are required)

2. VETERAN/SERVICE MEMBER NAME *(First, Middle Initial, Last)*

3. VETERAN'S SOCIAL SECURITY NUMBER *(SSN)*

4. HAVE YOU EVER FILED A CLAIM WITH VA?
○ YES   ○ NO   *(If "Yes," provide your file number in Item 5)*

5. VA FILE NUMBER

6. DATE OF BIRTH *(MM-DD-YYYY)*

7. VETERAN'S SERVICE NUMBER *(If applicable)*

8. SEX
○ MALE   ○ FEMALE

9. BDD CLAIMS *ONLY*: PROVIDE THE DATE OR ANTICIPATED DATE OF RELEASE FROM ACTIVE DUTY *(MM-DD-YYYY)*

10. TELEPHONE NUMBER(S) *(Optional) (Include Area Code)*
Daytime:
Evening:
Cell phone:

11. CURRENT MAILING ADDRESS *(Number and street or rural route, P.O. Box, City, State, ZIP Code and Country)*
No. & Street
Apt./Unit Number   City
State/Province   Country   ZIP Code/Postal Code

12. EMAIL ADDRESS *(Optional)*

○ 13. IF YOU ARE CURRENTLY A VA EMPLOYEE, CHECK THE BOX *(Includes Work Study/Internship). (If you are not a VA employee skip to Section II, if applicable)*

SECTION II: CHANGE OF ADDRESS

NOTE: If you are temporarily or permanently changing your address, complete Items 14A through 14C.

14A. TYPE OF ADDRESS CHANGE *(Complete if applicable) (Check only one box)*
○ TEMPORARY   ○ PERMANENT

14B. NEW ADDRESS *(Number and street or rural route, P.O. Box, City, State, ZIP Code and Country)*
No. & Street
Apt./Unit Number   City
State/Province   Country   ZIP Code/Postal Code

14C. EFFECTIVE DATE(S) OF NEW ADDRESS *(If your change of address is **temporary**, complete both the beginning and ending date of your temporary address) (If your change of address is **permanent**, please enter your effective data in the beginning date only)*

	Month	Day	Year		Month	Day	Year
BEGINNING DATE:				ENDING DATE:			

VA FORM
SEP 2019   **21-526EZ**   SUPERSEDES VA FORM 21-526EZ, MAR 2018.   Page 8

VETERANS SOCIAL SECURITY NO. [ ][ ][ ] — [ ][ ] — [ ][ ][ ][ ]

IMPORTANT: The following questions (Items 15A through 15F) should *only* be completed if you are currently homeless or at risk of becoming homeless. If this item does not apply to you, skip to Section IV.

15A. ARE YOU CURRENTLY HOMELESS?	15B. CHECK THE BOX THAT APPLIES TO YOUR LIVING SITUATION:
◯ YES *(If "Yes," complete Item 15B regarding your living situation)* ◯ NO	◯ LIVING IN A HOMELESS SHELTER ◯ NOT CURRENTLY IN A SHELTERED ENVIRONMENT (e.g., living in a car or tent) ◯ STAYING WITH ANOTHER PERSON ◯ FLEEING CURRENT RESIDENCE ◯ OTHER (Specify) [ ][ ][ ][ ][ ][ ][ ][ ][ ][ ]
15C. ARE YOU CURRENTLY AT RISK OF BECOMING HOMELESS?	15D. CHECK THE BOX THAT APPLIES TO YOUR LIVING SITUATION:
◯ YES *(If "Yes," complete Item 15D regarding your living situation)* ◯ NO	◯ HOUSING WILL BE LOST IN 30 DAYS ◯ LEAVING PUBLICLY FUNDED SYSTEM OF CARE (e.g., homeless shelter) ◯ OTHER (Specify) [ ][ ][ ][ ][ ][ ][ ][ ]
15E. POINT OF CONTACT *(Name of person VA can contact in order to get in touch with you)*	15F. POINT OF CONTACT TELEPHONE NUMBER *(Include Area Code)*
[ ][ ][ ][ ][ ][ ][ ][ ][ ][ ][ ][ ][ ][ ][ ][ ][ ][ ][ ]	[ ][ ][ ][ ][ ][ ][ ][ ][ ][ ]

16. LIST THE CURRENT DISABILITY(IES) OR SYMPTOMS THAT YOU CLAIM ARE RELATED TO YOUR MILITARY SERVICE AND/OR SERVICE-CONNECTED DISABILITY *(If applicable, identify whether a disability is due to a service-connected disability; confinement as a prisoner of war; exposure to Agent Orange, asbestos, mustard gas, ionizing radiation, or Gulf War environmental hazards; or a disability for which compensation is payable under 38 U.S.C. 1151)*

NOTE: List your claimed conditions below. **See the following three examples for guidance on how to complete Section IV.**

EXAMPLES OF DISABILITY(IES)	EXAMPLES OF EXPOSURE TYPE	EXAMPLES OF HOW THE DISABILITY(IES) RELATE TO SERVICE	EXAMPLES OF DATES
Example 1. HEARING LOSS	NOISE	HEAVY EQUIPMENT OPERATOR IN SERVICE	JULY 1968
Example 2. DIABETES	AGENT ORANGE	SERVICE IN VIETNAM WAR	DECEMBER 1972
Example 3. LEFT KNEE, SECONDARY TO RIGHT KNEE		INJURED LEFT KNEE WHEN BRACE ON RIGHT KNEE FAILED	6/11/2008

CURRENT DISABILITY(IES)	IF DUE TO EXPOSURE, EVENT, OR INJURY, PLEASE SPECIFY (e.g., Agent Orange, radiation)	EXPLAIN HOW THE DISABILITY(IES) RELATES TO THE IN-SERVICE EVENT/EXPOSURE/INJURY	APPROXIMATE DATE DISABILITY(IES) BEGAN OR WORSENED
1.			
2.			
3.			
4.			
5.			
6.			
7.			
8.			
9.			
10.			
11.			
12.			
13.			
14.			
15.			

VETERANS SOCIAL SECURITY NO. ☐☐☐ — ☐☐ — ☐☐☐☐

17 LIST VA MEDICAL CENTER(S) (VAMC) AND DEPARTMENT OF DEFENSE (DOD) MILITARY TREATMENT FACILITIES (MTF) WHERE YOU RECEIVED TREATMENT AFTER DISCHARGE FOR YOUR CLAIMED DISABILITY(IES) LISTED IN ITEM 16 AND PROVIDE APPROXIMATE BEGINNING DATE (Month and Year) OF TREATMENT.
NOTE: If treatment began from 2005 to present, you do not need to provide dates in Item 17B

A. ENTER THE DISABILITY TREATED AND NAME/LOCATION OF THE TREATMENT FACILITY	B. DATE OF TREATMENT (MM-DD-YYYY)	C. CHECK THE BOX IF YOU DO NOT HAVE DATE(S) OF TREATMENT
	☐☐ — ☐☐ — ☐☐☐☐	○ Don't have date
	☐☐ — ☐☐ — ☐☐☐☐	○ Don't have date
	☐☐ — ☐☐ — ☐☐☐☐	○ Don't have date
	☐☐ — ☐☐ — ☐☐☐☐	○ Don't have date

NOTE: IF YOU WISH TO CLAIM ANY OF THE FOLLOWING, COMPLETE AND ATTACH THE REQUIRED FORM(S) AS STATED BELOW.
(VA forms are available at www.va.gov/vaforms)

For:	Required Form(s):
Supplemental Claims	VA Form 20-0995, Decision Review Request: Supplemental Claim
Dependents	VA Form 21-686c and, if claiming a child aged 18-23 years and in school, VA Form 21-674
Individual Unemployability	VA Form 21-8940 and 21-4192
Post-Traumatic Stress Disorder	VA Form 21-0781 or 21-0781a
Specially Adapted Housing or Special Home Adaptation	VA Form 26-4555
Auto Allowance	VA Form 21-4502
Veteran/Spouse Aid and Attendance benefits	VA Form 21-2680 or, if based on nursing home attendance, VA Form 21-0779

SECTION V: SERVICE INFORMATION

18A. DID YOU SERVE UNDER ANOTHER NAME?

○ YES (If "Yes," complete Item 18B) ○ NO (If "No," skip to Item 19A)

18B. LIST THE OTHER NAME(S) YOU SERVED UNDER.

19A. BRANCH OF SERVICE

○ ARMY ○ NAVY ○ MARINE CORPS

○ AIR FORCE ○ COAST GUARD

19B. COMPONENT

○ ACTIVE ○ RESERVES ○ NATIONAL GUARD

20A. MOST RECENT ACTIVE SERVICE DATES (MM,DD,YYYY)

ENTRY DATE: Month ☐☐ — Day ☐☐ — Year ☐☐☐☐

EXIT DATE: ☐☐ — ☐☐ — ☐☐☐☐

20B. PLACE OF LAST OR ANTICIPATED SEPARATION

| 20C. DID YOU SERVE IN A COMBAT ZONE SINCE 9-11-2001? ○ YES ○ NO | 20D. ADDITIONAL PERIODS OF SERVICE (Indicate enlistment and discharge date(s), if applicable) | Enlistment Date(s): Month ☐☐ Day ☐☐ Year ☐☐☐☐ / Month ☐☐ Day ☐☐ Year ☐☐☐☐ |
| | | Discharge Date(s): Month ☐☐ Day ☐☐ Year ☐☐☐☐ / Month ☐☐ Day ☐☐ Year ☐☐☐☐ |

21A. ARE YOU CURRENTLY SERVING OR HAVE YOU EVER SERVED IN THE RESERVES OR NATIONAL GUARD?

○ YES (If "Yes," complete Items 21B thru 21F)

○ NO (If "No," skip to Item 22A)

21B. COMPONENT

○ NATIONAL GUARD

○ RESERVES

21C. OBLIGATION TERM OF SERVICE

From: Month ☐☐ — Day ☐☐ — Year ☐☐☐☐

To: ☐☐ — ☐☐ — ☐☐☐☐

21D. CURRENT OR LAST ASSIGNED NAME AND ADDRESS OF UNIT:

21E. CURRENT OR ASSIGNED PHONE NUMBER OF UNIT (Include Area Code)

21F. ARE YOU CURRENTLY RECEIVING INACTIVE DUTY TRAINING PAY?

○ YES ○ NO

22A. ARE YOU CURRENTLY ACTIVATED ON FEDERAL ORDERS WITHIN THE NATIONAL GUARD OR RESERVES?

○ YES (If "Yes," complete Items 22B & 22C)

○ NO

22B. DATE OF ACTIVATION: (MM,DD,YYYY)

Month ☐☐ — Day ☐☐ — Year ☐☐☐☐

22C. ANTICIPATED SEPARATION DATE: (MM,DD,YYYY)

Month ☐☐ — Day ☐☐ — Year ☐☐☐☐

23A. HAVE YOU EVER BEEN A PRISONER OF WAR?

○ YES (If "Yes," complete Item 23B)

○ NO

23B. DATES OF CONFINEMENT (MM,DD,YYYY)

From: Month ☐☐ — Day ☐☐ — Year ☐☐☐☐

To: Month ☐☐ — Day ☐☐ — Year ☐☐☐☐

From: Month ☐☐ — Day ☐☐ — Year ☐☐☐☐

To: Month ☐☐ — Day ☐☐ — Year ☐☐☐☐

VETERANS SOCIAL SECURITY NO. ☐☐☐ – ☐☐ – ☐☐☐☐

SECTION VI: SERVICE PAY (Retired Pay, Separation Pay, and Disability Severance Pay)

24A. ARE YOU RECEIVING MILITARY RETIRED PAY?	24B. WILL YOU RECEIVE MILITARY RETIRED PAY IN THE FUTURE?
○ YES *(If "Yes," complete Items 24C and 24D)* ○ NO	○ YES *(If "Yes," explain below (e.g. future Reserve/National Guard retirement, pending MEB/PEB and also complete Items 24C and 24D)* ○ NO

24C. BRANCH OF SERVICE	24D. MONTHLY AMOUNT	25. RETIRED STATUS
○ ARMY ○ NAVY ○ MARINE CORPS ○ AIR FORCE ○ COAST GUARD	$ ☐☐☐,☐☐☐.00	○ RETIRED ○ PERMANENT DISABILITY RETIRED LIST ○ TEMPORARY DISABILITY RETIRED LIST

IMPORTANT INFORMATION ON MILITARY RETIRED PAY (Includes all Uniformed Services Retired Pay):
Submission of this application constitutes a waiver of military retired pay in an amount equal to VA compensation awarded, if you are entitled to both benefits. Your retired pay may be reduced by the amount of VA compensation awarded. Receipt of the full amount of military retired pay and VA compensation at the same time *may* result in an overpayment, which *may* be subject to collection. If you qualify for concurrent receipt of VA compensation and military retired pay, the waiver of retired pay will not apply. If you do not want to waive any retired pay to receive VA compensation, you should check the box in Item 26.
Note that if you check the box in Item 26, you will not receive VA compensation, if granted. If you are currently in receipt of VA compensation and you check the box in Item 26, your VA compensation will be terminated, if you are also eligible for military retired pay.

IMPORTANT: VA COMPENSATION PAY IS NON-TAXABLE. THEREFORE, VA COMPENSATION PAY MAY BE THE GREATER BENEFIT.

○ **26. Do NOT pay me VA compensation. I do NOT want to receive VA compensation in lieu of retired pay.**

IMPORTANT INFORMATION ON SEPARATION/SEVERANCE PAY:
VA compensation, if granted, may be withheld to recoup any disability severance or separation pay such as involuntary separation pay, voluntary separation pay, or special separation benefit, you receive from your branch of service. In addition, if you receive a Voluntary Separation Incentive (VSI), your VSI payments may be reduced if you are awarded VA compensation. Receipt of VA compensation and VSI at the same time may result in an overpayment of VSI, which *may* be subject to collection.

27A. HAVE YOU EVER RECEIVED SEPARATION PAY, DISABILITY SEVERANCE PAY, OR ANY OTHER LUMP SUM PAYMENT FROM YOUR BRANCH OF SERVICE?

○ YES   *(If "Yes," complete Items 27B through 27D)*
○ NO

27B. DATE PAYMENT RECEIVED *(MM-DD-YYYY)*	27C. BRANCH OF SERVICE	27D. AMOUNT RECEIVED *(Provide pre-tax amount)*
☐☐ – ☐☐ – ☐☐☐☐	○ ARMY ○ NAVY ○ MARINE CORPS ○ AIR FORCE ○ COAST GUARD	$ ☐☐☐,☐☐☐.00

IMPORTANT INFORMATION ON INACTIVE DUTY TRAINING PAY:
You may elect to keep the active or inactive duty training pay you received from the military service department. However, to be legally entitled to keep your training pay, you must waive VA benefits for the number of days equal to the number of days for which you received training pay. In most instances, it will be to your advantage to waive your VA benefits and keep your training pay.

If you waive VA benefits to receive training pay by checking the box in **Item 28**, VA will retroactively adjust your VA award to withhold benefits equal to the total number of training days waived and at the monthly rate in effect for the fiscal year period for which you received training pay. This action may result in an overpayment of compensation, which *may* be subject to collection.

IMPORTANT: VA COMPENSATION PAY IS NON-TAXABLE. THEREFORE VA COMPENSATION PAY MAY BE THE GREATER BENEFIT.

○ **28. Do NOT pay me VA compensation. I do NOT want to receive VA compensation in lieu of training pay.**

SECTION VII: DIRECT DEPOSIT INFORMATION

The Department of the Treasury requires all Federal benefit payments be made by electronic funds transfer (EFT), also called direct deposit. To enroll in direct deposit, please attach a voided personal check, deposit slip, or provide the information requested below. If you **do not** have a bank account, please visit https://www.benefits.va.gov/benefits/banking.asp. This website provides information about the Veterans Benefits Banking Program (VBBP), and a link to banks and credit unions that may fit your needs. You may also call 1-800-827-1000. If you elect not to enroll, you must contact representatives handling waiver requests for the Department of the Treasury at 1-888-224-2950. They will encourage your participation in EFT and address any questions or concerns you may have.

○ **29. I CERTIFY THAT I DO NOT HAVE AN ACCOUNT WITH A FINANCIAL INSTITUTION OR CERTIFIED PAYMENT AGENT** *(If you check this box skip to Section VIII)*

30. ACCOUNT NUMBER *(Check only **one** box below and provide the account number)*

Account No : ☐☐☐☐☐☐☐☐☐☐☐☐☐☐☐   ○ CHECKING   ○ SAVINGS

31. NAME OF FINANCIAL INSTITUTION *(Provide the name of the bank where you want your direct deposit)*	32. ROUTING OR TRANSIT NUMBER *(The first nine numbers located at the bottom left of your check)*

VETERANS SOCIAL SECURITY NO. [ ][ ][ ] — [ ][ ] — [ ][ ][ ][ ]

VETERAN/SERVICEMEMBER CERTIFICATION AND SIGNATURE

I certify and authorize the release of information. I certify that the statements in this document are true and complete to the best of my knowledge. I authorize any person or entity, including but not limited to any organization, service provider, employer, or government agency, to give the Department of Veterans Affairs any information about me. For the limited purpose of providing VA with this information as it may relate to my claim, I waive any privilege that may apply and would otherwise make the information confidential and not disclosable.

I certify I have received the notice attached to this application titled, *Notice to Veteran/Service Member of Evidence Necessary to Substantiate a Claim for Veterans Disability Compensation and Related Compensation Benefits.*

I certify I have enclosed all the information or evidence that will support my claim, to include an identification of relevant records available at a Federal facility such as a VA medical center; **OR,** I have no information or evidence to give VA to support my claim; **OR,** I have checked the box in Item 1, on page 8, indicating I want my claim processed under the standard claim process because I plan to submit additional evidence in support of my claim.

33A. VETERAN/SERVICE MEMBER SIGNATURE (**REQUIRED**) *(Sign in ink)*	33B. DATE SIGNED *(MM-DD-YYYY)* [ ][ ] — [ ][ ] — [ ][ ][ ][ ]

SECTION IX: WITNESSES TO SIGNATURE

34A. SIGNATURE OF WITNESS *(Sign in ink)* *(Note: Only sign if veteran signed in Item 33A using an "X")*	34B. PRINTED NAME AND ADDRESS OF WITNESS
35A. SIGNATURE OF WITNESS *(Sign in ink)* *(Note: Only sign if veteran signed in Item 33A using an "X")*	35B. PRINTED NAME AND ADDRESS OF WITNESS

SECTION X: ALTERNATE SIGNER CERTIFICATION AND SIGNATURE
(NOTE: REQUIRED ONLY IF ITEM 33A IS BLANK)

I certify that by signing on behalf of the claimant, that I am a court-appointed representative; **OR,** an attorney in fact or agent authorized to act on behalf of a claimant under a durable power of attorney; **OR,** a person who is responsible for the care of the claimant, to include but not limited to a spouse or other relative; **OR,** a manager or principal officer acting on behalf of an institution which is responsible for the care of an individual; **AND,** that the claimant is under the age of 18; **OR,** is mentally incompetent to provide substantially accurate information needed to complete the form, or to certify that the statements made on the form are true and complete; **OR,** is physically unable to sign this form.

I understand that I may be asked to confirm the truthfulness of the answers to the best of my knowledge under penalty of perjury. I also understand that VA may request further documentation or evidence to verify or confirm my authorization to sign or complete an application on behalf of the claimant if necessary. Examples of evidence which VA may request include: Social Security Number (SSN) or Taxpayer Identification Number (TIN); a certificate or order from a court with competent jurisdiction showing your authority to act for the claimant with a judge's signature and a date/time stamp; copy of documentation showing appointment of fiduciary; durable power of attorney showing the name and signature of the claimant and your authority as attorney in fact or agent; health care power of attorney, affidavit or notarized statement from an institution or person responsible for the care of the claimant indicating the capacity or responsibility of care provided; or any other documentation showing such authorization.

36A. ALTERNATE SIGNER SIGNATURE (**REQUIRED**) *(Sign in ink)*	36B. DATE SIGNED *(MM-DD-YYYY)* [ ][ ] — [ ][ ] — [ ][ ][ ][ ]

SECTION XI: POWER OF ATTORNEY (POA) SIGNATURE
(NOTE: POA'S CANNOT SIGN FOR AN ORIGINAL CLAIM ONLY)

I certify that the claimant has authorized the undersigned representative to file this claim on behalf of the claimant and that the claimant is aware and accepts the information provided in this document. I certify that the claimant has authorized the undersigned representative to state that the claimant certifies the truth and completion of the information contained in this document to the best of claimant's knowledge.

NOTE: A POA's signature **will not** be accepted unless at the time of submission of this claim a valid VA Form 21-22, *Appointment of Veterans Service Organization as Claimant's Representative*, or VA Form 21-22a, *Appointment of Individual As Claimant's Representative*, indicating the appropriate POA is of record with VA.

37A. POA/AUTHORIZED REPRESENTATIVE SIGNATURE *(Sign in ink)*	37B. DATE SIGNED *(MM-DD-YYYY)* [ ][ ] — [ ][ ] — [ ][ ][ ][ ]

VA FORM 21-526EZ, SEP 2019

OMB Control No. 2900-0826
Respondent Burden: 15 minutes
Expiration Date: 08/31/2021

VA | Department of Veterans Affairs

	VA DATE STAMP (DO NOT WRITE IN THIS SPACE)

INTENT TO FILE A CLAIM FOR COMPENSATION AND/OR PENSION, OR SURVIVORS PENSION AND/OR DIC
(This Form Is Used to Notify VA of Your Intent to File for the General Benefit(s) Checked Below)

NOTE: Please read the Privacy Act and Respondent Burden below before completing the form.

SECTION I: CLAIMANT/VETERAN IDENTIFICATION

NOTE: You can *either* complete the form online or by hand. If completed by hand, print the information requested in ink, neatly and legibly to expedite processing of the form.

1. CLAIMANT'S NAME *(First, Middle Initial, Last)*

2. CLAIMANT'S SOCIAL SECURITY NUMBER

3. VA FILE NUMBER *(If applicable)*

4. VETERAN'S DATE OF BIRTH (MM,DD,YYYY)
Month   Day   Year

5. VETERAN'S NAME *(First, Middle Initial, Last)* **(If different from claimant)**

6. VETERAN'S SOCIAL SECURITY NUMBER

7. VETERAN'S SEX
☐ MALE   ☐ FEMALE

8. VETERAN'S SERVICE NUMBER *(If applicable)*

9. CURRENT MAILING ADDRESS *(Number and street or rural route, P.O. Box, City, State, ZIP Code and Country)*

No & Street

Apt./Unit Number   City

State/Province   Country   ZIP Code/Postal Code

10. HAS THE VETERAN EVER FILED A CLAIM WITH VA?
☐ YES   ☐ NO

11. TELEPHONE NUMBER *(Include Area Code)*

12. EMAIL ADDRESS *(If applicable)*

SECTION II: GENERAL BENEFIT ELECTION

IMPORTANT: *VA may not be able to use this form to establish an effective date for benefits if you do not select one or more of the general benefits listed below.*

13. I intend to file for the general benefit(s) checked below: *(Choose all that apply)*

☐ COMPENSATION   ☐ PENSION

NOTE: Only check the box below if you are a surviving dependent of the veteran.

☐ SURVIVORS PENSION AND/OR DEPENDENCY AND INDEMNITY COMPENSATION (DIC)

IMPORTANT. After receiving this form, VA will give you the appropriate application to file for the general benefit you select above. You can also apply for VA disability compensation online at www.va.gov. If you give VA a completed application for the selected general benefit within *one* year of filing this form, your completed application will be considered filed as of the date of receipt of this form. Only the *first* completed application for each selected general benefit that is received after you file this form will be considered filed as of the date of receipt of this form. You may indicate your intent to file for more than one general benefit on this form or you may submit a separate intent to file for each general benefit. Please complete as many fields in Section II as possible. VA cannot process this form if we cannot identify the claimant and veteran.

SECTION III: DECLARATION OF INTENT

By filing this form, I hereby indicate my intent to apply for one or more general benefits under the laws administered by VA. I acknowledge that: (1) this is *not a claim for benefits*; (2) I must file a complete application for each general benefit with VA before VA will process my claim; and (3) a complete application for the same general benefit(s) as indicated on this form must be received within one year of the date VA receives this form for my application to be considered filed as of the date of this form.

14A. SIGNATURE OF CLAIMANT/AUTHORIZED REPRESENTATIVE

14B. DATE SIGNED *(MM,DD,YYYY)*

15. NAME OF ATTORNEY, AGENT, OR VETERANS SERVICE ORGANIZATION *(Please Print)*
(NOTE: This form may only be completed by a Veterans Service Organization, attorney, or agent if a valid power of attorney has been completed.)

VA FORM
AUG 2018   **21-0966**   SUPERSEDES VA FORM 21-0966, MAR 2017.

**Department of
Veterans Affairs**

INFORMATION AND INSTRUCTIONS FOR COMPLETING DECISION REVIEW REQUEST: SUPPLEMENTAL CLAIM

IMPORTANT: Please read the information below carefully to help you complete this form quickly and accurately. Some parts of the form also contain notes or specific instructions for completing that part.

Use this form to request a SUPPLEMENTAL CLAIM of the decision you received that you disagree with. A **SUPPLEMENTAL CLAIM** is a new review of an issue(s) previously decided by the Department of Veterans Affairs (VA) based on submission of new and relevant evidence. For additional information on the **SUPPLEMENTAL CLAIM** process or other decision review options such as a higher-level review and appeal to the Board of Veterans' Appeals, visit https://www.va.gov/decision-reviews/.

Submit your **SUPPLEMENTAL CLAIM** request to the local VA office or processing center identified on your decision notification letter. I is important that you keep a copy of all completed forms and materials you give to VA. This form has several key components, which, when filled out completely and accurately, will decrease the amount of time it takes to process your **SUPPLEMENTAL CLAIM** request. This form may only be submitted for review of an issue(s) related to one benefit type *(Compensation, Pension/Survivors Benefits, Fiduciary, Insurance, Education, Loan Guaranty, Vocational Rehabilitation & Employment, Veterans Health Administration, or National Cemetery Administration)*. If you would like to file for multiple benefit types, you must complete a separate **SUPPLEMENTAL CLAIM** request form for each benefit type.

You may contact your accredited representative (attorney, claims agent, and Veterans Service Organizations (VSOs) representative) to assist you in completing this request form. If you have not already selected a representative, or if you want to change your representative, a searchable database of VA-recognized VSOs, VA-accredited attorneys, claims agents, and VSO representatives is available at https://www.va.gov/ogc/apps/accreditation/index.asp. Contact your local VA office for assistance with appointing a representative or visit www.ebenefits.va.gov.

You can also ask VA to help you fill out the form by contacting us at the number provided on your decision notification letter or at 1-800-827-1000. Before you contact us, please make sure you gather the necessary information and materials (decision notification letter, etc.), and complete as much of the form as you can.

SPECIFIC INSTRUCTIONS FOR DECISION REVIEW REQUEST: SUPPLEMENTAL CLAIM

Part I - Claimant's Identifying Information
Please note that it would assist VA if you provide all the personal information in Part I. However, if you provide certain information specific to the claimant such as the claimant's last name and Social Security Number or VA file number, VA will be able to identify the claimant in our system and would not necessarily consider this request incomplete if other information in Part I, such as the claimant's address and telephone number, is excluded. This request form may only be completed for review of an issue(s) related to one benefit type. **Select only one benefit type in Item 12.** If you would like to file for multiple benefit types, you must complete a separate **SUPPLEMENTAL CLAIM** request for each benefit type.

Part II - Information to identify the issues for SUPPLEMENTAL CLAIM
The purpose of this section is for you to identify, in item 13A, each issue decided by VA that you would like VA to review as a **SUPPLEMENTAL CLAIM**. Please refer to your decision notification letter(s) for a list of adjudicated issues. You should also enter the date of VA's decision notice letter for each issue, if possible. Only those issue(s) that you list on this form will be considered as part of your **SUPPLEMENTAL CLAIM**. For those issues you do not list on this form, you will still have *one* year from the date of the decision notification letter to file a **SUPPLEMENTAL CLAIM** for those issues to maintain eligibility for the earliest effective date for any granted benefits , or to have them reviewed in a different lane. For proper processing and in order to receive consideration for the earliest effective date possible, if you are filing a supplemental claim within one-year of a decision from the United States Court of Appeals for Veterans Claims, United States Court of Appeals for the Federal Circuit, or Supreme Court of the United States, identify the date of the court decision in item 13B and attach a copy of the decision with this form.

Upon receipt of a Statement of the Case (SOC) or Supplemental Statement of the Case (SSOC) in the legacy appeals system, you may elect to continue your appeal either in the legacy appeals system or in the modernized review system. Your decision notice contains further details. If you are filing this form to opt-in to the modernized review system for any issues decided in the SOC or SSOC, you must provide notice to VA of your decision to leave the legacy appeal process for those issues. To do so when using this form, please check the box for "**OPT-IN** from SOC/SSOC" in item 13 and list the issue(s) in the SOC or SSOC for which you are seeking review under item 13A as instructed above. Your selection of the **SUPPLEMENTAL CLAIM** option does not prevent you from changing the review option under the modernized review system (in accordance with applicable procedures) before VA renders the supplemental claim decision on an issue.

Please note that by checking the "OPT-IN from SOC/SSOC" box in item 13 you are acknowledging the following: I elect to participate in the modernized review system. I am withdrawing all eligible appeal issues listed on this form in their entirety, and any associated hearing requests, from the legacy appeals system to seek review of those issues in VA's modernized review system. I understand that cannot return to the legacy appeals process for the issue(s) withdrawn.

Part III - New and Relevant Evidence

For your **SUPPLEMENTAL CLAIM** application to be complete, you must submit additional evidence that is **NEW AND RELEVANT** to support granting the benefit(s) sought or you must identify existing relevant records that you would like VA to obtain. (**NEW** evidence means information not previously submitted to VA, and **RELEVANT** evidence means information that tends to prove or disprove a matter at issue.)

If you know of evidence not in your possession and want VA to try to get it for you, give VA enough information about the evidence so that we can request it from the person or agency that has it. List all relevant evidence in the custody of a VA medical center (VAMC) or other Federal department or agency in PART III of this application in items 15A and 15B. VA will retrieve relevant records from a Federal facility or VAMC, that you adequately identify and authorize VA to obtain. If the holder of the evidence declines to give it to VA, asks for a fee to provide it, or otherwise cannot get the evidence, VA will notify you and provide you with an opportunity to submit the information or evidence.

VA will make every reasonable effort to obtain relevant records **not held** by a Federal facility that you adequately identify and authorize VA to obtain. These may include records from State or local governments and privately held evidence and information you tell us about, such as private doctor or hospital records from current or former employers. Please review your decision notification letter for the appropriate authorization forms to complete and submit those forms to VA with this request form. The form is available at www.va.gov/vaforms.

Part IV - Certification and Signature

Please be sure to sign this **SUPPLEMENTAL CLAIM** application, certifying that the statements on the form are true and correct to the best of the claimant's or authorized representative's knowledge and belief.

For Compensation claims: If you are filing for review of an issue more than one year after VA provided notice of our decision, please visit https://www.va.gov/disability/how-to-file-claim/evidence-needed to review the 38 U.S.C. 5103 information regarding evidence necessary to substantiate your claim. Then, check the "**5103 Notice Acknowledgment**" box in item 16 to confirm your receipt of this information. If you cannot review the information online and would like the information mailed to you, do not check the box in item 16 and VA will send you this notice through the mail or other electronic communication.

OMB Control No. 2900-0862
Respondent Burden: 15 minutes
Expiration Date: 2/28/2022

VA Department of Veterans Affairs	VA DATE STAMP DO NOT WRITE IN THIS SPACE

DECISION REVIEW REQUEST: SUPPLEMENTAL CLAIM

INSTRUCTIONS: PLEASE READ THE PRIVACY ACT NOTICE AND RESPONDENT BURDEN INFORMATION ON PAGE 2 BEFORE COMPLETING THIS FORM.

PART I - CLAIMANT'S IDENTIFYING INFORMATION

NOTE: You can either complete the form online or by hand. If completed by hand, print the information requested in ink, neatly, and legibly to expedite processing the form.

1. VETERAN'S NAME *(First, Middle Initial, Last)*

2. VETERAN'S SOCIAL SECURITY NUMBER

3. VA FILE NUMBER *(If applicable)*

4. VETERAN'S DATE OF BIRTH *(MM/DD/YYYY)*

Month   Day   Year

5. VETERAN'S SERVICE NUMBER *(If applicable)*

6. INSURANCE POLICY NUMBER *(If applicable)*

7. CLAIMANT'S NAME *(First, Middle Initial, Last) (If other than veteran)*

8. CLAIMANT TYPE:

☐ VETERAN   ☐ VETERAN'S SPOUSE   ☐ VETERAN'S CHILD   ☐ VETERAN'S PARENT   ☐ OTHER *(Specify)*

9. CURRENT MAILING ADDRESS *(Number, street or rural route, City or P.O. Box, State and ZIP Code and Country)*

No. & Street

Apt./Unit Number   City

State/Province   Country   ZIP Code/Postal Code

10. TELEPHONE NUMBER *(Include Area Code)*

11. E-MAIL ADDRESS *(Optional)*

12. BENEFIT TYPE: **PLEASE CHECK ONLY ONE** *(If you would like to file for multiple benefit types, you must complete a separate request form for each benefit type.)*

☐ COMPENSATION   ☐ PENSION/SURVIVORS BENEFITS   ☐ FIDUCIARY   ☐ INSURANCE   ☐ VETERANS HEALTH ADMINISTRATION
☐ VOCATIONAL REHABILITATION AND EMPLOYMENT   ☐ LOAN GUARANTY   ☐ EDUCATION   ☐ NATIONAL CEMETERY ADMINISTRATION

PART II - ISSUE(S) FOR SUPPLEMENTAL CLAIM

13. YOU MUST LIST EACH ISSUE DECIDED BY VA THAT YOU WOULD LIKE VA TO REVIEW AS PART OF YOUR **SUPPLEMENTAL CLAIM**. *Please refer to your decision notice(s) for a list of adjudicated issues. For each issue, please identify the date of VA's decision (You may attach additional sheets of paper, if necessary. Include your name and file number on each additional sheet.)*

Check this box if any issue listed below is being withdrawn from the legacy appeals process. ☐ **OPT-IN from SOC/SSOC**

13A. SPECIFIC ISSUE(S)	13B. DATE OF VA DECISION NOTICE

VA FORM
FEB 2019   **20-0995**

Page 3

PART III - NEW AND RELEVANT EVIDENCE

14. To complete your application, you must submit new and relevant evidence to VA or tell us about new and relevant evidence that VA can assist you in gathering in support of your supplemental claim. If you have records in your possession, please attach the records to this form. Please list your name and file number on each page. If you would like VA to obtain **non-federal** records, please review your decision notification letter for the appropriate authorization forms to complete and submit those forms to VA with this request form.

15. DO YOU WANT VA TO GET FEDERAL RECORDS?

LIST BELOW ANY **VA MEDICAL CENTER(S) (VAMC), VA TREATMENT FACILITIES, OR FEDERAL DEPARTMENTS OR AGENCIES** THAT HAVE NEW AND RELEVANT EVIDENCE THAT YOU ARE AUTHORIZING VA TO OBTAIN IN SUPPORT OF YOUR SUPPLEMENTAL CLAIM: *You may attach additional sheets of paper, if necessary. Please list your name and file number on each additional sheet.*

15A. NAME AND LOCATION	15B. DATE(S) OF RECORDS

PART IV - CERTIFICATION AND SIGNATURE

NOTE: This section is **MANDATORY** and completion is required to process your claim, any omission may delay claim processing time.

VA AUTHORIZED REPRESENTATIVES ONLY: I certify that the claimant has authorized the undersigned representative to file this supplemental claim on behalf of the claimant and that the claimant is aware and accepts the information provided in this document. I certify that the claimant has authorized the undersigned representative to state that the claimant certifies the truth and completion of the information contained in this document to the best of claimant's knowledge.

NOTE: A POA's signature **will not** be accepted unless at the time of submission of this claim a valid VA Form 21-22, *Appointment of Veterans Service Organization as Claimant's Representative,* or VA Form 21-22a, *Appointment of Individual As Claimant's Representative,* indicating the appropriate POA is of record with VA.

16. I CERTIFY THAT the statements on this form are true and correct to the best of my knowledge and belief.

COMPENSATION BENEFIT CLAIMS ONLY:

☐ 5103 NOTICE Acknowledgement - I certify I have received the notice to this application titled, *Notice to Veteran/Service Member of Evidence Necessary to Substantiate a Claim for Veterans Disability Compensation and Related Compensation Benefits* as provided at https://www.va.gov/disability/how-to-file-claim/evidence-needed.
If the box is not checked, VA will send you this information through an electronic communication or written correspondence sent to the address on file with VA if your application is being submitted more than one year after VA provided notice of our decision for any issue listed in item 13.

16A. SIGNATURE OF VETERAN OR CLAIMANT OR VA AUTHORIZED REPRESENTATIVE *(Sign in ink)*	16B. DATE SIGNED

16C. NAME OF VA AUTHORIZED REPRESENTATIVE *(Please Print)*

ALTERNATE SIGNER CERTIFICATION AND SIGNATURE

17. I CERTIFY THAT by signing on behalf of the claimant, that I am a court-appointed representative; OR, an attorney in fact or agent authorized to act on behalf of a claimant under a durable power of attorney; OR, a person who is responsible for the care of the claimant, to include but not limited to a spouse or other relative; OR, a manager or principal officer acting on behalf of an institution which is responsible for the care of an individual; AND, that the claimant is under the age of 18; OR, is mentally incompetent to provide substantially accurate information needed to complete the form, or to certify that the statements made on the form are true and complete; OR, is physically unable to sign this form.

I understand that I may be asked to confirm the truthfulness of the answers to the best of my knowledge under penalty of perjury. I also understand that VA may request further documentation or evidence to verify or confirm my authorization to sign or complete an application on behalf of the claimant if necessary. Examples of evidence which VA may request include: Social Security Number (SSN) or Taxpayer Identification Number (TIN); a certificate or order from a court with competent jurisdiction showing your authority to act for the claimant with a judge's signature and a date/time stamp; copy of documentation showing appointment of fiduciary, durable power of attorney showing the name and signature of the claimant and your authority as attorney in fact or agent; health care power of attorney; affidavit or notarized statement from an institution or person responsible for the care of the claimant indicating the capacity or responsibility of care provided; or any other documentation showing such authorization.

17A. SIGNATURE OF ALTERNATE SIGNER *(Sign in ink)*	17B. DATE SIGNED

17C. NAME OF ALTERNATE SIGNER *(Please Print)*

PENALTY: The law provides severe penalties which include a fine, imprisonment, or both, for the willful submission of any statement or evidence of a material fact, knowing it to be false.

VA FORM 20-0995, FEB 2019

Department of Veterans Affairs

INFORMATION AND INSTRUCTIONS FOR COMPLETING DECISION REVIEW REQUEST: HIGHER-LEVEL REVIEW

IMPORTANT: Please read the information below carefully to help you complete this form quickly and accurately. Some parts of the form also contain notes or specific instructions for completing that part.

Use this form to request a HIGHER-LEVEL REVIEW of the decision you received. A **HIGHER-LEVEL REVIEW** is a new review of an issue(s) previously decided by the Department of Veterans Affairs (VA) based on the evidence of record at the time VA issued notice of the prior decision. The higher-level reviewer **WILL NOT** consider any evidence received after the notification date of the prior decision. This form must be submitted to VA **within one year** of the date VA provided notice of our decision. For additional information on the **HIGHER-LEVEL REVIEW** process or a list of review options that allow VA to consider new evidence and how to file, visit https://www.va.gov/decision-reviews/.

Submit your request for **HIGHER-LEVEL REVIEW** to the local VA office or processing center identified on your decision notice letter. It is important that you keep a copy of all completed forms and materials you give to VA. This form has several key components, which when filled out completely and accurately, will decrease the amount of time it takes to process your **HIGHER-LEVEL REVIEW** request. This form may only be submitted for review of an issue(s) related to one benefit type (Compensation, Pension/Survivors Benefits, Fiduciary, Insurance, Education, Loan Guaranty, Vocational Rehabilitation & Employment, Veterans Health Administration, or National Cemetery Administration). If you would like to file for multiple benefit types, you must complete a separate **HIGHER-LEVEL REVIEW** request for each benefit type.

You may contact your accredited representative (attorney, claims agent, and Veterans Service Organizations (VSOs) representative) to assist you in completing this form. If you have not already selected a representative, or if you want to change your representative, a searchable database of VA-recognized VSOs, VA-accredited attorneys, claims agents, and VSO representatives is available at https://www.va.gov/ogc/apps/accreditation/index.asp. Contact your local VA office for assistance with appointing a representative or visit www.ebenefits.va.gov.

You can also ask VA to help you fill out the application by contacting us at the number provided on your decision notification letter or at 1-800-827-1000. Before you contact us, please make sure you gather the necessary information and materials (decision notification letter, etc.). and complete as much of the form as you can.

SPECIFIC INSTRUCTIONS FOR DECISION REVIEW REQUEST: HIGHER-LEVEL REVIEW

Part I - Claimant's Identifying Information
Please note that it would assist VA if you provide all the personal information in Part I. However, if you provide certain information specific to the claimant such as the claimant's last name and Social Security Number or VA file number, VA will be able to identify the claimant in our system and would not necessarily consider this request incomplete if other information in Part I, such as the claimant's address and telephone number, is excluded. This request form may only be completed for review of an issue(s) related to one benefit type. **Select only one benefit type in item 12.** If you would like to file for multiple benefit types, you must complete a separate **HIGHER-LEVEL REVIEW** request form for each benefit type.

Part II - HIGHER-LEVEL REVIEW Options
You may request to have your HIGHER-LEVEL REVIEW conducted at either the same or a different office within the agency of jurisdiction that decided your issue(s). Please note that decisions on certain types of issues are processed at only a single VA office or facility. Accordingly, some issues cannot be reviewed at an office other than the office that decided your issue(s). For a list of these issue types visit VA.gov/decision-reviews. If we cannot fulfill your request, we will notify you at the time the **HIGHER-LEVEL REVIEW** decision is made.

You or your appointed representative may request an informal conference with the higher-level reviewer assigned to complete the review of your issue. The sole purpose of the optional telephone contact is to give you or your representative the opportunity to identify any errors of fact or law in the prior decision. VA may make up to two attempts to call you at the telephone number provided to VA to schedule your informal conference. If you would like VA to instead place the call to schedule your informal conference to your VA authorized representative you must place the representative's name and phone number in Box 14. If VA is unable to reach you or your representative, the higher-level reviewer will move forward with completing your request for higher-level review and will issue a decision.

Part III - Information to identify the issues for HIGHER-LEVEL REVIEW

The purpose of this section is for you to identify, in item 15A, each issue decided by VA that you would like as part of your higher-level review. Please refer to your decision notification letter(s) for a list of adjudicated issues. You should also enter the date of VA's decision for each issue, if possible. Only those issue(s) that you list on this form will be considered for **HIGHER-LEVEL REVIEW**. For those issues you do not list on this form, you will still have **one** year from the date of the decision notification letter to request a **HIGHER-LEVEL REVIEW** for those issues, or to have them reviewed in a different lane.

Upon receipt of a Statement of the Case (SOC) or Supplemental Statement of the Case (SSOC) in the legacy appeals system, you may elect to continue your appeal either in the legacy appeals system or in the modernized review system. Your decision notice contains further details. If you are filing this form to opt-in to the modernized review system for any issues decided in the SOC or SSOC, you must provide notice to VA of your decision to leave the legacy appeal process for those issues. To do so when using this form, please check the box for **"OPT-IN from SOC/SSOC"** in item 15 and list the issue(s) in the SOC or SSOC for which you are seeking review under item 15A as instructed above. Your selection of the **HIGHER-LEVEL REVIEW** option does not prevent you from changing the review option (in accordance with applicable procedures) before VA renders the higher-level review decision on an issue.

Please note that by checking the "OPT-IN from SOC/SSOC" box in item 15 you are acknowledging the following: I elect to participate in the modernized review system. I am withdrawing all eligible appeal issues listed on this form in their entirety, and any associated hearing requests, from the legacy appeals system to seek review of those issues in VA's modernized review system. I understand that I cannot return to the legacy appeals process for the issue(s) withdrawn.

Part IV - Certification and Signature

Please be sure to sign this request for HIGHER-LEVEL REVIEW, certifying that the statements on the form are true and correct to the best of the claimant's or authorized representative's knowledge and belief.

OMB Control No. 2900-0862
Respondent Burden: 15 minutes
Expiration Date: 2/28/2022

VA Department of Veterans Affairs

	VA DATE STAMP DO NOT WRITE IN THIS SPACE

DECISION REVIEW REQUEST: HIGHER-LEVEL REVIEW

INSTRUCTIONS: PLEASE READ THE PRIVACY ACT NOTICE AND RESPONDENT BURDEN INFORMATION ON PAGE 1 BEFORE COMPLETING THIS FORM.

PART I - CLAIMANT'S IDENTIFYING INFORMATION

NOTE: You can either complete the form online or by hand. If completed by hand, print the information requested in ink, neatly, and legibly to expedite processing the form.

1. VETERAN'S NAME *(First, Middle Initial, Last)*

2. VETERAN'S SOCIAL SECURITY NUMBER

3. VA FILE NUMBER *(If applicable)*

4. VETERAN'S DATE OF BIRTH *(MM/DD/YYYY)*

Month   Day   Year

5. VETERAN'S SERVICE NUMBER *(If applicable)*

6. INSURANCE POLICY NUMBER *(If applicable)*

7. CLAIMANT'S NAME *(First, Middle Initial, Last) (If other than veteran)*

8. CLAIMANT TYPE:

☐ VETERAN   ☐ VETERAN'S SPOUSE   ☐ VETERAN'S CHILD   ☐ VETERAN'S PARENT   ☐ OTHER *(Specify)*

9. CURRENT MAILING ADDRESS *(Number, street or rural route, City or P.O. Box, State and ZIP Code and Country)*

No. & Street

Apt./Unit Number   City

State/Province   Country   ZIP Code/Postal Code

10. TELEPHONE NUMBER *(Include Area Code)*

11. E-MAIL ADDRESS *(Optional)*

12. BENEFIT TYPE. **PLEASE CHECK ONLY ONE** *(If you would like to file for multiple benefit types, you must complete a separate request form for each benefit type.)*

☐ COMPENSATION   ☐ PENSION/SURVIVORS BENEFITS   ☐ FIDUCIARY   ☐ EDUCATION   ☐ VETERANS HEALTH ADMINISTRATION
☐ VOCATIONAL REHABILITATION AND EMPLOYMENT   ☐ LOAN GUARANTY   ☐ INSURANCE   ☐ NATIONAL CEMETERY ADMINISTRATION

PART II - HIGHER-LEVEL REVIEW OPTIONS

13. IF YOU WOULD LIKE THE SAME OFFICE THAT ISSUED YOUR PRIOR DECISION TO CONDUCT THE REVIEW, YOU CAN MAKE THAT REQUEST BY CHECKING THE BOX BELOW. IF YOU DO NOT CHECK THE BOX, VA WILL TAKE THAT AS A REQUEST TO HAVE A DIFFERENT OFFICE CONDUCT THE REVIEW. *(Please note VA may be unable to grant your request.)*

☐ If available, I would like **HIGHER-LEVEL REVIEW** conducted at the same office within the agency of original jurisdiction.

14. IN ADDITION, YOU OR YOUR AUTHORIZED REPRESENTATIVE MAY REQUEST AN INFORMAL CONFERENCE WITH THE HIGHER-LEVEL REVIEWER. *(This is a telephonic communication with the higher level reviewer for the sole purpose of pointing out errors of fact or law in the prior decision. VA will only conduct one informal conference associated with this request for higher-level review. Check the box below to request an informal conference.)*

☐ I, or my representative, would like an **informal conference** *(VA will make up to two attempts to call you between 8:00a.m. and 4:30p.m. Eastern Standard Time at the telephone number and time period you select below to **schedule your informal conference**. Please select up to two time periods you are available to receive a phone call.)*

☐ 8:00a.m. - 10:00a.m.   ☐ 10:00a.m. - 12:30p.m.   ☐ 12:30p.m. - 2:00p.m.   ☐ 2:00p.m. - 4:30p.m.

If you would like for VA to contact your representative, please provide your representative's name and telephone number where he or she can be reached at the above checked time.

297

15. YOU MUST INDICATE BELOW EACH ISSUE DECIDED BY VA FOR WHICH YOU ARE REQUESTING A HIGHER-LEVEL REVIEW. *Please refer to your decision notice(s) for a list of adjudicated issues. For each issue, please identify the date of VA's decision. You may attach additional sheets, if necessary. Please include your name and file number on each additional sheet.*

Check this box if any issue listed below is being withdrawn from the legacy appeals process. ☐ **OPT-IN from SOC/SSOC**

15A. SPECIFIC ISSUE(S)	15B. DATE OF VA DECISION NOTICE

PART IV - CERTIFICATION AND SIGNATURE

NOTE: This section is **MANDATORY** and completion is required to process your claim; any omission may delay claim processing time.

VA AUTHORIZED REPRESENTATIVES ONLY: I certify that the claimant has authorized the undersigned representative to file this higher-level review on behalf of the claimant and that the claimant is aware and accepts the information provided in this document. I certify that the claimant has authorized the undersigned representative to state that the claimant certifies the truth and completion of the information contained in this document to the best of claimant's knowledge.

NOTE: A power of attorney's (POA's) signature **will not** be accepted unless at the time of submission of this request a valid VA Form 21-22, *Appointment of Veterans Service Organization as Claimant's Representative,* or VA Form 21-22a, *Appointment of Individual As Claimant's Representative,* indicating the appropriate POA is of record with VA.

I CERTIFY THAT the statements on this form are true and correct to the best of my knowledge and belief.

16A. SIGNATURE OF VETERAN OR CLAIMANT OR VA AUTHORIZED REPRESENTATIVE *(Sign in ink)*	16B. DATE SIGNED

16C. NAME OF VA AUTHORIZED REPRESENTATIVE *(Please Print)*

ALTERNATE SIGNER CERTIFICATION AND SIGNATURE

17. **I CERTIFY THAT** by signing on behalf of the claimant, that I am a court-appointed representative, **OR**, an attorney in fact or agent authorized to act on behalf of a claimant under a durable power of attorney; **OR**, a person who is responsible for the care of the claimant, to include but not limited to a spouse or other relative; **OR**, a manager or principal officer acting on behalf of an institution which is responsible for the care of an individual; **AND**, that the claimant is under the age of 18; **OR**, is mentally incompetent to provide substantially accurate information needed to complete the form, or to certify that the statements made on the form are true and complete, **OR**, is physically unable to sign this form.

I understand that I may be asked to confirm the truthfulness of the answers to the best of my knowledge under penalty of perjury. I also understand that VA may request further documentation or evidence to verify or confirm my authorization to sign or complete an application on behalf of the claimant if necessary. Examples of evidence which VA may request include: Social Security Number (SSN) or Taxpayer Identification Number (TIN): a certificate or order from a court with competent jurisdiction showing your authority to act for the claimant with a judge's signature and a date/time stamp; copy of documentation showing appointment of fiduciary; durable power of attorney showing the name and signature of the claimant and your authority as attorney in fact or agent; health care power of attorney, affidavit or notarized statement from an institution or person responsible for the care of the claimant indicating the capacity or responsibility of care provided; or any other documentation showing such authorization.

17A. SIGNATURE OF ALTERNATE SIGNER *(Sign in ink)*	17B. DATE SIGNED

17C. NAME OF ALTERNATE SIGNER *(Please Print)*

PENALTY: The law provides severe penalties which include a fine, imprisonment, or both, for the willful submission of any statement or evidence of a material fact, knowing it to be false.

OMB Approved No. 2900-0674
Respondent Burden: 30 Minutes
Expiration Date: Feb. 28, 2022

VA Department of Veterans Affairs

DECISION REVIEW REQUEST: BOARD APPEAL
(NOTICE OF DISAGREEMENT)

PART I - PERSONAL INFORMATION

1. VETERAN'S NAME *(First, middle initial, last)*

2. VETERAN'S SOCIAL SECURITY NUMBER	3. VETERAN'S VA FILE NUMBER *(if different than their SSN)* C/CSS -	4. VETERAN'S DATE OF BIRTH

5. IF I AM NOT THE VETERAN, MY NAME IS *(First, middle initial, last)*	6. MY DATE OF BIRTH *(If I am not the Veteran)*

7. MY PREFERRED MAILING ADDRESS *(Number and street or rural route, P.O. Box, City, State, ZIP Code and Country)*   ☐ I AM HOMELESS

8. MY PREFERRED TELEPHONE NUMBER *(Include Area Code)*	9 MY PREFERRED E-MAIL ADDRESS	10. MY REPRESENTATIVE'S NAME

PART II - BOARD REVIEW OPTION *(Check only one)*

11. A Veterans Law Judge will consider your appeal in the order in which it is received, depending on which of the following review options you select. *(For additional explanation of your options, please see the attached information and instructions.)*

☐ 11A. Direct Review by a Veterans Law Judge: I do not want a Board hearing, and will not submit any additional evidence in support of my appeal. *(Choosing this option often results in the Board issuing its decision most quickly.)*

☐ 11B. Evidence Submission Reviewed by a Veterans Law Judge: I have additional evidence in support of my appeal that I will provide within the next 90 days, but I do not want a Board hearing. *(Choosing this option may add delay to issuance of a Board decision.)*

☐ 11C. Hearing with a Veterans Law Judge: I want a Board hearing and the opportunity to submit additional evidence in support of my appeal that I will provide within 90 days after my hearing. *(Choosing this option may add delay to issuance of a Board decision.)*

PART III - SPECIFIC ISSUE(S) TO BE APPEALED TO A VETERANS LAW JUDGE AT THE BOARD

12. Please list each issue decided by VA that you would like to appeal. Please refer to your decision notice(s) for a list of adjudicated issues. For each issue, please identify the date of VA's decision and the area of disagreement.

☐ Check here if you attached additional sheets. Include the Veteran's last name and last 4-digits of the Social Security number.

Check the SOC/SSOC Opt in box if any issue listed below is being withdrawn from the legacy appeals process. ☐ Opt In from SOC/SSOC

A. Specific Issue(s)	B. Date of Decision

PART IV - CERTIFICATION AND SIGNATURE

I CERTIFY THAT THE STATEMENTS ON THIS FORM ARE TRUE AND CORRECT TO THE BEST OF MY KNOWLEDGE AND BELIEF.

13. SIGNATURE *(Appellant or appointed representative) (Ink signature)*	14. DATE SIGNED

VA FORM FEB 2019 **10182**   PENALTY: THE LAW PROVIDES SEVERE PENALTIES WHICH INCLUDE A FINE, IMPRISONMENT, OR BOTH, FOR THE WILLFUL SUBMISSION OF ANY STATEMENT OR EVIDENCE OF A MATERIAL FACT, KNOWING IT TO BE FALSE.

INFORMATION AND DETAILED INSTRUCTIONS FOR COMPLETING
DECISION REVIEW REQUEST: BOARD APPEAL
(NOTICE OF DISAGREEMENT)

NOTE: Use this form ONLY if you received your VA decision on or after **February 19, 2019**, and you wish to appeal one or more issues to a Veterans Law Judge at the Board of Veterans' Appeals. *DO NOT USE THIS FORM to submit a Supplemental Claim (if you wish to have additional evidence reviewed by a VA rater) or request a Higher-Level Review (if you wish to have a new decision by a VA senior reviewer).*

If you have any questions about the filing deadline in your case, ask your representative or your local VA office. **Filing on time is very important. Failing to submit on time could result in you losing your right to appeal.**

When should I fill out a Notice of Disagreement? If you have received a decision from a local VA office or a higher-level adjudicator with which you disagree, and you would like one or more issues to be decided by a Veterans Law Judge, you **must** fill out and submit a Notice of Disagreement. You can choose to appeal all or only some of the issues previously decided, however, **ONLY** those issues that you list on your Notice of Disagreement will be considered on appeal.

How long do I have to submit my Notice of Disagreement? Your completed Notice of Disagreement must be post-marked or received by the Board within **one year (365 days)** from the day that your local VA office mailed the notice of the decision. If you do not provide all the information requested in the Notice of Disagreement, VA will consider your form incomplete and will contact you to request clarification and explain your options.

Contested Claim: If you are one of multiple people claiming the right to the same benefit, your completed Notice of Disagreement must be post-marked or received by the Board within **60 days** from the day that your local VA office mailed the notice of the decision. VA will notify you and provide additional information if you are a party to a contested claim.

What are my options for the Board's review? You must choose **one** of three options for how a Veterans Law Judge will review the issue(s) on appeal. Determine which of the below options best fits your situation. Please note that you may choose only one option for each issue you wish to appeal.

REVIEW OPTION	DESCRIPTION
Direct Review	- Choose this option if you do not want to submit additional evidence, and you do not want a hearing with a Veterans Law Judge. - The Veterans Law Judge and Board team will review the issue(s) you appealed, and make a new determination based on the evidence that the local VA office considered. - Choosing this option will often result in a Veterans Law Judge at the Board being able to issue its decision most quickly.
Evidence Submission	- Choose this option if you want to submit additional evidence, but you do not want to have a hearing with a Veterans Law Judge. - After 90 days, any additional evidence added to your claim will not be considered by the Board. - The Veterans Law Judge and Board team will review the issue(s) you appealed, considering the evidence that the local VA office considered, along with any additional evidence that you submit **within 90 days after** VA's receipt of your Notice of Disagreement.
Hearing Request	- **Please note that a Board hearing is optional, and may increase the wait time for a Board decision.** - Choose this option if you want a hearing with a Veterans Law Judge, which includes the option to submit additional evidence. - The Board will contact you to schedule your hearing and provide additional information. - After your hearing, the Veterans Law Judge and Board team will review the issue(s) you appealed, considering the evidence that the local VA office considered, along with your hearing testimony and any additional evidence that you submit **within 90 days** after the hearing.

Find more information on the review options at va.gov/decision-reviews

Where can I get help with filing my appeal? A Veterans Service Organization or a VA-accredited attorney or agent can represent you or provide guidance. Contact your local VA regional office for assistance or visit: va.gov/ogc/accreditation.asp.

Where do I submit my Notice of Disagreement once I have completed it? When you have completed the Notice of Disagreement, signed and dated it, you must send it to the Board at the address or FAX number below:

Board of Veterans' Appeals
P.O. Box 27063
Washington, DC 20038
FAX: 844-678-8979

What if I want to modify my Notice of Disagreement? You may make a request to modify your Notice of Disagreement for the purpose of selecting a different review option in Part II. Any such request must be made by submitting a new Notice of Disagreement form to the Board within one year (365 days) from the date of mailing of the notice of decision on appeal, or within 60 days of the Board's receipt of the Notice of Disagreement, whichever is later. *You cannot request to modify your Notice of Disagreement if you have already submitted evidence to the Board or testified at a hearing with a Veterans Law Judge.*

VA FORM
FEB 2019 **10182**

300

OVERVIEW OF NOTICE OF DISAGREEMENT FORM SECTIONS

If you decide to appeal to a Veterans Law Judge at the Board, these instructions will help you complete your Notice of Disagreement.

Part I - PERSONAL INFORMATION Please provide all the personal information in Part I. If desired, you may also enter the claimant's prefix (such as "Mr." or "Ms.") and/or suffix (such as "Jr." or "Sr."). If your address has changed recently or will change soon, please notify your local VA office. If you are homeless, please check the box in item 7. If you wish to include multiple addresses, you may attach additional sheets to the form, explaining how you would like VA to contact you.

Part II - REVIEW OPTION You must check one, *and only one*, of the boxes in Part II, Block 11, to choose how you would like the Board to review the issues identified in Part III. The Board will place your appeal onto a list for consideration in the order it was received. If you wish to request a different review option for one or more issues listed in Part III, you may attach additional sheets to the form, explaining your preference.

> **Box 11A - Direct Review by a Veterans Law Judge:** Check this box if you *do not* want to submit additional evidence and you *do not* want a Board hearing
>
> **Box 11B - Evidence Submission Reviewed by a Veterans Law Judge:** Check this box if you *do not* want a Board hearing, but you do want to submit additional evidence with this Notice of Disagreement or **within 90 days** following VA's receipt of your Notice of Disagreement.
>
> **Box 11C - Hearing With a Veterans Law Judge:** Check this box if you want a Board hearing with a Veterans Law Judge, which includes the option to submit additional evidence at your hearing or **within 90 days** following the hearing.

If you have already submitted a Notice of Disagreement, and wish to change your Board Review Option, please fill out this form completely, indicating your new choice in Part II.

Part III - SPECIFIC ISSUE(S) BEING APPEALED TO THE BOARD List the issue(s) you would like the Board to review in Block 12A, and the date of your decision notice in Block 12B. Please refer to your decision notice for a list of adjudicated issues. If you want to appeal more issues, you may attach additional pages as needed.

Upon receipt of a Statement of the Case (SOC) or Supplemental Statement of the Case (SSOC) in the legacy appeals system, you may elect to continue your appeal either in the legacy appeals system or in the modernized review system. Your decision notice contains further details. If you are filing this form to opt into the modernized review system for any issues decided in the SOC or SSOC, you must provide notice to VA of your decision to leave the legacy appeals system for those issues. To do so when using the Notice of Disagreement, please check the box for **"OPT IN from SOC/SSOC"** in item 12 and list the issue(s) in the SOC or SSOC for which you are seeking review under item 12A as instructed above. Your selection of the **BOARD APPEAL** option does not prevent you from changing the review option (in accordance with applicable procedures) before the Veterans Law Judge issues a decision on the issue(s).

Please note that by checking the "OPT IN from SOC/SSOC" box in item 12 you are acknowledging the following: I elect to participate in the modernized review system. I am withdrawing all eligible appeal issues listed on this form in their entirety, and any associated hearing requests, from the legacy appeals system to seek review of those issues in VA's modernized review system. I understand that I cannot return to the legacy appeals system for the issue(s) withdrawn.

Part IV - CERTIFICATION AND SIGNATURE Please sign and date the Notice of Disagreement, certifying that the statements on the form are true to the best of your knowledge and belief. An appointed representative may sign on the behalf of the appellant.

WHAT IF I WANT TO ADD ADDITIONAL INFORMATION? If you want to provide any additional information to VA, including why you believe that VA previously decided one or more issues incorrectly, you may check the box in Block 12 and attach additional sheets to the form. For each issue, please make sure to identify the date of VA's decision. The Board will not consider any new evidence unless you selected the "Evidence Submission" option in Part II, Block 11B. The Board will consider argument submitted with any Notice of Disagreement. Please number any additional pages and include the Veteran's last name and Social Security number (last four digits only).

PRIVACY ACT STATEMENT: Our authority for asking for the information you give to us when you fill out this form is 38 U.S.C. 7105(d)(3), a Federal statute that sets out the requirement for you to submit a formal appeal to complete your appeal on a VA benefits determination. You use this form to present your appeal to the Board of Veterans' Appeals (Board) It is used by VA in processing your appeal and it is used by the Board in deciding your appeal. Providing this information to VA is voluntary, but if you fail to furnish this information VA will close your appeal and you may lose your right to appeal the benefit determinations you told us you disagreed with. The Privacy Act of 1974 (5 U.S.C. 552a) and VA's confidentiality statute (38 U.S.C. 5701), as implemented by 38 C.F.R. 1.526(a) and 1.576(b), require individuals to provide written consent before documents or information can be disclosed to third parties not allowed to receive records or information under any other provision of law. However, the law permits VA to disclose the information you include on this form to people outside of VA in some circumstances. Information about that is given in notices about VA's "systems of records" that are periodically published in the *Federal Register* as required by the Privacy Act of 1974. Examples of situations in which the information included in this form might be released to individuals outside of VA include release to the United States Court of Appeals for Veterans Claims. if you later appeal the Board's decision in your case to that court; disclosure to a medical expert outside of VA, should VA exercise its statutory authority under 38 U. S.C. 5109 or 7109, to ask for an expert medical opinion to help decide your case; disclosure to law enforcement personnel and security guards in order to alert them to the presence of a dangerous person; disclosure to law enforcement agencies should the information indicate that there has been a violation of law; disclosure to a congressional office in order to answer an inquiry from the congressional office made at your request; and disclosure to Federal government personnel who have the duty of inspecting VA's records to make sure that they are being properly maintained. See the *Federal Register* notices described above for further details.

RESPONDENT BURDEN: VA may not conduct or sponsor, and the respondent is not required to respond to, this collection of information unless it displays a valid Office of Management and Budget (OMB) Control Number. The information requested is approved under OMB Control Number (2900-0674). Public reporting burden for this collection of information is estimated to average 30 minutes per response. including the time for reviewing instructions, searching existing data sources, gathering and maintaining the data needed, and completing and reviewing the collection of information. Send comments regarding this burden estimate or any other aspects of this collection. including suggestions for reducing this burden to: VA Clearance Officer (005R1B). 810 Vermont Ave , NW, Washington, DC 20420. **DO NOT** send requests for benefits to this address.

VA FORM
FEB 2019   **10182**

OMB Control No. 2900-0075
Respondent Burden: 15 minutes
Expiration Date: 12/31/2020

VA Department of Veterans Affairs

VA DATE STAMP
(DO NOT WRITE IN THIS SPACE)

STATEMENT IN SUPPORT OF CLAIM

INSTRUCTIONS: Read the Privacy Act and Respondent Burden on Page 2 before completing the form. Complete as much of Section I as possible. The information requested will help process your claim for benefits. If you need any additional room, use the second page.

SECTION I: VETERAN/BENEFICIARY'S IDENTIFICATION INFORMATION

NOTE: You will either complete the form online or by hand. Please print the information request in ink, neatly, and legibly to help process the form.

1. VETERAN/BENEFICIARY'S NAME *(First, Middle Initial, Last)*

2. VETERAN'S SOCIAL SECURITY NUMBER

3. VA FILE NUMBER *(If applicable)*

4. VETERAN'S DATE OF BIRTH *(MM/DD/YYYY)*

Month   Day   Year

5. VETERAN'S SERVICE NUMBER *(If applicable)*

6. TELEPHONE NUMBER *(Include Area Code)*

7. E-MAIL ADDRESS *(Optional)*

8. MAILING ADDRESS *(Number and street or rural route, P.O. Box, City, State, ZIP Code and Country)*

No. & Street

Apt./Unit Number

City

State/Province

Country

ZIP Code/Postal Code

SECTION II: REMARKS
(The following statement is made in connection with a claim for benefits in the case of the above-named veteran/beneficiary.)

302

VETERAN'S SOCIAL SECURITY NO. [ ][ ][ ] – [ ][ ] – [ ][ ][ ][ ]

SECTION III: DECLARATION OF INTENT

I CERTIFY THAT the statements on this form are true and correct to the best of my knowledge and belief.

9. SIGNATURE (Sign in ink)	10. DATE SIGNED (MM/DD/YYYY)

PENALTY: The law provides severe penalties which include fine or imprisonment, or both, for the willful submission of any statement or evidence of a material fact, knowing it to be false.

303

OMB Control No. 2900-0321
Respondent Burden: 5 minutes
Expiration Date: 02/28/2022

Department of Veterans Affairs

| VA DATE STAMP (DO NOT WRITE IN THIS SPACE) |

APPOINTMENT OF VETERANS SERVICE ORGANIZATION AS CLAIMANT'S REPRESENTATIVE

IMPORTANT: Please read the Privacy Act and Respondent Burden Information on Page 3 before completing the form.

NOTE: If you prefer to have an individual assist you with your claim instead of a veterans service organization, please complete VA Form 21-22a. *Appointment of Individual as Claimant's Representative.* When completed you can mail **or** fax this form to the appropriate intake center address shown on Page 4. VA forms are available at www.va.gov/vaforms.

SECTION I: VETERAN'S INFORMATION

NOTE: You can *either* complete the form online or by hand. If completed by hand, print the information requested in ink, neatly, and legibly to expedite processing of the form.

1. VETERAN'S NAME *(First, Middle Initial, Last)*

2. VETERAN'S SOCIAL SECURITY NUMBER (SSN)

3. VA FILE NUMBER *(If applicable)*

4. VETERAN'S DATE OF BIRTH — Month — Day — Year

5. VETERAN'S SERVICE NUMBER *(If applicable)*

6. INSURANCE NUMBER(S) *(If applicable) (Include letter prefix)*

7. VETERAN'S MAILING ADDRESS *(Number and street or rural route, P.O. Box, City, State, ZIP Code and Country)*

No. & Street

Apt./Unit Number — City

State/Province — Country — ZIP Code/Postal Code

8. VETERAN'S TELEPHONE NUMBER *(Include Area Code)*

9. VETERAN'S EMAIL ADDRESS *(Optional)*

SECTION II: CLAIMANT'S INFORMATION (If other than veteran)

10. CLAIMANT'S NAME *(First, Middle Initial, Last)*

11. CLAIMANT'S MAILING ADDRESS *(Number and street or rural route, P.O. Box, City, State, ZIP Code and Country)*

No. & Street

Apt./Unit Number — City

State/Province — Country — ZIP Code/Postal Code

12. CLAIMANT'S TELEPHONE NUMBER *(Include Area Code)*

13. CLAIMANT'S EMAIL ADDRESS *(Optional)*

14. RELATIONSHIP TO VETERAN

SECTION III: SERVICE ORGANIZATION INFORMATION

15. NAME OF SERVICE ORGANIZATION RECOGNIZED BY THE DEPARTMENT OF VETERANS AFFAIRS *(See list on Page 3 before selecting organization)*

16A. NAME OF OFFICIAL REPRESENTATIVE ACTING ON BEHALF OF THE ORGANIZATION NAMED IN ITEM 15 *(This is an appointment of the entire organization and does not indicate the designation of only this specific individual to act on behalf of the organization)*

16B. JOB TITLE OF PERSON NAMED IN ITEM 16A

17. EMAIL ADDRESS OF THE ORGANIZATION NAMED IN ITEM 15

18. DATE OF THIS APPOINTMENT *(MM/DD/YYYY)*

VA FORM FEB 2019 **21-22**   SUPERSEDES VA FORM 21-22, AUG 2015.   Page 1

VETERAN'S SOCIAL SECURITY NUMBER ☐☐☐ – ☐☐ – ☐☐☐☐

SECTION IV: AUTHORIZATION INFORMATION

19. AUTHORIZATION FOR REPRESENTATIVE'S ACCESS TO RECORDS PROTECTED BY SECTION 7332, TITLE 38, U.S.C. - By checking the box below I authorize VA to disclose to the service organization named on this appointment form any records that may be in my file relating to treatment for drug abuse, alcoholism or alcohol abuse, infection with the human immunodeficiency virus (HIV), or sickle cell anemia.

☐ I **authorize** the VA facility having custody of my VA claimant records to disclose to the service organization named in Item 15 all treatment records relating to drug abuse, alcoholism or alcohol abuse, infection with the human immunodeficiency virus (HIV), or sickle cell anemia. Rediscosure of these records by my service organization representative, other than to VA or the Court of Appeals for Veterans Claims, is not authorized without my further written consent. This authorization will remain in effect until the earlier of the following events: (1) I revoke this authorization by filing a written revocation with VA; or (2) I revoke the appointment of the service organization named in Item 15, either by explicit revocation or the appointment of another representative.

20. LIMITATION OF CONSENT - I authorize disclosure of records related to treatment for all conditions listed in Item 19 except:

☐ DRUG ABUSE ☐ INFECTION WITH THE HUMAN IMMUNODEFICIENCY VIRUS (HIV)

☐ ALCOHOLISM OR ALCOHOL ABUSE ☐ SICKLE CELL ANEMIA

21. AUTHORIZATION TO CHANGE CLAIMANT'S ADDRESS - By checking the box below, I authorize the organization named in Item 15 to act on my behalf to change my address in my VA records.

☐ I **authorize** any official representative of the organization named in Item 15 to act on my behalf to change my address in my VA records. This authorization does not extend to any other organization without my further written consent. This authorization will remain in effect until the earlier of the following events: (1) I file a written revocation with VA; or (2) I appoint another representative, or (3) I have been determined unable to manage my financial affairs and the individual or organization named in Item 16A is not my appointed fiduciary.

I, the claimant named in Items 1 **or** 10, hereby **appoint** the service organization named in Item 15 as my representative to prepare, present and prosecute my claim(s) for any and all benefits from the Department of Veterans Affairs (VA) based on the service of the veteran named in Item 1. I authorize VA to release any and all of my records, to include disclosure of my Federal tax information (other than as provided in Items 19 and 20), to my appointed service organization. I understand that my appointed representative will not charge any fee or compensation for service rendered pursuant to this appointment. I understand that the service organization I have appointed as my representative may revoke this appointment at any time, subject to 38 CFR 20.6. *Additionally, in some cases a veteran's income is developed because a match with the Internal Revenue Service necessitated income verification. In such cases, the assignment of the service organization as the veteran's representative is valid for only five years from the date the claimant signs this form for purposes restricted to the verification match. Signed and accepted subject to the foregoing conditions.*

SECTION V: SIGNATURES

NOTE: THIS POWER OF ATTORNEY DOES NOT REQUIRE EXECUTION BEFORE A NOTARY PUBLIC

22A. SIGNATURE OF VETERAN OR CLAIMANT *(Do Not Print)*	22B. DATE SIGNED *(MM/DD/YYYY)*
23A. SIGNATURE OF VETERANS SERVICE ORGANIZATION REPRESENTATIVE NAMED IN ITEM 16A *(Do Not Print)*	23B. DATE SIGNED *(MM/DD/YYYY)*

NOTE: As long as this appointment is in effect, the organization named herein will be recognized as the sole representative for preparation, presentation and prosecution of your claim before the Department of Veterans Affairs in connection with your claim or any portion thereof.

VA USE ONLY	COPY OF VA FORM 21-22 SENT TO:	DATE SENT	ACKNOWLEDGED *(Date)*	REVOKED *(Reason and date)*
	☐ VR&E FILE ☐ EDU FILE			
	☐ LG FILE ☐ INSURANCE FILE			

PENALTY: The law provides severe penalties which include fine or imprisonment, or both, for the willful submission of any statement of a material fact, knowing it to be false or for the fraudulent acceptance of any payment to which you are not entitled.

VA FORM 21-22, FEB 2019

Page 2

305

Membership in an organization is not a prerequisite to appointment of the organization as claimant's representative.

The following is a listing of national, regional, or local organizations recognized by the Secretary of Veterans Affairs in the preparation, presentation, and prosecution of claims under laws administered by the Department of Veterans Affairs.

African American PTSD Association	National Association of County Veterans Service Officers, Inc.
American Legion	National Association for Black Veterans, Inc.
American Red Cross	National Veterans Legal Services Program
AMVETS	National Veterans Organization of America
American Ex-Prisoners of War, Inc.	Navy Mutual Aid Association
American GI Forum, National Veterans Outreach Program	Paralyzed Veterans of America, Inc.
Armed Forces Services Corporation	Polish Legion of American Veterans, U.S.A.
Army and Navy Union, USA	Swords to Plowshares, Veterans Rights Organization, Inc.
Associates of Vietnam Veterans of America	The Retired Enlisted Association
Blinded Veterans Association	The Veterans Assistance Foundation, Inc.
Catholic War Veterans of the U.S.A.	The Veterans of the Vietnam War, Inc. & The Veterans
Disabled American Veterans	Coalition
Fleet Reserve Association	United Spanish War Veterans of the United States
Gold Star Wives of America, Inc.	United Spinal Association, Inc.
Italian American War Veterans of the United States, Inc.	Veterans of Foreign Wars of the United States
Jewish War Veterans of the United States	Veterans of World War I of the U.S.A., Inc.
Legion of Valor of the United States of America, Inc.	Vietnam Era Veterans Association
Marine Corps League	Vietnam Veterans of America
Military Officers Association of America (MOAA)	West Virginia Department of Veterans Assistance
Military Order of the Purple Heart	Wounded Warrior Project
National Amputation Foundation, Inc.	

Although agency titles vary, the following States and possessions maintain veterans service agencies which are recognized to present claims:

Alabama	Hawaii	Minnesota	North Dakota	Tennessee
American Samoa	Idaho	Mississippi	Northern Mariana Islands	Texas
Arizona	Illinois	Missouri	Ohio	Utah
Arkansas	Iowa	Montana	Oklahoma	Vermont
California	Kansas	Nebraska	Oregon	Virginia
Colorado	Kentucky	Nevada	Pennsylvania	Virgin Islands
Connecticut	Louisiana	New Hampshire	Puerto Rico	Washington
Delaware	Maine	New Jersey	Rhode Island	West Virginia
Florida	Maryland	New Mexico	South Carolina	Wisconsin
Georgia	Massachusetts	New York	South Dakota	Wyoming
Guam	Michigan	North Carolina		

VA FORM 21-22, FEB 2019

Page 3

FOR ALL **COMPENSATION** CLAIMS MAIL OR FAX THIS FORM TO THE FOLLOWING ADDRESS:

Mail your form to:
Department of Veterans Affairs
Claims Intake Center
P.O. Box 4444
Janesville, WI 53547- 4444
Or fax your form to:
Toll Free: (844) 531- 7818
Local: 248-524-4260

FOR **VETERANS PENSION** AND **SURVIVOR BENEFIT** CLAIMS MAIL OR FAX THIS FORM TO THE APPROPRIATE ADDRESS SHOWN BELOW:

Mail your form to:
Department of Veterans Affairs
Claims Intake Center
Attn: Milwaukee Pension Center
P.O. Box 5192
Janesville, WI 53547-5192
Or fax your form to:
Toll Free: (844) 655-1604

This Pension Center Serves The Following:

Alabama	Arkansas	Illinois	Indiana
Kentucky	Louisiana	Michigan	Mississippi
Missouri	Ohio	Tennessee	Wisconsin

Mail your form to:
Department of Veterans Affairs
Claims Intake Center
Attn: Philadelphia Pension Center
P.O. Box 5206
Janesville, WI 53547-5206
Or fax your form to:
Toll Free: (844) 655-1604

This Pension Center Serves The Following:

Connecticut	Delaware	Florida	Georgia
Maine	Maryland	Massachusetts	New Hampshire
New Jersey	New York	North Carolina	Pennsylvania
Rhode Island	South Carolina	Vermont	Virginia
West Virginia	District of Columbia	Puerto Rico	Canada

Countries outside of North, Central or South America

Mail your form to:
Department of Veterans Affairs
Claims Intake Center
Attn: St. Paul Pension Center
P.O. Box 5365
Janesville, WI 53547-5365
Or fax your form to:
Toll Free: (844) 655-1604

This Pension Center Serves The Following:

Alaska	Arizona	California	Colorado
Hawaii	Idaho	Iowa	Kansas
Minnesota	Montana	Nebraska	Nevada
New Mexico	North Dakota	Oklahoma	Oregon
South Dakota	Texas	Utah	Washington
Wyoming	Mexico	Central America	South America
Caribbean			

OMB Control No. 2900-0321
Respondent Burden: 5 Minutes
Expiration Date: 02/28/2022

Department of Veterans Affairs

VA DATE STAMP
(DO NOT WRITE IN THIS SPACE)

APPOINTMENT OF INDIVIDUAL AS CLAIMANT'S REPRESENTATIVE

IMPORTANT: Please read the Privacy Act and Respondent Burden on Page 2 before completing the form.

NOTE: If you prefer to have a veterans service organization assist you with your claim instead of an individual please complete VA Form 21-22, *Appointment of Veterans Service Organization as Claimant's Representative.* When completed you can mail **or** fax this form to the appropriate intake center address shown on page 3. VA forms are available at www.va.gov/vaforms.

SECTION I: VETERAN'S INFORMATION

NOTE: You can either complete the form online or by hand. If completed by hand, print the information requested in ink, neatly, and legibly to expedite processing of the form.

1. VETERAN'S NAME *(First, Middle Initial, Last)*

2. VETERAN'S SOCIAL SECURITY NUMBER *(SSN)*

3. VA FILE NUMBER *(If applicable)*

4. VETERAN'S DATE OF BIRTH
   Month   Day   Year

5. VETERAN'S SERVICE NUMBER *(If applicable)*

6. BRANCH OF SERVICE
   [ ] ARMY   [ ] NAVY   [ ] AIR FORCE   [ ] MARINE CORPS   [ ] COAST GUARD
   [ ] OTHER *(Specify)*

7. VETERAN'S MAILING ADDRESS *(Number and street or rural route, city or P.O., State and ZIP Code)*
   No. & Street
   Apt./Unit Number   City
   State/Province   Country   ZIP Code/Postal Code

8. VETERAN'S TELEPHONE NUMBER *(Include Area Code)*

9. VETERAN'S EMAIL ADDRESS *(Optional)*

SECTION II: CLAIMANT'S INFORMATION (If other than veteran)

10. CLAIMANT'S NAME *(First, Middle Initial, Last)*

11. CLAIMANT'S MAILING ADDRESS *(Number and street or rural route, city or P.O., State and ZIP Code)*
    No. & Street
    Apt./Unit Number   City
    State/Province   Country   ZIP Code/Postal Code

12. CLAIMANT'S TELEPHONE NUMBER *(Include Area Code)*

13. CLAIMANT'S EMAIL ADDRESS *(Optional)*

14. RELATIONSHIP TO VETERAN

SECTION III: SERVICE ORGANIZATION INFORMATION

15A. NAME OF INDIVIDUAL APPOINTED AS REPRESENTATIVE

15B. INDIVIDUAL IS *(check appropriate box)*
[ ] ATTORNEY   [ ] AGENT   [ ] INDIVIDUAL PROVIDING REPRESENTATION UNDER SECTION 14.630 *(*See required statement below. Signatures are required in Items 16A and 17A)*   [ ] SERVICE ORGANIZATION REPRESENTATIVE *(Specify organization below)*

*INDIVIDUALS PROVIDING REPRESENTATION UNDER SECTION 14.630
(Skip to Item 18, if the box for "Individual Providing Representation Under Section 14.630" was not checked in Item 15B)

The appointment of the individual named in Item 15A (the representative) authorizes that person to represent the individual named in Item 1 or 10 for a particular claim pursuant to the provisions of 38 CFR 14.630. By our signatures below, we, the representative and the veteran/claimant, attest that no compensation will be charged by or paid to the individual named in Item 15A.

16A. SIGNATURE OF REPRESENTATIVE NAMED IN ITEM 15A

16B. DATE OF SIGNATURE *(MM/DD/YYYY)*

17A. SIGNATURE OF INDIVIDUAL NAMED IN ITEM 1 OR 10

17B. DATE OF SIGNATURE *(MM/DD/YYYY)*

18. ADDRESS OF INDIVIDUAL APPOINTED AS CLAIMANT'S REPRESENTATIVE *(Number and street or rural route, city or P.O., State, and ZIP code)*

VA FORM FEB 2019 **21-22a**   SUPERSEDES VA FORM 21-22a, AUG 2015.   Page 1

VETERAN'S SOCIAL SECURITY NO. ☐☐☐ – ☐☐ – ☐☐☐☐

SECTION IV: AUTHORIZATION INFORMATION

19. AUTHORIZATION FOR REPRESENTATIVE'S ACCESS TO RECORDS PROTECTED BY SECTION 7332, TITLE 38, U.S.C. -
Unless I check the box below, I do not authorize VA to disclose to the individual named in Item 15A any records that may be in my file relating to treatment for drug abuse, alcoholism or alcohol abuse, infection with the human immunodeficiency virus (HIV), or sickle cell anemia.

☐ **I authorize** the VA facility having custody of my VA claimant records to disclose to the individual named in Item 15A all treatment records relating to drug abuse, alcoholism or alcohol abuse, infection with the human immunodeficiency virus (HIV), or sickle cell anemia. Redisclosure of these records by my representative, other than to VA or the Court of Appeals for Veterans Claims, is not authorized without my further written consent. This authorization will remain in effect until the earlier of the following events: (1) I revoke this authorization by filing a written revocation with VA; or (2) I revoke the appointment of the individual named in Item 15A, either by explicit revocation or the appointment of another representative.

20. LIMITATION OF CONSENT. My consent in Item 19 for the disclosure of records relating to treatment for drug abuse, alcoholism or alcohol abuse, infection with the human immunodeficiency virus (HIV), or sickle cell anemia is limited as follows:

21. AUTHORIZATION FOR REPRESENTATIVE TO ACT ON CLAIMANT'S BEHALF TO CHANGE CLAIMANT'S ADDRESS -
Unless I check the box below, I do not authorize the individual named in Item 15A to act on my behalf to change my address in my VA records.

☐ **I authorize** the individual named in Item 15A to act on my behalf to change my address in my VA records. This authorization does not extend to any other individual with out my further written consent. This authorization will remain in effect until the earlier of the following events: (1) I revoke this authorization by filing a written revocation with VA; or (2) I revoke the appointment of the individual named in Item 15A, either by explicit revocation or the appointment of another representative.

CONDITIONS OF APPOINTMENT

I, the person named in Item 1 or 10, hereby **appoint** the individual named in Item 15A as my representative to prepare, present, and prosecute my claims for any and all benefits from the Department of Veterans Affairs (VA) based on the service of the veteran named in Item 1. If the individual named in Item 15A is an accredited agent or attorney, the scope of representation provided before VA may be limited by the agent or attorney as indicated below in Item 23. If the individual indicated in Item 15A is providing representation under 14.630, such representation is limited to a particular claim only. I authorize VA to release any and all of my records (other than as provided in Items 19 and 20) to that individual appointed as my representative, and if the individual in Item 15A is an accredited agent or attorney, this authorization includes the following individually named administrative employees of my representative:

Signed and accepted subject to the foregoing conditions.

22A. SIGNATURE OF CLAIMANT *(Do Not Print)*	22B. DATE OF SIGNATURE *(MM/DD/YYYY)*

23. LIMITATIONS ON REPRESENTATION - AGENTS OR ATTORNEYS ONLY *(Unless limited by an agent or attorney, this power of attorney revokes all previously existing powers of attorney)*

24A. SIGNATURE OF REPRESENTATIVE	24B. DATE OF SIGNATURE *(MM/DD/YYYY)*

FEES: Section 5904, Title 38, United States Code, contains provisions regarding fees that may be charged, allowed, or paid for services of agents or attorneys in connection with a proceeding before the Department of Veterans Affairs with respect to benefits under laws administered by the Department.

PENALTY: The law provides severe penalties which include fine or imprisonment, or both, for the willful submission of any statement of a material fact, knowing it to be false or for the fraudulent acceptance of any payment to which you are not entitled.

PRIVACY ACT NOTICE: VA will not disclose information collected on this form to any source other than what has been authorized under the Privacy Act of 1974 or Title 38, Code of Federal Regulations 1.576 for routine uses (i.e., civil or criminal law enforcement, congressional communications, epidemiological or research studies, the collection of money owed to the United States, litigation in which the United States is a party or has an interest, the administration of VA programs and delivery of VA benefits, verification of identity and status, and personnel administration) as identified in the VA system of records, 58VA21/22/28, Compensation, Pension, Education, and Vocational Rehabilitation and Employment Records -VA, published in the Federal Register. Your obligation to respond is voluntary. However, failure to respond provide the requested information could impede the recognition of your representative and/or identification of disclosable records. Except for information protected by 38 U.S.C. 7332, your representative is not prohibited from redisclosing records. The responses you submit are considered confidential (38 U.S.C. 5701). Information submitted is subject to verification through computer matching programs with other agencies.

RESPONDENT BURDEN: We need this information to recognize the individuals appointed by claimants to act on their behalf in the preparation, presentation, and prosecution of claims for VA benefits (38 U.S.C. 5902, 5903, and 5904) and for those individuals to accept appointment. We will also use the information to verify consent for disclosure of VA records to the appointed representative (38 U.S.C. 5701(b) and 7332) Title 38, United States Code, allows us to ask for this information. We estimate that claimants and individuals appointed for purposes of representation will each need an average of 5 minutes to review the instructions, find the information, and complete this form. VA cannot conduct or sponsor a collection of information unless a valid OMB control number is displayed. You are not required to respond to a collection of information if this number is not displayed. A valid OMB control number can be located on the OMB Internet Page at www.reginfo.gov/public/do/PRAMain. If desired, you can call 1-800-827-1000 to get information on where to send comments or suggestions about this form.

VA Form 21-22a, FEB 2019

VA Department of Veterans Affairs | **REVIEW POST TRAUMATIC STRESS DISORDER (PTSD) DISABILITY BENEFITS QUESTIONNAIRE**

IMPORTANT - THE DEPARTMENT OF VETERANS AFFAIRS (VA) **WILL NOT PAY** OR **REIMBURSE** ANY EXPENSES OR COST INCURRED IN THE PROCESS OF COMPLETING AND/OR SUBMITTING THIS FORM. PLEASE READ THE PRIVACY ACT AND RESPONDENT BURDEN INFORMATION BEFORE COMPLETING THIS FORM.

NAME OF PATIENT/VETERAN

PATIENT/VETERAN'S SOCIAL SECURITY NUMBER

NOTE TO PSYCHIATRIST/PSYCHOLOGIST - Your patient is applying to the U. S. Department of Veterans Affairs (VA) for disability benefits. VA will consider the information you provide on this questionnaire as part of their evaluation in processing the veteran's claim. Please note that this questionnaire is for disability evaluation, not for treatment purposes. VA reserves the right to confirm the authenticity of ALL DBQs completed by private health care providers.

NOTE: If the Veteran experiences a mental health emergency during the interview, please terminate the interview and obtain help, using local resources as appropriate. You may also contact the Veterans Crisis Line at 1-800-273-TALK (8255). Stay on the Crisis Line until help can link the Veteran to emergency care.

The following health care providers can perform REVIEW examinations for PTSD: a board-certified or board-eligible psychiatrist; a licensed doctorate-level psychologist; a doctorate-level mental health provider under the close supervision of a board-certified or board-eligible psychiatrist or licensed doctorate-level psychologist; a psychiatry resident under close supervision of a board-certified or board-eligible psychiatrist or licensed doctorate-level psychologist; a clinical or counseling psychologist completing a one-year internship or residency (for purposes of a doctorate-level degree) under close supervision of a board-certified or board-eligible psychiatrist or licensed doctorate-level psychologist, or a licensed clinical social worker (LCSW), a nurse practitioner, a clinical nurse specialist, or a physician assistant, under close supervision of a board-certified or board-eligible psychiatrist or licensed doctorate-level psychologist.

SECTION I - DIAGNOSTIC SUMMARY

NOTE: This section should be completed based on the current examination and clinical findings.

1. DOES THE VETERAN NOW HAVE OR HAS HE OR SHE EVER BEEN DIAGNOSED WITH PTSD?

☐ YES ☐ NO *(If "Yes," continue to complete this Questionnaire)*
(If no diagnosis of PTSD, and the veteran has another Axis I and/or II diagnosis, then continue to complete this Questionnaire and/or VA Form 21-0960P-1, Eating Disorders Disability Benefits Questionnaire)

SECTION II - CURRENT DIAGNOSES

2A. LIST CURRENT DIAGNOSES

DIAGNOSIS #1: _____

    ICD CODE: _____ INDICATE THE AXIS CATEGORY: ☐ AXIS I ☐ AXIS II

    COMMENTS, IF ANY: _____

DIAGNOSIS #2: _____

    ICD CODE: _____ INDICATE THE AXIS CATEGORY: ☐ AXIS I ☐ AXIS II

    COMMENTS, IF ANY: _____

DIAGNOSIS #3: _____

    ICD CODE: _____ INDICATE THE AXIS CATEGORY: ☐ AXIS I ☐ AXIS II

    COMMENTS, IF ANY: _____

DIAGNOSIS #4: _____

    ICD CODE: _____ INDICATE THE AXIS CATEGORY: ☐ AXIS I ☐ AXIS II

    COMMENTS, IF ANY: _____

IF ADDITIONAL DIAGNOSES, DESCRIBE USING ABOVE FORMAT:

2B. AXIS III - MEDICAL DIAGNOSES *(to include TBI)*:

ICD CODE: _____

COMMENTS, IF ANY:

VA FORM MAY 2018 **21-0960P-3** | SUPERSEDES VA FORM 21-0960P-3, FEB 2015, WHICH WILL NOT BE USED | Page 1

PATIENT/VETERAN'S SOCIAL SECURITY NO. [ ][ ][ ] — [ ][ ] — [ ][ ][ ][ ]

SECTION II - CURRENT DIAGNOSES *(Continued)*

2C. AXIS IV - PSYCHOSOCIAL AND ENVIRONMENTAL PROBLEMS *(describe, if any)*:

2D. AXIS V - CURRENT GLOBAL ASSESSMENT OF FUNCTIONING *(GAF)* SCORE:

COMMENTS, IF ANY:

SECTION III - DIFFERENTIATION OF SYMPTOMS

3A. DOES THE VETERAN HAVE MORE THAN ONE MENTAL DISORDER DIAGNOSED?

[ ] YES   [ ] NO   *(If "Yes," complete Item 3B)*

3B. IS IT POSSIBLE TO DIFFERENTIATE WHAT SYMPTOM(S) IS/ARE ATTRIBUTABLE TO EACH DIAGNOSIS?

[ ] YES   [ ] NO   [ ] NOT APPLICABLE

(If "No," provide reason that it is not possible to differentiate what portion of each symptom is attributable to each diagnosis):

(If "Yes," list which symptoms are attributable to each diagnosis):

3C. DOES THE VETERAN HAVE A DIAGNOSED TRAUMATIC BRAIN INJURY *(TBI)*?

[ ] YES   [ ] NO   [ ] NOT SHOWN IN RECORDS REVIEWED   *(If "Yes," complete Item 3D)*

(Comments, if any):

3D. IS IT POSSIBLE TO DIFFERENTIATE WHAT SYMPTOM(S) IS/ARE ATTRIBUTABLE TO EACH DIAGNOSIS?

[ ] YES   [ ] NO   [ ] NOT APPLICABLE

(If "No," provide reason that it is not possible to differentiate what portion of each symptom is attributable to each diagnosis):

(If "Yes," list which symptoms are attributable to each diagnosis):

SECTION IV - OCCUPATIONAL AND SOCIAL IMPAIRMENT

4A. WHICH OF THE FOLLOWING BEST SUMMARIZES THE VETERAN'S LEVEL OF OCCUPATIONAL AND SOCIAL IMPAIRMENT WITH REGARDS TO ALL MENTAL DIAGNOSES? *(Check only one)*

[ ] NO MENTAL DISORDER DIAGNOSIS

[ ] A MENTAL CONDITION HAS BEEN FORMALLY DIAGNOSED, BUT SYMPTOMS ARE NOT SEVERE ENOUGH EITHER TO INTERFERE WITH OCCUPATIONAL AND SOCIAL FUNCTIONING OR TO REQUIRE CONTINUOUS MEDICATION

[ ] OCCUPATIONAL AND SOCIAL IMPAIRMENT DUE TO MILD OR TRANSIENT SYMPTOMS WHICH DECREASE WORK EFFICIENCY AND ABILITY TO PERFORM OCCUPATIONAL TASKS ONLY DURING PERIODS OF SIGNIFICANT STRESS, OR SYMPTOMS CONTROLLED BY MEDICATION

[ ] OCCUPATIONAL AND SOCIAL IMPAIRMENT WITH OCCASIONAL DECREASE IN WORK EFFICIENCY AND INTERMITTENT PERIODS OF INABILITY TO PERFORM OCCUPATIONAL TASKS, ALTHOUGH GENERALLY FUNCTIONING SATISFACTORILY, WITH NORMAL ROUTINE BEHAVIOR, SELF-CARE AND CONVERSATION

[ ] OCCUPATIONAL AND SOCIAL IMPAIRMENT WITH REDUCED RELIABILITY AND PRODUCTIVITY

[ ] OCCUPATIONAL AND SOCIAL IMPAIRMENT WITH DEFICIENCIES IN MOST AREAS, SUCH AS WORK, SCHOOL, FAMILY RELATIONS, JUDGMENT, THINKING AND/OR MOOD

[ ] TOTAL OCCUPATIONAL AND SOCIAL IMPAIRMENT

4B. FOR THE INDICATED LEVEL OF OCCUPATIONAL AND SOCIAL IMPAIRMENT, IS IT POSSIBLE TO DIFFERENTIATE WHAT PORTION OF THE OCCUPATIONAL AND SOCIAL IMPAIRMENT INDICATED ABOVE IS CAUSED BY EACH MENTAL DISORDER?

[ ] YES   [ ] NO   [ ] NO OTHER MENTAL DISORDER HAS BEEN DIAGNOSED

(If "No," provide reason that it is not possible to differentiate what portion of the indicated level of occupational and social impairment is attributable to each diagnosis):

(If "Yes," list which portion of the indicated level of occupational and social impairment is attributable to each diagnosis):

311

PATIENT/VETERAN'S SOCIAL SECURITY NO. ☐☐☐ — ☐☐ — ☐☐☐☐

SECTION IV - OCCUPATIONAL AND SOCIAL IMPAIRMENT *(Continued)*

4C. IF A DIAGNOSIS OF TBI EXISTS, IS IT POSSIBLE TO DIFFERENTIATE WHAT PORTION OF THE OCCUPATIONAL AND SOCIAL IMPAIRMENT INDICATED ABOVE IS CAUSED BY THE TBI?

☐ YES ☐ NO ☐ NO DIAGNOSIS OF TBI

(If "No," provide reason that it is not possible to differentiate what portion of the indicated level of occupational and social impairment is attributable to each diagnosis):

(If "Yes," list which portion of the indicated level of occupational and social impairment is attributable to each diagnosis):

SECTION V - CLINICAL FINDINGS

1. EVIDENCE REVIEW

5A. IF ANY RECORDS (EVIDENCE) WERE REVIEWED, PLEASE LIST:

2. RECENT HISTORY (SINCE PRIOR EXAM)

5B. RELEVANT SOCIAL/MARITAL/FAMILY HISTORY:

5C. RELEVANT OCCUPATIONAL AND EDUCATIONAL HISTORY:

5D. RELEVANT MENTAL HEALTH HISTORY, TO INCLUDE PRESCRIBED MEDICATIONS AND FAMILY MENTAL HEALTH:

5E. RELEVANT LEGAL AND BEHAVIORAL HISTORY:

5F. RELEVANT SUBSTANCE ABUSE HISTORY:

5G. SENTINEL EVENT(S) (OTHER THAN STRESSORS):

5H. OTHER *(If any)*:

VA FORM 21-0960P-3, MAY 2018

Page 3

312

SECTION VI - PTSD DIAGNOSTIC CRITERIA

NOTE: Please check criteria used for establishing the current PTSD diagnosis. The diagnostic criteria for PTSD, referred to as Criteria A-F, are from the Diagnostic and Statistical Manual of Mental Disorders, 4th edition (DSM-IV).

CRITERION A: The Veteran has been exposed to a traumatic event where both of the following were present

☐ The Veteran experienced, witnessed or was confronted with an event that involved actual or threatened death or serious injury, or a threat to the physical integrity of self or others.

☐ The Veteran's response involved intense fear, helplessness or horror.

☐ No exposure to a traumatic event.

CRITERION B: The traumatic event is persistently re-experienced in 1 or more of the following ways:

☐ Recurrent and distressing recollections of the event, including images, thoughts or perceptions.

☐ Recurrent distressing dreams of the event.

☐ Acting or feeling as if the traumatic event were recurring; this includes a sense of reliving the experience, illusions, hallucinations and dissociative flashback episodes, including those that occur on awakening or when intoxicated.

☐ Intense psychological distress at exposure to internal or external cues that symbolize or resemble an aspect of the traumatic event.

☐ Physiological reactivity on exposure to internal or external cues that symbolize or resemble an aspect of the traumatic event.

☐ The traumatic event is not persistently re-experienced

CRITERION C: Persistent avoidance of stimuli associated with the trauma and numbing of general responsiveness *(not present before the trauma)*, as indicated by 3 or more of the following:

☐ Efforts to avoid thoughts, feelings or conversations associated with the trauma.

☐ Efforts to avoid activities, places or people that arouse recollections of the trauma.

☐ Inability to recall an important aspect of the trauma.

☐ Markedly diminished interest or participation in significant activities.

☐ Feeling of detachment or estrangement from others.

☐ Restricted range of affection *(e.g., unable to have loving feelings)*.

☐ Sense of a foreshortened future *(e.g., does not expect to have a career, marriage, children or a normal life span)*

☐ No persistent avoidance of stimuli associated with the trauma or numbing of general responsiveness.

CRITERION D: Persistent symptoms of increased arousal, not present before the trauma, as indicated by 2 or more of the following:

☐ Difficulty falling or staying asleep.

☐ Irritability or outbursts of anger.

☐ Difficulty concentrating.

☐ Hypervigilence.

☐ Exaggerated startle response

☐ No persistent symptoms of increased arousal

CRITERION E: Duration of symptoms:

☐ The duration of the symptoms described in Criteria B, C and D is more than 1 month.

☐ The duration of the symptoms described in Criteria B, C and D is less than 1 month.

☐ Veteran does not meet full criteria for PTSD.

CRITERION F: Clinically significant distress or impairment:

☐ The PTSD symptoms described above cause clinically significant distress or impairment in social, occupational, or other important areas of functioning

☐ The PTSD symptoms described above do NOT cause clinically significant distress or impairment in social, occupational, or other important areas of functioning.

☐ Veteran does not meet full criteria for PTSD.

PATIENT/VETERAN'S SOCIAL SECURITY NO. ☐☐☐ – ☐☐ – ☐☐☐☐

SECTION VII - SYMPTOMS

7. FOR VA RATING PURPOSES, CHECK ALL SYMPTOMS THAT APPLY TO THE VETERAN'S DIAGNOSES:

- ☐ Depressed mood
- ☐ Anxiety
- ☐ Suspiciousness
- ☐ Panic attacks that occur weekly or less often
- ☐ Panic attacks more than once a week
- ☐ Near-continuous panic or depression affecting the ability to function independently, appropriately and effectively
- ☐ Chronic sleep impairment
- ☐ Mild memory loss, such as forgetting names, directions or recent events
- ☐ Impairment of short and long term memory, for example, retention of only highly learned material, while forgetting to complete tasks
- ☐ Memory loss for names of close relatives, own occupation, or own name
- ☐ Flattened affect
- ☐ Circumstantial, circumlocutory or stereotyped speech
- ☐ Speech intermittently illogical, obscure, or irrelevant
- ☐ Difficulty in understanding complex commands
- ☐ Impaired judgment
- ☐ Impaired abstract thinking
- ☐ Gross impairment in thought processes or communication
- ☐ Disturbances of motivation and mood
- ☐ Difficulty in establishing and maintaining effective work and social relationships
- ☐ Difficulty adapting to stressful circumstances, including work or a work like setting
- ☐ Inability to establish and maintain effective relationships
- ☐ Suicidal ideation
- ☐ Obsessional rituals which interfere with routine activities
- ☐ Impaired impulse control, such as unprovoked irritability with periods of violence
- ☐ Spatial disorientation
- ☐ Persistent delusions or hallucinations
- ☐ Grossly inappropriate behavior
- ☐ Persistent danger of hurting self or others
- ☐ Neglect of personal appearance and hygiene
- ☐ Intermittent inability to perform activities of daily living, including maintenance of minimal personal hygiene
- ☐ Disorientation to time or place

SECTION VIII - OTHER SYMPTOMS

8. DOES THE VETERAN HAVE ANY OTHER SYMPTOMS ATTRIBUTABLE TO PTSD (AND OTHER MENTAL DISORDERS) THAT ARE NOT LISTED ABOVE?

☐ YES   ☐ NO   *(If "Yes," describe):*

314

PATIENT/VETERAN'S SOCIAL SECURITY NO. ☐☐☐ – ☐☐ – ☐☐☐☐

SECTION IX - COMPETENCY

9. IS THE VETERAN CAPABLE OF MANAGING HIS OR HER FINANCIAL AFFAIRS?

☐ YES   ☐ NO *(If "No," explain):*

SECTION X - REMARKS

10. REMARKS *(If any):*

SECTION XI - PSYCHIATRIST/PSYCHOLOGIST CERTIFICATION AND SIGNATURE

CERTIFICATION - To the best of my knowledge, the information contained herein is accurate, complete and current.

10A PSYCHIATRIST/PSYCHOLOGIST SIGNATURE AND TITLE *(Sign in ink)*	10B. PSYCHIATRIST/PSYCHOLOGIST PRINTED NAME	10C. DATE SIGNED
10D. PSYCHIATRIST/PSYCHOLOGIST PHONE AND FAX NUMBERS	10E. NATIONAL PROVIDER IDENTIFIER (NPI) NUMBER	10F. PSYCHIATRIST/PSYCHOLOGIST ADDRESS

NOTE - VA may request additional medical information, including additional examinations, if necessary to complete VA's review of the veteran's application.

IMPORTANT - PSYCHIATRIST/PSYCHOLOGIST send the completed form to: _____
(VA Regional Office FAX No.)

NOTE - A list of VA Regional Office FAX Numbers can be found at www.benefits.va.gov/disabilityexams or obtained by calling 1-800-827-1000.

PRIVACY ACT NOTICE: VA will not disclose information collected on this form to any source other than what has been authorized under the Privacy Act of 1974 or Title 38, Code of Federal Regulations 1.576 for routine uses (i.e., civil or criminal law enforcement, congressional communications, epidemiological or research studies, the collection of money owed to the United States, litigation in which the United States is a party or has an interest, the administration of VA programs and delivery of VA benefits, verification of identity and status, and personnel administration) as identified in the VA system of records, 58/VA21/22/28, Compensation, Pension, Education and Vocational Rehabilitation and Employment Records - VA, published in the Federal Register. Your obligation to respond is voluntary. VA uses your SSN to identify your claim file. Providing your SSN will help ensure that your records are properly associated with your claim file. Giving us your SSN account information is voluntary. Refusal to provide your SSN by itself will not result in the denial of benefits. VA will not deny an individual benefits for refusing to provide his or her SSN unless the disclosure of the SSN is required by a Federal Statute of law in effect prior to January 1, 1975, and still in effect. The requested information is considered relevant and necessary to determine maximum benefits under the law. The responses you submit are considered confidential (38 U.S.C. 5701). Information submitted is subject to verification through computer matching programs with other agencies.

RESPONDENT BURDEN: We need this information to determine entitlement to benefits (38 U.S.C. 501). Title 38, United States Code, allows us to ask for this information. We estimate that you will need an average of 30 minutes to review the instructions, find the information, and complete the form. VA cannot conduct or sponsor a collection of information unless a valid OMB control number is displayed. You are not required to respond to a collection of information if this number is not displayed. Valid OMB control numbers can be located on the OMB Internet Page at www.reginfo.gov/public/do/PRAMain. If desired, you can call 1-800-827-1000 to get information on where to send comments or suggestions about this form.

OMB Approved No. 2900-0659
Respondent Burden: 1 hour 10 minutes
Expiration Date: 07/31/2020

Department of Veterans Affairs

VA DATE STAMP
DO NOT WRITE IN THIS SPACE

STATEMENT IN SUPPORT OF CLAIM FOR SERVICE CONNECTION FOR POST-TRAUMATIC STRESS DISORDER (PTSD)

IMPORTANT: If you or someone you know is in crisis, call the Veterans Crisis Line at 1-800-273-8255 and press 1, or visit https://www.veteranscrisisline.net/ to chat online, or send a text message to **838255** to receive confidential support 24 hours a day, 7 days a week, 365 days a year. Support for deaf and hard of hearing individuals is available.

INSTRUCTIONS: List the stressful incident or incidents that occurred in service that you feel contributed to your current condition. For each incident, provide a description of what happened, the date, the geographic location, your unit assignment and dates of assignment, and the full names and unit assignments of you know of who were killed or injured during the incident. Please provide dates within at least a 60-day range and do not use nicknames. It is important that you complete the form in detail and be as specific as possible so that research of military records can be thoroughly conducted. If more space is needed, attach a separate sheet, indicating the item number to which the answers apply.

SECTION I: VETERAN'S IDENTIFICATION INFORMATION

NOTE: You can *either* complete the form online or by hand. Please print the information requested in ink, neatly and legibly to help process the form.

1. VETERAN NAME (First, Middle Initial, Last)

2. SOCIAL SECURITY NUMBER

3. VA FILE NUMBER (If applicable)

4. DATE OF BIRTH (MM/DD/YYYY) — Month Day Year

5. VETERAN'S SERVICE NUMBER (If applicable)

6. TELEPHONE NUMBER (Include Area Code)

7. E-MAIL ADDRESS (Optional)

SECTION II: STRESSFUL INCIDENTS

8A. DATE *FIRST* INCIDENT OCCURRED (MM/DD/YYYY) — Month Day Year

8B. DATES OF UNIT ASSIGNMENT (MM/DD/YYYY) — FROM: Month Day Year TO: Month Day Year

8C. LOCATION OF INCIDENT (City, State, Country, Province, landmark or military installation)

8D. UNIT ASSIGNMENT DURING INCIDENT (Such as: DIVISION, WING, BATTALION, CAVALRY, SHIP)

8E. DESCRIPTION OF THE INCIDENT

8F. MEDALS OR CITATIONS YOU RECEIVED BECAUSE OF THE INCIDENT

VA FORM JUL 2017 **21-0781**

SUPERSEDES VA FORM 21-0781, AUG 2014, WHICH WILL NOT BE USED.

PAGE 1

316

VETERAN'S SOCIAL SECURITY NO. [ ][ ][ ] — [ ][ ] — [ ][ ][ ][ ]

SECTION II: STRESSFUL INCIDENTS (Continued)

NOTE: Information about persons who were killed or injured during the first incident *(attach a separate sheet if more space is needed.)*

9A. NAME OF PERSON *(First, Middle Initial, Last)*

9B. RANK *(If applicable)*	9C. DATE OF INJURY/DEATH *(MM/DD/YYYY)*			9D. PLEASE CHECK ONE
	Month	Day	Year	○ KILLED IN ACTION ○ WOUNDED IN ACTION ○ OTHER
				○ KILLED NON-BATTLE ○ INJURED NON-BATTLE

9E. UNIT ASSIGNMENT DURING INCIDENT *(Such as, DIVISION, WING, BATTALION, CAVALRY, SHIP)*

10A. NAME OF PERSON *(First, Middle Initial, Last)*

10B. RANK *(If applicable)*	10C. DATE OF INJURY/DEATH *(MM/DD/YYYY)*			10D. PLEASE CHECK ONE
	Month	Day	Year	○ KILLED IN ACTION ○ WOUNDED IN ACTION ○ OTHER
				○ KILLED NON-BATTLE ○ INJURED NON-BATTLE

10E. UNIT ASSIGNMENT DURING INCIDENT *(Such as, DIVISION, WING, BATTALION, CAVALRY, SHIP)*

11A. DATE **SECOND** INCIDENT OCCURRED *(MM/DD/YYYY)*			11B. DATES OF UNIT ASSIGNMENT *(MM/DD/YYYY)*						
Month	Day	Year	FROM: Month	Day	Year	TO: Month	Day	Year

11C. LOCATION OF INCIDENT *(City, State, Country, Province, landmark or military installation)*

11D. UNIT ASSIGNMENT DURING INCIDENT *(Such as, DIVISION, WING, BATTALION, CAVALRY, SHIP)*

11E. DESCRIPTION OF THE INCIDENT

11F. MEDALS OR CITATIONS YOU RECEIVED BECAUSE OF THE INCIDENT

VA FORM 21-0781, JUL 2017

PAGE 2

VETERAN'S SOCIAL SECURITY NO [ ][ ][ ] — [ ][ ] — [ ][ ][ ][ ]

SECTION II: STRESSFUL INCIDENTS (Continued)

NOTE: Information about persons who were killed or injured during the second incident *(attach a separate sheet if more space is needed.)*

12A. NAME OF PERSON *(First, Middle Initial, Last)*

12B. RANK *(If applicable)*	12C. DATE OF INJURY/DEATH *(MM/DD/YYYY)*			12D. PLEASE CHECK ONE
	Month	Day	Year	○ KILLED IN ACTION ○ WOUNDED IN ACTION ○ OTHER
				○ KILLED NON-BATTLE ○ INJURED NON-BATTLE

12E. UNIT ASSIGNMENT DURING INCIDENT *(Such as, DIVISION, WING, BATTALION, CAVALRY, SHIP)*

13A. NAME OF PERSON *(First, Middle Initial, Last)*

13B. RANK *(If applicable)*	13C. DATE OF INJURY/DEATH *(MM/DD/YYYY)*			13D. PLEASE CHECK ONE
	Month	Day	Year	○ KILLED IN ACTION ○ WOUNDED IN ACTION ○ OTHER
				○ KILLED NON-BATTLE ○ INJURED NON-BATTLE

13E. UNIT ASSIGNMENT DURING INCIDENT *(Such as, DIVISION, WING, BATTALION, CAVALRY, SHIP)*

14. REMARKS

SECTION III: VETERAN SIGNATURE

I HEREBY CERTIFY THAT the information I have given on this form is true and correct to the best of my knowledge and belief.

15. SIGNATURE	16. DATE SIGNED *(MM/DD/YYYY)*
	[ ][ ] — [ ][ ] — [ ][ ][ ][ ]

Department of Veterans Affairs | **INSTRUCTIONS FOR COMPLETING ENROLLMENT APPLICATION FOR HEALTH BENEFITS**

Please Read Before You Start . . . What is VA Form 10-10EZ used for?

For Veterans to apply for enrollment in the VA health care system. The information provided on this form will be used by VA to determine your eligibility for medical benefits and on average will take 30 minutes to complete. This includes the time it will take to read instructions, gather the necessary facts and fill out the form.

Where can I get help filling out the form and if I have questions?

You may use ANY of the following to request assistance:

- Ask VA to help you fill out the form by calling us at 1-877-222-VETS (8387).
- Access VA's website at http://www.va.gov and select "Contact the VA."
- Contact the Enrollment Coordinator at your local VA health care facility.
- Contact a National or State Veterans Service Organization.

Definitions of terms used on this form:

SERVICE-CONNECTED (SC): A VA determination that an illness or injury was incurred or aggravated in the line of duty, in the active military, naval or air service.

COMPENSABLE: A VA determination that a service-connected disability is severe enough to warrant monetary compensation.

NONCOMPENSABLE: A VA determination that a service-connected disability is not severe enough to warrant monetary compensation.

NONSERVICE-CONNECTED (NSC): A Veteran who does not have a VA determined service-related condition.

Getting Started: ALL VETERANS MUST COMPLETE SECTIONS I - III.

Directions for Sections I - III:

Section I - General Information: Answer all questions.

Section II - Military Service Information: If you are not currently receiving benefits from VA, you may attach a copy of your discharge or separation papers from the military (such as DD-214 or, for WWII Veterans, a "WD" Form), with your signed application to expedite processing of your application. If you are currently receiving benefits from VA, we will cross-reference your information with VA data.

Section III - Insurance Information: Include information for all health insurance companies that cover you, this includes coverage provided through a spouse or significant other. Bring your insurance cards, Medicare and/or Medicaid card with you to each health care appointment.

Directions for Sections IV-VI:

Financial Disclosure: ONLY NSC AND 0% NONCOMPENSABLE SC VETERANS MUST COMPLETE THIS SECTION TO DETERMINE ELIGIBILITY FOR VA HEALTH CARE ENROLLMENT AND/OR CARE OR SERVICES.

Financial Disclosure Requirements Do Not Apply To:

- a former Prisoner of War; or
- those in receipt of a Purple Heart; or
- a recently discharged Combat Veteran; or
- those discharged for a disability incurred or aggravated in the line of duty; or
- those receiving VA SC disability compensation; or
- those receiving VA pension; or
- those in receipt of Medicaid benefits; or
- those who served in Vietnam between January 9, 1962 and May 7, 1975; or
- those who served in SW Asia during the Gulf War between August 2, 1990 and November 11, 1998; or
- those who served at least 30 days at Camp Lejeune between August 1, 1953 and December 31, 1987.

You are not required to disclose your financial information; however, VA is not currently enrolling new applicants who decline to provide their financial information unless they have other qualifying eligibility factors. If a financial assessment is not used to determine your priority for enrollment you may choose not to disclose your information. However, if a financial assessment is used to determine your eligibility for cost-free medication, travel assistance or waiver of the travel deductible, and you do not disclose your financial information, you will not be eligible for these benefits.

Section IV - Dependent Information: Include the following:

- Your spouse even if you did not live together, as long as you contributed support last calendar year.
- Your biological children, adopted children, and stepchildren who are unmarried and under the age of 18, or at least 18 but under 23 and attending high school, college or vocational school (full or part-time), or became permanently unable to support themselves before age 18.
- Child support contributions. Contributions can include tuition or clothing payments or payments of medical bills.

VA FORM
JAN 2020   **10-10EZ**   *Complete only the sections that apply to you; sign and date the form.*   PAGE 1 OF 5

Continued ...

Section V - Employment Information:
- Veterans Employment Status
- Date of Retirement
- Company Name
- Company Address
- Company Phone Number

Section VI - Previous Calendar Year Gross Annual Income of Veteran, Spouse and Dependent Children

Report:
- Gross annual income from employment, except for income from your farm, ranch, property or business. Include your wages, bonuses, tips, severance pay and other accrued benefits and your child's income information if it could have been used to pay your household expenses.
- Net income from your farm, ranch, property, or business.
- Other income amounts, including retirement and pension income, Social Security Retirement and Social Security Disability income, compensation benefits such as VA disability, unemployment, Workers and black lung, cash gifts, interest and dividends, including tax exempt earnings and distributions from Individual Retirement Accounts (IRAs) or annuities.

Do Not Report:
Donations from public or private relief, welfare or charitable organizations; Supplemental Security Income (SSI) and need-based payments from a government agency; profit from the occasional sale of property; income tax refunds, reinvested interest on Individual Retirement Accounts (IRAs); scholarships and grants for school attendance; disaster relief payments; reimbursement for casualty loss; loans; Radiation Compensation Exposure Act payments; Agent Orange settlement payments; Alaska Native Claims Settlement Acts Income, payments to foster parent; amounts in joint accounts in banks and similar institutions acquired by reason of death of the other joint owner; Japanese ancestry restitution under Public Law 100-383; cash surrender value of life insurance; lump-sum proceeds of life insurance policy on a Veteran; and payments received under the Medicare transitional assistance program.

Section VII - Previous Calendar Year Deductible Expenses

Report non-reimbursed medical expenses paid by you or your spouse. Include expenses for medical and dental care, drugs, eyeglasses, Medicare, medical insurance premiums and other health care expenses paid by you for dependents and persons for whom you have a legal or moral obligation to support. Do not list expenses if you expect to receive reimbursement from insurance or other sources. Report last illness and burial expenses, e.g., prepaid burial, paid by the Veteran for spouse or dependent(s).

Section VIII - Consent to Copays and to Receive Communications

By submitting this application, you are agreeing to pay the applicable VA copayments for care or services (including urgent care) as required by law. You also agree to receive communications from VA to your supplied email, home phone number, or mobile number. However, providing your email, home phone number, or mobile number is voluntary.

Submitting Your Application
1. You or an individual to whom you have delegated your Power of Attorney must sign and date the form. If you sign with an "X", 2 people you know must witness you as you sign. They must sign the form and print their names. If the form is not signed and dated appropriately, VA will return it for you to complete.
2. Attach any continuation sheets, a copy of supporting materials and your Power of Attorney documents to your application.

Where do I send my application?
Mail the original application and supporting materials to the Health Eligibility Center, 2957 Clairmont Road, Suite 200, Atlanta, GA 30329.

PAPERWORK REDUCTION ACT AND PRIVACY ACT INFORMATION

The Paperwork Reduction Act of 1995 requires us to notify you that this information collection is in accordance with the clearance requirements of Section 3507 of the Paperwork Reduction Act of 1995. We may not conduct or sponsor, and you are not required to respond to, a collection of information unless it displays a valid OMB number. We anticipate that the time expended by all individuals who must complete this form will average 30 minutes. This includes the time it will take to read instructions, gather the necessary facts and fill out the form.

Privacy Act Information: VA is asking you to provide the information on this form under 38 U.S.C. Sections 1705,1710, 1712, and 1722 in order for VA to determine your eligibility for medical benefits. Information you supply may be verified from initial submission forward through a computer-matching program. VA may disclose the information that you put on the form as permitted by law. VA may make a "routine use" disclosure of the information as outlined in the Privacy Act systems of records notices and in accordance with the VHA Notice of Privacy Practices. Providing the requested information is voluntary, but if any or all of the requested information is not provided, it may delay or result in denial of your request for health care benefits. Failure to furnish the information will not have any effect on any other benefits to which you may be entitled. If you provide VA your Social Security Number, VA will use it to administer your VA benefits. VA may also use this information to identify Veterans and persons claiming or receiving VA benefits and their records, and for other purposes authorized or required by law.

OMB Control No. 2900-0091
Estimated Burden Avg. 30 min.
Expiration Date 12/31/2020

Department of Veterans Affairs

APPLICATION FOR HEALTH BENEFITS

SECTION I - GENERAL INFORMATION

Federal law provides criminal penalties, including a fine and/or imprisonment for up to 5 years, for concealing a material fact or making a materially false statement. (See 18 U.S.C. 1001)

1A. VETERAN'S NAME *(Last, First, Middle Name)*	1B. PREFERRED NAME	2. MOTHER'S MAIDEN NAME

3A. BIRTH SEX	3B. SELF-IDENTIFIED GENDER IDENTITY	4. ARE YOU SPANISH, HISPANIC, OR LATINO?	5. WHAT IS YOUR RACE? *(You may check more than one. Information is required for statistical purposes only.)*	6. SOCIAL SECURITY NO.
☐ MALE ☐ FEMALE	☐ MALE ☐ FEMALE	☐ YES ☐ NO	☐ ASIAN ☐ AMERICAN INDIAN OR ALASKA NATIVE ☐ BLACK OR AFRICAN AMERICAN ☐ WHITE ☐ NATIVE HAWAIIAN OR OTHER PACIFIC ISLANDER	

7. VA CLAIM NUMBER	8A. DATE OF BIRTH *(mm/dd/yyyy)*	8B. PLACE OF BIRTH *(City and State)*	9. RELIGION

10A. PERMANENT ADDRESS *(Street)*	10B. CITY	10C. STATE	10D. ZIP CODE	10E. COUNTY

10F. HOME TELEPHONE NO. *(optional)* *(Include Area Code)*	10G. MOBILE TELEPHONE NO. *(optional)* *(Include Area Code)*	10H. E-MAIL ADDRESS *(optional)*

11A. RESIDENTIAL ADDRESS *(Street)*	11B. CITY	11C. STATE	11D. ZIP CODE	11E. COUNTY

12. TYPE OF BENEFIT(S) APPLYING FOR *(You may check more than one)*	13. CURRENT MARTIAL STATUS
☐ ENROLLMENT/HEALTH SERVICES ☐ DENTAL	☐ MARRIED ☐ NEVER MARRIED ☐ SEPARATED ☐ WIDOWED ☐ DIVORCED

14A. NEXT OF KIN NAME	14B. NEXT OF KIN ADDRESS	14C. NEXT OF KIN RELATIONSHIP

14D. NEXT OF KIN TELEPHONE NO. *(Include Area Code)*	14E. NEXT OF KIN WORK TELEPHONE NO. *(Include Area Code)*	15. DESIGNEE - INDIVIDUAL TO RECEIVE POSSESSION OF YOUR PERSONAL PROPERTY LEFT ON PREMISES UNDER VA CONTROL AFTER YOUR DEPARTURE OR AT THE TIME OF DEATH *(Note: This does not constitute a will or transfer of title)*

16. I AM ENROLLING TO OBTAIN MINIMUM ESSENTIAL COVERAGE UNDER THE AFFORDABLE CARE ACT ☐ YES ☐ NO	17. WHICH VA MEDICAL CENTER OR OUTPATIENT CLINIC DO YOU PREFER? *(for listing of facilities visit www.va.gov/directory)*	18. WOULD YOU LIKE FOR VA TO CONTACT YOU TO SCHEDULE YOUR FIRST APPOINTMENT? ☐ YES ☐ NO

SECTION II - MILITARY SERVICE INFORMATION

1A. LAST BRANCH OF SERVICE	1B. LAST ENTRY DATE	1C. FUTURE DISCHARGE DATE	1D. LAST DISCHARGE DATE

1E. DISCHARGE TYPE	1F. MILITARY SERVICE NUMBER

2. MILITARY HISTORY *(Check yes or no)*	YES	NO		YES	NO
A. ARE YOU A PURPLE HEART AWARD RECIPIENT?	☐	☐	G. DO YOU HAVE A VA SERVICE-CONNECTED RATING?	☐	☐
B. ARE YOU A FORMER PRISONER OF WAR?	☐	☐	IF "YES", WHAT IS YOUR RATED PERCENTAGE _____ %		
C. DID YOU SERVE IN A COMBAT THEATER OF OPERATIONS AFTER 11/11/1998?	☐	☐	H. DID YOU SERVE IN VIETNAM BETWEEN JANUARY 9, 1962 AND MAY 7, 1975?	☐	☐
D. WERE YOU DISCHARGED OR RETIRED FROM MILITARY FOR A DISABILITY INCURRED IN THE LINE OF DUTY?	☐	☐	I. WERE YOU EXPOSED TO RADIATION WHILE IN THE MILITARY?	☐	☐
E. ARE YOU RECEIVING DISABILITY RETIREMENT PAY INSTEAD OF VA COMPENSATION?	☐	☐	J. DID YOU RECEIVE NOSE AND THROAT RADIUM TREATMENTS WHILE IN THE MILITARY?	☐	☐
F. DID YOU SERVE IN SW ASIA DURING THE GULF WAR BETWEEN AUGUST 2, 1990 AND NOVEMBER 11, 1998?	☐	☐	K. DID YOU SERVE ON ACTIVE DUTY AT LEAST 30 DAYS AT CAMP LEJEUNE FROM AUGUST 1, 1953 THROUGH DECEMBER 31, 1987?	☐	☐

APPLICATION FOR HEALTH BENEFITS
Continued

VETERAN'S NAME (Last, First, Middle)	SOCIAL SECURITY NUMBER

SECTION III - INSURANCE INFORMATION (Use a separate sheet for additional information)

1. ENTER YOUR HEALTH INSURANCE COMPANY NAME, ADDRESS AND TELEPHONE NUMBER (include coverage through spouse or other person)

2. NAME OF POLICY HOLDER	3. POLICY NUMBER	4. GROUP CODE	5. ARE YOU ELIGIBLE FOR MEDICAID? ☐ YES ☐ NO	6A. ARE YOU ENROLLED IN MEDICARE HOSPITAL INSURANCE PART A? ☐ YES ☐ NO 6B. EFFECTIVE DATE (mm/dd/yyyy)

SECTION IV - DEPENDENT INFORMATION (Use a separate sheet for additional dependents)

1. SPOUSE'S NAME (Last, First, Middle Name)	2. CHILD'S NAME (Last, First, Middle Name)	
1A. SPOUSE'S SOCIAL SECURITY NUMBER	2A. CHILD'S DATE OF BIRTH (mm/dd/yyyy)	2B. CHILD'S SOCIAL SECURITY NO.
1B. SPOUSE'S DATE OF BIRTH (mm/dd/yyyy) / 1C. SPOUSE SELF-IDENTIFIED GENDER IDENTITY ☐ MALE ☐ FEMALE	2C. DATE CHILD BECAME YOUR DEPENDENT (mm/dd/yyyy)	
1D. DATE OF MARRIAGE (mm/dd/yyyy)	2D. CHILD'S RELATIONSHIP TO YOU (Check one) ☐ SON ☐ DAUGHTER ☐ STEPSON ☐ STEPDAUGHTER	
1E. SPOUSE'S ADDRESS AND TELEPHONE NUMBER (Street, City, State, ZIP if different from Veteran's)	2E. WAS CHILD PERMANENTLY AND TOTALLY DISABLED BEFORE THE AGE OF 18? ☐ YES ☐ NO	
	2F. IF CHILD IS BETWEEN 18 AND 23 YEARS OF AGE, DID CHILD ATTEND SCHOOL LAST CALENDAR YEAR? ☐ YES ☐ NO	
3. IF YOUR SPOUSE OR DEPENDENT CHILD DID NOT LIVE WITH YOU LAST YEAR, DID YOU PROVIDE SUPPORT? ☐ YES ☐ NO	2G. EXPENSES PAID BY YOUR DEPENDENT CHILD FOR COLLEGE, VOCATIONAL REHABILITATION OR TRAINING (e.g., tuition, books, materials)	

SECTION V - EMPLOYMENT INFORMATION

1A. VETERAN'S EMPLOYMENT STATUS (Check one). ☐ FULL TIME ☐ PART TIME ☐ NOT EMPLOYED ☐ RETIRED	1B. DATE OF RETIREMENT	
1C. COMPANY NAME. (Complete if employed or retired)	1D. COMPANY ADDRESS (Complete if employed or retired - Street, City, State, ZIP)	1E. COMPANY PHONE NUMBER (Complete if employed or retired) (include area code)

SECTION VI - PREVIOUS CALENDAR YEAR GROSS ANNUAL INCOME OF VETERAN, SPOUSE AND DEPENDENT CHILDREN
(Use a separate sheet for additional dependents)

	VETERAN	SPOUSE	CHILD 1
1. GROSS ANNUAL INCOME FROM EMPLOYMENT (wages, bonuses, tips, etc.) EXCLUDING INCOME FROM YOUR FARM, RANCH, PROPERTY OR BUSINESS	$	$	$
2. NET INCOME FROM YOUR FARM, RANCH, PROPERTY OR BUSINESS	$	$	$
3. LIST OTHER INCOME AMOUNTS (e.g., Social Security, compensation, pension, interest, dividends) EXCLUDING WELFARE	$	$	$

SECTION VII - PREVIOUS CALENDAR YEAR DEDUCTIBLE EXPENSES

1. TOTAL NON-REIMBURSED MEDICAL EXPENSES PAID BY YOU OR YOUR SPOUSE (e.g., payments for doctors, dentists, medications, Medicare, health insurance, hospital and nursing home) VA will calculate a deductible and the net medical expenses you may claim.	$
2. AMOUNT YOU PAID LAST CALENDAR YEAR FOR FUNERAL AND BURIAL EXPENSES (INCLUDING PREPAID BURIAL EXPENSES) FOR YOUR DECEASED SPOUSE OR DEPENDENT CHILD (Also enter spouse or child's information in Section VI.)	$
3. AMOUNT YOU PAID LAST CALENDAR YEAR FOR YOUR COLLEGE OR VOCATIONAL EDUCATIONAL EXPENSES (e.g., tuition, books, fees, materials) DO NOT LIST YOUR DEPENDENTS' EDUCATIONAL EXPENSES.	$

APPLICATION FOR HEALTH BENEFITS **Continued**	VETERAN'S NAME *(Last, First, Middle)*	SOCIAL SECURITY NUMBER

SECTION VIII - CONSENT TO COPAYS AND TO RECEIVE COMMUNICATIONS

By submitting this application, you are agreeing to pay the applicable VA copayments for care or services (including urgent care) as required by law. You also agree to receive communications from VA to your supplied email, home phone number, or mobile number. However, providing your email, home phone number, or mobile number is voluntary.

ASSIGNMENT OF BENEFITS

I understand that pursuant to 38 U.S.C. Section 1729 and 42 U.S.C. 2651, the Department of Veterans Affairs (VA) is authorized to recover or collect from my health plan (HP) or any other legally responsible third party for the reasonable charges of nonservice-connected VA medical care or services furnished or provided to me. I hereby authorize payment directly to VA from any HP under which I am covered (including coverage provided under my spouse's HP) that is responsible for payment of the charges for my medical care, including benefits otherwise payable to me or my spouse. Furthermore, I hereby assign to the VA any claim I may have against any person or entity who is or may be legally responsible for the payment of the cost of medical services provided to me by the VA. I understand that this assignment shall not limit or prejudice my right to recover for my own benefit any amount in excess of the cost of medical services provided to me by the VA or any other amount to which I may be entitled. I hereby appoint the Attorney General of the United States and the Secretary of Veterans' Affairs and their designees as my Attorneys-in-fact to take all necessary and appropriate actions in order to recover and receive all or part of the amount herein assigned. I hereby authorize the VA to disclose, to my attorney and to any third party or administrative agency who may be responsible for payment of the cost of medical services provided to me, information from my medical records as necessary to verify my claim. Further, I hereby authorize any such third party or administrative agency to disclose to the VA any information regarding my claim.

ALL APPLICANTS MUST SIGN AND DATE THIS FORM. REFER TO INSTRUCTIONS WHICH DEFINE WHO CAN SIGN ON BEHALF OF THE VETERAN.

SIGNATURE OF APPLICANT
(Sign in ink)   DATE

Case Index

AB v. Brown, 6 Vet.App. 35 (1993) 181, 229

Acree v. O'Rourke, 891 F.3d 1009 (2018) 228

Akles v. Derwinski, 1 Vet.App. 118 (1991) 181, 182

Az v. Shinseki, 731 F.3d 1303 (Fed. Cir. 2013) 124

Baker v. West, 11 Vet.App. 163 (1998) 159

Baldwin v. West, 13 Vet.App. 1 (1999) 207

Barr v. Nicholson, 21 Vet.App. 303 (2007) 94, 229

Barrett v. Nicholson, 466 F.3d 1038 (Fed. Cir. 2006) xvii

Bell v. Derwinski, 2 Vet.App. 611 (1992) 172

Boone v. Lightner, 319 U.S. 561 (1943) 66

Bouton v. Peake, 23 Vet.App. 70 (2008) 207

Bove v. Shinseki, 25 Vet.App. 136 (2011) 63

Bradley v. Peake, 22 Vet.App. 280 (2008) 181

Brammer v. Derwinski, 3 Vet.App. 223 (1992) 93

Brown v. Gardner, 513 U.S. 115 (1994) 64, 66

Buchanan v. Nicholson, 451 F.3d 1331 (Fed. Cir. 2006) 94

Buie v. Shinseki, 24 Vet.App. 242 (2011) 181

Butts v. Brown, 5 Vet.App. 532 (1993) 54

Caluza v. Brown, 7 Vet.App. 498 (1995) aff'd, 78 F.3d 604 (Fed.
Cir. 1996) 92

Camarena v. Brown, 6 Vet.App. 565 (1994) 82

Capellan v. Peake, 539 F.3d 1373 (Fed. Cir. 2008) 184

Carpenter v. Principi, 15 Vet.App. 64 (2001) 253

Charles v. Principi, 16 Vet.App. 370 (2002) 168

Coffy v. Republic Steel Corp., 447 U.S. 191 (1980) 66

Cohen v. Brown, 10 Vet.App. 128 (1997) 112, 114, 117, 159

Cook v. Principi, 318 F.3d 1334 (Fed. Cir. 2003) 207

Coomer v. Peake, 552 F.3d 1362 (Fed. Cir. 2009) xvii

Cromer v. Nicholson, 455 F.3d 1346 (Fed. Cir. 2006)................... 161, 173

Cropper v. Brown, 6 Vet.App. 450 (1994)... 73

Cueva v. Principi, 3 Vet.App. 542 (1992)..173

Cushman v. Shinseki, 576 F.3d 1290 (Fed. Cir. 2009)......................65, 72

Darby v. Brown, 10 Vet.App. 243 (1997).. 266

DAV v. Sec. of Vet. Aff., 327 F.3d 1339 (Fed. Cir. 2003)............... 54, 69

Davis v. Principi, 276 F.3d 1341 (Fed. Cir. 2002) 64

Dela Cruz v. Principi, 15 Vet.App. 143 (2001)....................................158

DeLisio v. Shinseki, 25 Vet.App. 45 (2011) 228

Dennis v. Nicholson, 21 Vet.App. 18 (2007)..168

Dixon v. Derwinski, 3 Vet.App. 261 (1992)..173

Dizoglio v. Brown, 9 Vet.App. 163 (1996)..114

Donnellan v Shinseki, 24 Vet.App. 167 (2010) 185

Doran v. Brown, 6 Vet.App. 283 (1996) 115

Dover v. McDonald, 818 F.3d 1316 (Fed. Cir. 2016) 254

Dow Chem. Co. v. Stephenson, 539 U.S. 111 (2003) 144

Duro v. Derwinski, 2 Vet.App. 530 (1992) 79

Eddy v. Brown, 9 Vet.App. 52 (1996) 206

Elkins v. Brown, 8 Vet.App. 391 (1995) 90

Ferraro v. Derwinski, 1 Vet.App. 326 (1991).......................................156

Fishgold v. Sullivan Drydock & Repair Corp., 328 U.S. 275 (1946) 66

Flash v. Brown, 8 Vet.App. 332 (1995).. 206

Floore v. Shinseki, 26 Vet.App. 376 (2013)..178

Flores v. Nicholson, 476 F.3d 1379 (Fed. Cir. 2007)............................. 63

Fluharty v. Derwinski, 2 Vet.App. 409 (1992) 159

Forshey v. Principi, 284 F.3d 1335 (Fed. Cir. 2002).............61, 63, 69, 214

Gagne v. McDonald, 27 Vet.App. 397 (2015) 171

Garvey v. Wilkie (Fed. Cir. 2020).. 73

Geib v. Shinseki, 733 F.3d 1350 (2013) 178

Gilbert v. Derwinski, 1 Vet.App. 49 (1990)..183

Gleicher v. Derwinski, 2 Vet.App. 26 (1991) 159

Glover v. West, 185 F.3d 1328 (Fed. Cir. 1999).................................... 207

Golz v. Shinseki, 590 F.3d 1317 (Fed. Cir. 2010) 169

Green v. Derwinski, 1 Vet.App. 121 (1991)..177

Green v. McDonald, 28 Vet.App. 281 (2016).. 220

Haas v. Peake, 525 F. 3d 1168 (Fed. Cir. 2008)............................. 129, 137

Hamilton v. Brown, 4 Vet.App. 528 (1993) (en banc) aff'd, 39
F.3d 1574 (Fed. Cir. 1994)... 228

Hanna v. Brown, 6 Vet.App. 507 (1994) 267
Hansen v. Principi, 16 Vet.App. 110 (2002) 92
Harris v. Derwinski, 1 Vet.App. 180 (1991)..182
Harris v. Shinseki, 704 F.3d 946 (Fed. Cir. 2013).................................179
Hartman v. Nicholson, 484 F.3d 1311 (Fed. Cir. 2007).........................168
Harvey v. Brown, 6 Vet.App. 416 (1994) 79
Hatlestead v. Brown, 5 Vet.App. 524 (1993)..235
Hayes v. Brown, 5 Vet.App. 60 (1993)........................... 111-112, 185
Hayes v. Brown, 9 Vet.App. 73 (1996)..159
Hayre v. West Jr., 188 F.3d 1327 (Fed. Cir. 1999) 66
Henderson v. Shinseki, 562 U.S. 428 (2011) xvii
Hesley v. West Jr., 212 F.3d 1255 (Fed. Cir. 2000)............................... 68
Hickson v. West, 12 Vet.App. 247 (1999) 92
Hodge v. West, 155 F.3d 1356 (Fed. Cir. 1998) .... xvii, 66, 179
Holmes v. Brown, 10 Vet.App. 38 (1997) 77
Holmes v. Brown, 10 Vet.App. 38 (1997) 77
Holton & Bryant v. Shinseki, 557 F.3d 1362 (Fed. Cir. 2009) .. xvii, 88, 92
In re "Agent Orange" Prod. Liab. Litig., 597 F. Supp. 740
(E.D.N.Y. 1984) 143
In re "Agent Orange" Prod. Liab. Litig., 373 F.Supp.2d 7, 2005
WL 729177 (E.D.N.Y. 2005) 128
In re "Agent Orange" Prod. Liab. Litig., 517 F.3d 76 (2nd Cir.
2008) 128, 144
In the Matter of the Fee Agreement of Vernon, 8 Vet.App.
457 (1996)...253
Isaacson v. Dow Chem. Co. (In re "Agent Orange" Prod. Liab.
Litig.), 344 F. Supp. 2d 873 (E.D.N.Y. 2004) 144
Isaacson v. Dow Chem. Co., 129 S. Ct. 1523, 555 U.S. 1218 (2009)......144
Jackson v. Shinseki, 587 F.3d 1106 (2009)...182
Jandreau v. Nicholson, 492 F.3d 1372 (Fed. Cir. 2007) 94
Jaquay v. Principi, 304 F.3d 1276 (Fed. Cir. 2002) 68
Jensen v. Brown, 19 F.3d 1413 (Fed. Cir. 1994) 117
Jones v. Wilkie, 918 F.3d 922 (Fed. Cir. 2019)...................................169
Joyner v. McDonald, 766 F.3d 1393 (Fed. Cir. 2014) 64
Kays v. Snyder, 846 F.3d 1208 (Fed. Cir. 2017)..................................125
Kelly v. Nicholson, 463 F.3d 1349 (Fed. Cir. 2006).............................184
King v. Shinseki, 26 Vet.App. 433 (2014)... 207
Lathan v. Brown, 7 Vet.App. 359 (1995).. 268

Lind v. Brown, 3 Vet.App. 493, 494 (1992) 159
Locklear v. Nicholson, 20 Vet.App. 410 (2006).......................167-68, 177
Luallen v. Brown, 8 Vet.App. 92 (1995) 207
Masors v. Derwinski, 2 Vet.App. 182 (1992).......................................159
Mayfield v. Nicholson, 444 F.3d 1328 (Fed. Cir. 2006)......................168
McClain v. Nicholson, 21 Vet.App. 319 (2007)................................... 93
McGee v. Peake, 511 F.3d 1352 (Fed. Cir. 2008) 180
McKnight v. Gober, 131 F.3d 1483 (Fed. Cir. 1997) 66
McLendon v. Nicholson, 20 Vet.App. 79 (2006) 97, 176
Menegassi v. Shinseki, 638 F.3d 1379 (Fed. Cir. 2011)...................... 124
Moore v. Derwinski, 1 Vet.App. 356 (1991) 156
Moore v. Shinseki, 555 F.3d 1369 (Fed. Cir. 2009)............................235
Moreau v. Brown, 9 Vet.App. 389 (1996) 114, 124
Morgan v. Principi, 327 F.3d 1357 (Fed. Cir. 2003) 63
Moyer v. Derwinski, 2 Vet.App. 289 (1992)..159
Murincsak v. Derwinski, 2 Vet.App. 363 (1992) 159, 172
Myore v. Nicholson, 489 F.3d 1207 (Fed. Cir. 2007).......................88, 267
Nat'l Org. of Veterans Advocates, Inc. v. Affairs, 710 F.3d 1328
(Fed. Cir. 2013).. 68
Nieves-Rodriguez v. Peake, 22 Vet.App. 295 (2008)............................ 97
Norris v. West, 12 Vet.App. 413 (1999)..182
O'Hare v. Derwinski, 1 Vet.App. 365 (1991) 173
Ortiz v. Principi, 274 F.3d 1361 (Fed. Cir. 2001) 185
Ortiz-Valles v. McDonald, 28 Vet.App. 65 (2016) 156, 237
Padgett v. Nicholson, 19 Vet.App. 84 (2005)...................................... 62
Paralyzed Veterans of Am. v. Sec'y of Veterans Affairs, 345 F.3d
1334 (Fed. Cir. 2003)...176
Pederson v. McDonald, 27 Vet.App. 276 (2015) (en banc)...................157
Pelegrini v. Principi, 18 Vet.App. 112 (2004) 168
Porter v. Brown, 5 Vet.App. 233 (1993)... 207
Procopio v. Wilkie, 913 F.3d 1371 (Fed. Cir. 2019).......................46, 137
Quartuccio v. Principi, 16 Vet.App. 183 (2002)..................................168
Rankin v. Lull (W.D. Mich., 2017)..163
Ravin v. Wilkie, 31 Vet.App. 104 (2019)..253
Ray v. Wilkie, 31 Vet.App. 58 (2019)...156-158
Rice v Shinseki, 11 Vet.App. 447 (2009)..235
Richard ex rel. Richard v. West, 161 F.3d 719 (Fed. Cir. 1998) 72
Roberson v. Principi, 251 F.3d 1378 (Fed. Cir. 2001)................... 179, 182

Robertson v. Shinseki, 26 Vet.App. 169 (2013)...................................... 87

Robinson v. O'Rourke, 891 F.3d 976 (Fed. Cir. 2018)............................ 66

Robinson v. Shinseki, 557 F.3d 1355 (Fed. Cir. 2009) 179-180

Romanowsky v. Shinseki, 26 Vet.App 289 (2013)................................. 93

Russell v. Principi, 3 Vet.App. 310 (1992).. 206

Russo v. Brown, 9 Vet.App. 46 (1996)... 173

Sanchez-Navarro v. McDonald, 774 F.3d 1380 (Fed. Cir. 2014)........... 178

Saunders v. Wilkie, 886 F.3d 1356 (Fed. Cir. 2018)............................ 149

Schafrath v. Derwinski, 1 Vet.App. 589 (1991) 158

Schoonover v. Derwinski, 3 Vet.App. 166 (1992)................................ 268

Scott v. McDonald, 789 F.3d 1375 (Fed. Cir. 2015) 66

Serv. Women's Action Network v. Sec'y of Veterans Affairs, 815
F.3d 1369 (Fed. Cir. 2016).. 112

Shalala v. Schaefer, 509 U.S. 292 (1993).. 254

Shea v. Wilkie, 926 F.3d 1362 (Fed. Cir. 2019)................................... 179

Shedden v. Principi, 381 F.3d 1163 (Fed. Cir. 2004)....................... 92, 130

Sheets v. Derwinski, 2 Vet.App. 512 (1992) 90

Skoczen v. Shinseki, 564 F.3d 1319 (Fed. Cir. 2009)...................... 60, 65

Smith v. Brown, 35 F.3d 1516 (Fed. Cir. 1994) 66, 183

Smith v. Derwinski, 2 Vet.App. 241 (1992) 88

Snuffer v. Gober, 10 Vet.App. 400 (1997).. 177

Spencer v. West, 13 Vet.App. 376 (2000).. 79

Stefl v. Nicholson, 21 Vet.App. 120 (2007) 176

Stillwell v. Brown, 6 Vet.App. 291 (1994) 254

Swiney v. Gober, 14 Vet.App. 65 (2000).. 254

Swisher v. Wilkie (Fed. Cir. 2019) 172

Tarver v. Shinseki, 557 F.3d 1371 (Fed. Cir. 2009) 269

Thompson v. Derwinski, 1 Vet.App. 251 (1991)................................. 207

Turk v. Peake, 21 Vet.App. 565 (2008).. 174

Van Hoose v. Brown, 4 Vet.App. 361 (1993) 236

Vaughn v. Principi, 336 F.3d 1351 (Fed. Cir. 2003) 254

Ventigan v. Brown, 9 Vet.App. 34 (1996) 268

Veterans Justice Grp., LLC v. Sec'y of Veterans Affairs, 818 F.3d
1336 (Fed. Cir. 2016).. 196

Voerth v. West, 13 Vet.App. 117 (1999) 172

Walker v. Shinseki, 708 F.3d 1331 (Fed. Cir. 2013) 95, 101

Walters v. Nat. Assoc. of Radiation Survivors, 473 U.S. 305, 105
S.Ct. 3180, 87 L.Ed.2d 220 (1985) 64, 66

Wamhoff v. Brown, 8 Vet.App. 517 (1996).. 174
Washington v. Nicholson, 19 Vet.App. 362 (2005)................................ 92
Waters v. Shinseki, 601 F.3d 1274 (Fed. Cir. 2010).............................. 176
Wells v. Principi, 326 F.3d 1381 (Fed. Cir. 2003)................................ 176
West (Carlton) v. Brown, 7 Vet.App. 70 (1994) 124
Wilson v. Mansfield, 506 F.3d 1055 (Fed. Cir. 2007)........................... 168
Woehlaert v. Nicholson, 21 Vet. App. 456 (2007)................................ 62

Index

References are to Pages

AGENT ORANGE
Presumptive causation, 130
Presumptive exposure, 132

APPEALS
Generally, 209

ASSAULT
Post-traumatic Stress Disorder based on
  personal assault, 114, 124-25, 201

ATTORNEYS
Generally, 245

AUTHORITIES
Generally, 49
Case law, 55
  Court of Appeals for Veterans Claims
    (CAVC), this index
  Federal Circuit, this index
U.S. Constitution, 49
Regulations, 52
Legal hierarchy of authorities, 49
Statutes, 50

BOARD OF VETERANS APPEALS
Generally, 59

BURDEN OF PROOF
Generally, 107

CHRONIC DISEASES
Generally, 100

CHRONICITY and CONTINUITY
Generally, 98-99, 102-103

CLAIMS
How to file, 189

CLEAR and UNMISTAKABLE ERROR (CUE)
Generally, 206-207

COSTS AND FEES
Generally, 250
Fee agreements, 249
Permissible fees, 251-52
CAVC fees, 253
EAJA fees, 253

COURT OF APPEALS FOR VETERANS CLAIMS
Generally, 56, 61
Art. I Court, status, 56
Case law, 57
Scope of powers, 61-62
Statutory Authority, 61
Time limits on filing appeal
Generally, 62
Equitable tolling, 63

DISABLITY COMPENSATION

Generally, 71
Agent Orange exposure,
    presumptive service-connection, 130
Aggravation of preexisting
    condition, 105
Chronic diseases, presumptive
    service-connection, 100
Chronicity and continuity,
    presumptive-service connection, 98-99, 102-103
Clear and unmistakable standard
    of proof, 109
Current disabling condition, 91
Direct service-connection, claim
    Generally, 104
Disability Benefits Questionnaires
    (DBQs), 165-65
Herbicide exposure, presumptive
    service-connection, 130
In-service disease or injury
    Generally, 91
Line of duty requirement, 72
Medical opinion
    Connecting post-service
        condition to in-service disease or injury, 96
    VA's duty to provide medical
        opinion (see medical opinion, this index)
Mental health rating criteria, 203
Multiple disability ratings, 151-52
Nexus between current
    disability and in-service injury or disease
        Generally, 95
    Direct service-connection claim, 104
        Medical opinion post-service condition to in-service injury or disease, 115
Pain, undiagnosed, 149
Preexisting condition, aggravation of, 105
Presumptive service-connection
    Chronicity or continuity, 98-99, 102
In-service injury, 95
Rating disabilities
        Generally, 150

Multiple disability ratings, 151
Total disability based on individual
    unemployability (TDIU), 153
Secondary service connection, 106
Total disability based on individual
    unemployability (TDIU), 153
Toxic exposures, 105, 127
Tropical diseases, presumptive service
    connection, 101
VA's duty to provide medical examination
    or opinion. See Medical Opinion, this index

DISCHARGES

Generally, 73
Character of Discharge review, 77
Types of discharge from the military, 74

DUE PROCESS

Generally, 181
Protected property interest, 65, 72

EFFECTIVE DATES

Generally, 152

EQUAL ACCESS TO JUSTICE ACT (EAJA) FEES

Generally, 253
Prevailing party status, 254

EQUITABLE TOLLING

Time limits on filing CAVC appeal, 63

EVIDENCE

Generally, 93
Benefit of the doubt, 110
Competence
    Generally, 93
    Self-diagnosis of mental condition, 94

Lay evidence establishing diagnosis of
    condition, 94
Medical and lay evidence, 93-94
New evidence. See Revisiting
    Final Decisions, this index.
Post-traumatic stress disorder based on
    personal assault, corroborating evidence, 125, 126
Standards of proof, 888
Time, place and circumstances of service,
    consideration to be accorded, 108

EXPERTS

Medical Opinion, see this index

FEDERAL CIRCUIT

Generally, 63
CAVC and the Federal Circuit, 63
Jurisdiction
    Generally, 63

FEES

Costs and Fees, this index
Equal Access to Justice Act, this index

FINALITY

Adjudications, 206
Federal Circuit, 64
Revisiting Final Decisions, this index

FORMS

Disability Benefits Questionnaires
    (DBQs), 164
Notice of Disagreement (NOD), 207, 212, 299
VA's duty to provide free forms, 162

HERBICIDE EXPOSURE

See Agent Orange, this index

HISTORY OF VETERANS BENEFITS
Generally, 1-24
Organic era, 2-
    Colonies, 2
    Revolutionary War, 3
    Civil War, 8
Pre-modern era, 13
Modern era, 20

INTENT TO FILE CLAIM
Generally, 195

JUDICIAL REVIEW
Board of Veterans Appeals, this index
Court of Appeals for Veterans Claims
    (CAVC), this index
Federal Circuit, this index
Historical background, 17
Sympathetic development of claims, VA's duty, 178
Veterans benefits before judicial review, 17

JURISDICTION
Board of Veterans Appeals, this index
Court of Appeals for Veterans Claims
    (CAVC), this index
Federal Circuit, this index

LAWS
Generally, 49
Regulations, 52
Statutes
    Generally, 50
    Forms of a statute before becoming law, 50-52

LINE OF DUTY
Generally, 72
Disability compensation, line of duty
    requirement and misconduct, 89

LOST RECORDS

Records, this index

MEDICAL OPINION

Disability Benefits Questionnaires
(DBQs), 164
Duty to provide medical opinion
Generally, 175

MISCONDUCT

Disability compensation, line of duty
requirement and misconduct, 89

NEW AND RELEVANT EVIDENCE

Revisiting Final Decisions, this index

NOTICE TO CLAIMANTS

How to substantiate claim, VA's duty
to provide notice
Generally, 167
Clear and unmistakable error
(CUE), 206

PAIN

Service connection claim, undiagnosed pain, 149

POST-TRAUMATIC STRESS

DISORDER

Generally, 111
Corroborating evidence, PTSD based
on personal assault, 114, 122-126
Corroborating evidence, PTSD from
Combat, 114, 116-120

PREEXISTING CONDITION

Disability compensation, aggravation
of preexisting condition, 105

RATING DISABILITIES

Disability Compensation, this index

RECORDS

Lost records, 173
Relevant records, VA's duty to obtain
        Generally, 169-174
    Follow-up requirements, 171, 174
Social Security records, 172
Statutory duty, 169

RELEVANCE

Evidence, this index
Records, relevant, duty to obtain. See
        Records, this index

REVISITING FINAL DECISIONS

        Generally, 206
Clear and unmistakable error (CUE)
        motions, 206-207
New and relevant evidence
        Generally, 208, 210-11

SUBSTANTIATION OF CLAIM

VA's duty to provide notice to
        claimants. See Notice to Claimants, this index

TOXIC EXPOSURES

Agent Orange, this index
Causation, Presumption of, 130

TROPICAL DISEASES

Presumptive service connection, 101

UNEMPLOYABILITY

Total disability based on individual unemployability (TDIU), 153-160

VETERANS AFFAIRS

Adjudication process, veterans
    benefits, 60
Appeals, this index
Claims, this index
Hierarchy of authorities, 65
How to substantiate claim, VA's duty
    to provide notice. See Notice to Claimants, this index
Office of General Counsel,
    precedential opinions, 54
Regional offices, 60

VETERANS SERVICE ORGANIZATIONS

Historical background, 1-24
American Veterans, 18

9/11 Masquerade

a poem by Tyson Manker

★ ★ ★

We came from all around
Pledged allegiance with resound

And gave to Uncle Sam our rights away

A soldier corps
Built just for war
With ranks of those
Who yearned for more

Were drilled and taught to kill both night and day

We stood in line
Time after time
Were stripped of thoughts
Issued a mind

And told to hate and who to hate as well

As time went on
It wasn't long
All childhood innocence
Was gone

We new recruits bought all that they could sell

Over the years
We trained as peers
We worked as one
And shed our fears
We moved around
And often found

People sharing
Common ground

Then came the day
A frightful one
The day the planes
Blocked out the sun
We knew it then
Fate would befall
On us to answer
Battle's call

By then...

Patriotic pride had
Forged itself down deep inside

Within the breasts of we who stood to fight

Our nation we'd defend
If it took us to our end

Mattered not for why we joined meant doing right

Off to staging grounds we went
Determined not to die
Focused on the task at hand
Not once did we ask why

The cause for us to go to war
Was more than certain payback for
A cruel attack upon our land
A terrorist act that could not stand

But then again it could have been
The dreaded W M Ds
Yet all around they were not found
Despite the guarantees

Or was it freedom that we sought
For those who lived a life distraught
Surely order will return
After Saddam's been caught

It must have also been to kill
Extremist rebels armed with will
What right have they to guard their land
We come in peace please understand

With shock and awe we forged ahead
Democracy we vowed to spread
Justice for all became our cry
Shown in bullets we let fly

Once the dust had finally cleared
Such shameful dirty truths appeared
Contradictions of a kind
That cannot leave a person's mind
It wasn't long before we saw
The story's multitude of flaws
Iraq's invasion was illegal and
We must withdraw

But wait! our leaders yelp
They say we need to give it time
The best thing we can do to help
Is prosecute war crimes

So...

They grabbed their pens
And wrote new laws
Declaring theirs
A noble cause

They set to work and
Captured men

And tortured them
Time and again

"They have no rights," we'd often hear
"Besides, these methods aren't severe"

"We hope that soon they're going to talk
If not, we'll try electric shock"

They never stopped
For once to think
The world's support
Would surely shrink
That through their actions
Their own deeds
They had planted
Terrorist seeds

Yet awful as war is for some
For others rapid profits come
To them it brings utter delight
When boys and girls go off to fight

When sacrifice is in the air
It's not for them to share or care
They swoop in at the perfect time
With thoughts only to make a dime
Wartime profiteers
All gave the President three cheers
They knew they would not be condemned
'Cause after all he's one of them

By design the storyline
Was framed to then falsely assign
The blame away from those who cost
The treasure and the lives now lost

Resounding faith we had in those
Who told us where to find our foes
Yet when we looked we found instead
That all along we'd been misled

The dots were there for all to see
Indeed Mister Defense
But after I connect them
All the stories don't make sense

On and on for months and years
They preyed upon citizens' fears
Making all the people scared
With constant threat levels declared

Then they poured our money in
And miles away felt free from sin
Even lives were too outsourced
As long as profits were enforced

Now government can't pay the rent
Because of all the money spent
Engaging in wars without end
A mis-prioritizing trend

We look to see what side they're on
And find we're nothing more than pawns
They use to make themselves well off
They take our money while they scoff

Make it known to understand
The blood that stains the desert sand
Of murdered daughters, sons, and friends
Ever marks The Decider's hands

The only thing we have to fear
Is fear itself so let's be clear

Attempts to veil the truth are made in vain

We see the things officials do
We know their words to be untrue

Nothing within our minds shall we constrain

What's lost is gone
We can't get back
We must pursue
A different track
Now's the time
To take a stand
And rise above
To now demand

For those that fought and bled and died
And those who stayed at home and cried
For those who'll never shed the scars
And those remaining trapped by bars

Your sacrifices haven't gone
in vain We won't allow this con

Here on out we simply must
Put faith in reason and not trust
Those on top who preach the most
It's in themselves that they're engrossed

The next time that they want to fight
Let's come together and unite
Make peace and policy convene
Stand up against the war-machine

The power lies in all of us
To ask, question, dissent, discuss
And when our leaders go too far
We have to fuss and raise the bar

Since they've failed to lead upright
Let's show the true meaning of might
And take back long-abused powers
Remind them that this land is ours

★ ★ ★

Printed in the United States
By Bookmasters